GUIDES FOR AN AGE OF CONFUSION

Studies in the Thinking of Avraham Y. Kook and Mordecai M. Kaplan

JACK J. COHEN

Fordham University Press
New York
1999

Library of Congress Cataloging-in-Publication Data

Cohen, Jack, 1919–
    [Morim li-zeman navokh. English]
    Guides for an age of confusion : studies in the thinking of
Avraham Y. Kook and Mordecai M. Kaplan / Jack J. Cohen.—1st ed.
    p.   cm.
    Includes bibliographical references and index.
    ISBN 0-8232-2002-8 (hc).—ISBN 0-8232-2003-6 (pbk)
    1. Kook, Abraham Isaac, 1865–1935.   2. Kaplan, Mordecai Menahem,
1881–   .   3. Orthodox Judaism.   4. Reconstructionist Judaism.
5. Zionism and Judaism.   I. Title.
BM755.K66C6413   1999
296.3′092′2—dc21   99-16639
                                                                   CIP

Printed in the United States of America
03   02   01   00   99   5   4   3   2   1
First Edition

Guides for an Age of Confusion

To my grandchildren who have enriched my life:
Avishai, Noa, Avner, Gilad, Maya, Tamar, Ariel, Yael, Daniel.

CONTENTS

PREFACE

Many persons who had read the original Hebrew version of my book *Teachers for an Age of Confusion: Studies in the Thought of Avraham Yitzhak Hakohen Kook and Mordecai Menahem Kaplan* (Eked, Tel Aviv, 1993) urged me to translate it into English. I confess that I was reticent to do so. In the first place, the task was formidable. Second, when the Hebrew manuscript was published after many years of preparation, I felt that I had accomplished the purposes I had in mind when I decided to write the book. Among those purposes was my desire to give Israel's Jews a fair introduction to my teacher Mordecai M. Kaplan, as most of them have never had the opportunity to read any of his works. Then too I wanted to help clarify some of the confusion that prevails in the thinking of Israelis about the problems of the Jewish people, the State of Israel, and the future of Judaism under freedom.

My strategy of comparing and contrasting Kaplan's views with those of Avraham Yitzhak Hakohen Kook was motivated by several considerations: (1) I place Kook and Kaplan on opposite ends of the spectrum of reasonable Judaism. That is to say, the Judaism of the future will have to emerge from interaction between these two positive, creative, and contrasting interpretations of the nature and destiny of the Jewish people and its culture. Somehow, a dialogue must be established between the two positions. (2) One of the better ways of understanding a philosophy is to see it against the background of other options. Kook certainly provides such a foil for Kaplan, and vice versa. (3) Kook is famous in Israel, and I felt that the presentation of Kaplan's philosophy in the light of Kook's vision would open doors to the Israeli public that might otherwise be closed to an outlook that originated in the Diaspora. (4) I had gained great respect for Kook's intellectual prowess, and I wanted to respond to its challenge to my own naturalistic leanings.

All of these motivations operate differently when it comes to

English-speaking Jewries. Although since his death in 1983, Kaplan has been eclipsed in many intellectual circles by other responses to the Jewish condition, he is still a force to be reckoned with. Much of his vocabulary has become legal tender in American Jewish discourse, and several of his initiatives have been endorsed in the communal and religious practices of a large section of the liberal, English-speaking Jewry. Moreover, even his opponents and those who consider his ideas to be outdated still acknowledge that Kaplan merits serious study. It is against Kaplan's corpus that Kook, a complete stranger to most English-speaking readers, might well be given a respectful introduction.

In contrast to the emphasis on Israel in my Hebrew study, this new version relates more directly to the problems of diaspora Jewry. Simply providing a literal translation of the volume published in Hebrew was not satisfactory to me. The Kook-Kaplan confrontation presents a fruitful way to focus attention on the key issues of contemporary Judaism, for both of these men are distinguished by the broad scope of their visions. Even though Kook's point of departure was his messianic dream of the reunification of the entire Jewish people in Eretz Yisrael and of its return there to a Torah-true Judaism, his analysis of and programs for wide areas of Jewish life have had a profound bearing on Jewish lifestyles in the Diaspora.

This same breadth of reach characterizes Kaplan. Although he spent most of his century-long life in the United States, he sought ways of ensuring the creative continuity of the Jewish people everywhere, particularly in its homeland in Eretz Yisrael. The comparison with Kook should, therefore, cast light on where each of these men might lead Judaism in the Diaspora and in Israel.

I agreed to undertake this challenge because I realized that the Kook-Kaplan dialogue deserves further elaboration on the subject of the Diaspora than was done in the Hebrew book. In this introduction, therefore, I hope not only to present the two thinkers as objectively as I can but also to indicate how their insights must be taken into consideration in any disciplined effort to solve the problems of Jewish peoplehood and Jewish civilization in our confused and confusing modern world.

The reader will find no accounts of the interesting and busy lives of our protagonists. I limit their biographies to their similar origins and the different directions in which their fates and their temperaments took them.[1] After a brief introduction to their intellectual tempers and points of departure, I go directly to some of the issues that both deemed to be central to Jewish survival and the making of a full Judaism. I believe that the agenda I cover, although incomplete, will suffice to inform the reader of the broad, coherent insight of both thinkers as to what is entailed in enabling the Jewish people to cope with the intellectual and social hazards of the modern world. They both forthrightly confront such key questions as the following: What roles should Eretz Yisrael and the Diaspora play in fostering creative Jewish continuity? How should we relate to traditions such as Israel's election and covenant with God? What should be the status of the *Halakhah* (traditional Jewish law) in a democratic society?

Several chapters will be devoted to the theological concerns of both men—the idea of God, prayer, repentance, and several basic values of Judaism. I shall also delve into Kook's and Kaplan's views about education and the role of the esthetic dimension and the arts in Jewish life. Finally, I shall observe how their philosophies have influenced the status of women in the synagogue and public affairs.

Obviously, thinkers of the caliber of Kook and Kaplan do not grow or function in vacuums. They are stimulated and conditioned by their spiritual and intellectual antecedents. They, in turn, motivate disciples and arouse critics. After the death of inspiring thinkers, their message is often beclouded by the interpretations given to them by supporters and critics alike. Hence, to comprehend the full range and impact of the philosophies of Kook and Kaplan, we have to trace their intellectual heritage and correct the many errors made by their followers and detractors. Such a task, however, would require a different type of book from the one I wrote and which I now offer in revised form to English readers. I have chosen, as best I can, to concentrate on what Kook and Kaplan have to say and shall refer to interpretations and comments of other scholars only when such remarks and my reactions to them are likely to clarify the positions of the two thinkers. I have taken some steps to place Kook and Kaplan in their proper niches in the intellectual history of Judaism in the twentieth century, but the territory remains largely uncharted.[2] For now, I aim only to outline some of the agreements and disagreements of these seminal minds and to indicate how we Jews must take their philosophies into account as we confront the confusion of our age.

Finally, although I try my best to treat both men objectively and fairly, I do so as one of Kaplan's disciples. My bias is clear, and I make no attempt to hide it; however, I hope that I have written honestly and disinterestedly about both thinkers. Let the reader decide.

I apologize to the reader for what might appear to be inconsistencies in spelling. This is especially the case in regard to quotations, which contain words whose spelling differs from that in my own text. I preferred to present these passages in their original form. The inconsistencies are endemic to English language usage. I try to resolve the problem of gender-laden language by the use of plurals and neutral terms, but here and there I revert to the traditional "man" when my meaning is humankind. In a number of instances, I follow the lead of our two thinkers who use the masculine term in this all-inclusive sense. I also wish to point to a similar difficulty in the transliteration of Hebrew terms into English. Here, too, the transliterations in quotations are those of their authors, while my text follows my preference.

I also wish to express my deepest appreciation to Fordham University Press for its many kindnesses. Special thanks to Dr. Mary Beatrice Schulte, who helped me over many hurdles; to Anthony F. Chiffolo, who was responsive to my every need; and to Barbara Malczak, a marvelous editor, who saved me from many an error and who taught me how much I still have to learn about the English language.

NOTES

1. Readers who are interested in further details about the biographies of Kook and Kaplan can refer to the sketchy articles in the *Encyclopedia Judaica*. Jacob Agus has a few pages on Kook's life in his *Banner of Jerusalem* (New York: Bloch, 1946). Ben-Zion Bokser adds some items about Kook's career in his *Abraham Isaac Kook* (New York, Ramsey, Toronto: Paulist Press; 1978). The best source for Kaplan's life is the excellent

biography by Mel Scult, *Judaism Faces the Twentieth Century* (Detroit: Wayne State University Press, 1993).

2. The literature is voluminous—too vast to list here and of sufficient proportions to merit a study in itself. Interested students should refer to the libraries of Jewish theological seminaries or of universities in which there are departments of Judaic studies. Most of the references on Kook, however, are likely to be in Hebrew.

ABBREVIATIONS

WORKS BY KOOK

AT	*Arfelei Tohar*
DK	*Duat Kohen*
EK	*Ezrat Kohen*
KL	*Iggerot HaReiyah*
MA	*Musar Avikha*
MK	*Mishpat Kohen*
MR	*Maamarei HaReiyah*
OH	*Orat HaTorah*
OK	*Orot HaKodesh*
OR	*Olat HaReiyah*
OT	*Orot HaTeshuvah*
SH	*Shabbat HaAretz*
SR	*Shemuot HaReiyah*
ZR	*Zikhron Reiyah*

WORKS BY KAPLAN

FAJ	*The Future of the American Jew*
GJM	*The Greater Judaism in the Making*
INNW	*If Not Now, When* (with Arthur A. Cohen)
JC	*Judaism As a Civilization*
JT	*Judaism in Transition*
JWS	*Judaism without Supernaturalism*
MG	*The Meaning of God in Modern Jewish Religion*
NZ	*New Zionism*
QJA	*Question Jews Ask*
REN	*The Religion of Ethical Nationhood*

Guides for an Age of Confusion

1
Why This Confrontation? An Introduction

POPULAR AND EVEN SCHOLARLY WRITERS frequently err by hypostatizing the term Judaism. We often read passages that begin "Judaism says" or "Judaism declares." The prevalence of such rhetoric is a clear example of the ease with which many persons overlook the dynamic nature of all social enterprises. It is far simpler to handle a stable and stationary object than it is to grasp a moving phenomenon. Whether one is a particularist or a universalist, a democrat or a theocrat, a religionist or a secularist, a naturalist or a supernaturalist, one is called upon to define terms. So it is quite understandable that when affirming one's own position or when criticizing that of an opponent, it is preferable to deal with a fixed and clearly delineated subject.

However, every creation—whether material or spiritual—that distinguishes humankind from the rest of the experienced universe is a product of human initiative and activity. Judaism is one of these creations and is thus part of the ever-flowing stream of Jewish life. Throughout its long history, the Jewish people has wrestled with the circumstances of its existence and has sought to meet its physical, moral, spiritual, and esthetic needs in the midst of changing conditions. Judaism is the term generally applied to the total response to life on the part of Jews. Never has that response been uniform; nor is it ever likely to be. Pluralism is born out of the uniqueness of every individual, marked by differences in knowledge, experience, mental skills, and emotional drives. Thus, Judaism says many contradictory things to all of us.

The two thinkers whose works will be examined in these pages exemplify the above diversity in dramatic fashion. Avraham Yitzhak Hakohen Kook and Mordecai Menachem Kaplan were both loyal and passionate Jews. Yet few contributors to the advancement of Jewish culture differed so fundamentally in their personalities, in their interpretations of the Jewish past and present, and in their visions for the Jewish future. What purpose can be served, therefore, in bringing them together under one umbrella? Is it not obvious that they are bound to disagree about the essentials of Judaism? Will not a dialogue between them in regard to ensuring Jewish survival and enhancing Jewish tradition turn into nothing more than a shouting match? These are questions that must be addressed.

Kook and Kaplan were aware of the full scope of changes in modes of thought behavior and social postures that occurred during their lifetimes. Each knew, in his own way, that radical steps were required to correct the faults in all the extant responses to the Jewish condition. They had both the intelligence and the courage to see beyond the confines of their own commitments.[1] Dialogue between such men surely would have had the potential of being very fruitful.

Kook and Kaplan stand at opposite ends of the Jewish spectrum, along which can be found many attempts to react reasonably to the social and ideological challenges of our age.[2] To the right of Kook are those premodern Jews, religious extremists in varying degrees and forms, who see no reason to step beyond halakhic Judaism for any knowledge or assistance in mapping a direction for Jewish life. In the eyes of these Fundamentalists, there is absolutely no valuable wisdom beyond the confines of Jewish tradition. The outside world is impure, and Jews should distance themselves from it to the utmost extent. They consider Rav Kook to have been an enemy of his people, one who endangered authentic Judaism.[3] The Fundamentalist camp itself is splintered. While it includes a rabid group in Israel who would throw stones at those who travel in their cars on the Sabbath, it also includes quietists who isolate themselves and eschew, as much as possible, any contact with "modern" Jews. The rightists are to be found among Hasidim and their opponents, the Mithnagdim, and among Kabbalists and other mystical sects. Most of today's Fundamentalists are anti-Zionists. They share a deep animosity toward any Jew who departs from their narrow conception of halakhic Judaism.

The *Haredim*, as the Jewish Fundamentalists are known, are strange phenomena. While I do not read them out of the Jewish fold, I do assume that dialogue with them is virtually impossible, even as it was for such a confirmed traditionalist as Kook. Because he was tolerant of those to his right, he sought to embrace the *Haredim*; however, there could be no meeting of the minds with them.

To the left of Kaplan is an equally varied world of Jews. They have in common a negative attitude toward Jewish religious tradition and, for many of them, an antipathy to Judaism as a whole. They conclude that their Jewish heritage offers nothing that might contribute to normal modern life. One segment of these negators consists of Jews who acknowledge that it is psychologically inadvisable to sever all connection with the past. They affirm the need to study Jewish tradition solely for the purpose of acquiring insight into a dead culture that is of only historical interest. Such study helps them to justify their rejectionism. They and the outright assimilationists, who see no purpose to Jewish existence, do not intend to probe the Jewish religion for its possible relevance to their lifestyle.

This book is mainly directed toward Jews who are motivated by three purposes or wants: They want the Jewish people to survive as a creative, vital group; they want to heighten respect for past generations of Jewry by a serious study of their teachings and by making them accessible and relevant to themselves and their children; and they deem it important to wrestle with the eternal questions of human destiny and to search for the unifying force or principle that can confer meaning on human aspirations. It is my hope, therefore, that non-Jews will find this book of interest for the insight it might give them into the current state of the Jewish people and the human condition in general.

Kook and Kaplan, for all their differences, are united in their questions. Even though a chasm separates their philosophies, their conclusions grant them the same cultural identity. They are both Jewish to the core. This closeness is made possible by their common belief that striving for Jewish unity is necessary for a healthy Jewish future. Eliezer Schweid rightly comments, "There is an interesting parallel between HaRav Kook and Mordecai Kaplan from the standpoint of their recognition that Jews have to be united in their discernment of the partial truth that resides in every one of the divisions of the people."[4]

AGREEMENT AND DISAGREEMENT AMONG JEWS

Throughout the history of the Jewish people, its leaders have differed in their beliefs and opinions. The debate between Job and his friends reflected the disagreements that prevailed concerning theodicy and human dignity. Regardless of when the Book of Ruth was composed, its author disagreed with Ezra and Nehemiah in the matter of co-opting gentiles into the Jewish people. This dispute continued in the talmudic era and has not ceased. In the Middle Ages, Saadia Gaon, Yehudah Halevi, Maimonides, Crescas, and a host of other philosophers disagreed, often vehemently, about the fundamentals of Judaism. Finally, with the advent of the modern period, a burgeoning variety of schools of thought can be observed.

Of course, there have been times, some of them protracted, during which there was general agreement about the basic principles of Judaism. For instance, in spite of the serious differences between the schools of Hillel and Shammai, their ongoing debates were conducted within an ideological and spiritual consensus. They honored one another and found each other's children acceptable in marriage. Nor at any time did they call into question the other's Jewish legitimacy. It was said of them—and they themselves believed—that their words were equally expressive of the will of the living God.

However, not all views held by those acknowledged as scholars were accepted as part of the national consensus. Elisha ben Abuyah, who was known as Aher, the Other or the Outcast, was expelled from the Jewish ranks and ostracized. He had overstepped the bounds when he proclaimed heretical doubts about accepted theological assumptions. His colleagues were unable to consider him a legitimate participant in the arena of Torah. Not even Rabbi Meir, his student and friend, included him in the Jewish community. Whether Elisha ben Abuyah continued to regard himself as a Jew after his excommunication is not known. Did he think that his heterodox opinions should have been recognized as legitimate Jewish alternatives to the prevailing consensus? This answer, too, is unknown.

In contrast, there can be little doubt that Benedict (Baruch) Spinoza, a millennium and a half later, was not concerned with strengthening Jewish life when he conceived his philosophical system. He considered his orientation to be the antithesis of Judaism. Even if Spinoza had not been excommunicated, he could never have contemplated a Judaism that could absorb or tolerate his revolutionary ideas. For him, Judaism was a world apart from that in which he wanted to think and live. Yet, if Aher and Spinoza were to be in our midst today, they would undoubtedly be accorded opportunities to fill important posts in Jewish communal life or to teach or do research in the Jewish Studies Department of a Jewish university. It is not at all certain whether either of these "heretics" would *want* to identify himself as a Jew. A large body of opinion still posits that anyone who denies the authority of the Halakhah cannot be a "kasher" Jew (to use a term that Kook employed to describe halakhic loyalists). Honest, deviant intellectuals, therefore, are apt to conclude that they have no place in a Jewish setting. On the other hand, there are free-thinking Jews who resist such a skewed interpretation of Judaism and Jewish identity and who see their heterodox views as positive expressions of a changing and developing Jewish culture.

Both Kook and Kaplan were attuned to the far-reaching pluralism in Judaism; however, whereas Kook aspired to counter much of it,[5] Kaplan saw variety of thought and practice as a natural and desirable accompaniment of freedom. True, Kook envisaged a genuine role for pluralism—the prevention of intellectual petrifaction among halakhic scholars—but ultimately, Jews would have to be reunited under the banner of a single, uniform halakhic lifestyle. In contrast, Kaplan sought to achieve unity of a different kind. He too hoped for areas of agreement and for common standards of behavior. The precondition for such an eventuality would of necessity be for Jews to practice the art of compromise. At the same time, Kaplan opposed setting a goal or a criterion of Jewish legitimacy as a one-way return to the past.

KOOK AND KAPLAN CONFRONT THE TWENTIETH CENTURY

Kook and Kaplan were twentieth-century figures, exposed to the dramatic changes that swept through all Western society during their lifetimes. (Kook was born in 1865 and died in 1935. Kaplan's life span extended from 1881 to 1983.) Unlike the Fundamentalists to his right, Kook affirmed the study of secular subjects. He understood that it is impossible for any people to ignore the discoveries of science and the philosophic visions that so affect the way men and women perceive their destiny on earth. For Kook, of course, none of these novelties could negate a single iota of the Torah of Moses or of the Oral Law. The processes of research into, study of, and instruction in the expanse of world culture must be interpreted in such a way as to clarify and strengthen toraitic tradition. Under no circumstances can secular study be considered a replacement for *Talmud Torah*. Kook lived in and was part of the modern era, but he looked backward to locate the means for overcoming the weaknesses in contemporary Judaism.

It is difficult to determine whether this cautious conservatism expressed Kook's real outlook. It might have been a tactic to prevent any action, even a positive one, that the Jewish masses were not yet prepared to accept. Kook was passionate about preserving national unity, and he always strove to prevent splintering. He wrote:

> An important rule in human development is that any attempt to popularize and implement an idea, which is far broader than the prevailing conceptions of contemporary society, will not be helpful and will do harm! Its message will not be appreciated and will stir up vociferous opposition, tumult, confusion, and reaction. It will delay the advent of the good beyond what might have been the case without this act of impatience. Furthermore, it will deprive many generations of the treasure that would have been theirs in greater measure, were it not for this forbidden effort. Such (untimely behavior) can only postpone the achievement of our objective.[6]

This passage illustrates Kook's pragmatism. He wanted to find practical outlets for his most abstract thoughts. He realized, however, that a leader must not run too far ahead of his people. Unfortunately, Kook revealed little of the thought and actions that he felt should await their times. I can recall only one instance—his support of vegetarianism—when he did so. In this instance, he specifically stated that any effort to enforce a ban on eating meat would be counterproductive.

Any serious student of Kook's writings learns that every word, every sentence, every paragraph must be read carefully. Kook's meaning is often obscure. Yosef Ben-Shelomo, in his excellent series of lectures on Kook delivered on Radio Kol Yisrael, attributes the difficulty in reading Kook's writings to the latter's reluctance to artificially restrain his stream of consciousness. Ben-Shelomo cites Kook's statement, "The soul of every creative person has to be entirely unfettered from the chains of logic. Reason shackles ideation and stifles poetry."[7] There is a good deal of truth in this explanation. Yet the matter is more complicated.

Kaplan's work, too, cannot be understood when read on the run; the difficulty in his case, however, stems from his style rather than from obscure thinking or his reticence to disclose his real views. He hides nothing. Although he rarely displays Kook's propensity for combining disparate ideas into lengthy sentences, his prose is often too forbidding for the general reader. Once over that hurdle, however, Kaplan's intent is clear.

Such is not the case with Kook. One can admire his courageous demand that human imagination be free to search for transcendent truth. Why, then, should he regard reason or logic as a rein on the spirit or on its responsible functioning? Is it his unsystematic way of thinking that produces obscure passages, or is it possible that at least some of his difficult passages conceal elements of doubt or uncertainty and, perhaps, a trace of fear of the very freedom he espouses? Admittedly, this is conjecture, a suspicion that cannot be proved. Nonetheless, since, according to Ben-Shelomo's testimony, Kook wanted to influence all Jews, as is manifest in his thousands of letters and responsa, should he not have gone to greater lengths to write in a more orderly fashion? Many of his letters and halakhic responsa demonstrate that he had the ability to organize his ideas clearly and forthrightly. Hence the suspicion grows that when the time came to publish some of his radical ideas, Kook did not, indeed could not, state them clearly for himself or for the masses.[8]

In contrast, Kaplan entered the realms of science, philosophy, and art without hesitation, and he drew and applied the conclusions to which his studies led him. He became convinced that there could be no future for the Jewish people unless it could honestly confront the rich general culture that is being created everywhere. Kaplan stood squarely in the modern world and directed his attention to the future. He entered the following thought in his *Diaries*: "A stubborn will resists, a strong will persists; a stubborn will allies itself to tradition, a strong will to purpose; a stubborn will keeps to the past, a strong will builds for the future."[9]

Thus, the gap between Kook and Kaplan is reflected in both their manner of thinking and their style of expression.[10] Kaplan wrote systematically, thoroughly, and coherently. One gets the impression that Kook's thoughts came upon him like a mighty stream, the direction of its flow determined by the very banks it had hewn out. There is hardly a sentence in Kook's entire corpus that is not full of ideas, hints, and echoes of the Bible or the Sages; his thinking was conditioned by this vast flow of tradition. Kaplan's mind was totally focused on a well-defined item of interest, and he was determined to exhaust all of its relevant connections.

Kook strove to uncover all the secrets that lie hidden in the thoughts of the moment. Kaplan endeavored to analyze specific problems and to propose solutions for them. Kook looked at the world while standing solidly within the Jewish circle. He felt compelled to anchor his innovations and his radical conceptions in Jewish sources. Kaplan stood astride both the worlds of Judaism and those of other cultures. He had an eclectic view and did not hesitate to adapt his thinking to the best in all cultures. Equally, he sought to make available for the rest of humankind that which is unique and valuable in Jewish civilization. Moreover, he was not afraid to recommend the uprooting from Jewish life of anything that, in his opinion, had become harmful or anachronistic. Furthermore, he was always prepared to add something of value to fill a vacuum.

What, if anything, can two such different minds have in common? Both sought to foster a Judaism with universalist aspirations. Kook, for all his parochialism, valued the positive accomplishments of non-Jews, although he was convinced that all that is good in foreign cultures has been inherent in Judaism from its inception. The bad, on the other hand, is foreign to Judaism's essential character.[11] Kaplan could not go along with the view that any culture, including Judaism, has matured completely and that by probing its depths, one can find everything one needs for a full life. On the contrary, there is no way to avoid the eternal tension between the worthy and the unworthy in every culture.

Kook apparently read or knew about the philosophies of Kant, Schopenhauer, Nietzsche, and other modern thinkers, but only rarely does he mention a non-Jewish name and, as far as I can recall, never does he quote directly from non-Jewish sources. This, of course, is in sharp contrast to his extensive citations from the entire range of Jewish tradition. Kaplan's style is utterly different. He draws whatever insights he can from the wells of Judaism and from those of other civilizations. In his effort to portray the problems of the Jewish people and to devise possible solutions, he postulates that no individual and no people can afford to turn away from any potential fountain of truth and wisdom. In contrast, Kook thinks that he can locate in toraitic Judaism all the wisdom needed for his spiritual enterprise; he requires no outside help. For him, the Torah is perfect and all embracing. Nonetheless, at times, Kook cannot avoid being unconsciously affected by the *Zeitgeist*, or the spirit of the age.[12]

Kaplan, too, loves the entire range of the Torah; it is, after all, the lifeblood of his people. However, since Judaism, like every culture, is constantly evolving, it must be perceived within the perspective of humankind's expanding knowledge. In addition, Kaplan insists that the strengths and weaknesses of Judaism have to be evaluated by the standards of verified knowledge and intellectual honesty. Nonetheless, while his sources are often found in the far reaches of the earth, Kaplan tries never to lose touch with the treasures obtainable in Jewish tradition.

Kook suffered from criticism leveled against his relative openness to general studies. The Fundamentalists feared that by opening the door to such studies, Kook was also admitting heresies into the Jewish home. In his own defense, Kook held that only through broad knowledge would Torah-true Jews be able to safeguard the tradition against the growing number of skeptics. Yet

the extent of Kook's support of non-toraitic learning must not be
exaggerated. He did not regard the study of the exact and social
sciences, general history, foreign languages, or other such disciplines as possessing independent value. He suggested their study
only when they could aid the spiritual quest in consonance with
classical Judaism.

It would appear that Kook considered attention to these subjects as an important strategy in his effort to bridge the gap between the modern, free-thinking Zionist pioneers and the
halakhists. He could not countenance the idea that the absorption
of secular knowledge might necessitate uprooting, changing, or
amending even a fragment of the classic tradition. This is the current position of many modern Orthodox Jews. They manage to
live simultaneously in two worlds, that of halakhic Judaism and
that of science and free thought. In their minds, no tension exists
between these two disparate systems. They see no need to reexamine any of the foundations of their version of Judaism in the
light of what, to other Jews, appear to be the contradictory or
more plausible conceptions of science and advanced intellection.
On the contrary, they have devised ways to use the latest findings
and theories to strengthen the protective wall surrounding their
form of Jewish ideology and practice. For example, instead of
permitting a critical study of the Bible to undermine belief in its
divine origin, they conclude that scientific biblical research has
validated the trustworthiness of the biblical text, and that, in turn,
adds credence to the biblical vision of God, man, and Israel. Or,
to illustrate further, instead of exposing the faults in some interpretations of human nature by talmudic Sages, the social sciences
are employed by modern Orthodox scholars to highlight the wisdom of the Tannaim (sages of the Mishnaic period, ending about
200 CE) and the Amoraim (sages of the period between 200 and
500 CE). In their grasp of human motivations, the latter are depicted as leading the way to and even outstripping contemporary
psychologists.

Most of us do not easily surrender that which has become part
of our personalities. Rather, we frequently try to reinterpret hallowed ideas or devise new ways to buttress our position. This
human characteristic should serve as a caution against the assumption that progress in one branch of human knowledge will force

adjustments in other areas or even lead to a reexamination of accepted conventions. Of course, some thinkers invariably tend to believe that life is always in flux and that change in one aspect of knowledge, particularly a radical change, is bound to evoke adjustments in the whole range of human existence, with the emphasis on the workings of the mind. Kaplan was such a thinker. He called for nothing less than a revolution in the way Jews think. For him, it was a moral responsibility.

In the upcoming chapters, the common denominators in the philosophies of Kook and Kaplan will be explored, as well as their serious differences. The plethora of schools of thought and movements that inform the Jewish community of this era range between these two arresting positions. True, it is difficult, perhaps impossible, to define "balanced"and "reasonable," but the presumption here is that a lucid person tries to convince an opponent of the soundness of his or her position by means of reasoned argument and not by coercion of any kind. It may be that Kook chose the path of persuasion not because he favored full freedom of thought and expression as a matter of principle, but rather because his humaneness propelled him to a high degree of tolerance. Kook, the man, was often more liberal than his ideal. He wanted to preclude further attenuation in the ranks of Orthodoxy. He feared that Orthodoxy's dropout rate would increase if the Rabbinate were to use coercive methods. But why guess? All signs indicate that Kook never deviated from his efforts to bring Jews closer to one another. He did so without hiding his criticism of the way of life of most self-proclaimed, secular *halutzim* (agricultural settlers). Because of the warmth he exuded for these pioneers, and indeed for all segments of the Jewish community, and because of the respect he showed his opponents in the struggle for the mind of the Jewish public, Kook succeeded in gaining a hearing among non-Orthodox Jews and in creating a human basis for a continued dialogue between the secular and halakhic communities. No mean achievement! Unfortunately, Kook's tolerance did not generate an ongoing dialogue between halakhic and non-halakhic Jews.

Kaplan, too, strove throughout his professional life to effect the unity of the Jewish people. He also had firm standards from which he never departed. Among them was his insistence that a new kind of unity must be created. This new unity was to result from a constant, respectful interchange between ideological opponents who, despite their disagreements, accept one another and want to share a common fate. For several decades, Kaplan called for a reformulation of the Jewish covenant that would affirm unity without uniformity. Nonetheless, pluralism must not become anarchy. Kaplan posited the need for legislation—he even called it *Halakhah*—in matters that bear directly on the social stability of the Jewish polity. He was referring to the questions of personal status such as marriage and divorce, inheritance, conversion, and the like. Kaplan held that in a free society, such laws must be enacted by democratic methods and should be subject to amendment or repeal by duly elected representatives of the people. Between Kook and Kaplan is a gap that stretches from a theocratic nomocracy to a democratic polity. The issue will be examined in greater detail in the chapters on *Halakhah* and democracy.

This distance between the two thinkers, living in the same historical period and universe of discourse, educated with the same classical Jewish texts, and buffeted by the same or similar intellectual currents, has its antecedents in the history of Jewish thought. However, since the seventeenth century, the distance between some of the disputants has widened to the verge of a split. It is difficult to discern how the approaches of both Kook and Kaplan can be credited with the designation, "These and these are the words of the living God" (B. Eruvin 13b). Can we imagine a single religious framework within which both thinkers could function? From the standpoint of many halakhists, Kaplan was a heretic and a candidate for excommunication. Indeed, in 1945, a number of Fundamentalist extremists took this action against him. If other, more moderate, Orthodox rabbis did not follow suit, their silence can be attributed to the fact that the penalty of excommunication has lost all force in the Jewish community at large. The area of belief and conflicting ideas, beyond which we enter the territory of heresy, has expanded to such an extent as to render excommunication an anachronism.

Hardly a single non-Orthodox Jew today is free of the taint of *apikorsut*, or heresy. But it should be noted that in Israel and the free Diaspora, there are different degrees of tolerance toward deviations. Kaplan was excommunicated in New York City by ideological critics in a camp with which he did not identify and with which he had lost contact. Moreover, no one in the American Jewish community who was not already alienated from Kaplan paid the slightest attention to the ban. In Israel, however, excommunication is likely to be pronounced more readily against Jews within the halakhic camp than it is against outright secularists and nonreligionists. In 1920, Kook himself was excommunicated by a small group of extremists. They took exception to the daring views expressed in his book *Orot*, published in that year.[13]

Whereas Kaplan saw no need to react to his excommunication, except with sorrow that Jews could be so benighted, Kook apparently found it necessary to soften or explain some of his rhetoric. An equally blatant example of the power of intolerance in Israel today is the pressure that was placed upon the outstanding scholar Adin Steinsalz. In 1992, Steinsalz was forced to remove from the market a book he had written, in which he approached certain biblical heroes in somewhat heterodox terms. Halakhic right-wingers threatened to ban his new commentary on the Talmud in all Fundamentalist circles. Because he wanted his work to benefit all segments of Jewry, Steinsalz yielded to the threat.

Kaplan created his system to include the whole spectrum of Jewry, from the many free-thinkers on his left, whom tradition would exclude from the world-to-come, to those who stand to the right of Kook. This global inclusiveness is an innovation of the pluralist approach, namely, that the right to Jewish identity and participation in Jewish affairs must not be denied any Jew because of divergence from traditional beliefs or practices. Kaplan does not proclaim that all ideas and forms of behavior are of equal worth, but he argues that the determination of what is or is not of value should be made through debate and public opinion. Clearly, Kook would not and could not consent to the compromises that would be required for him to relate to the likes of Kaplan as a partner in a joint venture.

The current social tensions of the Jewish people are as serious as at any time in history. In the past, even when Jewish scholars and thinkers were divided by ideological differences, they shared the same platform. They agreed that they had to function within the *Halakhah*. Today, even many of those who pledge allegiance to Jewish law have difficulty in justifying its structure of authority or defending its theological basis. The overwhelming majority of Jews are no longer to be found within the halakhic arena. Their lives are inspired by influences that negate the authority and method of the *Halakhah* and a large portion of its contents. Kook and Kaplan agree on the need for all Jews to achieve respect for our tradition and to study it in depth, but Kook could not contemplate the kind of extensive selectivity and willingness to amend, change, and add that men like Kaplan deemed necessary. Kook believed that the renascence of Judaism would evolve from a large-scale return to halakhic ways. Kaplan reasoned that return alone, without revaluation of principles and substantive changes in Jewish mentality and habits, could not lead to a vital survival. This polarity is widening among the Jewish masses. In generations to come, the ideological split is apt to assume proportions whose consequences will be more dangerous to the integrity of the Jewish people than the division between the Rabbanites and Karaites over a millennium ago.

How can this tragic outcome be forestalled? This disturbing question has no easy answer. In the absence of a solution that would be acceptable to the opposing parties, only *Ahavat Yisrael*, the love of all Jews for one another, can be appealed to, but the will to maintain close ties with fellow Jews has weakened. However, the social breach can be narrowed between persons like Kook and Kaplan. Thinkers of their cast can possibly prevent further loss of communication between the disputants. Fortunately, many human beings can live with paradoxes, dilemmas, and problems lacking visible solutions. It is this quality that enables them to avoid pressing some of their sincerest beliefs to the ultimate degree. Delay in implementation is undoubtedly distressing to ideological activists. Nevertheless, it is preferable to continue the debate rather than to curtail it artificially by coercing one side or the other into surrender without conviction. Such a resolution can lead only to bitterness and further unrest.

Kook made an important contribution to reasoned debate when he wrote, "[T]he pure and righteous do not complain about wickedness; they add to the measure of righteousness. They do not cry out against heresy; they increase faith. They do not draw attention to ignorance; they increase wisdom."[14]

I repeat. I do not pretend to be a neutral observer. More than sixty years ago, I became a disciple of Mordecai Kaplan. However, respect for my teacher imposes a moral obligation on me to be objective about his views and to be as open as possible to criticism of my own position. In the spirit of the School of Hillel and of Kaplan himself, I shall attempt to state respectfully and fairly what Kook has to say and, when it is relevant to do so, the opinions of other thinkers, before expressing my own opinion on a subject. Moreover, I have acquired enormous respect for Kook and regard his thought as one of the major intellectual achievements of twentieth-century Jewish theology and philosophy. Much in his work challenges Kaplan's supporters and other modernists to examine more closely some of the assumptions of such non-Orthodox outlooks. No doubt Kook's inspiration will continue to play a role in the Judaism of the future. Thus, despite the criticism that I level at many of Kook's ideas, I am duty-bound to describe his thought as it is, in its own terms, and as comprehensively as is possible in a single volume. I do not expect my interpretations of either Kook or Kaplan to be acceptable to all readers, but it is my hope that I shall not be accused of subjectivity, tendentiousness, or blind partisanship.

NOTES

1. I disagree with the opinion of Yosef Ben-Shelomo that Kook alone seriously addressed the changes in Jewish life that resulted from secularization and from Zionism. Kaplan was even more far-sighted, for he had a better grasp than Kook did of the impact of general culture and the worldwide spread of Jewish communities. See Ben-Shelomo's *Shirat Hayyim: Perakim B'mishnato shel HaRav Kook* (Tel Aviv: Ministry of Defense, 1989, p. 9). The book is available in English under the title *Poetry of Being* (Tel Aviv: Mod Books, 1990). The reference here is to page 11.

2. See *Toledot Hahagut Hayehudit Bameah Ha-20* (*A History of Jewish Thought in the 20th Century*) by Eliezer Schweid (Tel Aviv: Dvir, 1990, p. 261). Schweid categorizes Kaplan's conception of Judaism as secularist, as opposed to Kook's religiosity. Schweid is expressing the viewpoint of most Israelis, including those who see themselves as having no connection with religion, who take religion to be synonymous with belief in a supernatural God and in the historicity of the revelation at Mt. Sinai,

and who accept the *Halakhah* as totally authoritative. Denial of any of these fundamentals is regarded as an admission ticket into the secular world. In contradistinction to Schweid, I shall attempt to demonstrate that Kaplan, as well as Kook, belongs thoroughly in the religious medium. There is no reason to negate the validity of Kaplan's self-identification as a religious Jew. His program was intended to vitalize Jewish religion by strengthening the ties between Jews of all description and by honest examination of the established and changing elements in tradition. It is true that Schweid does not argue that secularism is necessarily antireligious, but in this book at least, he makes no attempt to examine Kaplan's contribution to the understanding of religion.

3. See Menachem Friedman, *Hevrah V'dat: Haorthodokziyah Ha-lo Zionit B'Eretz Yisrael* (*Society and Religion: Non-Zionist Orthodoxy in Eretz Yisrael*) (Jerusalem: Yad Yitzhak ben Zvi, 1978).

4. Schweid, op. cit., p. 261.

5. Kook's well-known availability and graciousness to everyone mislead some readers to regard him as a liberal and a pluralist. But it is sufficient to note his reaction to common practices in non-Orthodox synagogues in the United States to realize his uncompromising opposition to all deviations from *Halakhah* and ancestral custom. In a responsum written in 1923, he pronounced single-mindedly: "God forbid that any Jew should be among the sinners and join a congregation like this that casts off holy restraints. It is absolutely forbidden to enter and to pray in synagogues like this" (*Orah Mishpat* [*The Way of Law*], Jerusalem: Mosad HaRav Kook, 1978, p. 48). The issue involved synagogues that practiced family seating and had mixed male-female choirs.

6. "Afikim Banegev" ("River Beds in the Negev") in *HaPeles*, 1903, p. 656.

7. *Poetry of Being,* p. 20.

8. See also the comments of Benjamin Ish-Shalom in his important study, *HaRav Kook: Bein Razionalism Umistikah* (*Rabbi Kook: Between Rationalism and Mysticism*) (Tel Aviv: Am Oved, 1990).

9. *Diaries*, October 10, 1917. Since I shall quote extensively from Kaplan's *Diaries*, I should mention that they have not yet been published. The original hand-written volumes are found in the Library of the Jewish Theological Seminary of America in New York. Incomplete copies are located in photocopied or microfilm form at the Reconstructionist Rabbinical College in Philadelphia; the Hebrew Union College in Cincinnati and Jerusalem; and the Hebrew University of Jerusalem. Professor Mel Sculpt is preparing three volumes of selections, which will soon be published. The *Diaries*, which are contained in about twenty-five notebooks of three hundred pages each, are a mine of philosophical

cogitation, recordings of reflections on the historic events of Jewish life during the Kaplan century, comments on leading Jewish and non-Jewish figures and ordinary people whom he knew, outlines of sermons or articles in preparation, literary criticism, unsparing self-analysis, random thoughts, and more.

10. Kook had a facile pen, but Kaplan says about himself: "It is difficult for me to express easily whatever enters my mind, whether I write in English or in Hebrew. My pen is heavy in both languages" (*Diaries*, June 29, 1935).

11. Jacob Agus skillfully describes Kook's attitude toward secular studies and foreign cultures. He writes: "His was a peculiarly selective mind which intuitively drew from Western philosophy and literature only those elements that enriched and deepened his religious beliefs" (*Great Jewish Thinkers of the Twentieth Century* [Washington, D.C.: B'nai B'rith, 1963, p. 76]). In this way, Kook was able to convince himself that his absolute faith could only benefit from reading the works of the great philosophers. They could not undermine an iota in the Torah of Israel. Kook knew how to adapt specific ideas from these sources for inclusion in the halakhic framework.

12. Ish-Shalom declares that Kook was familiar with the leading philosophers of his day, whether through reading their works or learning about them from essays that appeared in Hebrew journals. Doubtlessly, he also breathed the atmosphere of the intellectual environment of the time.

13. Bezalel Naor records the entire affair in the Introduction to his translation of *Orot* (Northvale, London: Jason Aronson, 1993). See Note 1, Chapter 2.

14. *Arfelei Tohar* (*Clouds of Purity*) (henceforth, AT) (Jerusalem: Zvi Yehudah Kook Memorial Institute, 1987, p. 39).

2
Two Worlds

IDEAS HAVE LIVES of their own. Once thrust into the arena of human discourse, they stand on their own, regardless of who formulates them. However, should one want to understand, at least to some extent, how an idea evolves, it is necessary to know something about its author. In such a context, one must enter the world the author experienced and consider the ways in which the environment affects outlook. This is by no means a simple task. For instance, consider the cases of R. Yehudah Halevi and R. Moses ben Maimon (Maimonides or Rambam), on one hand, and Kook and Kaplan, on the other.

Halevi and Maimonides were born fifty years apart—Halevi, in 1085, and Rambam (the acronym for R. Moses ben Maimon), in 1135. At death they were separated by almost sixty-five years, as Halevi died in 1140, and Maimonides, in 1204. Thus, while over a generation separated these two great figures, their lives were conducted in virtually the same world of thought and interaction with a non-Jewish environment that was sometimes accepting of and available to talented Jews. In contrast, Kook was born only fifteen years before Kaplan but died almost fifty years earlier than Kaplan did. Despite the proximity of their births, their lives were light years apart when compared with the lives of the medieval philosophers.

KOOK'S WORLD

Kook was born in Grieve, a small town near Dvinsk, Latvia, in 1865. Kaplan was born in Sventzian, Lithuania, in 1881. Although their births were close in time and their birthplaces were in geographical proximity, their worlds of experience were vastly different. Kook studied long years in yeshivot, schools for Talmudic studies, most notably in Volozhin, and served as rabbi of several communities until he became the Chief Rabbi of Jaffa in 1904. While on a mission during World War I, Kook was trapped in Europe and was unable to return to Eretz Yisrael until the hostilities ended. He spent part of that time as rabbi of an important congregation in London. In 1921, soon after resettling in Jaffa, Kook was elected to the post of the first Chief Rabbi of Ashkenazi Jewry. He took up residence in Jerusalem and there continued his distinguished career for the rest of his life. Kook's biography is that of a great scholar, a *talmid hakham*, whose entire education and activities were conducted within the realm of Jewish experience. Virtually all of his knowledge of the non-Jewish world came from reading and from what he gleaned from secondary sources. In his rabbinical capacity, of course, he had to relate to non-Jewish authorities, but his contacts with them stemmed from his professional responsibilities rather than from any sense of occupying the same space.

Kook was more than an observer of the social and political revolution in which the Jewish people was involved during the last decades of the nineteenth century and the first decades of the twentieth. He imbibed love for Eretz Yisrael in his home and developed his own brand of political and cultural Zionism. Kook faced fierce opposition to his Zionist stand from right-wing religious extremists, especially after his election to the post of Chief Rabbi. Particularly repugnant to these strict halakhists was Kook's positive attitude toward the new type of Jew that he encountered after his arrival in Jaffa. Kook strove to fathom the mentality of the secularist halutzim. He soon communicated to these "new Jews" his appreciation of their dedication to the revitalization of Eretz Yisrael. He was convinced that their performance of this *mitzvah*, or meritorious action, would eventually bring them to religious observance.

Socially, Kook kept his distance from the non-Jewish world, but he was extremely interested in its currents of thought. In this study, I shall not attempt to speculate on the identities of the European thinkers who appear in Kook's writings. I leave this subject to academicians more capable than I. Suffice it to say that traces of Spinoza, Schopenhauer, Bergson, and other philosophers seem to have influenced some of Kook's ideas. As I have noted, it is difficult to determine whether their impact came from Kook's reading of original sources, from essays that appeared frequently in Hebrew periodicals, or from unconscious absorption of the intellectual atmosphere of the time (see Note 8, Chapter 1). Among his Orthodox colleagues, Kook stood out as a person who understood that Judaism could not be blind to the truths that were being discovered beyond the Jewish world.

Nevertheless, Kook found complete fulfillment in the study and practice of Torah. Nothing in classic Judaism was beyond his scope of interest, but he did not permit the walls of the yeshivah to protect him from what was happening outside. Jewish life was being revolutionized. Both political and cultural Zionism had created new forms of Jewish expression for traditional and deviant Jews alike. The social experiments of the kibbutz (collective settlements) and the moshavim (cooperative settlements) were conceived by their theoreticians as superior moral, spiritual, and cultural alternatives to the Judaism of their forebears. Kook devoted much time and effort in arguing the Zionist cause among halakhic Jewry and the halakhic cause among the growing so-called secular community. He succeeded in neither direction. The Fundamentalists viewed the restoration of Eretz Yisrael as God's responsibility, while the free-thinking settlers turned a deaf ear to Kook's appeals for their return to the Judaism of old. The Fundamentalists hated him and the halutzim loved him; but the conflict between the two different visions of Judaism continued unabated.

KAPLAN'S WORLD

Kaplan's life was played out on another planet. When he was six years old, his father, Rabbi Israel Kaplan, emigrated to New York City, where he was appointed by the Orthodox Chief Rabbi, Yaakov Yosef, to supervise kashrut (the Jewish dietary regulations) in the State of New York. As was common among Eastern European Jewish families of that era, Rabbi Kaplan preceded his wife and children to the United States. Two years later, they were reunited after the family had spent the second year in Paris, where Mordecai's mother had a brother who supported his sister, her daughter Sophie (known as Shprinze), and her son. Upon arriving in the United States, Kaplan studied with private teachers who were expected to train him to be a devout Jew and to become steeped in the classic Jewish texts. Mordecai Kaplan recalled with special fondness the many hours he spent with his learned father, who taught him Talmud. At the age of twelve, Kaplan entered the Jewish Theological Seminary, from which he eventually earned his rabbinical ordination. A fellow graduate was Joseph Hertz, later the Chief Rabbi of the British Empire.

For all his piety, Kaplan's father was a broad-minded man who maintained contact with scholars whose approaches to Torah were distinctly scientific and non-Orthodox. One of these scholars was Arnold Ehrlich, who, in his major work *Mikra Kifshuto*, sought to identify the plain meaning of the Bible by applying the lessons of its scientific study. He was a frequent visitor to the Kaplan household and often turned to Israel Kaplan, Mordecai's father, for help with talmudic sources that might aid in the understanding of various biblical passages. Mordecai was captivated by Ehrlich's approach to the Bible. Despite his openness, however, Israel Kaplan had no intention of letting his son abandon Orthodox tradition. He employed a pious teacher to instruct Mordecai in the thought of Rambam. The tactic failed. The son plunged enthusiastically into the modern world. In addition to his study at the Seminary, Kaplan received degrees from City College and from Columbia University. At Columbia, Kaplan was offered a stipend that would have enabled him to undertake advanced study in anthropology, leading to an eventual academic career. Israel Kaplan's efforts bore fruit, however, as Mordecai rejected the attractive offer; he decided to devote his talents to the Jewish people and the advancement of Judaism.

Following his ordination, Kaplan served as principal of the Hebrew school and preacher of English sermons under Rabbi M. Z. Margolis in Kehillat Yeshurun, an Orthodox congregation in New York City. Conscience soon forced Kaplan to admit that he could not in all honesty minister to an Orthodox group. Even though he had no alternative in mind, he resigned his position. Fortunately, he was invited by Solomon Schechter, the renowned scholar of the Cairo Genizah and, at the time, the head of the Jewish Theological Seminary of America, to organize the Teachers Institute of the Seminary and stay on as its principal.

In 1909, Kaplan began his career of training teachers for Jewish schools and serving as an instructor in the Rabbinical School of the Jewish Theological Seminary. For about sixty years Kaplan taught *Midrash* (rabbinical commentaries), homiletics, and philosophies of religion. During these exciting decades, he participated in virtually every area of Jewish communal life—in Zionism, education, community centers, social welfare, and other Jewish concerns. He formed the Society for the Advancement of Judaism, which was intended to be the focus of a new nationwide approach to creative Judaism, but which, in effect, functioned as a synagogue where Kaplan was able to proclaim and test his ideas about religion and worship. In the 1930s, the Society advanced beyond its own walls and began to publish a periodical, *The Reconstructionist*. Kaplan and his colleagues organized a school of thought through the agency of the Jewish Reconstructionist Foundation.

Kaplan readily acknowledged his indebtedness to scores of Jewish and non-Jewish scholars, scientists, and thinkers. His organic thinking, which sought the connections between phenomena, resulted from and stimulated the catholicity of his reading and study. No field of knowledge escaped his interest, for he believed in the interconnectedness of all phenomena. Such breadth of concern can easily lead to superficiality and oversimplification. Kaplan recognized this danger, but he compensated for his limited knowledge in many fields by taking into account the limits of each discipline. However, as an adventurer in ideas, he refused to surrender to the pessimism of those who claim that field theories and cross-disciplinary understanding cannot be attained. The forest is there even if one can see only a few of its trees.

Despite his care in trying to avoid overreliance on the authority of science, Kaplan hurt his own case by not sufficiently clarifying the distinctions between the natural and exact sciences and the human and social sciences. Too often he gave the impression of crediting the latter with greater exactitude and certitude than they can actually achieve.

Kaplan had far too many mentors to list here. All students of Kaplan's thought know of his indebtedness to Halevi, Maimonides, Spinoza, Krochmal, Emerson, Ahad HaAm, Dewey, Durkheim, Wieman, and, indeed, a parade of seminal thinkers in the long history of human cognition. Kaplan was as much a product of his time as were all those who chose to live philosophically in the twentieth century, but that does not mean that he rejected the knowledge and ideas of the past as automatically passé or that a latter-day opinion is necessarily superior to what was taught in previous ages. Occasionally, he protested that when he quoted from another person he was merely providing support for or an illustration of an idea that he had previously arrived at independently. He stated as much in regard to Durkheim, denying that he had adopted his social approach to religion from the Jewish French sociologist. Nor do I think that Kaplan was always or even mostly original. The same applies to Kook. My objective is to outline and assess their positions on a number of issues in contemporary Judaism.

Kaplan maintained extensive contacts with non-Jewish thinkers and was considered one of the leading contributors to democratic education and liberal religion in America. Without in any way limiting his love for the Jewish people or its evolving civilization, Kaplan extended his horizons to the far regions of human knowledge and wisdom. Without question, the free cultural atmosphere of the United States was a decisive factor in the development of Kaplan's system. Kook, in contrast, had neither the opportunity nor the urge to engage in direct contacts with such a multicultural environment. Even the sojourn in England did not enable Kook to experience the full impact of freedom and openness that enriched Kaplan's life.

The World in Common

Yet, to a great extent, the two worlds were united. Although Kook did not seek direct contact with the outside world, he did exhibit great interest in what was happening beyond the borders of Judaism. He and Kaplan agreed that humankind must see itself in the broadest possible perspective, namely, that of a divine, holy universe. Only through such a perspective can humans make sense of their lives. Only love of God, Kook and Kaplan believed, can motivate people to overcome evil and feel that the venture is not in vain. The two men also stood together in placing the Jewish people—its positive features and its faults, its ideals and dreams, its past and future—at the center of their concern. They saw no contradiction between their cosmic outlook and their nationalist devotion. In Kook's rhetoric, love of Israel implied love of all people.[1] For Kaplan, "Jewish religion would have Jewish civilization make for the enhancement not only of Jewish life but of the life of mankind. . . ."[2] Neither Kook nor Kaplan perceived any contradiction between universalism and Jewish particularism.

It follows from the above that we are dealing with two men who thought about life comprehensively and organically. For them, there is a reciprocal relationship between the cosmic whole and its parts, between a people and its individuals, and between a civilization and its components. For example, Kook writes, "*Teshuvah* and redemption of the world eventuate if the world would busy itself with the light of Torah in a way which would enable the spiritual soul to recognize the proper connection between the disparate units and the spiritual whole."[3] He adds, "One can apprehend the essence of Torah study only by acquiring the understanding of and feeling for the desirable holiness of every detail of Torah. One must also observe that the universal light which brings life to the cosmos invades each and every unit."[4]

In a similar vein, Kaplan remarks about the organic character of Jewish culture, saying that it

> is maintained as long as all the elements that constitute the civilization play a role in the life of the Jew. Any attempt to live or transmit only certain elements in Judaism to the neglect of others is bound to end in failure, since in Judaism as a civilization the normal functioning of each element is bound up with and conditioned by the normal functioning of every other.[5]

Through it all, Kook and Kaplan differed significantly about the structure of cosmic organicity. Kook posited that the earth is divided into parcels of soil that belong to specific peoples. Eretz Yisrael is the natural habitat of the Jews. As long as there is no ingathering of the exiles, the people cannot be resurrected. Furthermore, foreign soil defiles any Jew who dwells there and prevents his or her restoration to spiritual health. For his part, Kaplan wanted a mass return of Jews to the homeland, but he eschewed attributing essential qualities to Eretz Yisrael that are denied to other lands. Kook was persuaded that Eretz Yisrael has supernatural powers, whereas Kaplan credited it only with the powers characteristic of all other soil. That *only*, however, is not to be taken lightly, for it is that power of a land to attract a group and galvanize it to creativity that converts it from a mere stretch of soil into a homeland.

Kook looked at nations through the lens of comparison, that is, between Israel and other peoples. This perspective is reflected in a statement contained in a sermon he delivered on Shabbat Vayetze, in 5689 (1928):

> There is an eternal conflict between Israel and the nations of the world. Judaism says, "The holiness of man can and must be part and parcel of natural existence. . . ." The nations, however, believe that holiness has to be separate from the life of nature. They conceive of nature as being opposite from and in opposition to holiness.[6]

The flaws in such comparisons and in Kook's unfounded description of other peoples will be examined later, but to describe Kook's world, it is important to call attention to his train of thought. On the one hand, he asserted that the door to salvation is open to all humankind, and all peoples will ultimately attain a pure faith and come to recognize and worship the God of Truth and adopt a way of life consonant with that belief. On the other hand, he maintained that the current spiritual level of the rest of humankind is far below the standards of Judaism. Therefore, Israel and the nations relate to one another in conflict. The inference is that Jews are best advised to have as little to do with gentiles as possible. Kook sees no contradiction between this attitude and his eagerness to learn what he can about the non-Jewish world and its advances.

Kaplan tried to avoid comparisons, regarding them as harmful. He took pride in Jewish contributions to the moral and spiritual growth of humankind, but in his mature thought he never argued that God revealed these inventions as exclusive gifts to the Jewish people or that other peoples lacked the same responsibility to strive for moral and spiritual perfection. The potential for improvement is innate in all peoples.

Kook's attitude toward Eretz Yisrael has been mentioned. Here, too, he was not satisfied to express his love for the land and to describe the unique landscape and historical associations that evoked his devotion and that of the people as a whole. It was not the Jewish people, he emphasized, that conferred upon Eretz Yisrael its special status as its homeland. This was God's doing. He blessed the soil of this land with unique, even supernatural, capacities not possessed by any other territory in the world. All Creation was planned and executed by God. Only this premise can help us to understand the essence of the nations and their lands.

Conversely, Kaplan envisaged the Jewish people and the Land of Israel as natural phenomena. In no way does this deprive the Jewish people of its uniqueness. Uniqueness inheres in the very otherness of individuals and groups and is synonymous with individuality. Of course, Israel and Eretz Yisrael differ from other nations and their lands in many ways, but these marks of uniqueness are no indication of inherent or permanent superiority or inferiority. In the same vein, Israel's Torah is unique and, according to arguable standards, might at certain times even be considered more advanced than the teachings of other traditions. But, according to Kaplan, this, too, is a tenuous matter. Cultures change and have to be judged in the light of their adjustment to new demands. Comparisons with other cultures can only mislead because all peoples face different circumstances. Above all, Kaplan rejected the idea that the fate and faith of all peoples are God's will. Such a theology, which would seem to be implicit in Kook's observations concerning Israel and the nations, raises unanswerable doubts about God's justice.

The disagreement between Kook and Kaplan on the special qualities of the people of Israel, its land, and its Torah will be examined more closely later. However, in describing their worlds, it is useful to delve more fully into the theme of comparison as a strategy for restoring national morale and commitment. Those who argue for the superiority of Judaism tend to assume that loyalty to a people is contingent on confidence that it is endowed with attributes unmatched by other groups and that its culture embodies a larger measure of truth, goodness, and beauty than any other tradition. Why should one remain a Jew unless Judaism has more to offer than any other culture? Indeed, many nations operate on the assumption that the enhancement and progress of all cultures result only from competition to outdo one another. Most education is based on the idea that without the goal of achieving superior excellence, students of all ages would never put forth their maximum effort to learn. The ideal of *Torah lishmah*, that is, study for its own sake, is likely to appeal only to those to whom the content of that study is, ab initio, of extreme worth. This is the mood in the traditional yeshivah.

Kook's world is one of a Jewry firm in its belief that it has the ability to reach moral and spiritual heights that are unattainable by any other nation. Other peoples, it is true, can climb to higher rungs on the ladder of achievement, but only Israel is duty-bound by its nature to become an ideal people. This concept is repeated in many passages throughout Kook's works. I shall cite just a few lines from one of his essays, "Israel and its Renascence":

> The might of the God of the universe, Israel's God . . . is most clearly manifest and increases through the exalted actions of the Jewish people. It shines forth as a basic characteristic of this nation; in its passion for redemption, it is aroused and flourishes. . . . *No other nation in the world has a spiritual psyche that can apprehend* this *earth-shaking truth.* . . . The vital center of Israel's soul is in the Source of holiness. We were born in the way of truth and faith, and in it we continue to mature. Our values are not disparate. Unity pervades us, and the light of the One God is in our being. The laws of the living God's Torah *distinguish us from all nations. Holiness acts within us, and our finest aspirations are directed toward its attainment. There are tricklings of holiness in every people, but not all their life-values stem therefrom. Not so, in regard to Israel.* . . . The God-quest of Torah has remained a precious trait of Israel which is manifest in its eternal, universal nature and which shines forth in Eretz Yisrael, the land of its inheritance, the locale of the light of the holy treasure.[7] (Italics, JJC)

From these lines it is evident that it was important for Kook not only to proclaim the unique qualities of Israel but to deny the possibility that they might be possessed in substantial measure by other peoples or religions.

Nevertheless, Kook was equally assertive in his criticism of chauvinistic nationalism. He believed that the Torah enabled the Jewish people to avoid this danger.

> Nationhood in the spirit of Torah is protected from the kind of thick-headedness that eventuates in riotous nationalism, when a

people strays from the straight road of national loyalty. There is no sentiment more calculated than nationalism to evoke in a people vitality and light, but it can easily deteriorate into coarse and ugly self-infatuation. Our nationalism, however, rests on the exalted toraitic foundation of the highest morality. . . .[8]

In his determination to judge Israel in the most positive way, Kook overlooked elements in traditional Judaism that bear the seeds of chauvinism.

Kaplan fled from the outlook best exemplified in a remark by the German historian, Oswald Spengler: "A people is such only in relation to other peoples." In contradistinction to this idea, Kaplan wrote: "Nationhood must henceforth be based on the principle that a people is mainly such in relation to its individual members. . . . Only secondarily and under stress of attack should nationhood operate vis-à-vis other peoples."[9] That is to say, every nation is unique, in ways that are conditioned by its historical development. These ways result from internal and external circumstances, past and present, that are only partially under the nation's control. However, according to Kaplan, every nation has the same responsibility, no more and no less, to ensure that its vocation is used to train men and women worthy of the designation "made in the image of God."

The comparative approach leads to other distortions. If descriptions of national differences were such that each added a special tint to the colorful fabric of human civilization, there would be nothing wrong in pointing out such differences. Both Bach and Beethoven can be appreciated without comparing them. It is also legitimate to criticize Christianity for the measure of anti-Semitism that remains in the theology of some of its denominations, just as it is correct to see the self-ghettoization of many Jews as a sign of weakness and a refusal to tackle the problem of living under freedom. But statements of fact are not what believers in their religious superiority have in mind. They are convinced that their religion contains more of the knowledge of God and His will than any other faith. This state of mind was expressed by the medieval Jewish philosopher Joseph Albo. Every person is capable of grasping reality in what he called "natural religion," and every people creates its own way of life in keeping with its understanding of what is best for human welfare. Albo termed the social enterprise, unique in form from group to group, "conventional religion." The highest form of religion (*dat,* best translated as law), is "divine religion." This form of religion, based on God's revelation of His will for all humankind, is in Israel's sole possession. In summary, comparisons between peoples and cultures generally do not encourage self-criticism. They are intended to prove the superiority of the ingroup.

In comparisons of this type, who is to determine the standards by which the merits of different groups are to be determined? The comparer? Is it not standard procedure for judges not to adjudicate in cases in which they are involved? In our instance, even assuming that the criteria for comparisons are formulated by an objective, honest judge, who can guarantee that what holds today in evaluating cultural levels will pertain tomorrow? Kook himself called his readers' attention to the fact that *Ahavat Yisrael,* the love that every Jew should have for the Jewish people, "should not blind him from criticizing all its defects."[10]

In every nation one can always find a broad spectrum that extends from sinners to those who live by the universal norms of human behavior. In this respect, we Jews are no different from other groups. Kook cannot deny the fact that there is a mixture of saints and scoundrels in Jewish ranks as well as among other peoples. But he adopts the strategy of comparing the nations, not as they actually are, but as ideal, timeless entities. In this way, Kook places Israel beyond all possibility of evaluation according to the criteria that apply to the other nations. In the transcendent realm that Israel occupies, the Jewish people is the only treasured people. The views of Kook and Kaplan on the historic and cosmic significance of the Jewish people will be discussed further below.

Reference has been made to the ethnocentrism of the two thinkers. As a result of their different experiences and their intuitive predilections, they arrived at conflicting conclusions about the meaning and implications of their common theological focus. Kook was a mystic; Kaplan, a rationalist. This is the manner in which Shmuel Hugo Bergmann depicted the spirit of Kook's thought:

> Rational reflection and analysis can at best provide us with disconnected scenes of various aspects of life; they cannot give us a picture

of the whole of reality nor envisage the dynamic, unifying substance that underlies the whole of experience. Ultimately, man can
grasp reality and perceive truth only through the non-rational faculty of his inner vision and the power of his imagination.[11]

The universe is refracted through a human being's senses and
reason as a collection of collisions and contradictions of unconnected, ever-changing units. In the midst of all this dissonance,
human beings realize their unity and uniqueness. Kook strove to
rise above the cosmic divisions and to experience the divine unity,
to go beyond the rational and to reach the higher reality beyond
the observable world. He believed that this aim can be fulfilled
only in mystic experience, and he was apparently endowed with
this talent. He expresses this view several times in both his philosophical and his poetical works. Here is one example taken from
a poem titled "Aspiration":[12]

> My soul's desire, my heart,
> Please tell me,
> Tell me, my soul
> The secret of this riddle.
>
> My soul aspires,
> My spirit flutters,
> Whence? To a goal.
>
> The destination is lofty,
> There in the high heavens
> And very glorious.
>
> Who will answer my question,
> That I might see above the clouds
> Perhaps there I shall observe my target
> Face to face.
>
> Perhaps from the beauty of her eyes
> Rays will strike me
> And bring light and life
> With her flames to my cold heart.

Turning to Kaplan, we again pass into another realm, one no
less pervaded with love of God and a passionate desire to experi-

ence something beyond what meets the eye. However, the unity that Kook sought to experience through mystic flights is in Kaplan's view to be approximated—only approximated—with the aid of the instruments of reason and wisdom, including disciplined imagination. Kaplan never expects to see God face to face. He is satisfied with the hints about God's existence that penetrate his consciousness in the course of manifold experiences. He, too, uses poetic prayer to express his longing to buttress his faith in God's unity. A few stanzas will suffice to illustrate what Kaplan shares with Kook, as well as what sets the two men apart.[13]

> God is the oneness
> That spans the fathomless deeps of space
> And the measureless eons of time.
> Binding them in act,
> As we do in thought.
>
> He is the sameness
> In the elemental substance of stars and planets,
> Of this our earthly abode
> And of all that it holds.
>
> He is the unity
> Of all that is,
> The uniformity of all that moves,
> The rhythm of all things
> And the nature of their interaction.

Briefly, the universe as visualized by Kook under the influence of Lurianic Kabbalah lost its pristine unity at the moment of Creation. Man and the rest of Creation are destined to be restored to that primal unity in the end of days. The material cosmos is but a shadow of the true world. The phenomena that man encounters on earth have only a secondary, evanescent significance. Every person is obligated to try as hard as possible to gain freedom from the chains of time and substance and to seek reunion with the One God, the *Makom* (the Place) of all existence.

Kaplan also perceives the unity of, and in, the universe but not in the vision of a God from Whom Creation separated and to Whom it is fated to return and to lose its distinct identity. Instead, Kaplan locates unity in the unchanging laws that dominate the world of phenomena.

In Kook's view, people achieve perfection by clinging to God and underplaying their individuality. Kook's ideal is the restoration of God's aloneness. According to Kaplan, salvation or fulfillment is achieved when a person satisfies a large proportion of his or her needs and implements a goodly number of his or her native talents. Human salvation is a ceaseless effort, whose success can only be proximate. Salvation, it might be said, depends as much on finding satisfaction in playing the game as in winning it. In this connection, Kaplan makes a crucial distinction between needs and wants. Human fulfillment is in another dimension from that of ego-satisfaction. Needs are the inherent requirements for the healthy functioning of the human body and psyche. However, inasmuch as humans are limited creatures and can never reach perfection, they must at least try to avoid identifying wants and appetites as always consonant with needs. Wants are subjective; needs are the ineluctable requirements of an orderly life.

KOOK AND KAPLAN: THE ISSUES AT STAKE

Let me clarify the issues at stake in the debate between Kook and Kaplan on the question of cosmic unity. Both men affirm the unity of God and that of the universe we know. Each responds positively, both intellectually and emotionally, to the call, "Sh'ma Yisrael, Adonai Eloheinu, Adonai Ehad" ("Hear, O Israel, the Lord our God, the Lord is One") (Deut. 6, 6). They are united in their pain at the suffering of decent men and women. They believe that much of this evil can be overcome. But their methods of correction differ widely as a result of their distinctive conceptions of cosmic unity. They each start by asserting that the path to God is through the gate of ordinary daily experiences. Kook puts it this way:

> It is necessary to locate the path to be followed in order to gain access to the reception hall—through the gate. The gate is the Godhood as revealed in the world in all its beauty and splendor, in every spirit and soul, in every living thing and insect, in every plant and flower, in every nation and realm, in the sea and its waves, in the heavenly canopy and the majestic lights, in the cadences of conversation, in the ideas of every author, in the images of every poet and

the musings of every thinker, in the emotions of every sensitive person and in the tempestuous bravery of every hero.[14]

Note that the experiences and phenomena Kook mentions do not prove the existence of a First Cause or Creator. Unity is first and foremost the intuitive faith of a believer. Kook's list provides only hints about God's existence and unity, but God is presupposed in each item. Theology, like science, is based on a feeling of unity that precedes all attempts to give it rational content and substantiation. This emotional factor, in turn, is undoubtedly conditioned by those experiences that thrust persons toward faith. Despite all the discontinuities in nature, human beings are moved by the many examples of continuity to surround themselves with a magic circle of emotional faith in the world's unity and of an intellectual effort to prove this very premise. Kook does not have to break out of this circle because he sees no need for rational evidence. Cosmic unity becomes manifest to him in moments of mystical union or communion with God.

Meanwhile, although Kaplan insists on a rational stance regarding knowledge of the world, he acknowledges that the instruments of the senses and the mind used to apprehend the outside world are imperfect and inexact. Successive discoveries or new insights are bound to change the way men and women, including the greatest scientists and philosophers, think about the universe. But these innovations, far from discouraging faith in the underlying unity of reality, increase one's confidence that the cosmic flux is ruled by permanent laws.[15] A person's experience supports the view that many suppositions about the operation of the universe can be validated through disciplined research. Each generation adds credence to the belief in cosmic unity. But, Kaplan argues, this unity has meaning for humankind only when it can be seen as a process that offers hope that human needs can be fulfilled sufficiently to make life worthwhile.

Kaplan explains his position as follows:

Our intuition of God is the absolute negation and antithesis of all evaluations of human life which assume that consciousness is a disease, civilization a transient sickness, and all our efforts to lift civilization above the brute only a vain pretense. . . . The human mind cannot rest until it finds order in the universe.[16]

At first glance the similarity between this passage and Kook's comments is surprising, considering Kook's mystical predilections and Kaplan's rationalism. However, if we probe more deeply, the difference becomes apparent. Kaplan criticizes mysticism and writes:

> *While the immediacy and the dynamic of God-Awareness are, no doubt, indispensable to vital religion, their value is dangerously overstressed by those of a romantic or mystic turn of mind.* (Italics, MMK)
>
> Nothing less than the deliberate refusal to be satisfied with the negation of life's inherent worth is likely to keep our minds in a receptive mood for the belief in God. But being in a receptive mood is not enough. We shall not come to experience the reality of God unless we go in search of Him. To be seekers of God, we have to depend more on our own thinking and less upon tradition. Instead of acquiescing passively in the traditional belief that there is a God, and then deducing from that belief conclusions which are to be applied to human experience and conduct, we must accustom ourselves to find God in the complexities of our experience and behavior.[17]

Kaplan implores us not to draw simplistic conclusions from this orientation to faith. We must continue to open each door that we come upon after successfully passing through the one to which we have just found the key. Above all, Kaplan distanced himself from the supposition, founded in faith, that God exists as a supernatural Being and that Israel is not subject to the laws of behavior that guide the destiny of other nations.[18]

Clearly, what divides Kook and Kaplan theologically is not faith in God, which each assumes to be the natural state of mind of a healthy person. They part company when it comes to the *object* of that faith, namely, the idea of God. This matter will be discussed in detail in the chapter dealing with the search for God. At this point, though, it may be helpful to examine three concepts that are pivotal in every theological debate. These terms are "immanent," "supernatural," and "transcendent." For Kook, in the last analysis, everything is in the hands of a supernatural God, so the terms transcendent and supernatural are synonymous in meaning. In this cosmology, nature is a name for the usual order of things—*minhago shel olam*. But that regularity is not autonomous. God can cause miracles. Ultimately, God's unity will prevail, and disparate reality will be reconstituted into its primal state of oneness.

Kaplan and Kook agree that knowledge begins with the apprehension of immanent phenomena, with the experience of the senses and of mental processes. All that a person can know comes from the existential reality of which he or she is a part. That reality, however, extends beyond the scope of the senses and is not exhausted by the many ways in which the human mind pictures the connectedness of these immanent experiences. There is always a further novelty to immanent reality. The creative flux continues. If it were not for one's ability to imagine an all-embracing realm of principles, laws, standards, and other uniting factors, humanity's reach could not extend beyond the experience of the here and now. Without the positing of transcendent possibilities and restrictions, one could make no plans for the future, even for the very next second. Nor could one relate to one's fellows in rational trust. It is this transcendent quality of reality which guarantees that the cosmos operates in an organic fashion and that the search for meaning and fulfillment need not be in vain.

For Kaplan, these two categories—immanence and transcendence—are sufficient to enable people to unravel some of the secrets of the universe and to make sense of their lives. Of course, the secret of Creation itself is beyond human understanding. Nor are humans qualified to tap into a supernatural generator and identify its effects as the word of God. For it is the individual human who formulates what is attributable to God and then tries to foist these views on others as authoritative descriptions of divinity. Immanence and transcendence are also manmade categories, but they are by definition never absolute and are always subject to refinement and correction, thereby, assuring that the damage caused by error is minimized. To Kaplan, this is a better way to lift humans above their present stage of knowledge. The supernaturally founded criteria of truth and goodness force Kook to believe that the Torah is entirely good and true. How can the word of God be mistaken? Kaplan, conversely, is free to reconsider the Jewish heritage in the light of new, verified findings and insights, without having to feel that he is disloyal to his ancestors. They, after all, were not privy to what we know about reality and cannot be blamed for the errors of their ignorance. No generation ever attains omniscience.

Ours is an age in which many persons seek to recapture the sense of holiness that has been virtually eliminated from humankind's view of the universe and of itself. Life has become an endless struggle for power, which is to be used ruthlessly. Carnal satisfaction and pleasure are now the overriding goals of human endeavor. Holiness is an anachronism or an exercise in the absurd. To yearn or search for the holy is a sure road to frustration; however, Kook and Kaplan meet the challenge head on.

In our era, the struggle between the sacred and the profane, the religious and the secular, has reached a critical period, one that is even more threatening than similar periods in the past. The dispute between Kook and Kaplan on the subject is especially enlightening because both men resist turning back the clock to a time when a sharp dichotomy existed between heavenly rule and nature. The last century was one in which a division occurred between those religious theorists who have sought to restore or to buttress belief in a heteronomous universe and those who have tried to adapt religion to the reality of an autonomous nature. Both Kook and Kaplan have grappled with this problem, which received its definitive analysis in the discussion on the sacred and the profane by G. Van der Leeuw[19] but which has been one of the main items on the agenda of theologians of all stripes. Kaplan seeks holiness in the structure of the cosmos; Kook finds it there, too, but only as a manifestation of the periodically employed power of the Creator. For Kaplan, existence is a continuous process; for Kook, God creates anew every day.

Both men, however, regard the holy and the profane in human affairs as relative to human intelligence and experience. This is to be expected in Kaplan's vision. His whole philosophy assumes that men and women define what is holy. It was the Jewish people who sanctified the Bible. It is Jews who declare that God made sacred the Shabbat and all the holidays in the Jewish calendar. Of course, it is not a matter of pure subjectivity. Holiness is conferred on occasions, places, conceptions, documents, and the like that have played important roles in the life of the Jewish people. Thus, Kaplan regards holiness as an interplay between a people and the character-molding elements in its history, environment, and culture.

Kook's assertion that the difference between the holy and the profane is dependent on the intellectual and spiritual levels of human beings is unusual. Because he is a traditionalist, we might expect him to point to what the Torah declares to be holy and to leave the matter at that. But Kook was a man of the world who sought to rescue the sparks of holiness, which he regarded as lying hidden in the shattered vessels of Creation. Although it is easy to trace this vision to Kook's kabbalistic roots, I have the feeling that he was equally touched by his humanistic instincts. He wanted a better world, and he must have sensed that there are stretches of holiness that exist beyond the range of Torah.

Thus, Kook occupied a two-story world—immanent and supernatural. Kaplan's cosmic home was a ranch-style, one-story structure that housed immanence and transcendence as complementary aspects of the same level. Kook had to reach the second flight through mystical ascent. No other substantial means were available to him, since all the steps in a staircase could, in theory at least, be whisked away arbitrarily from under his feet. In Kaplan's one-story home, reality is studied through the contemporaneity of the two complementary foci of immanence and transcendence. Every phenomenon requires the application of both epistemological tools to be understood and set into a useful context.

It is the nature of theological controversy never to be terminated. Who can prove or disprove that natural law is governed and can be repealed by an inscrutable Being, or that it is an autonomous, unchangeable order? Whether temperament or logic determines many of our choices in life is a matter of opinion. Nevertheless, truth and goodness cannot be ascertained arbitrarily. Every person is intellectually and morally obligated to support his or her position with fact, when it is available, and to justify the consequences of his or her stand. The person who chooses the example of either Kook or Kaplan as the guide to the Jewish future must bear that responsibility in mind. In subsequent chapters, a number of the more salient aspects of the two approaches will be amplified, along with indications of some of the likely consequences of each.

Kook and Kaplan have similar views of the social and ideological changes of the twentieth century and the impact of these developments on the inner life of the Jewish people. However, the two thinkers comprehend these developments in different ways, which has an important bearing on the utility of their systems. Precisely because their conceptions are so different, it is of great interest to note their similarity in spirit and content.[20] Kook points to three major changes in modern thought, relating to social vision, cosmology, and evolution.[21] He notes that nations realize their interdependence. Humankind is no longer observed or conceived solely in terms of the immediate environment. Even the Jewish people understands or should be aware of the fact that beyond Jewry is an influential reality. Until recently, we had been a nation apart, as a result of persecution that, as Kook says, conditioned "the essential difference between our spiritual life and behavior and those of every other nation on the face of the earth. . . ."[22]

Kook perceives the variety in a positive light, for "the human spirit is universal."[23] Despite all the dissimilarity between Israel and other peoples of the world, they are united by a common impulse to better themselves and to draw ever closer, individually and collectively, to the universal, godlike image. All this, Kook states,

> was always known to exceptional persons, but today the masses too recognize the closeness of the human family. Social perception has widened. Every individual feels that he is not alone and not completely confined in one space, and that *he functions in and is moved by extensive groups* from strange and foreign surroundings. No person should think that it is unnecessary for him to pay attention to these others because they are located far away.[24] (Italics, JJC)

Kook senses that this new social reality poses a danger to traditional Judaism, but unlike other halakhic loyalists, he is convinced that it has to be confronted courageously. Hiding our heads in the sand is no solution. Nevertheless, Kook is torn on this issue. Despite his determination to face facts and to learn from the expanding sources of knowledge, he never entirely loses his fear of the negative effects of this openness. Only his faith in his fellow halakhic scholars and their ability to ward off the effects of modernity enables him to enter the arena of advancing knowledge. To his credit, Kook admits that the problem exists, and he does his best to deal with it.

Similarly, Kook does not try to hide from the cosmological revolution brought about by science. The physical universe has broadened and demands drastic changes in our conception of its dimensions and its nature. Kook's dilemma, then, is how to digest these new facts without harming the bases of the ancient vision. For a traditionalist, the problem is especially difficult because the new information reaches not only the experts, who, in Kook's view, are best qualified to handle its effects, but also the masses. Faced with these altered circumstances, Kook tries to hold on to both ends of the rope, accepting the facts while not relinquishing an iota of the halakhic tradition.

Nevertheless, Kook, who affirmed the need to face the consequences that result when scientific conclusions are validated, now beclouds his own daring stand. He asserts that life can proceed successfully without human consistency and without putting scientific discoveries to work. For example, he claims that despite scientific proof that the earth is not the center of the universe but rather is only one of the countless bodies whirling through space, multitudes of men and women still ignore this fact and continue to behave as though nothing new has been learned. Kook criticizes this group when he says, "the fact that not many persons take an interest in such research does not mean that it is of slight value and that it is of no consequence which picture of the universe one accepts."[25] Yet, if Kook had thought and acted in consonance with the view he just expressed, he would have suggested that tradition be reinterpreted or amended to reflect this new direction. But it was exactly this border that he did not dare to cross. The future will take care of itself; meanwhile, the main body of the people can perpetuate the old pattern. It did no harm in the past and is unlikely to do damage now. "As for the other dimensions of thought and behavior: the poets sang, the philosophers cogitated, and life went its wonted way."[26]

With regard to evolutionary thought, Kook repeats his view that the problem is acute because the theory of evolution has become widespread. Exceptional Jewish sages always related to a "graded order of development"[27] and were accustomed to seek the relationships that bound together material and spiritual events. The average person, however, is unable to fathom evolution's significance. Kook does not evade the problems raised by evolutionary theory. He avoids subtle interpretations that would circumvent the challenge to faith that is innate in autonomous, natural evolution. If nature goes its own way, where is God? He proclaims, "A crass form of faith . . . cannot last."[28] In the face of the new image of humans and of all living things, merely matching biblical verses will not suffice to convince most Jews that the tradition can remain unaffected.

Of course, Kook did not conclude from his analysis that anything had to be uprooted from the Torah or that solutions need to be sought beyond the halakhic borders. He firmly believed that "sages devoted to toraitic logic and methodology"[29] are capable of meeting the challenge without harming a single verse of the time-honored Law.

Thus, Kook's intellectual daring was not bold enough to transform him into a new type of being. As has been discussed, Kook followed the revolutionary developments of the nineteenth and twentieth centuries, and he knew that the Jewish people could not avoid their impact. Nonetheless, he denied that any of the fundamentals of the theory or practice of Judaism required alteration. He concluded that the traditional machinery could absorb all the latest discoveries of science and inventions of technology without having to be overhauled. Kook was a modernist in his perceptions but a premodernist in his proposals to stabilize the mental health of the Jewish people. It was not that Kook was torn by an internal struggle from which he tried consciously to escape, or that he deeply repressed his doubts. However, anyone who considers Kook's life and thought must be struck by the incongruence between his courageous confrontation of modernism in the midst of a community steeped in the past and his faltering response to the revolutions that were occurring in all branches of knowledge.

Turning to Kaplan, we once again enter the dangerous world in which unbending traditionalism and adventurous radicalism, belief and disbelief, faith and cynicism, do battle. It is a world where both the impossible and the unconventional can be explored and where a new synthesis of ideas and values can be conceived.[30] From the moment he realized his heterodoxy and his inability to think in a halakhic mode, in the usual sense of that term, Kaplan had to find another way, in keeping with his mind and heart, to deal with the many problems placed on the Jewish and general human agenda. In the ensuing chapters, some of the details of Kaplan's spiritual struggle will be presented. What can be observed above all was his uncompromising determination not only to analyze the current Jewish condition but to effectuate what he concluded to be the necessary changes. In the first few decades of the twentieth century, such forthrightness was unusual among Jewish theologians and educators. Kaplan, the educator, approved of a teacher's admitting that he or she did not have an answer to a pupil's question, but he did not approve of a teacher who hid personal doubts or provided an answer that he or she knew was false or evasive.

Kaplan opens his magnum opus, *Judaism as a Civilization*, with the following words: "Judaism is a problem to those who have to teach it, and what Jew is exempt from teaching it?"[31] Kaplan then goes on to say that every Jew who is eager to ensure the Jewish future must be able to present his ideas clearly and cogently. This observation is not Kaplan's invention. "The Sages builded better than they knew when they included in the liturgy a prayer not only for the knowledge of the Torah but also for the ability to teach it."[32] In the past, he states, the knowledge of the tradition dictated the present and future conduct of the people. There was no gap between the Torah and the average Jew's outlook on life. Not so today. Every idea or custom that claims a place in the Jewish present and future has to be justified in the light of the most rigorous standards of reason and probity. That is why Kaplan—perhaps with exaggeration—wrote that we must rely more on our ability to think than on our confidence in the inherent rightness of our heritage. In the confrontation between tradition and evolving thought, Kaplan primarily gave precedence to reason validated by experience. However, in many instances tradition is itself a compelling standard of judgment and deserves preference. In each case, the decision requires objectivity and the ability to discern reliable evidence. Only in this way can the modern Jew live Judaism wholeheartedly.[33]

The air that Kaplan breathed was composed of a different proportion of tradition and science from that breathed by Kook. Kaplan considered science—more its method than its findings and conclusions—as the major fulcrum on which human civilization

must rest. For him, the scientific way of thinking was more reliable than any other method in the search for knowledge and
truth. It is best suited to prepare men and women to think independently and to arrive at convincing conclusions. However,
Kaplan did not deem science to be an ultimate value. He did not
view it as a replacement for religion.[34] Eliezer Schweid criticizes
Kaplan for what he thinks is an exaggerated reliance on science.
But the charge misleads in two ways. In the first place, Kaplan
was no reductionist. According to him, human consciousness
should not be conceived solely as pursuing objective truth. Nature does not have the only say about human destiny. Moral values—justice, equality, and the like—are often opposed or
irrelevant to nature; science has no authority over them. Science
has neither the capacity nor the right to dictate the purposes or
the values that humans set for their lives. Kaplan dissociated himself vigorously from scientism, which distorts the complex
makeup of both humans and the universe at large. While it is
likely that the cosmos is guided by unalterable laws, much space
is left for spiritual, moral, and esthetic creativity; for the overcoming of evil; and for giving form to the chaos that is prevalent in
physical and human nature.[35]

Second, as mentioned above, Schweid conceives religion rather
narrowly. He leaves little or no room for a naturalist theology to
be considered a legitimate religious option. But religion need not
be identified with any single God-concept. For Kaplan, "Religion is the process by which a People or Church seeks to enable
its members to fulfill the purpose of human life, as it conceives
that purpose."[36] Clearly, this definition confers functions on religion that cannot be fulfilled by science, which has no tools to fix
the meaning of human salvation.

The worlds outlined in this chapter indicate dramatically how
greatly Kook and Kaplan disagreed in regard to the complicated
issues of Jewish life. Consider, for instance, the symbiosis of people and culture. In what sense does a people create its culture, and
in what ways is it a product of the creations of its past? Is a culture,
or can it be, independent of the current needs of a people? Must
a people regard its heritage as demanding unstinting loyalty and
obedience and as the sole arena of its life? Does stepping beyond
its heritage in certain matters necessarily deprive a people of con-

tact with the source of its spiritual strength? Or perhaps, is it just this expansion of horizons and search for other sources of inspiration that vitalize a people?

Kook tended to limit freedom to what is permissible within the *Halakhah*. Within it, he surmised, Jewish continuity and survival could be guaranteed. Beyond it lurked danger. Kook neither advocated a ghetto nor tackled the full challenge of freedom.

In contrast to Kook's reserve, Kaplan fully endorsed the notion that the vitality of the Jewish people depended on its ability and willingness to improve its tradition. The inheritance must be deepened, changed, enhanced, and sometimes corrected. Jewish culture, including religion, must be continuously refined in the crucible of living Jewish experience. Kaplan's Judaism cannot be autonomous. The Jewish heritage cannot be the sole determinant of Jewish destiny. Judaism must inevitably include the contributions of generations past, present, and future. At the same time, if Jews wish to preserve their individuality, they have to love and respect their tradition, study it, expose its inner light, and practice whatever in it is worthy of implementation. The Jewish people and Judaism are in constant tension. There are periods when the heritage acts as a force for the perpetuation of Jewish life and for fostering the ethical sensitivity of the Jewish individual. For example, when Jews are persecuted, their natural and justifiable tendency is to observe stringently those *mitzvot*, or commandments, which, under freedom, might be deemed to have little spiritual salience and are therefore dispensable. When the gates are open and Jews are quietly welcomed into the general social and cultural matrix, it becomes necessary to fashion a Judaism that retains its otherness and uniqueness and yet absorbs worthwhile elements from the outside. A vital Jewry can be expected to be an influential force of its own, affecting the thought and behavior of its neighbors. Judaism cannot mark time. Even the reading of its past is always in flux. Israel's Torah was born in the body of the Jewish people and was thrust forth from its womb. By studying the works of Kook and Kaplan, one can clearly see the two main alternatives for preparing the Jewish world for the next few generations.

Judaism in the twenty-first century will evolve in unforeseen ways. People like Kaplan will introduce innovations as they see fit. Others, like Kook, will guard against precipitous abandonment of what to them remain hallowed ideas and practices. But the conditions surrounding their choices will be determined by the outcome of current ideological encounters.

NOTES

1. *Orot* (Jerusalem: Mosad HaRav Kook, 5723, p. 18). "Israel is full of supernal strength and splendor; its consciousness of them is suffused with eternal wisdom, with the life of grace and love of all creatures." (In translating passages from *Orot*, I acknowledge my indebtedness to the fine rendition in English by Bezalel Naor [Northvale, N. J. and London: Jason Aronson, 1993]. While I have preferred to do my own translating, I have consulted Naor and have benefited from some of his phrasing.) As early as 5661 (1901–1902), Kook gave strong expression to this motif: "The plain truth is that all men are truly brothers, children of one God and one spiritual Father. The sense of honesty demands that they return to a life of peace and pleasantness and seek wholeheartedly to secure the good of their neighbors, as befits spiritual brothers. . . . And should the human population increase drastically, there is no rational reason why this should eliminate the feeling of brotherhood" ("Teudat Yisrael U'leumiyutah"—"Israel's Mission and Its Nationhood," in *HaPeles*, p. 85).

2. The *Future of the American Jew* (henceforth, FAJ) (New York: Macmillan, 1948, p. 229). Concern for the other is a product of the interdependence of humankind. This reciprocal reliance is itself an accompanying factor of cosmic organicity. Kaplan states this view in various ways. As one illustration, he writes: "Human life can be . . . little conceived without social cooperation . . . [a person] must therefore depend on the conscious recognition of an organic social relationship in which all men are involved, and he must see in every man an organ of a common life. . . . If one man oppresses another and thus thwarts the growth and creativity of his personality, he is interfering with the healthy functioning of the organism as a whole. . . ." *The Meaning of God in Modern Jewish Religion* (New York: Reconstructionist Press, 1962, pp. 212–213). First published by Macmillan, 1937; henceforth, MG.

3. AT, p. 1.

4. Ibid., p. 2.

5. *Judaism as a Civilization* (henceforth, JC) (New York: Schocken, 1967, p. 515). First published in 1934 by Macmillan.

6. *Shemuot Hareiyah* (*A Listener's Reports of Sermons by HaRav Kook*), edited by Kalman Eliezer Frankel (Jerusalem: Hassneh, 5699). The book contains summaries of the Rav's talks, rendered by Frankel and others who heard his sermons and later recorded from memory what he had said. Although the sanctity of the Shabbat or holiday prevented a more accurate recording, there is little doubt that the summaries faithfully capture Kook's message.

7. *Orot,* selected passages from the Hebrew edition, pp. 18–21.

8. "Teudat Yisrael U'leumiyutah," *HaPeles*, p. 237.

9. JC, pp. 242–243.

10. *Orot*, p. 149.

11. *Faith and Reason* (Washington, D.C.: B'nai B'rith Hillel Foundations, 1961, p. 125). Kook never strayed from his early reservations about rationalism. He wrote shortly after his *aliyah*, "The essence of spirituality cannot be captured by any (rational) search or research. Opinion, intellectual exploration, philosophy—these can point only to the external signs of life. Even when they deal with the inner life, they perceive only its shadows and not its real essence. All the prowess of these intellectual methods only pave the way for the spirit to draw nearer to the entrance hall. . . ." From: *HaNir*, 5666/1907, reprinted in *Maamarei HaReiyah* (*Essays of HaRav Kook*) (henceforth, MR) (Jerusalem: privately published by Golda Katz Memorial Fund, 5744/1984, p. 41).

12. *Orot HaReiyah* (*Lights of HaRav Kook*) (Jerusalem: Mosad HaRav Kook, 5730, pp. 26–27).

13. *Sabbath Prayerbook* (New York: Jewish Reconstructionist Foundation, 1946, pp. 381–390).

14. *Orot*, p. 119.

15. To be more exact, many problems are unresolved in modern science. Perhaps one of the most dramatic is in the field of physics; it is articulated most notably in Heisenberg's Principle of Indeterminacy. Physicists have until now been unable to simultaneously predict the velocity and the location of subatomic matter and are therefore unable to know if the behavior of these particles follows any set of laws. However, for our purposes, the evidence is overwhelming that one can achieve a large measure of fulfillment during the span of one's life. Such fulfillment depends on the degree to which one reckons with the demonstrated laws of nature and proposes values and purposes that commend themselves to lovers of humanity.

16. MG, p. 27.

17. Ibid., p. 31.

18. Emanuel Goldsmith writes: "Kaplan believed that nothing so threatened the future of humanity, generally, and of the Jewish people,

in particular, than the dogmatism, chauvinism, fanaticism, and intolerance of supernatural religion." From his essay, "Mordecai Kaplan's Synthesis of Judaism and American Religious Naturalism," *American Journal of Theology and Philosophy*, Vol. 1, p. 7.

19. *Religion in Essence and Manifestation* (London: Allen and Unwin, 1938).

20. In a similar vein, Joseph Soloveitchik tries to synthesize both worlds in a new way that, to him, seems called for by the *Halakhah*. Soloveitchik is conscious of the serious contradictions and conceptual and behavioral conflicts that exist between halakhic Judaism and the general culture, but he claims, "The perspectives on man and the world presented by the social sciences and contemporary society not only do not disturb the halakhic view of man and the duties it thrusts on him, but they are the very *same* perspectives from a different point of view" (from: "Hermeneutics in the Theology of J. B. Soloveitchik," by Pinchas Peli, *Conservatism Judaism*, Vol. XLI, No. 3, Spring 1989, p. 25).

21. *Orot Hakodesh* (The Sacred Lights) (henceforth, OK) (Jerusalem: Mosad HaRav Kook, 5724, Vol. 2, pp. 538–542).

22. Ibid., p. 539.

23. Ibid. Note that the uniqueness of Israel is to be expected from the nature of mortals. "For all men differ from one another in spirit and inclination. They are born with different wills and passions" (*HaPeles*, p. 85).

24. *Orot Hakodesh*, Vol. 2, p. 540.

25. MR, p. 10. Reprinted from *HaNir*, Vol. 1, No. 1, 5666.

26. Ibid.

27. OK, Vol. 2, p. 541.

28. Ibid., p. 542.

29. Ibid.

30. Kaplan muses, "Why are we not satisfied with the old way of life? Because it is out of harmony with the rest of our thinking in scientific, historical and comparative terms, because it conflicts with our sense of right and wrong, and because it obstructs the free and many-sided development of human creative ability" (*Diaries*, December 11, 1938).

31. JC, p. XI.

32. Ibid.

33. Kook and Kaplan epitomize most of the late nineteenth- and twentieth-century philosophers of Judaism. They wrestle with the challenges posed by the scientific, moral, and esthetic achievements of the enlightened societies of this period. Unfortunately, Kook's efforts were cut short before the establishment of the State of Israel. Their responses, as I have already indicated, are often in sharp conflict, but the compari-

son between them will present a useful map to anyone trying to find his or her way in contemporary Judaism.

In no way do I wish to belittle the value of examining the works of many of the other brilliant thinkers of the last hundred years. A long list of distinguished names, including Hermann Cohen, Buber, Rosenzweig, Baeck, and Heschel, would have to be considered if it were my intention to exhaust the latter-day visions of Jewish destiny. I shall just mention Soloveitchik as an Orthodox thinker who dipped far more than did Kook into the well of science and modern thought, in an effort to demonstrate that the foundations of Judaism are not threatened. A more complete study than this would have to offer an extended analysis of both the enlightened Orthodox position and that of the so-called liberals of various persuasions.

Kook attempts to elicit all that is holy in the profane. He attaches a Jewish label to all that is good and true in non-Jewish cultures. Everything worthwhile is already in Judaism, but, he adds, we should all rejoice when sparks of holiness are discovered among non-Jews. Kaplan holds that real contradictions exist between aspects of Judaism and the implications of science and modern enlightenment. In his view, these contradictions can be overcome only by forthright adjustments in Jewish thought and practice or by well-founded demonstrations that Jewish tradition does, indeed, provide more satisfactory answers to the human condition than are available elsewhere.

34. *A History of Jewish Thought in the 20th Century*, p. 260.

35. Examine the limits that Kaplan places on science in his FAJ, especially pp. 294–339, and the discussion on scientism, p. 462. Other references to this subject are scattered throughout Kaplan's works.

36. *Questions Jews Ask* (henceforth, QJA) (New York: Reconstructionist Press, 1965, p. 158). The interested reader will find dozens of formulations by Kaplan of his basic premise that religion is socially based and inevitably changes with the metamorphoses of the group in which it is rooted. Science is only the latest method employed by religious men and women who seek the meaning of their lives in a universe better known to them, but no less elusive than it was to past generations.

3

The Mystic and the Rationalist

WE MUST TAKE one more preliminary step before examining how
Kook and Kaplan approached specific problems of Jewish life.
Thus far, we have observed their perceptions of the social and
intellectual environments to which the Jewish people must respond intelligently if it wishes to survive as a vital and creative
entity. We have also touched on some of the main directions of
their thinking. In this chapter, I shall examine their intellectual
moods in greater depth.

In academic circles it is customary to seek the proper philosophical pigeonhole in which to categorize thinkers. In that way,
it becomes easier to follow their train of thought. Conventional
thinking thereby classifies Kook somewhere among the mystics
and Kaplan in the ranks of the rationalists. It is true that every
person has a basic temperament, intellectual tendency, and characteristic manner of expression; however, a superior intellect cannot easily be put into a cognitive straitjacket. Kook and Kaplan
belong to this class of independent minds.

I should qualify my objection to classifying Kook and Kaplan
by acknowledging that their moods are certainly different. Kook
frequently talks about feeling, exaltation, communion with God,
secrets of Torah, and the like. The influence of the Kabbalah, one
of the main streams of Jewish mysticism, is apparent in both the
form and the content of all his writings, albeit, as I have said, he
adapted this mystical trend to his own original purposes. Every
one of Kaplan's pages is replete with terms such as reason, wisdom, logic, experience, and intellectual honesty. He does not hide
his distaste for popular mysticism. Why, then, should I dispute
what seems to be such a proper classification—Kook, the mystic,
and Kaplan, the rationalist? Do they not belong to two distinct
universes of discourse?

These questions are not easy to answer, because the definitions of mysticism and rationalism are themselves matters of considerable disagreement. However, if we are ever to bring about a genuine and respectful dialogue between the schools of Jewish thought, we have to explore the extent to which their ability was able to rise above the major emphasis of their intellectual bias. Were they able to see the limits of their own methods and the possibilities in other systems?

A GLANCE AT MYSTICISM AND RATIONALISM

Let us first review the meaning of mysticism, or, in the semantics of Jewish tradition, the doctrine of the hidden or the secret. Frequently, Jewish mysticism is designated as Kabbalah, which, although it is only one of its forms, has become a trade name for mysticism in general because of its popularity. I define popular mysticism as a quest to experience God directly, often accompanied by irrational or pseudo-rational recommendations for achieving this aim. It is usually marked by a feeling of ecstasy stemming from the search itself. Many will dispute this definition. For instance, Gershom Scholem, the great scholar who established the discipline of research into the history of Jewish mysticism, was one of those who admitted that attempts at definition fill a large catalog.[1]

Mysticism is not devoid of rationality. As Benjamin Ish-Shalom reminds us, "A considerable part of mystical literature deals only with experiences that are not necessarily irrational. In any case, the literature is not confined only to cosmological and anthropological theosophies."[2] That is to say, the mystic experience per se includes a measure of reason or at least an attempt at logical explanation.

I believe that my proposed description of mysticism encompasses the common aspects of this form of mental behavior as depicted by most savants. However, my purpose is to enable the reader to grasp why thinkers like Kook and Kaplan avoid relying solely on reason or emotion as a means of understanding life's meaning. Each in his own way realizes that he must seek a balance between both faculties of consciousness.

My presentation raises a number of questions. What is an experience of God and how is such an experience generated? Is the first step a rational procedure—setting a goal, analyzing the seeker's present state of mind, formulating a strategy, and determining the specific means of attaining the goal? Or is the desire to feel God's presence aroused by an unusual emotional experience that suggests to the person a possibility that had never occurred to him or her before? As a result of such an experience, is it likely that the person will conclude that there is a need to trust more in the power of an emotional tidal wave than in the calm application of the human mind to a sense-induced contact with the natural environment? Should one distance oneself from nature and its "illusions"? What are the indications that a human is standing before God? How can a person know when he or she has achieved communion with the Deity?[3] Clearly, one can answer these questions with contradictory responses. But one thing holds true for all of them. They all testify to the human wish not only to *know* but also to *feel* the bond of unity between God, humankind, and the cosmos. The mystic feels that the unity being sought once characterized all of Creation. If only we can acquire the appropriate instruments, we shall be able to restore that ideal cosmic condition.

The rationalist, in a quest for meaning and truth, refuses to rely on historical revelation, on intuition that lacks any basis in experience and disciplined thought, or on any other method of cognition that ignores the canons of elementary proof. The rationalist rules that religion must be subject to the same standards of historical and scientific judgment that are customary in the analysis and evaluation of other human endeavors. Rationalism is usually envisioned as leaving no room for miracles and as insisting that the rule of natural law is total.[4] But rationalism, like mysticism, cannot properly be depicted in such simplistic terms. The mind is a remarkable but imperfect instrument. The numerous disagreements among intelligent men and women are ample proof that reason, too, must be subject to critical scrutiny. Its findings, despite our confidence in their correctness, are only first, tentative steps in the direction of greater knowledge.[5] What, then, is the advantage of the rational faculty over the other tools of consciousness—imagination, instinct, intuition, emotion? And how is reason supposed to function in regard to values? Can reason prove that the moral values of one person or group are closer to God's will than those of others? Is the determination of normative standards a matter of reason? Perhaps the preference of one good over another depends on the character of each individual and each society.

Kook and Kaplan knew the limitations of the mind. They were aware of the imperfections of reason, and they realized that emotions could easily lead to corrupt behavior. Both men constantly sought to achieve a balance between the faculties of consciousness, but their conceptions of the desirable harmony differed. Let us examine how they perceived the roles of cognition (acquisition of knowledge) and conation (desire and volition) in religious faith.

Kaplan posits that the essence of traditional Jewish religion is not to be found in

> the cognitive element of its God-idea, but from the *conduct* in which that idea has found expression. Jewish religious behavior requires an idea of God, but were it contingent on a particular idea of God, the continuity of the religious process would be broken. Since, however, the Jewish civilization succeeded in retaining its own continuity and that of its religion, despite the changes in the God-idea, it has proved itself exempt from the necessity of commitment to one authoritative conception of God. . . . [Jewish civilization] cannot afford to become secular and omit the God-idea altogether.[6]

In this passage, Kaplan speaks in a traditional spirit—practice, not theory, is the basic principle. He and Kook agree on this point. But from his theological perspective, Kaplan argues that in an enlightened Jewish religion, Jews will conceive of God in many, sometimes conflicting ways. There always have been and most likely always will be a variety of Jewish theologies. However, the current theological debate differs from those of the past in the extent of the disagreements. Moreover, according to the Kaplanian stand, a fair hearing, if not legitimacy, has to be accorded to all concepts. Whereas in the past, overt naturalistic tendencies were likely to be branded as heresy, today the number of religious Jews who somehow locate God in the orderly processes of nature is too large to be dismissed cavalierly as a religious option. These Jews feel that a naturalistic approach provides a better theoretical basis for a vital Jewish life than any of the traditional supernaturalistic options. Nevertheless, Kaplan goes on to declare, "*There is nothing in Judaism viewed as a civilization to preclude an anthropomorphic or any other God-idea, provided its emotional and conative expression in religious behavior makes for what are now recognized as the highest ends of human aspiration.*"[7] (Italics, MMK)

Kaplan's rationalism is thus basically pluralistic. This does not imply that he was a relativist regarding truth or the concept of God. He was convinced that the era of belief in the historicity of the theophany at Sinai has been eclipsed and that the quest for God must henceforth rely heavily on the scientific study of the past and present. However, humans differ in their emotional tendencies and intellectual capacities, and it would be absurd to force upon a whole people a single faith or a uniform way of thinking. We have to get used to the fact that Jews will continue to disagree about religious issues. Jewish unity cannot be built on uniformity.

Kook, too, stated that there are many paths to God. He witnessed the fanaticism of which devoted Jews could be guilty when they were absolutely certain that they possessed the sole keys to the Kingdom. He personally suffered greatly from the passion of the extreme Fundamentalists. Yet even though he served a community of Orthodox believers, he was convinced that a certain amount of freedom of thought was desirable. He maintained, "Only through complete freedom of ideas can man attain completely pure intellectual communion with God."[8] Despite this radical comment, which, incidentally, is repeated several times in his writings, Rav Kook was not consistent regarding the rule of reason in the determination of what is Jewishly correct. In the final analysis, reason could not be free to take the Jew beyond the *Halakhah*. Moreover, in addition to his conviction that reason had to submit to the traditional restraints, he believed the rational workings of the mind had limited effectiveness in grasping truth. Emotion has an important role to play.

Kook claims:

There is one kind of rational procedure which men are accustomed to use in following the path of God; and there is another type which is based more on the feeling of goodness. Both of them constitute what we call "the good heart." For the person who relies on the method of intellect, the most important thing is arriving at a pure concept.[9]

In contrast to reason, feeling directs a person toward "improving the quality of his practice."[10] Thus, despite the important role that Kook assigns to reason, emotional conviction about the truth of the Torah is the better route to right behavior. (In passing, I call attention to the fact that when Kook talks about reason or intellect, he is frequently referring to the mental activity involved in the study of toraitic texts. At such moments, it is clear that Kook attaches little significance to the free functioning of the mind.) Philosophically minded persons are satisfied with ideas and often see no need to draw any conclusions from them for their way of life. Kook, of course, rejects this way of thinking. His attitude has deep roots in the history of Jewish philosophy. For example, in *The Kozari*, Yehudah Halevi, at the conclusion of his lecture on the philosopher, puts the following words (which are undoubtedly his own opinion) into the mouth of the king: "I see merit in your words, but they are not suited to the purpose I have in mind."[11] And what is it that the Kozari wants if not instruction concerning proper behavior? That information cannot come from abstract philosophy, no matter how well intended.

A chasm exists between the feelings of Kook and Kaplan, as well as between their views on the utility of reason in handling a broad range of human questions. Inasmuch as Kook regards Torah as the linchpin holding together the wheel of human endeavor, particularly as regards the search for truth, the main objective in activating reason should be to decipher the messages of the toraitic heritage. Kook argues for the desirability of acquiring knowledge of certain general or secular disciplines, but only as aids to the study of Torah. Independent reason can contribute nothing basic to the truth that is already contained in Israel's Torah. Certainly, reason may not pass judgment on the Torah, diminish it, or add anything to it that is not in the spirit of the tradition. This approach is filled with paradoxes and inconsistencies, and it fails to offer independent criteria of truth outside the magic circle of the Torah itself.

In his pursuit of truth, goodness, and God's presence, Kaplan tries to effect a synthesis between reason and emotion, experience and tradition, and rationalism and mysticism. However, he argues that without acceptable norms for the utilization of mysticism, metaphysics, and moral theory, we shall not be able to fashion a reasonable religion or a well-founded God-idea. The norms have to support and supplement one another. Kaplan cautions us to resist the tendency to regard inconsistency as a virtue. He writes:

> If we are not to lose ourselves in the obscurities of word-worship, we have to rely upon inner consistency as a brake on our uncontrolled imaginings. If a norm in one field of religious philosophy is permitted to contradict a norm in one of the other fields, the mind becomes involved in inner conflict. When people accept such inner conflict resignedly, they help to create a state of society in which conflicting social ideals and institutions are the order of the day.[12]

If these differences were to exhaust the agenda of the dispute between the rationalist and the mystic, the work of analysis would be fairly simple. We could then classify the former as one who subjects the whole of tradition to the judgment of historical and scientific criticism. The latter, we could then say, accepts without reservation the divine origin of every letter in the written Torah and in the great halakhic enterprise to which it gave rise. In this simplistic fashion, we could declare that the rationalist sifts through the Jewish past not only in search of its spiritual treasures but also to locate its mistakes and limitations. Such individuals are not reticent about recommending corrections or innovations, even if they have to go beyond halakhic restraints.

It is equally common to oversimplify the nature of the mystic. A mystic can be defined as one who sees no contradiction between loyalty to one's traditional heritage and one's readiness to read into the words of the wise men of the past fantastic ideas that cannot legitimately be extrapolated from their vision. Such a definition applies only in regard to the most extreme forms of mysticism. Both mysticism and rationalism are far more complex than these descriptions would lead us to believe. The interplay between intellect and emotion in both styles of thinking cannot be reduced to facile categorization.

In the rest of this chapter, I shall largely confine myself to the mysticism and rationalism of Kook and Kaplan. I am not interested, for the purpose of this study, in the academic question of where each one belongs in the various mystical and rationalistic schools.[13] I shall merely try to sketch the major lines of their thinking.

KOOK'S MYSTICISM

Jacob Agus, who wrote one of the first and most penetrating studies of Kook's philosophy, remarks, "[T]he whole world-view of Rabbi Kuk was merely an elaboration and an interpretation of the magnificent mystical phenomena that occurred to him in the Holy Land. Thereafter, religion was for him not merely a matter of external authority, but of inner life."[14]

Even before settling in Eretz Yisrael, Kook had undergone mystical moments that helped to deepen his faith. It is doubtful whether his soul was capable of experiencing anything superficially. All the testimonies we have indicate that from his childhood on, Kook at prayer was virtually a disembodied soul. In these ecstatic moments, he lost contact with the material world. Men who knew him in those early years describe Kook as passionately eager to fly off to mysterious realms. They claim that he frequently succeeded. Moreover, Kook himself testifies that his loftiest moments in the Diaspora were as nought compared to the wondrous illuminations of his soul in Eretz Yisrael. In one of his letters, he writes:

> There is an essential difference between the Torah of Eretz Yisrael and that of the Diaspora. In Eretz Yisrael, an abundance of the Holy Spirit bursts out and descends on every scholar who studies Torah for its own sake. This holds true far more for the scholarly community as a whole. The general spirit flows with increasingly broad profusion. From above, it subdues each individual and dictates all proper conduct. This is not so in the Diaspora. There, where the air and the earth are impure, it is impossible to breathe the general Holy Spirit. At most, each item of Torah emits, a spark, a slight illumination that enables the individual to draw closer to the living God whose Spirit resides with His people in the land of life. . . . This is the kind of delightful light of holiness that shines on scholarly seekers of God in Eretz Yisrael. It is not present at all elsewhere. I sense this in my entire being.[15]

Kook expresses what he actually experiences. He sees the study of Torah as more than an intellectual venture. It is accompanied

by feelings and experiences that he could record but whose content he could not describe. Kook's testimony is far-reaching.
Every student of Torah in Eretz Yisrael enjoys the supernatural
inspiration of the Land. Kook stresses again and again that the
creative influence of Eretz Yisrael on students of Torah is God's
doing. The election of this country is no less an initiative and an
act of God than is the choice of Israel to teach God's will to the
rest of the nations. Kook never peers beyond the arbitrary will of
God for an explanation of why and how it is that Eretz Yisrael is
able to elicit the creativity of the collective Jewish people to an
extent unknown in any other place on earth. Apparently, historical, psychological, and social factors have nothing relevant to say
about the dynamics of a people's love for a particular spot on
earth. Yet the ancient rabbis knew the arbitrary power of love.
And just as the beloved is beautiful in the eyes of the lover, so a
poor land like Eretz Yisrael can hold in an unbreakable embrace
countless generations of the Jewish people. Kook was madly in
love with the Land, but this natural emotion does not explain the
romance between the Jews and their homeland. Again, Kook
points to God as the instigator of this love match.

Kook negates the Diaspora without feeling that he has to explain his position. He could have argued that anti-Semitism is
endemic to the non-Jewish world and that Jews should return to
their homeland for their own safety. He might have used the well-
worn argument that a minority group cannot withstand the attractions of the majority culture, particularly when the latter is
enlightened. Such arguments are irrelevant to Kook. No land except Eretz Yisrael can be a homeland for Jews, even if it offers
ideal conditions for a full and good life. From the vantage point
of Jewish peoplehood, all other lands are impure. Dwelling in
them can only destroy the Jewish spirit.

The above concept is known as mystical nationalism. But Kook
goes beyond using a mystical explanation of the connection between Israel and its land. For whatever happens to Israel is tied in
with the nature and destiny of the human race and the entire
cosmos.

Ben-Zion Bokser offers an explanation for Kook's fascination
with the reality and the idea of light. Bokser declares that in
Kook's eyes, "[t]he force which directs the world toward the ab-

solute good that pulsates throughout existence is a spiritual illumination from the Divine source of all existence."[16] This
illumination is not only symbolic, it is embodied in cosmic energy, in the form of spiritual lights that influence human behavior
in very concrete ways. Kook's belief, typical of mystics, led him
to some daring thoughts. It was most unusual for a traditionalist
like Kook to proclaim the need for a good Jew to go beyond the
study of the classic texts and take notice, even in a circumscribed
fashion, of other founts of knowledge and concern. Bokser mentions Kook's criticism of secular nationalism, but he also points
out that Kook emphasized that Jewish leaders "must be deeply
spiritual personalities for whom contact with the Divine spirit is
a living experience, and who bring new light and vitality to the
entire fabric of Jewish life."[17]

At first glance, there is nothing novel about the idea of a new
light. Does not the pious Jew pray daily, "Cause a new light to
shine on Zion) / And may we all soon be worthy of its radiance"
(a verse in the morning service of the traditional prayer book).
People can interpret this "light" as they see fit—a symbol of the
redemption of the individual or the nation, a new heart or a new
spirit, or a transformed reality. Kook, however, envisages the light
as the everlasting and unceasing presence of God and His infinite
effulgence. The holy lights suffuse the entire cosmos, but the ability of humans to observe and to comprehend them and to be
purified by their inspiration entails enormous spiritual and intellectual effort. Without the divine lights, there can be no hope for
humankind, but they are also dangerous. Only scholars of moral
and spiritual stature can guarantee that the lights will be good for
the Jewish people and for all humankind. Even for scholars,
though, there is no guarantee of success. Kook's mysticism was
tempered by a certain amount of skepticism and pragmatism.

Whenever Kook repeats the word "light," it is as if he were on
the verge of an emotional explosion. His passion for God is so
overpowering and his confidence that communion with Him is
within the grasp of a "kasher" Jew is so strong, that it is easy for
him and others to overlook a vital fact. Like many mystics, Kook
does not and cannot detail the nature of the light, the meaning of
the union with God, or even the difference between God's light
and that of Satan. One of the characteristics of mysticism is the

tendency to be verbose about the secrets of reality and to avoid
the peril of exact description.[18] On the contrary, the moment one
lowers the mystic experience to the level of communicable data
and substantiation, it loses its imaginative value. Poetry then becomes prose. Infinity is contracted into the limits of time and
space.

Several examples summarize the spirit of Kook's philosophy. I
choose one of his early statements that characterize his suggestive
but often obtuse thinking throughout the rest of his career. It is
taken from his important essay "The Road to Renewal," which
was published early in this century. One must read this piece not
only for its message but also for its emotional tension.

> It is impossible to fathom spiritual existence by means of the most
> careful investigation and research. Knowledge, intellectual inquiry
> and philosophy can merely touch the externals of life. Even when
> they attempt to penetrate to life's inner regions, they see only its
> shadows. All that rational proofs can accomplish is to pave the road
> that enables man to approach the anteroom of the experience of
> spiritual reality. As long as humanity is tied to the senses, with their
> narrow limitations, we cannot know that reality. These faculties
> can only reveal weak shadows. If a person mistakes these shadows
> for actual existence, they become a heavy burden and lessen both
> his physical and spiritual powers. We must learn to flee from their
> harmful influence.
>
> But no matter how much a person tries to flee the shadows, they
> pursue him. There is only one avenue of escape, and that is by
> means of increased light.
>
> Additional light cannot be generated merely by apprehending
> the inner essence of spiritual being, for which man lacks the psychic
> means. He can rely only on the depth of his faith in divinity. This
> is the loftiest knowledge and the grandest emotion. They unite
> man's existential and mundane spirituality with infinite, faultless
> supernal life.[19]

This passage illustrates Kook's struggle with the tension between reason and emotion. From one vantage point, we have to
exercise our intellectual capacities to reach the outskirts of spiritual being. But here is the rub! Do we reach only the outskirts or,
as Kook says, the anteroom? Beyond the entrance resides the spiritual reality of our longing, at which we can arrive only by inscru-

table means and by applying vague concepts, such as extra light and profound faith in God. Actually, as Kook has said, the whole enterprise is doomed to failure as long as we are restricted by our senses—a reminder of the interpretation by Maimonides of the biblical verse, "Man cannot see Me and live" (Ex. 33, 20). Rambam interprets this verse to mean that man can experience God directly only after his death.[20] Kook insists, nevertheless, that man can resist the exaggerated influence of the senses on his spirit. In this battle, both reason and emotion have a role. However, Kook does not detail the essence of the supernal life, even though he regards that existence as more real and more desirable than the day-to-day life on earth. In the end, it is the mystic's emotional conviction that the path being followed will lead to the true spiritual life that lies at the basis of his outlook. For all its importance, reason plays a secondary role.

Nonetheless, Kook's mystical theory is not anti-intellectual. In truth, with the exception of the magical trends in Kabbalah and other streams of Jewish mysticism, the tension between emotion and intellect does not generally result in conflict between the two emphases. For the most part, the tension leads the mystic to question the distance that can be traveled with reason before it is necessary to leave that path and trust in the power of imagination, faith, and feeling. I think that this same problem pertains to the rationalist as well, albeit with different emotional involvement and conceptual conclusions.

Kook's mysticism is central to his perception of the Jewish people. (Additional details are provided in Chapter 8 on the idea of election.) Without feeling the need to substantiate his claim, Kook announces:

> God's psychic illumination, which fills heaven and earth and embraces eternally all of the alterations in time and space, strengthens all of the nation's properties—its heredity, language, land, life-style. God's light grants delicacy, pleasantness, power and richness.
>
> The preparation of the nation's soul for unification with the cosmic psyche is based on the traditional, exalted Torah, revealed to the people through the medium of its moral habits, its wisdom and its humanizing *mitzvot.* . . . The divine purpose of goodness stands out in every corner of this eternal Torah.[21]

On the surface, Kook does not wander far from the generally accepted norms of the rationalistic and mystical traditions in Judaism. Everything is subject to God's will, from Creation to the end of all flesh. Israel is as much God's creation as every individual human being. Although Israel is responsible for acting in its own behalf, its ultimate fate is determined by God and is not the outcome of a natural historical process. The "Divine Psyche provides all the appurtenances of Jewish culture," and the Torah is the light whose rays penetrate into the depths of the collective national soul. However, the light of Torah can succeed in its mission only when people are in their proper location and equipped to absorb the rays. Paradoxically, that light can blind as well as illumine and enlighten. When parts of the earth turn away from the sun, they become dark; similarly, when people stare into the glare of the sun, they are blinded. The study of Torah is an arduous, even dangerous career.

Since Kook envisages the Torah as filled with mystery, he cannot study it by a routine method. Only when the student is divested of silly fantasies and evil desires and acquires broadmindedness can he or she enjoy the full benefit of "the flow of divine spirituality which manifests itself more in the activities of practical life than in methods of [textual] study."[22] Kook is ever eager to disclose the hidden secrets of Torah by means of an openness not possessed by the average student of his period. (For further clarification, see the analysis of *Shir Vasiah* in Chapter 10 on education.) Therefore, he never retreats from his position that the fountain of reason contains the fresh waters of Torah. One must drink them in order to be fully nourished by the living Jewish heritage. Still, reason alone is an inadequate means of probing God's truth. It is only one instrument in a complicated endeavor. Kook comments:

> [S]cientifically oriented culture, based on inferential reasoning and sense perception, and the natural morality derived from them, prepares mankind to absorb the light emanating from the universal spiritual psyche. Then, under the impact of this light, the direction of our culture with its roots in reason, instinct and natural moral sense, will take on great vigor and an abiding divine stability. Not so if the emanation of light reaches us without the preparation of the cultivated method of scientific culture and conventional moral-

ity. Without such readiness, this very light will beget only darkness.[23]

I conclude that Kook's mysticism must be interpreted as having deep roots in reason. However, lest he give the impression of elevating scientific reasoning to the highest epistemological level, Kook does an about-face and carries us into the realm of vivid imagination, feeling, and myth. By way of illustration, let us examine his commentary on a section of the hymn, "Adon Olam" ("Eternal Lord"). This adoration, whose origin is in rationalistic philosophy, becomes in Kook's hands a mystical vision of the destiny of the cosmos. For our purpose, I shall refer only to Kook's treatment of the verse, "And when all comes to an end, the Awful One will reign alone."

In rationalistic philosophy, whose classic Jewish expression is that of Maimonides, we find a series of arguments in proof of God's existence. In his *Mishneh Torah*, Maimonides offers, among other proofs, the following scale of logical points:[24]

> Should it enter your mind that except for Him there are no existents, bear in mind that He will continue to exist even if all other existents are abolished. For all other existents need Him, while He, may He be blessed, is independent of each and every one of them. Therefore, the truth of His existence is unique.

Typically, Rambam adds a biblical confirmation to his argument. "This is what the prophet meant when he said, 'And the Lord God is truth' (Jer. 10, 10). He alone is truth, and there is no truth like His. This is what the Torah says: There is none except Him. There is no true existent except for Him alone." These sentences are part of a chain of arguments intended to prove God's existence by logical inference. Maimonides buttresses his position by quoting (often out of context) those biblical verses that seem to provide the authority of revelation needed to silence the opposition to his views on the part of conventional thinkers. Nonetheless, it is evident that Maimonides himself was convinced that rational proof of God's existence sufficed. The essence of Rambam's metaphysical method is to be found in logic and not in the biblical support. Nothing in the foregoing statements from the *Mishneh Torah* was intended to picture what is likely to happen or should happen "when all comes to an end."

Kook sketches a completely fanciful picture of God, the One and Only. According to Lurianic Kabbalah, a major branch of Kabbahah, Creation is defective. Our world is not the ideal state of existence or the embodiment of God's truth. Kook writes: "The Creation we experience was wrought from above by God's will, from the highest region of exalted, unlimited possibility, and from the infinite heavens, to the lowly, limited and graduated confines. . . ."[25] That is to say, Creation is limited and damaged by its materiality. One of the main functions of the Jewish people is to correct this cosmic fault. Most pious Jews interpret this vocation to mean that they are obligated to contribute to the improvement of human behavior, which, in turn, will mark the coming of the Messiah and the advent of universal peace. Although Kook, too, starts from the assumption that the universe cannot remain as it is, he states:

> [E]verything was made to achieve great majesty and high estate in the abode of ultimate Power and to attain a magnificence infinitely greater than that of our contracted domain. Creation has the possibility of calling the Name of God and embodying His Kingdom. This climb, involved in the restoration of being to its highest peak is what is meant by "when all comes to an end." This is not the end that is associated with destruction and deprivation, but of "My flesh and my heart fail (come to an end); / But God is the rock of my heart and my portion forever" (Ps. 73, 26). This return of the entirety of all being to the most exalted region of its desire, dwelling above the limited and contracted state of being, is the royal crown in its absolute sublimity. . . . And after all comes to an end, the Awful One will reign.[26]

Briefly, Kook imagines that the cosmic process of contraction (*tzimtzum*, as it is known in Kabbalah) will be reversed. The universe will be restored to its pre-Creation condition. Humankind and the cosmos will cease to exist, and God alone will be, in all His uniqueness. The I (*ani*) becomes Nothing (*ayin*). Obviously, this mystical image raises many questions, but they are not the kind to be usefully debated. Kook's vision is a fanciful and fascinating flight of imagination on the part of a great lover of God who is devastated by the flawed condition of mundane existence. What can one say to a man who strained throughout his life to experience the nearness of God? Kook believed with all his heart that alongside the Holy One, blessed be He, there is no other true being, even that of the *tzaddikim* (perfectly righteous humans). Only God can be Absolute.

KAPLAN'S RATIONALISM

How utterly different is Kaplan's conception of reality! He sees it as a process of eternal change. Even the capacity of the human mind is subject to change. At times it advances, but it deteriorates as well. The classical rationalism and method of thinking of Maimonides and other medieval Jewish philosophers resembled those of their Christian and Moslem counterparts. The rational wisdom of that era assumed that the

> respective religious traditions had been supernaturally revealed by God. Their validity was beyond question. Hence they could not possibly be in conflict with reason, since both revelation and reason sought to enable mortals to know the true or authentic way of life by which they could achieve salvation. Accordingly, the function of reason in pre-modern times was regarded as being merely that of confirming the validity of the religious tradition, not only as a whole, but also in all its details of belief and practice.[27]

Today, Kaplan observes, reason plays a different role. Whereas in the past its job was to preserve ancestral heritage and substantiate its premises, reason is now frequently employed to criticize tradition, exposing its intellectual and moral deficiencies. Kaplan, in the name of reason, calls for "a complete transformation of our habits of thought and action as Jews."[28] Reason, as understood by Kaplan, is a dynamic force, undergoing constant sharpening and refinement. When it is applied to the preservation of a people, it does its work, not by guarding the status quo but by appropriating what is still relevant in tradition and searching for coherent ways to relate the people to the changing world. Culture is a process and not a stationary artifact. Nonetheless, Kaplan recognizes that reason is imperfect. We must not exaggerate its power, for it often fails us. But it has one advantage over all other mental faculties— its capacity for self-correction.

Kaplan applies his conception of reason to his analysis of the nature of religion. He asserts:

A genuine understanding of religion is precluded by the conventional notions about it. (Italics, MMK) They all boil down to the assumption that, whereas politics, economics, science, technics, art and morals have their respective sources in normal and communicable experience, and tend to improve with the growth of experience, religion derives from a source of truth that transcends that kind of experience, and is not affected by it. Only those who have access to that transcendent [meaning, supernatural, JJC] source of truth are supposed to be able to mediate it to their fellowman. It is generally assumed that for the masses religion must remain an object of vicarious and not of direct experience. It is therefore to be exempt from the kind of free inquiry to which we ordinarily subject experiences of a secular character.[29]

In summary, Kaplan regards religion as similar to every other human endeavor, in that it sprouts in the daily activities and experiences of men and women. As such, the transcendent gates of religion are open, at least potentially, to every human being. Of course, humans are endowed with unequal talents. Only exceptional persons are able to quaff deeply from the pure waters of spirituality. But their success is akin to that of those graced with special capabilities in other spheres of activity. Kaplan concludes that religion is subject to the same rational discipline that is demanded in every effort to adjust oneself to the cosmic setting.

The fact that religion possesses no independent source of truth is no indication that it lacks a function of its own. Religion is no substitute for science, art, or any other human discipline; conversely, none of these disciplines can fill the role of religion. However, Kaplan denies that religion or any other human instrumentality can establish direct communication between humans and God. The theophany at Sinai, historical revelation, Torah from heaven, exclusive access to God's will—these claims of traditional Jewish religion, all of which epitomize mystical thinking, have now been rejected or significantly reinterpreted by the bulk of Jewry. Kaplan regards such deviation from tradition as a positive development. It is not heresy at all, but rather a fitting response to the advance of knowledge. In his time, Maimonides was hesitant to publicly question the historicity of the giving of the Torah, perhaps because he still believed it, but also, I suspect, because he knew that the people were not ready to accept such a radical deviation. For a latter-day rationalist like Kaplan, captivated by the scientific study of the Bible, the deviation was unavoidable. He believed that the creative future of the Jewish people depends on finding a natural explanation for the evolution of Judaism.

Kaplan outlines three stages in the development of the human mind.[30] He identifies the first stage as spontaneous thinking, which antedates the emergence of individual intellection. The second stage is marked by the evolution of individual speculation. We are now in the midst of the third stage, the era of scientific thought.[31] It is apparent that if the development of the mind were only chronological and linear, the first two stages would already have disappeared. However, the fact is that all three forms of cognition continue to function everywhere, to a greater or lesser extent, even in advanced societies. The most knowledgeable and sophisticated men and women find it hard at times to relinquish the mental habits of bygone ages. Moreover, Kaplan claims that the earlier mentalities can still prove useful, provided that they do not violate the standards of probity and fact cultivated by scientific method. Kaplan realizes there is no point in arguing with those who are satisfied with pre-scientific thought. Their minds are not attuned to the scientific manner of reflection. Furthermore, there is no one-to-one relationship between methods of thinking and moral perception and behavior. Outmoded ways of thinking per se are no bar to moral stature.

Kaplan focuses his attention on those who relish the scientific atmosphere. He explains, "The general public, whether Jewish or non-Jewish, by dint of their cultural lag, manage to live complacently, with their minds divided between their intelligence which they use on weekdays and their will to believe which they exercise on Sabbaths."[32] This attitude renders religion irrelevant to hordes of men and women who prefer coherence and consistency and who are uncomfortable with the ambivalence of those who bracket their intellect while enjoying a modicum of mysticism and supernaturalism.

In the light of Kaplan's stand, we might expect him to throw his full weight behind science. Like Kook, however, his thinking has some surprising turns. Although he considers science to be one of the most magnificent achievements of the human mind, science that is unguided by mature ethical and spiritual judgment can easily lead humankind to destruction. Without moral and spiritual values in mind, scientists can distort science itself, as was the case with the scientism of the Nazis. Knowing for its own sake can bring a certain satisfaction, but it cannot help men and women become more human or more at peace with themselves, unless it is placed in the context of the search for life's meaning. Science needs religion as a partner to tame its potential arrogance, and religion needs science to prevent its claims from assuming unwarranted authority and certainty. Science cannot tell humans what is good or teach them to control their greed. These are among the functions of religion and other branches of the humanities. This is where we run into trouble. In order for religion and its humanistic associates to do their job of improving the quality of life, they have to eschew the supernatural approaches that flagrantly ignore verified knowledge and experience. Thus, having called upon scientists to recognize the limits of their disciplines, Kaplan now asks that religion focus on natural experience. Recourse to a supernatural God, about whom we have no information but whose word we profess to believe, makes interreligious communication a matter of conflict or competition. Humankind needs theologies that create opportunities for mutual enrichment. Kaplan urges us to direct the energies of our respective religious groupings to the discovery of and obedience to the cosmic laws, about which we can learn something and that impel and guide us to our human destiny.

Unless we read him carefully, we might be seduced by Kaplan's viewpoint into an error that is sometimes found in the history of philosophy. I refer to Aristotle's assertion that knowledge is virtue. It is simply untrue. There is no straight path from the "is" to the "worthy" or the "ought." Kaplan tries to avoid this trap. However, he does argue that knowledge of the facts of nature, especially human nature, is essential to avoid declaring worthy what is patently false or evil or destructive of the human essence. A person must know the facts about the physical and psychic composition of human beings. In this sense, knowledge can help men and women to avoid doing damage to themselves and to others. It is likely that mortals are destined never to become perfect, but we can improve ourselves and not repeat our mistakes.

(In a conversation I had with Kaplan in 1962, he accepted my observation that, according to his position, he could not legitimately speak of human perfectibility, but only human improvability.)

Further, Kaplan finds constructive places for mysticism in human consciousness, in general, and in the Jewish mind, in particular. He declares, "Mystic lore formed a part of Jewish civilization, as it was part of all other civilizations. . . ."[33] This was so, Kaplan argues, because mystic lore develops from man's need to adapt his environment to his desires. Impelled by the need to transform their environment, the Jews resorted to such lore

> in the hope of discovering the theurgic formulas and practices that would help to bring about, as it were, the forcing [of] the hand of God to redeem his people, by sending the Messiah and restoring them to their land. . . . In the tense spiritual struggle that centered about the *Kabbalah*, the yearning for the return to *Eretz Yisrael* and the resumption of national life constituted the most meaningful part of Jewish life during the centuries of exile.[34]

Along with Kook, Kaplan sensed the power of emotion over the individual and the group. Intelligent reasoning cannot effect change in life, whether for good or evil, without the stimulation or support of some emotional drive. Furthermore, emotion, no less than reason, is rooted in a field of consciousness in which the as yet unknown outweighs the revealed. Life, after all, is a mystery in itself. Hence, Kaplan concedes, we have to use all the resources of consciousness as responsibly as we can. But we must also evaluate carefully what each has to offer. When it comes to cognition, Kaplan grants greater authority to reason; mysticism fuels action, but this very power makes it imperative that its resort to emotion and imagination be constrained by the standards of experiential knowledge.

Kaplan expresses his view on mystically founded myths as follows: "'Myth' was once a term to denote anything which was so intrinsically irrational as to be unbelievable. Nowadays we use the term to denote anything which is believed in with such emotional intensity that there is no need of explaining it rationally."[35] However, Kaplan avoids associating mysticism with irrationalism. He cautiously acknowledges the role that mysticism plays in investigating those problematic aspects of reality that lie beyond reason's ability to unravel. Kaplan proclaims, "The test of genuine mysticism is that it communicate some coherent state of mind. Any other kind of mysticism is quackery."[36] Kaplan is dogmatic in this declaration, and Arthur Cohen criticizes his unwavering faith in the ability of reason to apprehend the logic embedded in existence. In his dialogue with Kaplan when the latter was ninety years old, Cohen comments, "One of my fundamental disagreements with you has always been that you have wanted to make reality more rational than I believed it could be made."[37] Cohen confuses Kaplan's faith in cosmic order with his belief that Kaplan equated that order with the most up-to-date scientific claims. Scientists, too, make mistakes, but they know their errors can be corrected. Scientists have that confidence in their ability to make those corrections because they assume the cosmic order is there but has been misread. Obviously, Kaplan was fully aware of many of the unexplained discontinuities and accidents in nature. Admittedly, however, some of his rhetoric lends itself to the type of criticism that Arthur Cohen leveled against him.

Bridging Rationalism and Mysticism?

The dispute between rationalism and mysticism involves several factors, only four of which I mention here: the tension between reason and emotion; the chasm between supernaturalism and naturalism; the different perspectives of theism and humanism; and the theological distance between defining God ideationally and experiencing Him in communion. Although their basic premises contrast, both Kook and Kaplan attempt to navigate between the above-mentioned poles. Kook pilots his boat closer to the shore of feeling, supernaturalistic theism, and communion. Kaplan sails closer to the opposite shore. However, I have to add some reservations. Kaplan views theism and humanism as two sides of the same coin. In regard to the other contrasts, however, Kook and Kaplan often travel in close proximity. They both affirm a rationalism that takes mystery into account and know that imagination must be anchored in part in reason and experience if mystical speculation is not to distort reality.

Kook and Kaplan have a common problem. Both are wary of the hubris of defining God, but they also want to experience God so as to avoid the empty feeling that Deity is only a figment of their imagination. Kook looks to mysticism to escape the dilemma, while Kaplan chooses the rationalist alternative. The latter claims that "the God who is the object of Jewish belief is conceived as being near and generally accessible. It would follow from this that there is nothing mystical or metaphysical in that experience."[38] The very longing to see signs of holiness in the universe, which permeates the spirituality of Kook and Kaplan, leads the latter to seek them in normal, daily activities that can be interpreted by means of scientific method, logical inference, and informed wisdom. But to him, as to Kook, God remains elusive, never to be captured by the tools of consciousness. What person can ever claim possession of absolute truth? Nonetheless, Kaplan argues, it is better to err in theorizing about God than to make fantastic claims about receiving His will through the certainty of mystical experience or emotion. Conceptualization can always be corrected; mystical experience cannot be disputed except by equally dogmatic counterexperience. Thus, Kaplan says that the real problem of religion is "not one of returning to a lost faith in God but of where to look for him, so that we might actually experience his reality."[39] "God is nigh to all who seek Him" (Ps. 145, 18), implying that God is to be found in the normal affairs of human beings. Therefore, Kaplan has no need for supernatural, mystical revelations. Words like miracles, ineffable, and ecstasy appear in his vocabulary as states of mind but not as categories of cognition or as explanations for complex phenomena.

In rejecting supernaturalism, Kaplan in no way denies the role of transcendence in the search for God. Rather, he emphasizes that every person must be capable of rising above his or her present state of being. He or she must be able to perceive the universe as a changing whole, as being more than its current appearance. Cosmic transcendence is manifest in the fact that the whole is greater than its parts. Kaplan calls this feature of reality "holiness," a concept about which I shall add a few lines later in this chapter. The assumption that the cosmos is an organic entity, that its phenomena are somehow related to one another in an orderly way, seems to be part of the nature of most humans. Hence, they search for evidence to prove this belief. They know that this goal will remain beyond their reach, but they are driven by their faith that the cosmos supports their effort to give meaning to their lives. This faith is also a kind of mysticism, an instinctive reaction to the experience of nature. But the feeling is not blind; it is substantiated by ordinary experience and by scientific discoveries and self-corrections.

Kaplan's conception of things will not satisfy those who see Judaism as stemming from a Source beyond nature. This is illustrated in the way in which he and Kook interpret the *mitzvot*. Kook regards them as bridges over which the Jew travels to God. The *mitzvot* lead the Jew to contact with supernatural forces and open the road to *tikkun*, the repair of our damaged world. In contrast, Kaplan sees the *mitzvot* as educational instruments in the effort to purify human behavior. Symbols, holidays, customs of eating and dressing, ways of praying and studying Torah—all these are fruits of the collective imagination of the nation, no different in kind from similar folk creations of other peoples. This demythologization of the *mitzvot* does not devalue them as aids in the spiritual and moral education of the Jew.

Although they travel along separate paths, Kook and Kaplan follow a bipolar Jewish tradition. The *mitzvot* were designed to train the Jews to become decent human beings and to draw them closer to God. But whereas Kaplan emphasizes the humanistic aspect, Kook looks upon moral improvement as only the first step toward the ultimate goal of actual union with God. Thus, Kook and Kaplan turn from one another in the emphases they place on reason and mystical emotion in the efforts of men and women to become fully human.

In conclusion, our two thinkers belong to the camp of Jews who love God, Israel, and Torah. In this sense, they are mystics. All love has this emotional quality, and when it is present in men's and women's feeling about life, they can engage in useful dialogue about what lies behind the mystery of existence, the role of Israel among nations, and the proper content of its culture. Without love of life, neither the way of reason nor the way of feeling will unite Jews in bonds of fraternity. With the threefold love, the debate between Kook and Kaplan, and between ideological opponents in general, becomes one for the sake of Heaven. Only love can testify to the holiness that pervades the cosmos.

NOTES

1. *Main Streams in Jewish Mysticism* (New York: Schocken, 1961, p. 4). Scholem doubts whether mysticism can be defined. He writes, "[N]o one except the mystics themselves knows what mysticism is, each mystic according to his own grasp." He states: "If we are talking about mysticism as unmediated unification with God, then there is no such thing as Jewish mysticism." (See also Scholem's comment in *Devarim Bego* [*Explications and Implications: Writings on Jewish Heritage and Renaissance*] [Tel Aviv: Am Oved, 1975, p. 72.])

2. *HaRav Kook—Bein Ratzionalism L'mystikah* (*HaRav Kook—Between Rationalism and Mysticism*) (Tel Aviv: Am Oved, 1990, p. 198).

3. For example, as Kaplan proclaims, "Habituate yourself to the idea that it is no more possible to be aware of God in any single experience than it is to sense all of electricity in a single shock. The fallacy of identifying any one experience or even a cluster of experiences as the revelation of Deity in his fullness gives rise to idolatry (*Diaries*, July 13, 1936).

4. Differences of opinion about natural law and miracles pervade Jewish thought for at least a millennium. For instance, Shem-Tov Ibn-Falkira mentions philosophers who "have many opinions concerning physics which contradict some of the teachings of Torah, such as their saying that the world is eternal and that nature cannot change." (Quoted by Raphael Jospe in his *Torah and Sophia* [Cincinnati: Hebrew Union College, 1988, pp. 51–52].) There remains considerable disagreement among rationalists concerning the act of Creation, but the consensus against miracles holds.

5. Ish-Shalom, for example, distinguishes between rationality and rationalism. The former demands having "good and sufficient reasons for maintaining a position." Rationalism, on the other hand, is the view that "in the world there is a structure of law and order which only human reason can apprehend" (op. cit., p. 195). Given this usage, it is evident that neither rationality nor rationalism can guarantee certainty.

6. JC, p. 397.

7. Ibid. Kaplan is one of the few Jewish theologians who dared to call upon fellow Jews to surrender the belief in a supernatural God. Unlike Scholem, he believes that naturalistic religion has a future. He denies that abandonment of belief in the divine revelation of Torah would lead to religious anarchy. He feels that religious experience need

not be mystical. Although it was not his intent, Kaplan's theology might be seen as a response to Scholem's views in the essay cited above in Note 1.

8. Cited by Ish-Shalom, pp. 247–248.

9. *Olat Reiyah* (henceforth, OR), Vol. 1, p. 27. I think Jacob Agus exaggerates when he writes: "The starting point of Kuk's thought is the conviction that reason is incapable of revealing truth" (in *Great Jewish Thinkers of the Twentieth Century,* p. 89). It appears to me that Kook was ambivalent and did not wish to surrender entirely the strength inherent in reason in the definition and pursuit of truth.

10. Ibid.

11. *The Kozari,* paragraph 2.

12. FAJ, p. 169.

13. For the reader interested in an in-depth treatment of Kook's mysticism, I strongly recommend the book by Ish-Shalom.

14. *Banner of Jerusalem* (New York: Bloch, 1946, p. 69).

15. *Letters of Reiyah* (Jerusalem: Mosad HaRav Kook, 5722, Vol. 1, pp. 112–113).

16. Introduction to Bokser's translation of Kook's essay, "The Road to Renewal," which appeared in *Ha-Nir,* 5669. The translation was published in *Tradition,* Vol. 13, No. 3, Winter 1973.

17. Ibid.

18. Compare Kaplan's criticism of the mystics: "There is much more of the case for humanity and for that cosmic unity and creativity which gives meaning to life in the social idealists of the last three centuries than in the self-intoxicated mystics, who if they really got at the secret of godhood were unable to communicate it in spite of their proliferate verbosity and their bizarre actions" (*Diaries,* August 13, 1935).

19. *Ha-Nir,* 5666, p. 1. Cited in MR, 5744, p. 1. The version in the *Essays* is slightly different from that in *Ha-Nir.* My quotations contain a combination of both sources.

20. *Hilkhot Yesodei Hatorah,* 1:10.

21. MR, pp. 3–4.

22. Ibid., p. 10. Kook would have the study of Torah use all the tools of consciousness. Torah study can be helped by scientific research, but it is an independent discipline with a unique hermeneutics. Its method does not necessarily accord with the standards that apply to other humanistic branches of learning. Kook mentions the utility of science, but he objects to the idea that rational instruments suffice to enable us to experience communion with the divine or to fulfill a spiritual purpose. Nevertheless, the intellect plays an important role in the life of the spirit. Kook reflected unceasingly on the accomplishments and limitations of rational cogitation.

23. MR, pp. 1–2. The translation is that of Ben-Zion Bokser. See Note 16.

24. *Hilkhot Yesodei Hatorah*, 1:3–4.

25. OR, Vol. 1, p. 47.

26. Ibid.

27. *The Purpose and Meaning of Jewish Existence* (henceforth, PMJE) (Philadelphia: Jewish Publication Society, 1964, p. 298).

28. Ibid., p. 303.

29. Ibid., pp. 303–304.

30. Ibid., p. 307. There is also a similarity between Kook and Kaplan in regard to this point. To illustrate, Kook writes: "As the universe settles down and the human spirit develops, we observe life advancing from instinct to wisdom" (MR, p. 29).

31. Kaplan returns several times to the theme of the evolution of thought. He never seems to have been satisfied with the various theories as to the nature of the thought process. Here is just one illustration of his concern: "Our biblical ancestors managed in their wisdom to anticipate some of the most important moral and spiritual dimensions of life. However, the Greeks were the first to be concerned with the problems of reality and appearance and with problems of how to think. It was only when philosophy gave way to science that people began learning *what* to think, and only then did they begin to learn what to think concerning human behavior. They then began to understand the function of religion and the meaning of God. It is of the very nature of philosophy as such to render one who indulges in its pursuit *vulnerable*. What is philosophy if not the immaculate conception of thought not sired by experience?

"Truths of value are the subject matters of wisdom. Wisdom deals with factors, reason deals with facts, intelligence deals with artifacts. God is not merely a fact; God is a factor. God creates facts." Mordecai M. Kaplan and Arthur Cohen, *If Not Now, When?* (henceforth, INNW) (New York: Schocken, 1973, pp. 20–21).

32. PMJE, p. 308.

33. JC, pp. 270–271.

34. Ibid.

35. *Not So Random Thoughts* (henceforth, NSRT) (New York: Reconstructionist Press, 1966, p. 192).

36. Ibid.

37. INNW, p. 16.

38. Ibid, p. 31.

39. Ibid., p. 37. Kaplan distinguishes between faith, which is basically in the category of emotion, and reason or idea. In a Hebrew entry in his

Diaries (March 24, 1938), Kaplan comments: "The more I reflect on education, the clearer it becomes to me that the success of an educator depends on his ability to learn properly the functions of faith and reason in human life. The function of faith is to infuse man with confidence that his striving for goodness will ultimately be successful. The function of reason is to correct the imbalance which generally exists between the true and the good."

4

Halakhah and Modern Society

COMMUNICATION IS ACCOMPLISHED most effectively through a common language, provided there is agreement on the meanings of the words, signs, or symbols that are used. There are, of course, other methods of interaction. beside verbal ones. Facial expressions (Shalom Aleichem says somewhere that "the nose can kill"), cries of love, joy, or anger, music, dance—these are just a few ways in which men and women speak to and with one another. But the word is the main instrument by which humans transmit their ideas and wishes to one another. Scriptures and the talmudic Sages taught that God created the world and continues to fashion it through His speech. "Blessed be He who spoke, and the world came into being" is repeated daily by the devout Jew. The Bible is a centuries-long conversation between God and the Jewish people. However, the word is a double-edged sword. It can be used not only to clarify but also to hide meaning, to mislead, and to distort reality.

The purpose of this brief discourse on semantics is to emphasize the importance of clarity and terminological exactitude. Many useless debates are conducted because the disputants attribute different meanings to words. Consequently, they argue at cross-purposes. Sometimes, as a result of semantic deficiency, the disputing parties fail to understand the real issue that divides them. A consideration of the views of Kook and Kaplan concerning the viability of the *Halakhah*, traditional Jewish law, should open windows to the current controversies on this subject.

I realize that this debate is unbalanced. For Kook, the viability of the *Halakhah* is a nonquestion. Nothing in God's world is more important than the *Halakhah*. True, Kook knows the Jews. Most of them violate many practices mandated by halakhic tradition. While Kook does not deny the legitimacy of their status as Jews, they are nonetheless sinners. He believes that it is his duty and that of all observant Jews to restore the sinners to full obedience to halakhic norms—albeit by using gentle persuasion. But Kook denies that there is anything in the Jewish thought or lifestyle of nontraditional Jews that merits his intellectual concern, let alone agreement. There is no basis for deliberation between the Torah of truth and the pseudo-Torah of the wrongdoers.

Surprisingly, Kook acknowledges that heresy and freedom of thought play a role in the furtherance of the tradition.[1] Without the challenge of deviations in thought, the *Halakhah* would become static. However, this dialectical "justification" has to be seen in its proper light. Heresy remains heresy, and there is no room for departures from the fundamentals of the *Halakhah*, even for the sake of intellectual honesty.

Kaplan agrees that the observance of *mitzvot* (not *the mitzvot*) is essential to a full life, but he has serious reservations about their status in contemporary Judaism. He loves Israel's Torah but maintains that some of its principles and theoretical foundations, as well as some of its practices, have to be altered.

Is it possible to encourage change in Judaism without weakening the cause of Jewish continuity? In the confrontation between Kook and Kaplan on this question, we shall be hearing most strongly the voice of the latter. Kook's stand is virtually self-understood: The Jewish people have no future except with and within the *Halakhah*. In Kaplan's view, the Jewish future requires carrying the *Halakhah* along with the rest of our traditional baggage, but only by refurbishing its containers and making drastic alterations in its contents.

THE MEANING OF *HALAKHAH*

First, we must accurately describe the sense in which the term "*Halakhah*" is understood in these pages. It is a universe in itself, almost equivalent to the whole of traditional Judaism and hence a subject for description rather than precise definition.

Let us try, at least, to outline its boundaries. My revered teacher, the great Talmudist Louis Ginzberg, once wrote:

It would be impossible within the compass of anything less than a substantial volume to present an analysis of the ideas comprised or implied in the term Halakah, or even to set forth the various senses in which the term has been employed. It has often been observed that the more claim an idea has to be considered living, the more various will be its aspects; and the more social and political is its nature, the more complicated and subtle will be its issues and the longer and more eventful its course. The attempt to express the "leading idea" of the Halakah I must perforce leave to those whose forte is omniscience and whose foible is knowledge.[2]

Despite Ginzberg's reticence, there can be no constructive discussion of the status of the *Halakhah* unless the participants can agree on the questions at stake and unless they can arrive at some mutually held premises about the essence of traditional Jewish law. I shall try, then, to sketch some of the key points about the *Halakhah* that I believe are involved in all attempts to establish its role in contemporary Jewish life.

1. Halakhah is founded on belief in divine revelation. All the halakhic fundamentals based on this assumption are eternal. In the spirit of Maimonides, HaRav Kook decisively clarifies this issue:

> The eternity of Torah is inherent. It was determined by the state of the world at the time the Torah was given. Nothing departs from the Torah, even though mundane affairs change. The prophecy of Moses, our Teacher, is not part of the ordinary spirituality of existence, like that of the rest of prophecy which . . . manifests itself as a natural phenomenon. The prophecy of the Master of all Prophets is a miracle, like the creation of the cosmos out of nothing. And just as that moment of creation accompanies the ongoing flow of time and will brook no change in the rules of its process, so the Torah, too, does not change.[3]

Note what follows in the next paragraph:

> Although, according to him [Maimonides], everything depends on the recognition of the divinity of the Torah, it is permissible to change some item, if the time demands it. But, in allowing ourselves to make such changes, we must affirm that the Torah is God-given, for that is its essence. Therefore, the whole enterprise exists forever, and change is possible only under certain conditions, most particularly [when it is introduced as] a provisional amendment by a prophet or an authorized court, or the like.[4]

2. Although the Oral Torah or Law is based on the Written Law (basically, the Pentateuch), it is the former, paradoxically, that determines the Jewish way of life. Kook articulates this point as follows:

> Oral Law is the very essence of the nation that was blessed by the revelation of the Written Law. The revelation of Oral Law is subordinate to that of the Written Law, for its source is in the latter. . . . But internally, since the Torah was given to Israel because of its exalted inner quality, this deeply-imbedded character causes divine Torah to descend upon it. As a result, the Oral Law is raised to a higher level than that of the Written Torah. The teachings of the Sages are more precious than those of the Written Torah.[5]

3. The *Halakhah* is total. All Jews are subject to its authority from the moment they awaken until the second they fall asleep at night. All of their thoughts and movements have halakhic significance, for each of them is subject to halakhic judgment.

4. The authority of the *Halakhah* applies equally to the individual and to the people as a whole.

5. The *Halakhah* is of Israel and is legislated by Israel for the conduct of its own life. The non-Jew has no role in halakhic legislation or in its judicial functioning. But should the non-Jew fall under Jewish jurisdiction, he or she is assured of being granted basic human rights under the law. It is conceivable that the *Halakhah* can be adapted to the needs of a sovereign, democratic Jewish state like Israel, but this would require a revolution in the halakhic theory of government and in its conception of the status of non-Jews under a Jewish majority. Meanwhile, there is an absolute contradiction between democracy and *Halakhah* in regard to the kind of polity that should be sponsored by sovereign Jews in the State of Israel.

6. There is no difference in principle in the application of *Halakhah* to human relations and to humanity's duties to God. That is to say, ritual practices are to be viewed as divine commands, transmitted to the people through halakhic authorities; they are not folkways that spring from the creative genius of the folk and its spiritual virtuosi. This theological claim explains why, on the one hand, the *Halakhah* is considered to be a supernatural phenomenon and, on the other, it is subject to interpretation, change,

and development. God supplies what is fixed and certain, and people introduce the novelty that is essential to keep up with life's fluidity.

7. The *Halakhah* seethes with spirituality, morality, and concern for human rights. It is not a codex of dry laws. Each act of legislation is founded on moral and spiritual values. Every Jew is unreservedly duty-bound to obey the *mitzvot* but must know that the law's purpose is to purify his or her moral performance.

8. Who has halakhic authority? This status is potentially conferred on every Jew who masters the legal literature and has the necessary intelligence and spirituality. In practice, a few scholars rise to eminence and become recognized as authorities. Although it is desirable for halakhic experts to acquire competence in one or more fields of general knowledge, such as philosophy, foreign languages, natural sciences, and human sciences, their status as a *posek* or legislator, judge, or commentator is dependent on their halakhic erudition and not on their qualifications in other areas. The broad-minded halakhist will consult with outside experts, even non-Jews, when their information is considered relevant, but no one except the halakhic authority can have a say in the determination of the law.

In a more far-reaching analysis of *Halakhah,* each of the above paragraphs would require documentation and broader analysis. But I believe that my sketchy outline enables us to follow the responses of Kook and Kaplan to today's challenges to the halakhic system.

The *Halakhah* has always been under challenge from the environment. One of its most severe tests came in the Middle Ages when Greek philosophy spread in various forms throughout Europe, northern Africa, and western Asia. The Arabs, in particular, addressed the theological and scientific implications of Greek thought, and they drew into the circle of these concerns intellectuals from many societies, including that of the Jews. What had previously been taken as self-evident—God's existence and His attributes, the theophany at Sinai, prophecy and the world to come—had now to be proved, clarified, or reformulated. Only against this background can we understand the astounding introduction with which Rambam begins the section on the foundations of Torah in his halakhic code, the *Mishneh Torah*. He apparently realized that to shore up the foundations of the *Halak-hah*, he had to provide the intellectually alert student with an additional rationale to the claim of historical revelation. Thus, before he organized and summarized the enormous corpus of law, he offered proofs of God's existence and responded to other theological questions in the spirit of Greek philosophy. His vocabulary consists of concepts such as motion, that which moves the heavenly bodies, infinity, matter and form, and so on. The terminology of the talmudic sages and their questions and methods of thinking were inadequate to cope with the new universe of discourse. Rambam's daring brought upon him the wrath of the Fundamentalists of his era. The history of Jewish law is replete with similar challenges and controversies.

In contrast to those who accuse halakhists of ossifying the law were the visionaries within the system who insisted that the Torah had to be progressive. They adjusted its intellectual rationale; they applied strict or loose construction to its demands, according to the circumstances of the moment; they issued intelligent and courageous decrees; and they even resorted to legal fictions when prescribed methods proved inadequate. We should not be surprised to discover that Kook has a similar problem in trying to navigate between the pre-modern *Halakhah* and the urgent needs of our fast-changing world.

KOOK'S HALAKHISM

In one matter, Kook finds no problem. Every decision has to be made within the *Halakhah* itself, not only because this is self-evident to anyone purporting to live by halakhic norms, but because all the problems of life can presumably be solved within the system. Kook's faith in the *Halakhah* is illustrated by the manner in which he deals with the problem of *Shemittah*, the sabbatical or fallow seventh year, which occurs seven times in the Jubilee cycle and is designed to minimize economic inequality. With the restoration of national life in Eretz Yisrael, the laws relating to Jewish conduct in and on the ancestral soil once again became vital halakhic concerns. *Shemittah* was and is no longer a theoretical issue, as is still the case for diaspora communities. Kook recognized that it would be economically disastrous for an entire country to refrain from growing crops for a whole year. It would also be spiritually unworthy to rely on non-Jews or the largesse of diaspora Jews to survive. This is not the place to describe the halakhic means by which Kook sought to enable all Jews to carry on their farming in accordance with the principles of *Shemittah*. His detailed analysis is to be found in his lengthy responsum, *Shabbat Haaretz*.[6] My point is that Kook, motivated by concern for the growth of Eretz Yisrael, was able to find a halakhic category— preventing financial hardship—that would serve as the basis of his effort to enable Jews to overcome biblical limitations on plowing the soil in the seventh year. Like many other halakhists, Kook believed that Jewish law is to be based on and to advance ethical, national ideals.

Kook assigned to halakists the duty to direct the masses ever closer to a rational, ethically sound life. He believed that the quality of life is itself a halakhic category, to be applied in structuring and conducting an ideal community. The *Halakhah*, therefore, can be used to harmonize the various ethical outlooks among Jews. He believed that this could be accomplished without reading personal opinions into the *Halakhah*. One need not step out of the halakhic circle to solve the most difficult problem.

To prove his case, Kook sought to extrapolate the full measure of insights from the classic literature. To do so, he often had to weigh the plain letter of the law against a value that is also embodied in the Torah but which had not previously been brought into play in specific instances. Thus, when mercy or pity could be applied, Kook weighted the scale in its favor. In the *Shulhan Arukh*, we find the following: "Whoever violates any toraitic law and does not repent need not be sustained" (*Yoreh Deah*, 251:1). Kook comments:

> This rule applies when we know that the person acts intentionally. But generally, we treat such a person as having acted innocently. We must feed him without further investigation. . . . Today, we have to relate mercifully to all Israel. Due to the troubles that beset us, we must view as innocents those who appear to be sinning on purpose.[7]

Kook was not naive. He perceived that intentional violation of the *mitzvot* was widespread. The sinners knew exactly what they were or were not doing. Kook hoped that the way of mercy would prove effective. So out of a feeling that moral considerations should lead a *posek* (a halakhic decision-maker) to eschew strict rulings as much as possible, he chose to ignore the stark reality. Nevertheless, we should not conclude that the halakhist is free to rule leniently in all cases, on the basis of mercy or some other humane principles. Rabbi Hayyim Hakohen Kook, the brother of the Reiyah, records in the name of the latter that one must be extremely cautious in family law and rely only on the opinion of experts. Hayyim Kook cites his brother's reasoning, saying,

> To effectuate the real correction of the world's faults, we should turn to the great scholars of Israel who seek ways to permit, whenever circumstances allow. However, when there are no grounds for leniency, we have no right to be more merciful than God Himself. The Holy one, blessed be He, will protect His people from all trouble and affliction and save all who are in distress. For only He can redeem the troubled ones.[8]

Kook's moral tension is circumscribed by the halakhic walls. To illustrate: a civil court can, after a period of time prescribed by law, free an *agunah* (a woman whose husband's fate or location is unknown or whose husband refuses to grant her a divorce), to remarry. A rabbinical court, however, has no such option, even if the judges are moved by the plight of the unfortunate woman. I acknowledge that a truly liberal halakhist can find a way to circumvent the laws of the *agunah*—by legal fiction or by decree. However, such maneuvers would strain to the limit the self-imposed legal restrictions of traditional halakhists, loose and strict constructionists alike.

The law in every ethically oriented system of justice dictates the degree of flexibility to be permitted to judges and administrative officials. Kook's moral dilemma is essentially the same as that of the authorities in every society. A tension often arises between the law and the moral sense of one person or another on the ladder of authority. No law can satisfy the need of every citizen. In view of this fact, we can ask the question to which Kook and Kaplan offer divergent answers: Is it desirable today to enforce the *Halakhah*, with its entire conception of authority, its legal procedure, and its moral and spiritual assumptions? Perhaps we should strive to transpose the whole halakhic tradition into a democratic key? Or, put differently, while Kook hopes to persuade the Jewish people to create a halakhic polity and way of life in Eretz Yisrael, Kaplan seeks to determine what in the halakhic tradition is suitable for a democratic State of Israel and in the conduct of Jewish life in the disparate diaspora communities.

Luckily, despite their differing views, Kaplan and Kook can accompany one another for long stretches of the road. They share many values and practices of the Written and Oral Laws: the sanctity of life and respect for the individual, the interdependence of all Jews and their responsibility for their welfare and that of non-Jews, acts of loving-kindness, observance of the Shabbat and holidays, the duty to rebuild Eretz Yisrael, and other elements of the halakhic tradition. This broad agreement, emanating from their mutual love of God, Israel, and Torah, suffices to enable the two men to dwell together in the same society. The ideals they proclaim are precisely those that have enabled Zionism to perform its historic mission. It was in the Zionist movement that large segments of religious and secular Jewry were able to cooperate in the efforts to induce Jews to return to Zion and to revive the Jewish homeland. But the Jewish consensus today does not seem broad enough to enable the ideological rivals to agree upon the principles of a Jewish public domain or to arrive at a workable conception of Judaism that would unite the two ends of the reasonable Jewish spectrum. In this chapter on *Halakhah*, I attempt to disclose some of the reasons for this condition.

As I have stated, the *Halakhah* is total, but the growth of freedom and voluntarism has made it impossible for Jewish law to dominate every aspect of life. Most Jews no longer favor the universal imposition of law in all matters. In effect, modern voluntarism forestalls the high degree of uniformity that characterized the traditional Jewish community. This is true both in the Diaspora and in Israel. In the latter, attempts are constantly but unsuccessfully being made to reduce the number of legitimate behavioral options. The extent of halakhic authority, although still potent because of the need to form political coalitions, has been severely curtailed. For instance, a sanction such as excommunication scarcely affects the one who is banned or the overwhelming bulk of the citizenry. A loving and conciliatory person like Kook succeeded here and there, by virtue of his winning personality and charisma, to convince some laborers to stop working before the advent of Shabbat.[9] In 1914, Kook led a mission of rabbis to some of the northern settlements. They surveyed the state of Jewish observance in some of the town's agricultural settlements. Kook persuaded a few farmers to observe aspects of *Shemittah*, separating tithes, and the like. But while Kook gained their respect, his influence over the halutzim never led to the single-minded return to traditional Judaism that he had sought.

The Jewish people today are split between those who observe the *mitzvot* as divine dictates and those who deny that assumption and therefore practice only those *mitzvot* to which they can give their intellectual, moral, and esthetic consent. Many of these Jews view themselves as religiously observant, even though they take exception to the sovereignty of the *Halakhah* in the determination of the content, form, and application of the *mitzvot*. For example, such Jews—and they are legion—argue that they can celebrate Shabbat while riding to the synagogue or to a hospital to visit a loved one. They regard such practices not as *hillul Shabbat* (violation of the Sabbath) but as proper ways of sanctifying the day. They see the traditional *lo taaseh* (prohibition) in instances like these, which prevent them from fulfilling a spiritual need and deny them the chance to perform an act of loving-kindness, as the opposite of what should be expected from a devoted Jew. The concept of the observant Jew has been broadened. It is no longer possible to treat the *Halakhah* as the sole authority in the determination of the scale of *mitzvot*. The conception of halakhic totality has been shattered, along with popular belief in the inherent relevancy and worth of some of its practices. Perhaps most significant is the fact that law is today inapplicable in certain areas of individual choice and taste. Voluntarism is the rule in matters of ritual.

Kook places the responsibility for reversing this trend upon the halakhic authorities. They must take advantage of every opportunity to prove that the *Halakhah* has greater validity and worth than other legal and cultural systems. Kook deemed the halakhic problem to be merely one of explaining the spirit and content of Jewish law to the uninitiated. He was confident that if people would listen to the halakhists, they would be convinced to follow the way of Torah. Therefore, wherever an internal halakhic controversy arose, Kook tried his best to get agreement, so that the law would shine forth clearly. Without clarity, it would be difficult for the community to accept halakhic authority. If the halakhists cannot agree, what can we expect from the general public?

In his search for an effective halakhic method, Kook suggested:

> We must see the plain sense of things and in what direction majority opinion is heading in a specific case. If the matter spreads over the Babylonian and Jerusalem Talmudim and the Tosefta, we must then review the attitude of the Bavli. If opinion in the Bavli is balanced, we have to refer to the other relevant halakhic sources— and the Tosefta—and seek to distill the majority opinion among the early Sages. We then come upon the content of the *Halakhah*, as it has become manifest among the people. Whenever we discover indecision among the Sages, we must look beyond their opinions and endeavor to disclose the majority trend in all the versions at our disposal. On the basis of all these clear and simple procedures, we must then decide the law.[10]

In summary, halakhic disputes are resolved completely in accord with the internal logic of the *Halakhah* itself. There is not the slightest hint that one can have recourse to outside authority of any kind. Although elsewhere Kook does point to the desirability of seeking expert testimony in matters of fact about physical phenomena, his openness does not permit going beyond the *Halakhah* in the adjudication of any case. One might and should use relevant evidence from expert sources, but if that evidence contradicts a halakhic principle, its truth or suggestiveness is irrelevant and of no worth. Outside evidence that is theoretical and not yet substantiated by the senses is to be avoided.

For instance, although medical advances impressed Kook, he was skeptical about the claims made by medical researchers and physicians. He comments:

> Every discussion among the decisors (*poskim*) in regard to the trustworthiness of doctors, revolves around the question of the reliability of medical science. We doubt the validity of some of the assertions of doctors. It is well known that from time to time, they disprove their own scientific positions. I stated long ago that one should act favorably only on medical opinion based on the evidence of the senses, concerning which the doctors themselves are

certain. I adopt the view of the Rabbis (Shabbat 85a), who said that certain agricultural measurements had been learned by their Israelite ancestors from the descendants of Seir the Horite, who were knowledgeable about the cultivation of the soil. The Israelite settlers relied on the testimony of the Horites. The latter were described as "smelling the land." Similarly, the Hivites, who "tasted the soil," were to be trusted to impart what they learned through their sense of smell or taste. The behavior of the soil and the beings who dwell upon it is better learned in this way than from theoretical wisdom. Furthermore, conventional wisdom leads us to assume that an artisan will not say or do anything that might damage his professional reputation.[11]

From this we can infer that while Kook deems halakhic debates to be spiritual encounters in which all sides express truth, the scientists and the philosophers "cast axes" against one another. Extra-halakhic disagreements render the assertions of secular authorities untrustworthy. Only the evidence of a science that is based on sense perception—a capability potentially accessible to all ardent students of Torah—is acceptable to Kook and to traditional halakhists. They cannot or will not give credence to the possibility that the quest for the divine requires openness to all branches of wisdom. They do not accept the premise that the conventions of the past and the decisions of Torah experts sometimes have to be subject to radical revision. Kook would never consent to deliberately uprooting any item from the Torah, even if halakhic sages were convinced of its immorality or irrationality. Only halakhic warranty could legitimize such a move.

Kook approaches the *Halakhah* as an organic whole. The particular has to be understood in the context of this whole and has no significance except in that connection. In the same vein, while the fulfillment of each Jew is subject to the workings of the *Halakhah*, its main thrust is to guarantee the special status of the Jewish people. In one of his responsa, in which he deals with the behavioral deviations of righteous men, Kook accuses the righteous of not

having proclaimed that Israel is blessed with a holiness not conferred on any other nation. The main aim of other peoples is to provide for the good of the individual, but the group as a whole has no independent essence. The relations between average nations are basically those of a partnership, in which the main concern of the partners is to insure that the association redounds to the benefit of each party. For Israel, however, community and partnership are two distinct concepts . . . for in the community of Israel are a holiness and general reality that cannot be measured in terms of individual interest. The Jewish community defies division. . . .[12]

The burden of the *Halakhah* on individuals is heavy indeed. Jews acquire their identity by virtue of their belonging and their loyalty to the Jewish people. But according to the concept discussed above, their every move is circumscribed by the ambience of that group. We cannot expect that the creativity of the greatest genius will alter any fundamental of the tradition, if the product of that talent deviates from it in any way.[13] Kook fought against what he considered to be the exaggerated individualism of the open society, but he was apparently unaware of the equal danger of the power and authority that he claimed for the people as a unit and for the unbreakable totality of Jewish law.

The exclusiveness of the halakhic concern for the interests of the Jewish people explains why Kook considers the presence of non-Jews to be essential to Jewish welfare. Paradoxically, without the "Shabbos Goy," that is, the non-Jew who is enlisted to perform necessary chores that the Jew is forbidden to do on Sabbaths and holidays, life in a halakhic society would be extremely difficult. But Kook never questions whether the non-Jew will always be available or whether he or she will consent to be the paid servant of Jewish religiosity. To illustrate, Kook decreed that milking cows on Shabbat is absolutely forbidden to Jews:

> this is an activity that has to be undertaken by non-Jews, as has been the practice of our ancestors throughout time. Of necessity, a few non-Jews must be present in every Jewish settlement in order that chores that are permitted to gentiles on Sabbaths and holidays might be done. The laws of our holy Torah are undoubtedly stronger beyond all measure than the folkways invented by men. . . .[14]

Kook's Israelocentrism and his unstinting support of the institution of the "Shabbos Goy" deprive his halakhic vision of some of its moral quality and its practicality. For example, what should and can Kook's disciples expect of a Christian or a Moslem when a holiday such as Christmas or a holy occasion such as Id al-Fitr falls on the Sabbath or on a Jewish holiday? Is it fair to expect the Christian or the Moslem to surrender his or her holiday in favor of Jewish need? A law that is not based on the complete autonomy and self-sufficiency of the Jew and the Jewish community hardly befits a modern, enlightened society. Certainly, we should hope, not the State of Israel.

In contrast to his general leniency in matters of human relations, Kook tended to be strict in regard to ritual, prayer, and other *mitzot maasivot* that deal with the individual's relationship with God. To him family seating in the synagogue was scandalous, and he wanted to uproot the practice. He viewed placing the reading desk in front of the ark instead of in the midst of the worshipers as a step toward deculturation. All his life, Kook worried about the kashrut of the *ethrog*, the citron used during Sukkot, and he tried to convince all Jews to purchase only ungrafted citrons. He fought vigorously against the slightest act that might cast suspicion on the kashrut of hotel kitchens. When he noted that hotels were violating those halakhic standards unrelated to food regulations, he recommended establishing two types of kashrut certificates. He wrote:

> In any case, we should distinguish between two types of authorization: hotels with an unqualified *hekhsher* and those which have rabbinical supervision in regard to food but are not really "kasher" in the complete sense. [That is to say, there are violations of Shabbat in other matters, such as smoking or collecting fees. This arouses suspicion that the formal supervision does not suffice to guarantee the complete kashrut of the food.] But on Shabbat, the presence of the *mashgiah* [supervisor] must be more assiduous, inasmuch as the hotel management is under suspicion. It is important to stop up this breach before it widens. Clearly, the supervision of such places has to be stricter and more persistent and detailed. It should also extend to watching how dishes are washed, and the like. Even this second certification should be tied to the condition that the hotel promise not to collect payments on Sabbaths and holidays. Otherwise, I think that we cannot sustain such violators of the law, even with the placement of a permanent supervisor. For by supporting such a business, we contribute to the violation of the Sabbath.[15]

From the halakhic standpoint, Kook's strict supervision was not in vain. He had no choice, given his premises, but to watch for deviations such as those I have mentioned. At a time when heresy is widespread, the only road that a halakhic loyalist can take is that of extreme conservatism. Just as a woman cannot be partially pregnant, so too does the acceptance of the burden of the Law impose on the halakhically minded Jew total obedience to its demands. If Kook were alive today, he would unquestionably find the prevailing procedure of kashrut certification to be unsatisfactory.

Nonetheless, we can assume that Kook's issuance of lenient halakhic decisions in ritual matters was motivated by his understanding of the relevant laws and by the fact that many of the cases involved problems of human need and human relations.[16] For instance, despite his uncompromising opposition to equalizing the status of women, he allowed women to sew together the segments of parchment following the completion of the writing of a Torah scroll. His remarks at the outset of his responsum on this subject are enlightening:

> Regarding the disqualification of the product of someone who is not authorized to write [a sacred text], the Rambam does not explain his source (H. Tefillin, ch. 3). Undoubtedly, his ruling was taken from a Rabbinic source that he forgot. Be that as it may, it is only miderabbanan [a ruling of the Rabbis, of lesser authority than a biblical decree]. That being the case, since the core of the disqualification of women from writing a Torah Scroll is shrouded in doubt . . . and since it is a Rabbinical doubt, we ought not initially put ourselves into this frame of mind. . . .[17]

Kook goes on to show that the talmudic sages permitted women to lay their hands upon a sacrifice, even though they themselves were forbidden to offer it. The rabbis were motivated, says Kook, to provide some spiritual satisfaction for the women. Similarly, Kook says that if a woman truly wants to participate in the preparation of a Torah scroll, it is inhumane to deny her that pleasure. Kook is able to open the door to leniency by making use of the possibility, in a halakhically legitimate way, of bypassing a technicality and uncertainty in favor of the fulfillment of an ethical ideal. Kook was so greatly motivated by his humanitarianism that he strained to find a legal way to accomplish this purpose.

We have just seen how a humane morality can expose the unfairness of certain halakhic restrictions and how a sensitive halakhist can amend a law or correct a practice by reference to that morality. But the history of ethics indicates that every set of moral values, whether secular or religious, has to be reviewed and occasionally revised in the course of time. Efforts by theologians, philosophers, and clergy to establish the universality and the absoluteness of the morality they espouse have been unsuccessful. It is true that humankind has reached agreement on certain principles that guide its slow advance toward a universal humanity, but the understanding of those principles differs from nation to nation and religion to religion. It is also unclear how each moral value is to be embodied in social structure and behavior. Thus, it is not Kook but the halakhic system that has to be judged. Kook was bound by its restraints. When put this way, however, we can see how much morality is historically conditioned and how even a courageous person like Kook cannot always live up to the moral standards he deems to be ideal. The *Halakhah* is morally concerned, but it often falls short of being an acceptable criterion of ethical worth. I raise a few points to support this assertion.

The *Halakhah* discriminates against women. It does not accord them some of the civil rights granted in enlightened societies. The same discrimination applies to ritual. Kook justifies the daily benediction recited by a Jewish man, thanking God for not having made him a woman. He accepts the restrictions on women as witnesses in a court. He finds reasons for the separate and unequal position of women in the traditional synagogue. And he looks upon women as passive creatures as compared to the activism of men. These and Kook's other pre-modern views are founded in anachronistic biological and sociological conceptions of historical revelation. Much of the content of the Sinaitic dispensation has been undermined by the accumulated findings of modern science and ethical research.

This criticism does not contradict my opinion of Kook as an open-minded, tolerant, and loving person. But Kook's humaneness is not the issue. It frequently happens that a person's character is superior to his or her philosophy, and vice versa. I need not belabor the point. The real problem confronting the Jewish people today is to decide in which universe of discourse it ought to live. On one side is the world of traditional knowledge and morality; on the other side is the world outlook that respects tradition but wants to adapt it to the values of freedom and critical judgment. We should not underestimate the worth of Jewish tradition, which embraces many truths and high moral values. However, some of its psychological and physiological foundations are distortions of fact. The halakhists, therefore, continue to issue judgments based on shaky grounds. Many myths about human nature, still extant in halakhic thought, have no standing outside halakhic circles. Even if we reserve judgment as to the validity of recent findings about the nature of the sexes and question the wisdom of some of the ways in which those findings are used, we can no longer be confident that the *Halakhah* is superior to all other methods of ethical striving. The best we can do is to demonstrate where halakhic values are, indeed, worthy of emulation. But we must also be prepared to admit its failings.

Kook exhibited considerable compassion toward and empathy for Arabs, "the Ishmaelites," as he called them. But the *Halakhah* is paternalistic about the status of Arabs and other non-Jews in Eretz Yisrael. His attitude could be born out of a sense of superiority or a fear of the impact of the outgroup if it is granted full equality.

On another plane, does halakhic morality cope with the full depth of the dilemmas of modern warfare? There is no doubt that the talmudic sages tried to deal with the moral problems of war. They sought to implant in all Jewish soldiers the image of God that resides both in them and in the enemy. Nevertheless, under today's conditions of total warfare, is it still advisable to speak of *milhemet mitzvah*, traditionally, a war to fill out the borders of Eretz Yisrael or a war of defense, as divinely mandated? I do not intend to analyze the many facets of the problem.[18] However, I am impelled to insist that the halakhic approach omits important considerations, some of which are time-bound and others, indicative of a basic moral obtuseness. For instance, a distinction has to be made between a justifiable war and an unavoidable war. Given the indiscriminate and destructive power of modern weapons, is it legitimate to *justify* war under any circumstances? Self-defense may compel a nation to take military action, but can one call the killing of innocent men, women, and children—the inevitable outcome of missile attacks or bombings from the air—anything except manslaughter or murder, however unintentional these deaths might seem to be to the attackers? In another vein, can any nation today justify a military initiative in order to acquire or regain territory that was at one time under its sovereignty? Kook, in keeping with the *Halakhah*, gave thought to training the Jewish warrior to be humane in battle.[19] But war today is mainly conducted at long distance. Most soldiers never know whom their weapons are likely to strike down. Therefore, progressive morality demands that all peoples try to avoid going to war. This calls for a new social psychology and stepping beyond the *Halakhah*.

The waging of war is a concern of every individual. In Jewish society it is a matter that cannot be left in the hands of halakhic scholars or any other single group of experts. Halakhic wisdom should play a role in military decisions, but it is the duly elected representatives of the nation who must make the fateful decision, after due consultation with the best minds in all the relevant disciplines. Kook's stand regarding the authority of the *Halakhah* testifies to its pretension. He posits:

> [W]e have to attend to the fact that divine thought embraces every old or new idea. Therefore, every phenomenon for good can be attributed with surety to toraitic insights, among which are to be found the sources of universal moral awareness and knowledge, as well as a lifestyle of just laws and judgments.[20]

Kook's confidence in the omniscience of halakhic wisdom is a misreading of the history of ideas. The ancients were no less intelligent than moderns, but they could not know what we know. A classic example is a statement by Maimonides. When he wanted to illustrate an idea that is inconceivable, that is, completely irrational and beyond the possibility of implementation, he mentioned "an iron ship travelling through space."[21] There is no basis for the assumption that all knowledge or goodness can be located in the Torah. Nor can we say that whatever is in the Torah is automatically to be considered true or good.

In summary, Kook was convinced that Judaism and the *Halakhah* are identical. There is no other legitimate way in the Jewish purview. Kook wanted a vital and viable system of Jewish law, but he was totally subservient to what he believed were divine principles. The *Halakhah* determines human destiny, and human purposes do not always match God's plan. Jews can frequently find sustenance for their wants in the law, but their will cannot determine the truth or the value of the *Halakhah*. "In any case," Kook quotes, "the *mitzvot* are not given for enjoyment."[22] If Jews do find pleasure in them (Sukkot is "our joyous season"; "Soon there will be heard in the cities of Judea and the streets of Jerusalem the sounds of joy and happiness"), this is a sign of God's unsolicited kindness and is not a necessary outcome of the observance of the *mitzvot*.

KAPLAN ON HALAKHAH

In Kook's vision, *Halakhah* is the thrust of God's will into human affairs, an intrusion of eternity into time. Kaplan, on the other hand, portrays the halakhic system as a great achievement of Jewish ingenuity that has to be superseded by a new conception of the governance of life for the Jewish group and the Jewish individual.

Kaplan has deep respect for tradition, but he sees it as a field that has to be replowed and weeded, its stones removed, its soil reseeded and refertilized. Similarly, tradition has to undergo periods of interpretation and reinterpretation, to uproot stale or outmoded ideas and generate fresh concepts and creative innovations. Kaplan insists that tradition has to be heard, but it should not be granted veto power over today's decisions. He demands that

> the living generation assume full responsibility for its own decisions, and use tradition as affording data on which to base present judgments, but not as being itself decisive. When we let the past prejudge a present situation, we are governed by prejudice. We abdicate our responsibility, when we yield to the authority of the past.[23]

We note that Kaplan assigns a major role to tradition in the preservation of Jewish life. However, the present and future are not merely continuations of the past. Cultural growth has moments of discontinuity, conflicting stresses, and innovations that do not always receive the approval of the past. One should not discard the past or alter it before one understands it intellectually and emotionally. Neither should one permit tradition to act as the final judge of what is appropriate for the present day. The court of history consists of a panel of judges representing different ages and interests.

If we agree that the core of the *Halakhah* is in law and *mitzvah*, we quickly come to a parting of the ways between our two thinkers. Kaplan rejects the idea that all of life can or should be subsumed under the halakhic establishment. He acknowledges that cult-related practices are suitable instruments for transmitting spiritual values from person to person and from generation to generation. Nevertheless, given the differences in capacities and tastes among men and women, and in view of the need to protect freedom of thought and expression, Kaplan would remove rituals of all kinds from the category of law. Implicit in this approach is his abandonment of the belief in their divine source. Just as all peoples develop their own language, so too they create their own ritual forms. Every practice evolves as part of the natural vitality and growth of the group. Kaplan remarks:

> Ritual helps us to identify ourselves with the People to which we belong and to read the spiritual meaning for us of its historic experience. *We can as little do without observances and practices that symbolize the religious meanings of our civilization as we can do without language to communicate our ideas and feelings to one another.*[24] (Italics, MMK)

This process is natural, and each of its products has only that authority, power, and influence which are exercised by any work of human initiative. As soon as we accept this premise, it follows that the observance of these customs or, in Kaplan's rhetoric, "folkways," depends on the free response of individuals to their message and tone. This means that the creation and preservation of all symbolic acts and artifacts have to be transferred from law to educational, moral, spiritual, and artistic expression.

Unquestionably, this naturalization of the *mitzvot maasivot* makes the possibility of having a single and uniform system of Jewish ritual less likely, but pluralism, Kaplan asserts, is one of the inevitable by-products of the growing freedom in civilized societies. Two considerations determine Kaplan's readiness to pay this price. First, he prizes freedom to such an extent that he cannot conceive of human advancement without it. Second, since the purpose of the *mitzvot* is "to purify human beings," to draw them closer to God and to devotion to truth, goodness, and beauty—all rabbinic views that Kaplan cherishes—each custom must pass the test of effectiveness. The theological or metaphysical assumptions behind ritual cannot dictate its realization in daily conduct. Where there is freedom, implementation will depend on the ability of each ritual to speak to the heart and mind of every Jew. In the Bible, God is often depicted as addressing the individual, as in the instance of the Ten Commandments (better translated as Words or Principles). Even though the Words are uttered in the presence of the entire people and are meant for the group as a whole, they are drafted so as to impress on each individual his or her personal responsibility to obey the divine dictates. If the individual is not convinced of the rightness of certain laws, commands, or symbols, of what value can they be? The *mitzvah* has to speak for itself. If its content and form are unconvincing, free men and women will not be coerced into practicing it.

Kaplan encouraged efforts to seek what can still be effective and inspiring in traditional customs. He wanted to revive the creative process of breathing life into *mitzvot* that have spiritual potential, to amend or reconstruct them as needed, and to introduce new practices, as the times demand. It was this type of development that produced the magnificent Hebrew calendar and its rich treasure of holy days. At the same time, Kaplan perceived the danger of anarchy and sought to prevent it. Freedom does not mean that each person may "make Shabbat for himself." Freedom imposes on those who enjoy its blessings the duty to learn the art of compromise, to cooperate in common endeavors, and to conduct civilized debate with those who hold differing or conflicting views.

The formulation of an effective ritual system has to be the work of a congregation or community and not of isolated individuals. In a setting composed of a group of men and women who need and want one another and who respect the tradition that brings them together, the chances are good that a blend of tradition and novelty can be achieved. A grass-roots development of this kind should be circumscribed by national standards that are democratically established. To reach a consensus under freedom, both disparate congregations and the people as a whole have to exercise considerable patience. They should avoid the temptation to set up minimal standards, lest they become too rigid. Kaplan writes:

> It would be unwise to define minimum standards, because conditions vary so greatly for different individuals that what might amount to a minimal sacrifice for some might amount to an intolerable burden for others. . . . What every Jew should seek in adjusting his beliefs and observances to conditions is not a quantitative minimum or maximum, but an optimum standard. He should hold himself to account for making the best possible creative adjustment to those conditions that affect his effort to fulfill himself as a Jew.[25]

Obviously, Kaplan's openness and flexibility raise the question as to who should wield the authority to alter tradition? The problem is twofold: Who is to have power in governmental matters, and who should handle practices relating to the dialogue between humankind and God? The answer to the first question is clear enough. The establishment of the State of Israel created a totally new situation, which has no counterpart in Jewish history. (I shall treat this development at greater length in Chapter 13 on Judaism and Democracy.) Democracy and *Halakhah* are political opposites. A democratic state, by definition, is one in which all citizens have the right and duty to participate in the choice of their government and in which citizenship is open to all, regardless of race, religion, or ethnic origin. The *Halakhah* restricts legislative and judicial authority to Jews and is manifestly unfit to answer the needs of a pluralistic society.

Nevertheless, the *Halakhah* can contribute to the framing of law in the State of Israel. The halakhic corpus contains innumerable conceptions and laws that deserve to be incorporated into the theory and practice of a democratic government. The *Halakhah* can be one of the sources of legislation and adjudication in the State of Israel, alongside what is borrowed from Ottoman, English, American, and other legal systems. This entails the secularization of the *Halakhah* and its transposition into the key of a modern universe of discourse.[26] Kook wanted the Jewish state to be a halakhic domain, whereas Kaplan, who was wholeheartedly in favor of democracy, felt that the best way to preserve what is worthwhile in the *Halakhah* is to entrust its treasures to a system of democratic government and religious volunteerism. This means that political rule in a multiethnic society cannot be placed in the hands of halakhic scholars. As for the Jewish community itself, Kaplan calls for the creation of a new, democratically elected body that would deal with matters affecting the integrity of the Jewish people. However, he leaves such concerns as prayer, home rituals, and holiday celebrations to the free choice of individuals and their free associations. In such matters of the spirit, each person must be guided by education and by the inspiration of influential leaders.

The second question concerning who has the right to alter any of the *mitzvot maasiyot* is another matter, for it touches on the inner life of the entire Jewish people, those in the Diaspora as well as in Israel. Kaplan distinguishes between two types of authority. One relates to all aspects of worship and the other to human relations. Authority in the area of the God-human relationship

> will have to reckon with the principle of the freedom of conscience, and will not be able to apply public sanctions to enforce uniform behavior. It will, however, be able to offer the guidance of professional personnel familiar with Jewish religious and cultural values, whose advice will have weight, because of their learning and because of their understanding of Jewish values and Jewish needs.[27]

In Kaplan's perspective, prayer, observance of the Sabbath and holidays, and public religious practices and restrictions should all be subject to group decision, in which each person will have an equal voice. But Kaplan expects the tone of the communal religious expression to be influenced by the input of rabbis of all streams, educators, artists, and recognized spiritual leaders. A consensus will gradually emerge from the many attempts at infusing the religious tradition with new vitality. The period of transition between traditional norms and the consensus of the future will have to be one of search and trial and error. Naturally, this fluidity and pluralism will alienate those Jews who adhere to every detail of the ancestral heritage. They can see in Kaplan's approach only the destruction of Judaism. Nonetheless, his vision is a formidable response to the current spiritual malaise.

The Jewish people has to make a fateful choice. Is it better to try and restore the relative uniformity of the past or to search for God by encouraging the creation of a variety of options for worship and celebration? If the latter alternative is selected, how does one determine which of the new options are worthy replacements of or supplements to the hallowed tradition? Clearly, newness is not a synonym for merit. Therefore, we shall have to examine Kaplan's attempt to steer a course between continuity and change.

Those who charge halakhic-minded Jews with automatically rejecting all manner of change in Jewish practice are misguided. The *Halakhah* has always been a fluid system of adjustment between an authoritative tradition and the needs of the hour. However, the method, scope, and speed of adjustment have become increasingly unsatisfactory. The exaggerated need to find precedents in the *Halakhah* in order to justify change is too cumbersome. Any system that is subject only to criticism from within or is reluctant to grant authority to foreign wisdom is bound to lag behind the times or to employ inefficient or unsavory methods to accomplish obviously needed goals. Taking verses out of context, deliberately ignoring the law's intent, resorting to anachronisms, or having recourse to *ormah* (subtle manipulation or legal fiction) are among the ways in which halakhists attempt to keep the law abreast of the times. Kaplan, despite his admiration for the halakhic achievement and its great contribution to Jewish survival, could not stomach these instruments. He was fascinated by the creative originality of the halakhists and their many lasting insights, but he was not enamored of some of the means they used. He refused to be chained to what he considered the intellectual and moral errors of the halakhic system. Therefore, he called for forthright rejection of what is unacceptable. He tried to work out a system of adjustment between past and present, always bearing in mind the dangers that lurk along the way. One of these dangers is a method that he called "passive adjustment." This approach is

> motivated by the purpose of making life easy and comfortable, without any serious concern with issues and consequences beyond one's own convenience. Thus, the complete neglect of Sabbaths and holidays, when their observance interferes with our worldly ambitions, is characteristic of the passive adjustment, which always follows the path of least resistance.[28]

Conversely, Kaplan declares:

> Creative adjustment seeks not only to preserve, but even to en-
> hance the spirit of the tradition. It reckons with environmental
> conditions by trying to overcome obstacles they present, and to
> take advantage of the opportunities of improvement that they af-
> ford. Thus, when the climate of opinion makes it impossible to
> maintain a religious belief in its traditional form, creative adjust-
> ment would seek, wherever possible, to reinterpret it in terms of
> modern thought.[29]

Kaplan cites the example of the concept of the world-to-come.
Instead of referring to life after death, the concept would come
to mean the striving for fulfillment by participation in causes that
are geared to making life more peaceful and richer in experience
for future generations. Although Kaplan follows the path of Maimonides, there is one important difference. Kaplan reveals his intent, whereas the great medieval philosopher leaves us in doubt
as to whether the world-to-come is in an earthly existence or in
the afterlife.

Creative adjustment seeks to preserve as much as possible of the
form and content of the *mitzvot maasivot,* even as the force of
modernity pushes us toward radical change. Thus, when the
Temple was destroyed and the sacrificial system had to be dis-
carded, the people created the synagogue as a substitute and included in the prayers many references to the sacrifices. In this way
they were able to bear the shock of their loss, preserve the memory of past glory, and exhibit hope for its future restoration. The
synagogue proved to be more than a substitute. It led the people
to new levels of spirituality. Similarly, today we are witness to the
remaking of society. The growing equalization of the status of
men and women is forcing societies throughout the world to re-
structure. In the synagogue, this means that egalitarianism has become an essential step in the advance toward spiritual maturity.

Inasmuch as Kaplan rejects the revelational basis for Jewish religious culture, he has to find another rationale for its continuation.
He identifies himself with the continuous effort of our ancestors
to fathom God's will and to behave according to its dictates. But
the search is endless, and one can never arrive at a final station.
Clearly Kaplan's vision is open to error and hubris, and it invites

doubt and unrest. Anyone seeking security and certainty will not find them in Kaplan; however, Jews who revel in broadening their horizons will find his thought to be a great challenge.

Kaplan did not rest with theory.[30] He knew that a people's vitality is discerned in its sancta—the sacred symbols, days, places, and customs that draw the attention of each person to the values cherished by the nation—in brief, to that which the group considers to be holy. Kook, surprisingly for a staunch traditionalist, thought that the difference between the sacred and the profane, the holy and the secular, is only relative. Kaplan went further and declared that even the definition of the holy is conditioned by the historical experience and the intellectual and spiritual levels of the people. But he opposed all anarchy. Freedom does not permit one to do whatever one wishes without regard to circumstances, consequences, and transcendent norms.

Kaplan had to deal with the problem of how men and women can conceive freedom so as to always choose only those actions that accord with truth and goodness as perceived by the most advanced wisdom. No less difficult is the problem of how to ensure that freedom and creativity will engender a beauty that is the final and fitting stage of the harmonious working of the human soul. Kook saw the *mitzvot* as the commands of an Absolute Deity. Kaplan saw them as norms that are distilled from the past and present experiences of the Jewish people. He realized that the accumulated heritage of the Jewish people and the free intercourse between generations of Jews could lead to mistakes. Innovators can easily ignore or misread old ideas and practices that deserve to be preserved for present and future generations. As a force for conservation, Kook's method is surer, but it is also full of unwarranted certainty. In the hands of souls less spiritual than Kook, it can become a source of nationalistic arrogance.

Kaplan's road is less certain, but it encourages self-criticism and self-correction. Jews today face the problem of whether or not these two systems can exist side by side. Are their supporters wise enough and courageous enough to learn from the positive elements in the seemingly incompatible "other" vision?

Even the nonlegalistic approach to ritual and worship requires criteria for changing formulas of prayer and ritual practices and for providing new contents and forms for other sancta. Kaplan and his colleagues formulated a *Guide for Jewish Ritual Usage* to "indicate along what lines traditional practices may be changed and new practices instituted, without endangering the entire structure of Jewish religious life."[31] The following principles are proposed in the *Guide:*

1. Ritual change cannot be so radical as to destroy the entire fabric of the religious culture and convert it into an abstract ethic.

2. Only a minority of Jews will accept the view that since ritual is God's dictate, it must not be altered. The determination of the minority must not deter the majority from acting upon their convictions.

3. In the effort to vitalize and enrich the *mitzvot maasiyot*, we must maintain a balance between the needs of the community and the legitimate wants of the individual. *"A satisfactory rationale for Jewish usage is one that would recognize in it both a method of group survival and a means to the Personal fulfilment, or salvation, of the individual Jew."*[32] (Italics, MMK)

4. It is to be expected that not all Jews will find equal satisfaction in this or that custom. The life experiences of each individual are different and will affect his or her soul accordingly. Equally significant are his or her genetic and learned traits of character. Therefore, it is absurd to believe that an entire people can be satisfied with a uniform set of ritual practices and symbols. Hence, while loyalty to tradition must be measured by respect for the heritage of the past and the standards of the contemporary community, attention must be given to the spirit, temperament, intelligence, and need satisfaction of the individual.

5. As already stated, ritual should be removed from the category of law. According to Kaplan, natural law governs the operations of the physical universe, while conventional law conditions the relations of men and women in society. He writes:

> In a Jewish commonwealth, religious usages could be embodied into the law of the land, only insofar as they had social repercussions, as, for instance, in matters of Sabbath observance, where it would be necessary to insure the opportunity for such observance to all who desire it, and marital law, where the social efficacy of the family has to be protected.[33]

6. Removal of ritual from the legal category does not mean leaving it entirely in the hands of the individual. Nor can we

await the establishment of an authoritative, democratic, and fully representative body that would recommend ritual standards and legislate in matters that involve the entire collective. It is almost certain that the Jewish people will not be psychologically prepared to create such an authority within the foreseeable future. Instead of holding on to an idle dream—a failing of which Kaplan was often guilty—the *Guide* encourages initiative on the part of rabbis, research scholars, and experts in various aspects of human behavior. They are called upon to cooperate in strengthening ritual observance through casting new light on or revising old practices and suggesting new content and alternative forms. Obviously, the efforts of such teams would require a broad consensus concerning the premises of ritual practice. Among those presuppositions are the following:

a. Uniformity is both unattainable and undesirable. In place of uniform practice, we should strive to achieve a common purpose, which is *"the preservation and maintenance of a Jewish group life that shall be experienced by the individual as making his own life as a Jew worthwhile."*[34] (Italics, MMK) We want the Jew to feel that his or her own fulfillment is achievable within the context of a Judaism that is itself on the road to self improvement. Independence and patriotism should be complementary and not contradictions in terms. All this should be within the context of unity in diversity.

b. Flexibility has to have minimal and maximal limits. Kaplan understood that if most Jews choose only minimal forms of ritual observance, their Judaism would be shallow and lack the power to survive. Equally undesirable is an exaggerated ritualism.

c. Kaplan seeks a change in the folk psychology. By and large, negative commands have had greater force in Jewish tradition because their violation is a sin of commission subject to punishment. On the other hand, failure to perform a positive command is an act of omission for which there is no obvious penalty. Instead of this attitude, Kaplan maintained, *"the moment we get away from the legalistic approach, we treat Jewish observances as religious folkways designed to insure the enhancement of the value of Jewish life, the affirmative injunctions assume the more important role.*"[35] (Italics, MMK) This new psychology focuses attention on the content of religious practices. Henceforth, Jews will perform the *mitzvot* because of their inherent worth and not because they are imposed on them by divine fiat. Kaplan rejects the opinion of R. Yehudah who declared, "Greater is he who is commanded and obeys than he who acts voluntarily."[36] Readiness to obey commandments out of reverence for God or some respected human authority is commendable, provided that what is commanded does not violate one's conscience. For example, we are all prepared to honor reasonable requests of our parents. Their wish is our command. But even parental authority is not sufficient to compel us to violate norms that are sacred to us. Values such as freedom and equality may not be set aside for the sake of parental approval or traditional discipline.

d. Kaplan warned against hasty and mindless abandonment of certain restrictive *mitzvot*, even if they seem to serve no high moral or spiritual purpose. Discarding traditional practices is always difficult because we are often uncertain as to the standards by which to evaluate them. For instance, a Pesah seder with bread on the table is an oxymoron. Even one who detests negative commands must be sensitive to the fact that the seder would lose much of its educational value if this symbolic restriction is not retained. Kaplan recommends the deliberate elimination of this or that traditional practice only when a matter of principle is at stake. But a natural discarding of customs is bound to occur as perceptions and styles change. Therefore, it is necessary to fill the vacuum with new ceremonies or revisions of the old.

Several illustrations will document Kaplan's consistency. One is his introduction of a Bat Mitzvah ceremony for girls. His innovation, in 1922, was bitterly opposed at first, but it has now been widely adopted. Kaplan was one of the few theologians who went beyond preaching in an effort to heighten the devotion of worshipers in the synagogue. His main action in this regard was to revise the Sabbath and holiday prayer books and to prepare additional prayers and readings. He and his associates issued a revised *Haggadah* for Pesah, which brought upon him the wrath of his colleagues on the faculty of the Jewish

Theological Seminary of America. But with the exception of the Orthodox, Jews everywhere felt the need for more relevance, and the Reconstructionist effort inspired the preparation of other *Haggadot*. Kaplan's other recommendations remain to be implemented, such as his call for Shabbat eve booklets of stories, prayers, and inspirational texts. Kaplan wanted to strengthen family ties by enlivening the Sabbath meal in much the same way that the seder functions on Pesah. He wanted to introduce a new ceremony, called Ben-Torah and Bat-Torah, to be conducted at some point during or after matriculation in college. This occasion would mark the rededication of the celebrant to Jewish life, after further study and on a more mature level than is possible at the age of Bar or Bat Mitzvah.

Kaplan's suggestions were sometimes naive. He overlooked the degree to which any Jews want to retain rituals without having to think about their meaning. He underestimated the large number of Jews, including participants in the liberal denominations, who prefer to keep things as they are. However, he was aware of the difficulty in reaching indifferent Jews who want no part of Jewish practice. His approach has the greatest appeal to committed Jews who want to observe the *mitzvot* not as habit but as inspiration.

e. Strict laws and those of lesser importance, Torah-based and Rabbinic laws, positive and negative commandments— these have to give way to or at least be supplemented by modern standards. A free mind will not be coerced by heteronomous legal norms that rest on the belief in an ancient revelation. Kaplan suggests a threefold division of ritual practices. There are those, such as reading the Torah in the synagogue or reciting and discussing the Pesah *Haggadah*, that are meaningful in both form and content. In another type, such as putting on *tefillin* (phylacteries) or affixing a *mezuzah* (scroll of parchment attached to the doorpost) the form is arbitrary but the content is meaningful. A third type, for example, the laws of kashrut, are obscure both in form and in content. Innumerable explanations have been devised to inject spiritual significance into the practices of *tefillin* and kashrut, but it is obvious that some of these efforts are interpolations rather than extrapolations from the essence of these *mitzvot*.

The *Guide,* however, sets forth criteria that help to establish an order of priorities among the *mitzvot.* The first class deserves our greatest concentration and the third, the least; but all three categories have constructive roles to play in Jewish life. Customs whose rationale is weak or vague and whose form is outdated can nonetheless add a distinctive, interesting tone to Judaism, provided they have an esthetic charm and are morally inoffensive. All peoples have distinctive practices, clothing, and expressions of politeness and beauty that they preserve out of habit. Kaplan sees no reason to disrupt these stabilizing, constructive elements in an age-old Jewish culture, except "when either their form or content is objectionable on esthetic or moral grounds or when circumstances make their observance a practical impossibility."[37]

Kaplan's proposed *Guide* differs from the *Shulhan Arukh* and other traditional codes in its openness to pluralism and periodic revision. It is also distinguished by its attempt to clarify the purpose of each practice. Halakhic-minded persons, although also eager to understand the reason for every ritual, observe the *mitzvot* in obedience to a command that transcends any and every humanly mediated norm. Liberal Jews, on the other hand, want a ritual culture that symbolizes ideas and ideals to which they can commit themselves without reservation. Kaplan addresses those Jews who have distanced themselves from belief in historical revelation and supernaturally commanded customs. He accepts the fact that many Jews are committed to these beliefs and find much pleasure in the way of life dictated by the commandments. Most of these Jews also attribute inherent value to the *mitzvot.* But even if it were the case that no such worth could be found, the command would have to be acknowledged and obeyed. Kaplan's *Guide* has never been officially approved by any of the denominations, but it is an accurate description of the way in which open-minded religious Jews approach ritual observance.

In our observations about Kaplan's approach to *Halakhah,* we have concentrated on the *mitzvot maasiyot.* What about those aspects of the halakhic system that must continue to be legislated and administered under communal authority? Kaplan's position can be summarized briefly. The *Halakhah* should be democratized. As a political system, the *Halakhah* cannot be the method of government in an enlightened state, although, as I have already suggested, many of its laws and legal practices can and should be adapted and adopted by the democratic leadership. But since the *Halakhah*, by definition, is entirely in Jewish hands, it cannot be the basis of an egalitarian commonwealth. Furthermore, in purely internal Jewish concerns, such as marriage and divorce, inheritance, Jewish education, communal funding, and the like, which pertain to diaspora communities as well as Israel. Kaplan urges that control be transferred to elected bodies. For the time being, Kaplan's proposal does not have the slightest chance of being implemented. However, it offers a criterion of criticism of the current combination of free but shallow pluralism (in the Diaspora) and state-imposed, partial theocracy (in Israel).

Kook and Kaplan sought to sweeten Jewish tradition for all Jews, even while their paths would lead the Jewish people toward different horizons. Nevertheless, as long as they can find a common point of departure in the Jewish heritage and as long as they both strive to enrich and vitalize it, they and their followers can remain together within the Jewish consensus. The power of symbols—and rituals are symbols—lies in their ability to absorb new content in old, sanctified vessels. Kaplan and Kook have indicated that many sancta form the basis of their Jewish identity, even though their meaning may be subject to conflicting interpretations. The followers of Kook and the Kaplan might, therefore, still be able to engage in dialogue, but unity on the basis of voluntarism and pluralism is far-fetched. All we can do is encourage civilized dialogue between Jews who respect one another and who are prepared to listen to each other's opinions. Continuing conversation is itself a modus vivendi that will enable Jews to remain one people while continuing to disagree on fundamental issues.

NOTES

1. For example, in a typical observation, Kook says, "God's light is revealed only through free thought" (MR, p. 41).

2. *Students, Scholars and Saints* (Philadelphia: Jewish Publication Society, 1929, pp. 109–110).

3. AT, p. 22.

4. Ibid.

5. Ibid., p. 78.

6. *Shabbat Haaretz* (*Sabbath of the Land*) (Jerusalem: Mosad HaRav Kook, 5739).

7. *Daat Kohen* (henceforth, DK) (Jerusalem: Mosad HaRav Kook, 5729, R. 131, p. 245). DK is one of several volumes of Kook's responsa, that is, learned answers that he gave to halakhic questions sent to him from many quarters. The titles given to these volumes are extremely difficult to translate because of their multiple meanings, all suggested by Kook's status as a Kohen. In this book, I bring passages from *Daat Kohen, Mishpat Kohen,* and *Ezrat Kohen.*

8. *Ezrat Kohen* (henceforth, EK) (Jerusalem: Mosad HaRav Kook, 5729, R. 107, p. 392).

9. Many instances of Kook's conciliatoriness and liberal tendencies can be cited. Here are just two of them: "Wherever it is customary for the people to be lenient, we pay no attention to those who would be strict, even if they be supported by Elijah, may his memory be blessed" (DK, R. 45, p. 101). The purpose of this ruling is to strengthen an ancient Israelite tendency toward leniency. In another place, Kook writes: "We do not rule strictly in regard to issues in which we already have lenient opinions. Anyone who does so acts in disparagement of our holy Rabbis. His character is then marked by strictness, concerning which it has been said, 'Do not be ultra-righteous' " (DK, Ibid. p. 117).

10. *Mishpat Kohen* (henceforth, MK) (Jerusalem: Mosad HaRav Kook, 5726, R. 96, p. 185).

11. DK, R. 191, p. 366. Kook maintains that the notions of the classic Sages "are more trustworthy than those of the doctors whose knowledge is pure conjecture. It is well known that the doctors, claiming it is dangerous, tried to abolish the sucking out of blood [during circumcision]. But all our scholars ruled that their opinions cannot be trusted in comparison with those of our Sages, whose wisdom comes from God and is eternal" (DK, R. 84, p. 189). Another illustration of his limited respect for science and scientists is the following: "Regarding species, we should not rely on agronomists, for what they designate as belonging to a certain species can be differently identified by the Sages" (DK, R. 234, p. 607). These citations underscore Kook's ambivalence about the usefulness of science within the halakhic context. S. Z. Shragai oversimplifies matters when he states that Kook's resort to Kabbalah testifies to his favorable attitude toward science. (Incidentally, it should be recorded that neokabbalists today look upon science as a direct continuation of Kabbalah. Kaplan echoed this view. However, this is a subject for another study.) Shragai claims, "Looking at the whole of reality, including that which is

still hidden and yet to be revealed daily through science, one senses God's supernal, holy light." (See his essay, "Kabbalah and Hasidut in the Thought of Hareiya Kook," in *Zikhron Reiya—Remembrance of HaRav Kook* [Jerusalem: Mosad HaRav Kook, 1986, p. 144].) Whatever was positive in Kook's feelings about science came from his opinion that every idea that becomes common currency succeeds because it has good in it. Shragai overlooks the fact that Kook denies that science can uncover truth to the extent that it can be found in Torah.

12. MK, R. 124, p. 273.

13. Kook maintains that no prophet can introduce something novel into the Torah. He may side with one party or another in a dispute when no one seems to know in what direction the law should go. Then he can decide by means of the "divine spirit." "But," Kook rules, "when even the parameters of the doubt are unclear, the prophet may not introduce any novelty, even if it negates nothing in the Torah. For it would then appear to be a new Torah" (MK, R. 92, p. 174).

14. DK, R. 235, p. 427.

15. DK, R. 61, p. 154.

16. Kook, like all halakhists, assumed that the *mitzvot* in their entirety are meant to educate and refine all Jews. Rabbi Y. L. Maimon sums up Kook's attitude to ritual observances as follows: "The Torah strengthens the love between a man and his neighbor, by providing them with a practical base. The observance of the *mitzvot* exercises an egalitarian effect on the desires and ambitions of the folk and helps develop a general will. Only in the light of this conception should one regard the *mitzvot* and the many fences that protect them and whose rationale is often difficult to grasp. Everyone has the duty, through obeying all the *mitzvot*, to equip himself as a moral being. Each *mitzvah*, even one which applies only to the life of the most modest person, contains a profound national secret. With the fulfilment of each individual, Israel, too, will achieve maturity and will be able to teach the way of God to the nations" (*Ha-Reiyah*, 5725, pp. 70–71).

17. DK, R. 169, p. 313.

18. For a scholarly analysis of halakhic approaches to war and peace, see *Love Peace and Pursue Peace* by Bradley Shavit Artson (New York: United Synagogue of America, 1988).

19. MK, R. 143, especially pp. 315–316.

20. *Iggerot Reiyah* (*The Letters of HaRav Kook*, henceforth, IR) (Jerusalem: Mosad HaRav Kook, 5722, Vol. 1, p. 86).

21. Shemonah Perakim, ch. 1.

22. MK, R. 2, p. 1. (The saying, "*mitzvot* are not intended to provide enjoyment," is found in Eruvin 31a.) Yeshaiah Leibowitz insists that

in this spirit, there is no connection between human need and ritual observance. The latter is imposed upon a loyal Jew, who obeys out of a sense of obligation and with no expectation of reward.

23. QJA, p. 152.

24. Ibid., p. 229.

25. Ibid., p. 230.

26. For elaboration on this point, see my essay, "Is the Halakhah Viable? The View from Jerusalem," in *Jewish Civilization: Essays and Studies*, ed. by Ronald Brauner (Philadelphia: Reconstructionist Rabbinical College, 1979).

27. QJA, p. 232.

28. Ibid., p. 234.

29. Ibid., p. 235.

30. "To deal with the economic, social and ideological factors which account for the breakdown of the traditional way of life, something more is needed than repeated homiletical harangues urging Jews to remain loyal to their heritage" (FAJ, p. 413).

31. Ibid., p. 414.

32. Ibid,. p. 418.

33. Ibid., p. 419.

34. Ibid., p. 422.

35. Ibid., p. 424.

36. FAJ, p. 426.

37. Ibid.

5

The Search for God

EVERY SOCIETY has its intoxicated seekers of God. They are often seen as dangerous because they tend to destroy the protective fences of accepted tradition. Only infrequently do they succeed in their quest and, even then, only for a passing, ecstatic moment. Then the ecstasy subsides and remains only in a memory of some vague divine illumination, revelation, or communion. It is like a dream, vivid during sleep but faded and frequently forgotten upon awakening.

If the God-hunt were a concern solely of the individual, humankind would not be as torn apart by it, as it has been throughout the ages. But believing in God and trying to conceive God have far-reaching social consequences. The outcome has been a ceaseless conflict between those who regard the results of their speculation as God's revelation and those who attack such a conclusion as dangerous to clear thinking and social harmony. Let us see how Kook and Kaplan grapple with this complex issue.

THE PATH TO GOD

Paradoxically, the true believer is filled with hesitation and doubt. The believer knows that the line separating communion with God from idolatry is extremely thin. Therefore, he or she has to be cautious and try to refrain from exaggerated claims. Kook and Kaplan heed this warning.

Kook asserts, "It is possible to find a firm foundation for the human spirit only in a godly context."[1] The human soul in all its actions must recognize its dependence on God. "If a person is satisfied with a status lower than this, he is quickly buffeted around like a ship in a stormy sea. . . ."[2] Confident reliance on God would seem to be simple and obvious for a religious thinker like Kook. However, after this affirmation, he comes up against roadblocks on his journey to God. He indicates:

> God is beyond all reality that can possibly become part of our cognition or feeling. Whatever transcends our intellectual and emotional grasp has no value for us. But the mind cannot bear nothingness. Therefore, scholars who search for God become spiritually exhausted.[3]

The paradox is profound. Only in God can we find our way and achieve satisfaction. Yet the path to God is endless. We have to search for that which can never be found. The target moves uninterruptedly and in a direction away from the archer. Even when we think that we are behaving according to the highest moral standards, or when we discover some truth or experience beauty in its most sublime form, we feel choked. The world appears constricted. Nonetheless, we have no choice. We must continue our quest, which, it turns out, is itself our reward. Here and there, we come upon moments of pure joy. The supernal God descends "to the world and penetrates it, and we discover Him and rejoice in His love. In His serenity, we find repose and peace. . . ."[4] However, it is our fate to return to stark reality. The moment of inspiration, revelation, and communion is "an evanescent condition; the lightning will pass, and we descend to sit in the courts of God but not inside His palace."[5]

Kook, the pietist and the quintessential halakhic man, could not gain satisfaction by being simply an exemplar of the classical *Matmid*, the eternal Torah student.[6] He had to relate to the godly in all creatures and in unconscious nature. I refer the reader to the passage cited in Chapter 2, in which Kook locates the gate to God in the wonders of human experience.[7]

There is something unclear about Kook's emphasis on the gate to God rather than on a direct meeting with Him. To avoid the danger in defining God, Kook often speaks of *Elohut* (Godhood), which can be taken as synonymous with *Elohim* (God), whose form suggests a more abstract connotation. Kook writes, "All denotative definitions of Godhood lead to heresy. Definition is spiritual idolatry. . . ."[8] Kook points out the danger inherent in the appellations by which we designate the Deity, for a name is a definition in itself. Therefore, Kook does not define Godhood;

he only calls attention to the results of divine action. If it were not for the fact that the Name became known through revelation, it too would be a source of idolatry. I believe that Kook deluded himself in trying to escape completely from the semantic peril, for pointing to the divine traces in the physical world and in human behavior is also a kind of definition, or at least a step toward it. Whether my observation is correct or not, Kook deserves praise for two reasons. First, his warning against defining God makes us less likely to propose absolutes about the nature of deity. Second, this cautious view does not prevent Kook from looking beyond the classic Jewish texts for signs of God. Of course, he drew extensively from Jewish sources. One need only observe his heavy reliance on Rambam. But it is worth comparing his lyrical description of the gate to God with the following excerpts from "Gitanjalill," by Kook's contemporary, the renowned Hindu poet, Rabinadrath Tagore (1861–1941):

> God, where shall I find Thee,
> Whose glory fills the universe?
> Behold, I find Thee
> Wherever the ploughman ploughs his furrow through
>   the hard soil, . . .
>
> Wherever the mind is free to follow its own bent,
> Wherever words come out from the depth of truth. . . .
>
> Wherever men struggle for freedom and right,
> Wherever the scientist toils to unbare the secrets of nature,
>
> Wherever the poet strings pearls of beauty in lyric lines,
> Wherever glorious deeds are done.
>
> Behold, I find Thee
> When comes the dawn with its golden cornucopia,
> Or when evening falls, bringing peace and rest from the
>   Western ocean of rest,
> Thou art in the joy that streams from heaven with the
>   morning light,
> In the current of life that courses day and night
>   through my sinews and through all nature,
> In the life that throbs exultant in the dust of the earth
>   and through the blades of grass innumerable,

And that flows, in a multitude of tempestuous waves,
   through the leaves and flowers.[9]

There is a startling similarity between this poem and Kook's description of the gate of passage to God's domain. Both images indicate that religious thinkers in all traditions cannot be constrained by conventional theologies. But Kook, who was steeped in the Torah and its unique system, could not draw conclusions from his personal experiences or those of others that would carry him beyond the toraitic borders. On the contrary, his contacts with nature and his fellow Jews only confirmed his faith in the Torah as the embodiment of God's will. He refused to accept the thought that halakhists might have to radically adjust the toraitic vision to take into account some of the new scientific views about the nature of reality. He saw no reason to examine in depth the possibilities for the Jewish future that might ensue from all the experiences that he identified as bringing people close to God. Although he referred to other trustworthy sources, he did not act on their implications regarding belief in God and the idea of God.

Kaplan also adopts the premise that the purpose and meaning of life can best be grasped in the context of belief in God. In one of his many reflections on the subject, he says, "The qualitative or value aspect of life derives from Reality taken as a whole. Unless we contemplate man against a cosmic background, his life becomes too unimportant to try and improve it."[10] However, Kaplan does not leap from this assertion to empty attempts to define the essence of God.

Both Kook and Kaplan exhibit intellectual modesty in regard to claims about God.[11] Kaplan posits, "That God, as ultimate reality, is unknowable is a commonplace of all thinking other than that which is entirely naïve."[12] Or, in other words, "when we come to think of God in terms of infinity, and therefore as altogether beyond the power of human comprehension, we must either adjust our notion of communion with God, or do away altogether with religious observances."[13] Expansion of knowledge brings in its wake theological rethinking. The new adjustments will have their greater or lesser period of survival before giving way to further refinements. Nonetheless, Kaplan argues, humankind must respond to the most up-to-date and authoritative information and not hold onto anachronistic notions. Therefore, the function of theology becomes not to define God but to clarify the sense in which the term "God" is employed in religious discourse. Kaplan states: "*It is the business of religion not to give a metaphysical conception of God, but to make clear what we mean by the belief in God, from the standpoint of the difference that belief makes in human conduct and striving.*"[14] (Italics, MMK)

Changes in our understanding of reality need not interfere with our continued belief in God.

> Some people, gifted with a spiritual insight that is usually identified with mysticism, are not in the least troubled by the realisation of God's infinite nature. Can we not enjoy the light and warmth of the sun now, though we know that it is almost a million times the size of the earth, as when we thought that it was a large fiery chariot racing across the sky? Instead of dismissing such communion as an illusion, we may regard it as a more sensitive functioning of the human organism.[15]

The rationalist, too, by adjusting the idea of God to the new reality, can retain complete faith in God's existence. Kaplan argues:

> [E]ven without the faculty for mystic experience, for direct communion with God, it is possible to be in rapport with those situations that seem to make God manifest. Any situation which has the power of enlarging our sympathies, widening the perspective of our thought, calming our mind, sweetening our disposition and strengthening our will, should reveal God to us.[16]

Kaplan's functionalism is apparent in the above passages. Kook's approach resembles this functionalism, insofar as it gives preference to exploring God's works over metaphysical speculation as the better way to picture God. However, Kaplan is more forthright in searching for and identifying signs of divinity. He more readily accepts the scientific disclosure of cosmic order and evidences of moral law as reflections or hints of divinity. Fearing idolatry, Kook suspends judgment about the claims of reason, while simultaneously affirming the need to accord science limited authority. Kook's functionalism leads only to the threshold. As long as we remain tied to ordinary experience, our search will be unsuccessful. The only certain identification of God is in communion, which is totally dependent on God's will.

Thus, like Kook, but more forthrightly, Kaplan follows the path of human experience in his search for God. But since it is hard to predict which experiences are apt to act in a revelatory fashion, we must remain alert to everything that occurs around us and dare to attach the name of God to that which most commands a sense of truth, goodness, and beauty. Kook, as a mystical functionalist, awaits the revelatory moment that can accord with reason but cannot be generated by it.

Kaplan attempts to elicit the educational implication of his experientialist approach to the quest for God. We must try as best we can

> to cultivate what may be described as the beginning of a cosmic feeling, an appreciation of the immensity, the sublimity, the beauty and order of nature. Where, if not in the religious school, should the child be imbued with a sense of humility in the presence of the awe-inspiring phenomena of life? How else is he ever to receive a sense of proportion which is needed to correct the natural egocentrism with which everyone commences life? . . . If [the child] has not learned to find in anything he actually experiences something *that points to what we mean by God*, his cosmic feeling is likely to dissolve into vague sentimentality.[17] (Italics, JJC)

Kaplan claims that human experience reveals not God but the phenomena that should be identified as signs of God and His creative acts.

In summary, then, Kook and Kaplan agree that the paths chosen by men and women in their quest for God can lead to a clarification of what they mean by the word "God" or its equivalents, but not to God Himself. However, why do certain phenomena seem to us to have the stamp of divinity, while others appear to be satanic or to obliterate God's presence? Is not any attempt to identify signs of divinity as dangerous as seeking definition, against which both thinkers warned?

BELIEVING IN AND CONCEIVING GOD

Thus far, we have followed Kook and Kaplan as they seek God through experience. Their effort makes sense only on the presupposition that they have a chance to succeed. Kaplan says:

The objective study of religion the world over has proved beyond a doubt that the belief in God originated neither in speculative reasoning nor in any supernatural revelation. *Gods have to be believed in before they can be beheld, imagined or proved to exist.* Had this fact been recognized centuries ago, thinkers would have been spared an immense amount of mental effort to prove the existence of God. All that effort was apparently in vain, since unbelievers seldom become believers as a result of logical arguments.[18] (Italics, MMK)

Unanimity about the concept of God is impossible. Differences in age, intellectual ability, education, and experience are so great as to render any such agreement a chimera. What does unite human beings in their search for God is their common feeling that their aspirations are not pursuits of illusions. Humans are in the theistic arena when they believe that their purposes—at least a goodly portion of them—can be fulfilled by appropriate adherence to a built-in cosmic order. This belief requires no uniform cognition. Young and old, rich and poor, sage and fool—all can be sustained by a confident belief in the ultimate achievement of good. They are also all equally subject to loss of faith when they are struck with tragedy or sorrow or when they see the evil that people inflict upon one another. Faith, however, is a spiritual condition with which the normal person is endowed; but like other genetic functions, it can be diseased and turned into melancholia or despair. Basically, the restoration of faith is not an intellectual enterprise. Rather, it is a psychological process of recuperation resulting from an accumulation of constructive experiences. Faith in God is thus a person's emotional response to the vicissitudes of life. It is this psychic reaction that enables humans of differing dispositions to declare with equal sincerity that they believe in God.

The foregoing is only part of the theological problem. Humans are not satisfied with feeling alone. They want to authenticate their emotions in cognitive terms and to put them into a reasonable perspective. They need to learn how to mourn courageously and to rejoice wisely, to keep their eyes on universal values when the environment promotes thoughtless hedonism or permissiveness, and to retain a stable morale when others around them have lost their way. In looking to achieve this broad perspective, Kaplan turns his back on supernaturalism. He presumes that many, perhaps most, people have not left the circle of belief in divine revelation, miracles, divinely ordained systems of law, and the like. Such believers will turn a deaf ear to him. His message thus is directed to the confused but open-minded of our era and to those who are already in the field of science with its objective thinking, that is, those who seek answers to the contradictions and paradoxes of life that leave many persons unperturbed.

The conflict between Kook and Kaplan is sharp on this point. For Kook, the Torah is a distinct discipline that provides the means for men and women to acquire all the truth and goodness needed for their careers on earth. There is no conflict between Judaism and science because the source of truth and goodness is the One God. If something seems to be missing, there is no cause for worry. God will supply the missing piece in good time. All is in God's hands. Nature is a miracle, and a miracle is no less natural than the usual order of things. In Kook's opinion,

> [w]e should regard the connection between nature and miracle in the context of cosmic unity. All phenomena stem from God's unity. Whatever is lacking in nature is supplied by miracle. Therefore, miracle is attached to nature and is not something apart from it. The existence of miracles teaches us that there is no accident in reality. For everything that occurs is ordered by the divine wisdom.[19]

According to Kook, the contradiction is apparent between his views that the Torah contains all truth ("Turn it and turn it over again, for everything is in it"—*Sayings of the Fathers* 5:25) and those who believe that the most reliable source of truth is the observation of nature and human behavior. Kook believes there is no room for conflicting conclusions. Perception of the natural order can only be a supplement to what is hidden in the secrets of the Torah. Kook cannot accept the view that nature is an autonomous process.

Kaplan is deeply moved by the wonders of nature. He is touched by the blessing of thanksgiving that is found in the *Amidah* prayer (the Eighteen Benedictions). In this blessing, we thank God "[f]or the life granted to us and for our souls in your care, and for the daily miracles and the wonders and kindnesses, at all times, evening, morn and noon."[20] For Kaplan, the miracles mentioned in this prayer are synonymous with the wonders of the natural order. If this order were to be disrupted by a willful act of a supernatural God, humans would be unable to rely on their own judgment and talents as an efficient means of gaining fulfillment. Nonetheless, those talents are gifts from the divine Process, without whose order human efforts would be pure guesswork. Kaplan endeavors to infuse his readers with gratitude for the gift of life. Everyone must fight against taking for granted the cyclical and regular behavior of the planets, the seasons, the rising and setting of the sun, the phases of the moon, sleeping and awakening, and the numerous indications of an orderly cosmos. A miracle is natural, and nature is miraculous, but not in the way that Kook conceived both nature and miracle. Kaplan sees no departure from natural law. The consistent behavior of the cosmos enables us to learn ever more about the grandeur and the inexhaustible secrets of nature. God is to be sought in the amazing connectedness of phenomena. Our abilities warrant our faith that we can achieve fulfillment on earth. But, says Kaplan, human destiny is not a final, stationary destination. Rather it must be conceived as an endless series of steps in self-improvement.

Although their outlooks differed, Kook and Kaplan tried to formulate an authentic and relevant Jewish theology. Therefore, it behooves us to look for whatever points of contact can be found in their thought that might prove helpful for this generation and those to come.

Toward a Consistent Theology

The Bible starts with the declaration, "In the beginning, God created the heavens and the earth." God's existence is taken as self-evident. About three thousand years later, Rambam opens his discussion of the foundations of Torah with the statement that the basic principle of wisdom is to acknowledge that there is a first existent.[21] Thus, Rambam implies that God's existence should not be taken for granted. It has to be proved by logical demonstration. Note that before he mentions "God," Rambam feels obligated to indicate how the first existent comes to be identified with the Ruler of the entire universe. Apparently, Rambam finds

solid footing for his theology in the existence of the cosmos. Intellectually, God is to be inferred and not assumed.

The tradition of Maimonides courses through the thought of
Kook and Kaplan. They both explain the connection between
God and the universe in a way that will do the least harm to the
demands of reason. Theologically and philosophically, of course,
it is possible to portray God without the cosmos. This is what
Rambam did. "Should it enter your mind that none of the existents exist except for Him, know that He will continue to exist
even should these existents disappear. For all existing things require Him, but He, may He be blessed, does not need them."[22]
This abstract, logical argument does little to answer the question
that bothered our two theologians. Their concern about God and
the cosmos paralleled their primary question regarding the role of
God in human life. Whether God can exist without the cosmos
or its creatures is totally irrelevant. What is central is what men
and women mean when they affirm or deny belief in God. That
is, how is God conceived in relationship to human destiny?

The essence of Kook's response is found in his commentary on
the hymn "Adon Olam" ("Eternal God"); we have already cited
his commentary on one verse of this hymn. Concerning the verse
that describes God as King before the world was created, he asks
himself how could God reign before there was anything or anyone to rule? Kook begins his answer by explaining what is meant
by sovereignty:

> Supernal sovereignty, the most exalted and infinite kingdom, is the
> absolute ability to create and shape everything. It is the unceasing,
> eternal creative process of activity, originating in the might of abso-
> lute lordship and true kingship, that lies beyond all possibility of
> being named or expressed. For to [divine] potentiality there is no
> end and to omnipotence, no definition or limit.[23]

Here Kook refers to God before Creation. The appellation,
King, is inapplicable, inasmuch as He alone exists. It is absurd to
say anything about Him. Before Creation, who is present to praise
God? Therefore, anything said about Him at this stage is only
conjecture, "as it were." Only in this sense does Kook hint at
God's eternal omnipotence. It is only after God, out of His free
will, loving-kindness, and absolute power, creates the world and

its creatures, including humans who dominate all living things, that he can truly be called King. "Only with the formation of creatures in their potentiality and actuality, which bespeak His awful power, can the term refer to its modifier. When God's glory is revealed, then it is permissible to say that His Name is announced as King."[24] It follows that Kook realized that the God of religion—in contrast to the metaphysical God—has meaning only in connection with humankind. Only the human mind can think about Him, search for Him, try to describe Him, and address Him.[25]

Two main roads can be followed in the quest for God. The first leads to a conception of that Power in or beyond the universe on which humans must rely for the fulfillment of their destiny. The second is a metaphysical route toward an understanding of God Himself. There is no inherent contradiction between these two theological dispositions, although thinkers tend to prefer one emphasis over the other. Kook, the mystic, persists in searching for the hidden God who, though He is beyond the reach of humans, demands obedience to His commands. The *mitzvot* are the only way by which the gap between God and the average person can be partially closed. Only exceptional souls can hope to gain an inkling of God's essence.

Kaplan, on the other hand, prefers to reflect on God in relation to human needs. Since the distance between humans and God's essence is so vast, Kaplan eschews abstract metaphysics and tries to infer the divine will from a close examination of the Creation. Kaplan repeatedly expresses his dislike of metaphysical theology, not because he opposes imagining the principles on which cosmic existence rests, but because he rejects the idea that a way of life for an individual or a group can be constructed without the benefit of concrete experience.

The disparity between the two points of view can be demonstrated by an examination of the idea of "the hidden God." There is a fundamental difference between a "hidden God" and a "hiding God." Both thinkers concede that God is always opaque to humans, who must devote their lives to trying to resolve as much of the mystery as they can. Success will never be more than partial. But Kook and Kaplan part company when the former attributes to God the will to hide, either for reasons beyond human ken or as a conscious response to human perversity. It is the difference between supernaturalism and naturalism.

Human knowledge is limited to what men and women can learn from their senses, reason, and intelligence. How can we expect mortal creatures to unlock all the divine secrets? But supernatural theology claims to know that God often hides Himself in order to teach or punish humans or to prevent their redemption. One version of this theology declares that the eclipse of God is a strategy to bring humans to repentance and to purify their will. In this way humans can induce God to cancel the "evil decree."

Kaplan protests against the blurring of these concepts. How can humans *know* the will of God? Human experience has amply demonstrated that natural evil (floods, earthquakes, volcanic eruptions, disease, and other disasters) usually has little or nothing to do with immoral behavior. Only when humans violate the ecological balance can we infer that nature takes its "revenge." Mostly, however, natural catastrophes are accidents that occur within the natural order. Kaplan admits that in an important sense, God is hidden. The actuality of evil is a mystery of Creation. But so is the goodness that leads to human fulfillment. The question "Why?" is unanswerable. Nature obliterates the lives of the righteous and the wicked. If God is conceived as a hiding God, then the unanswerable question becomes a theological horror. For how can a sane mind absorb the possibility that an omnipotent, good God would permit or intentionally cause the torture of innocent beings? Therefore, Kaplan withdraws natural evil from the category of Providence, of reward and punishment.

Kook has to affirm Providence, inasmuch as he denies autonomy to nature. Suffering at the hands of nature is essentially no different from the social destruction and misery that ensue in the wake of evil deeds. Kaplan cannot resort to this explanation, for the hiding God is the God of miracles. They have no place in his cosmology.

In the commentary to "Adon Olam," discussed above, Kook considers God's unity ("He is One, and there is no other"). This is a purely metaphysical question, for humans experience only endless variety. God's unity can be conceived solely as a transcendent reality. This conundrum causes many a rationalist to declare that the divine unity has no counterpart in the existence we know. "God is One" means that God is unique. We can only guess at the secret. But in every generation, there are men and women who try to solve the dilemma, obsessed by the desire to be united with God.

Kook was one of these personalities. We are not surprised, therefore, at his daring interpretation of the verse, "And after all reality shall cease to be, / In dread lone splendor He shall reign," to which we have already referred. Kook writes:

> The created reality that we sense descended from the heavenly heights at the transcendent behest of the omnipotent, unlimited exalted One. It has come to a constricted region which has fallen on all levels. This fallen state and disgrace will not last forever. Everything has been created in order to ascend to the highest pinnacle of the hiding place of supernal power. All will attain an infinitely greater measure of splendor and purpose than is possible in the precincts of divine contraction, where it is possible to pronounce the royal Name. This ascent, this return of being to its loftiest summit, is the cessation of All, not in the sense of destruction and deprivation, but in that of the Psalmist, "My flesh and heart fail; / But God is the rock of my heart and my portion for ever" (73, 36). This restoration of the entirety of existence to its longed-for, supernal abode, far above contracted, limited existence, is the crown of the exalted Kingdom in its absolute awfulness. . . . The infinite supernal Kingdom is the source of revelation of all realms, so that after all reality comes to its end, The Awful One will reign alone. And on that day, God alone will be exalted.[26]

Kook transplants a rationalistic reflection into kabbalistic soil. He offers a concept of God that makes the human career a minor, passing episode in the cosmic drama.

Even one who thinks that Lurianic Kabbalah raises more questions than it answers can be fascinated by the vision of divine contraction, breaking of the vessels, and the process of cosmic repair. The hope for unity is one of the guiding impulses of human endeavor. But a solution evades us. Science has no answer for Creation or for the emergence of matter from spirit or spirit from matter. However, science can and does provide a description of their functioning. Nonetheless, this knowledge fails to satisfy human curiosity. Where the unknown still perturbs, mortals, depending on their propensity, will either continue their disciplined research into the secrets of nature or resort to myth-making. Since men and women are apparently born with different temperaments, they will respond idiosyncratically to the variety of mythic explanations of cosmic unity. It is not at all surprising that many persons should believe that God's Kingdom should be restored by the observance of the rituals. This myth confers on the Jewish individual and Jewry as a whole a clear and glorious vocation. As long as humankind exists, the election of Israel is the central factor in its advancement or retrogression. If Israel fulfills its mission, the world will come closer to its ultimate redemption; if not, salvation will become more remote.

Kook's vision enlivens the past, in the spirit of "Renew our days as of old" (Prayer Book). Completeness is regarded as a quality of ancient times. The future must be a reconstruction of what was—a return to Eden, to the innocence of birth, to the wholeness of the vessels before they were broken in the act of Creation. This is not only a theological conception but also, and perhaps primarily, an emotional response to reality and a daring stab at life's purpose. There have always been those persons who resign themselves to an undetermined and undeterminable future and those who want the comfort of an ideal, former state. An illustration of this division is the debate among the Schools of Hillel and Shammai over the following question: Is it more desirable to have been born or not to have been born? I say *among* rather than *between* because the text is unclear as to whether the disagreement is between the schools or whether it cuts across the lines. In any case, it was concluded that it is better not to have been born, but since we are alive, "we must set our houses in order, and some say, we must examine our behavior."[27] Rashi interprets these similar phrases as follows:

> Setting one's house in order—one must examine the deeds one has already performed, remind oneself of one's sins, confess and repent; examining one's conduct—when confronted by the possibility of performing a *mitzvah*, one should not refrain from doing it because one thinks that the disadvantage of carrying it out will outweigh the immediate reward. For the full reward will come in the long run. And if the possibility arises of doing a misdeed which has an immediate reward, give thought to the retribution that is sure to come.

It is hard to believe that debate will cause either school to change its view. Although movement away from or toward a basic perception of life does sometimes occur, such a change of mind is almost always motivated by psychological stress rather than intellectual challenge. Similarly, the choice of a rationalistic or mystic position is no less attributable to psychological and temperamental factors than the attitude toward the value of life. Thus, Kook's vision befits his personality, a fact that, as we shall see, is equally true of Kaplan.

Kaplan's theology is based on his assumption that humans can satisfy enough of their needs and purposes to make their earthly careers worthwhile. He believes that efforts to discover the immanent forces and to conceive the transcendent laws that make for human fulfillment need not be in vain. In one of his aphorisms, Kaplan describes the relationship between the striving for perfection and belief in God: "The will to salvation implies that what can be ought to be. The belief in God implies that what ought to be can be."[28]

However, human fulfillment, to the extent that it is possible, is in the future. The past was not that ideal state described in the Garden of Eden myth. Instead, Kaplan views it as the childhood of the human race.

> Man has not fallen from a higher estate, but has risen from a lower one. He has evolved from an animal ancestry and is still largely dominated by beastly urges and impulses that are a part of his natural heritage. These tendencies are imbedded in his unconscious mind and also tend to pervert and corrupt a great part of his conscious thinking.[29]

Kaplan's objection to the theory of the deterioration of the cosmic order is implicit in his rejection of supernaturalism. According to the supernaturalist's perception, miracles and revelations were not accidents but were willed for the sake of Israel from its birth until today.

> The logic behind that fact is that there was something intrinsically sacrosanct about the past which rendered it worthy of having harbored all those eye-witness proofs of the reality and greatness of God. . . . But the mere fact that God chose to reveal Himself in the early past, and has remained "hidden" ever since, is sufficient to sanctify that past.[30]

As an example Kaplan quotes Rashi's interpretation of a verse in *Kohelet*, "Say not; 'How is it that the former days were better than these?' / For it is not out of wisdom that you inquire about this" (7, 10). Rashi treats the verse antithetically from its plain meaning. "Do not wonder about the beneficences that befell the earliest righteous men, such as the generations of the desert and of Joshua and David. For you do not ask wisely—everything happens according to the merit of the generations."

Supernaturalism has many versions, and some of them do not consider the past to be superior to the present, even in the plain sense of the verse from *Kohelet*. However, there can be no doubt that the Kabbalists, with whom Kook agreed, assigned to the Jewish people the responsibility for restoring the cosmos to its pristine condition. Kaplan, on the other hand, looks to a future of continuous creativity, in which men and women would find their satisfaction in the act of exercising all their faculties and talents. He acknowledges that no one can attain perfection because all are constricted by their creaturely nature. Kaplan thus tries to formulate a conception of human nature that would induce large numbers of persons to aspire to perfection, but he does not make it sufficiently clear that they will have to be satisfied with only a reasonable degree of self-improvement and less than perfect social justice. These limited objectives are attainable, and they suffice for a Kaplanian temperament. Once humans accept their mortality, they should live realistically but adventurously. This is a vision for the brave and the idealistic.

Many theologians claim to see humans through the eyes of God, so to speak. Kaplan seeks to understand God by inference from his grasp of humans and the natural order. Let it be said at once: Kaplan's humanism is not meant to imply that humans are the measure of everything. He says, "Not man, but nature's God is the measure."[31] In what sense, then, is Kaplan a theological revolutionary? In two ways. First, he insists that all theologies and religious cultures are human constructions and, as such, must be subject to the same criticism of experience and logical coherence that apply to other manmade ideational creations. Theologies that purport to transmit God's will uncritically are indications of impudence. This means that while the claims of the historical religions might have some measure of truth and wisdom, they have to be examined objectively. At best they might merit only critical and reserved acceptance as divine manifestations. Second, while man is not the measure, he is the *measurer*. Therefore, God–ideas should be conceived out of the most informed and established information about man and nature. True, one cannot arrive directly at the *ought* from the *is*, but theologies that lack a basis in experience are apt to mislead morally and spiritually. The history of theology is rife with examples of errors resulting from failure to keep abreast of advancing knowledge. Among such mistakes was the instinctive and strong opposition to the Copernican theory—a case of dogma against scientific investigation.

Kaplan tries to discover the common denominator among the countless concepts of God. To what phenomenon or experience do men tend to apply the designation "God"? Kaplan maintains that the term always relates to that Power that drives men and women to seek salvation and makes its attainment possible. But what is salvation, and what is God's role in its achievement?

The question of salvation—variously termed in Jewish philosophical writings as perfection, ultimate purpose, success, peace of mind or redemption—deserves a separate study. Here, we can give only a bare outline of the significance of the concept.

In the Bible, salvation often refers to national continuity and the implementation of Israel's vocation as a just and law–abiding people. The Bible, unlike later Jewish tradition, gives no credence to individual salvation in life after death. A person is "gathered unto his ancestors," but there seems to be no concern as to what happens to that person after he or she has left this earth. "The dead shall not praise Yah" (Ps. 115, 17). "The dust shall return to the earth, as it was, and the spirit shall return to God who gave it" (Koh. 12, 7).[32] This seemingly morbid conception persisted through the biblical era of more than a millennium and then gave way to the rabbinic vision of the world-to-come. It is hard to determine why the change occurred. The argument that it was caused by contact with other nations is weak, because other-worldliness was common in the Middle East during the entire biblical period. Why were our ancestors unimpressed for so long by the hope for life beyond the grave? Whatever the reason, the world-to-come became a fixture in Jewish thought from the last biblical days until today. Even Jews who have returned to biblical realism find it difficult to dispense with the semantics of the Garden of Eden, resurrection of the dead, and immortality of the soul.[33]

The location of salvation in this world or the next has a decisive impact on the conception of God as Savior. Rambam noted the disparity between the various views of the theologians about the afterlife and those of the philosophers, who saw salvation as primarily a this-worldly, intellectual grasp of God. The philosophers sought the delights of the soul and not of the body. Knowing was the highest bliss, and this was something that could be enjoyed on earth. This was true salvation. Nonetheless, this idea of salvation is unlikely to satisfy the masses, who are incapable of entering the lofty regions of philosophical speculation. They require bodily satisfactions. Abstract knowledge is secondary to their mundane interests. Rambam responded to their need by opening the gates to Eden, resurrection, and immortality, but one gets the impression that, for him, metaphysical insight was the optimal fulfillment.

Kaplan extends the image of Maimonides. He concentrates his thought on the reality that conditions one's experience and toward whose improvement one has the ability and the duty to contribute. Kaplan regards the rabbinic view as an unfortunate deviation from what he considers to be the wiser biblical vision of this-worldly salvation.

In keeping with biblical realism, Kaplan calls for a theology that starts with the most authoritative account of human needs that one can find. Modern men and women, he asserts, have at their disposal tools of learning that were unavailable to their forebears. If they use these tools skillfully and honestly, they can come closer than their ancestors to the detection of human destiny. But this new knowledge about humanity necessitates adjustments in conceptions of nature and God.[34] We now know how closely the human body, mind, and behavior are tied to other natural processes. Science is not a discipline that is completely disconnected from religion. If religion ignores the former's findings, it will bring humankind to despair. Therefore, Kaplan strives to discover whether there is or can be an organic connection among the various disciplines. He is impatient with Jewish scholars who have revolutionized our understanding of the Jewish past but who refuse to draw the conclusions that such knowledge demands for the Jewish future. He sees the danger in tampering with an ancient, sacred tradition, but he calls attention to the equal danger of ignoring the need for constant development. Of course, creative change should be predicated on careful study of both the Jewish heritage and the new conditions. People make mistakes. They should be cautious, but they should not fear error. As Goethe put it, "Es irrt der Mensch so lang er strebt" ("As long as men strive, they are bound to err"), but courageous men and women will not give up the effort to improve themselves and their societies.

What is human completeness to Kaplan, and what is the connection between that answer and the idea of God? Kaplan states, "The real problem of religion is not how to prove the existence of God but how to make sure that human beings, both individually and collectively, are being impelled and helped in their efforts to achieve what is most important to them—salvation or self fulfillment."[35] Kaplan postulates that if we can identify our true needs—as opposed to unimportant needs or often destructive greed—we shall learn how to fit them into the divine structure of the cosmos or, if you will, the laws of physical and human nature.

Kaplan assumes that human needs are balanced in the outer world by a concomitant source for their satisfaction. This assumption is a matter of faith. Thirst, for example, must be slaked, but drought is also a fact of nature. Therefore, it does not follow that a thirsty person will necessarily find water. Needs and their satisfaction in nature are often unbalanced. On the other hand, if it were not for our belief that solutions can be found for water shortages, we should not be blessed with reservoirs, dams, cloud seeding, desalinization, and the like, all of which do seem to indicate a cosmic polarity between need and response. Hope for salvation is thus a reasonable way to react to the manifest uncertainties and discontinuities of life. At the same time, humans are obligated to avoid the idolatry of pretending that greed is synonymous with needs.

Kaplan lists needs as follows:

(1) biological needs for health, security and mating, the satisfaction
of which is experienced as well-being; (2) psycho-social needs for

appreciation and influence, the satisfaction of which yields a sense of power; and (3) spiritual needs, which constitute the human differential, and which are the needs for directing and controlling human efforts in satisfying biological needs without indulgence in lust and in satisfying psycho-social needs without surrender to greeds. To satisfy the need for control and direction, the individual requires involvement with his self-governing and perpetuating organic community, such as family, clan, tribe, nation or people.[36]

To satisfy all these needs, people have to depend on outside support and aid. This same saving force also affects the direction and the degree of satisfaction.

Therefore, Kaplan suggests that humankind's search for sources of help proceeds in accordance with the wisdom and intelligence of the human race as a whole. In the distant past, imagination dominated human feelings and will. This resulted in the creation of myths. Later, intelligence matured, refined the myths, and uncovered more reliable methods of need satisfaction. We are now on the verge of a new era beyond supernaturalistic monotheism. Kaplan explains the new wisdom: *"God's divinity manifests itself in the fulfillment of the human in man, and man's humanity is realized to the extent that it cooperates with the divinity of God."*[37] (Italics, MMK) Thus, "God" is one of the words by which people of faith identify the cosmic forces that make for their salvation. Faith in the efficacy of this cosmic support system is buttressed by progressive knowledge about its constitution.

Kaplan is always criticized for using "God" as an appellation for a natural process. He has been accused of being an atheist or a pantheist. This charge indicates how great is the need for semantic clarity in theological discourse. I have already noted that Kook seeks God in natural phenomena and in human behavior. We recall that Kook and Kaplan follow one of the well-traveled paths in Jewish theology. It is true that Kook does not veer far from the supernatural strand in Jewish tradition. The Chosen People, the Promised Land, the revealed Torah, miracles—indeed, everything that happens in the universe is wrought by the living God. In Kook's vision, God can be grasped, so to speak, in the semantics that derive from human behavior. God speaks, legislates, and judges. Kook does not enter into the problematics of anthropomorphism; instead, he is satisfied to follow Maimonides. The latter had declared that God's actions might be described to a certain extent, even though His essence is secret. The Torah speaks in human language. Kook stands astride two different theologies.

Kaplan is more forthright. He does not accept a God-idea that is built on a paradox—an omnipotent, good God up against cosmic evil, a universal God who chooses one people to bear His message, a God of natural law who performs miracles, a God of impeccable morality who punishes the children of an adulterous mother and commands His people to commit genocide. Must one be called an atheist if one identifies God's actions with cosmic orderliness, while admitting that the divine essence is not only ineffable but unknowable?

Kaplan avoids paradox, but he cannot escape some other serious problems. How can one pray to an objective Process? Is Creation a nonquestion? Kaplan is forced to pay the price of his consistency. He has to bracket Creation and confine himself to creativity. He has to foster a new style of worship, both theoretically and practically. The next chapter will discuss this subject. The problem of prayer was one of the main factors in Yehudah Halevi's rejection, in his book *The Kozari,* of the philosopher's argument. If God is unchangeable and does not listen to or hear prayer, then prayer has no purpose. Kaplan does not agree. He reconstructs the whole theory and practice of prayer.

The theological problems of Kook and Kaplan differ. Yosef Ben-Shelomo comments on an anomaly in Kook's system—the contradiction between the necessary existence of God and the tentativeness of Creation. Nothing in God's essence is necessary except His existence. Creation is thus an act of God's free will. As Ben Shelomo writes, "God's free will breaks through . . . His absolute necessity, so that He becomes the source of every manifestation of freedom in the universe, in general, and of man's will, in particular."[38] Will, both divine and human, is a Pandora's box, in that it opens the way to arbitrary and even immoral behavior that does not seem to befit the ideal characters of either God or humans. In the end, Kook has no explanation for some of God's arbitrary acts that cause misery to His creatures. We can only try to find some meaning in natural evil that will leave God's goodness intact. The paradox disappears, replaced by justification of God's every deed—and by ignorance.

Natural evil is an inescapable problem for theologians, but it has no metaphysical solution. The severity of the issue is mitigated somewhat for Kaplan, however, because he does not regard evil as the product of a willful, omnipotent, and good God. According to him, humans can take advantage of natural law to secure their fulfillment. To the extent that human freedom is limited, it is not an inscrutable God who is the cause; rather, it is the same order that makes salvation possible. We are free to the extent that we know the connection between cause and effect and act accordingly.

Kaplan does not have to resort to paradox to make peace between a good God and the flawed world He created. He does not assume that the cosmos was created as a perfect reality. We must all admit our ignorance about Creation. We are best advised to be ignorant as to God's purpose or purposes in causing natural existence. To Kaplan, natural evils are aspects of the process of cosmic evolution, which is far from completed. But, says Kaplan, human suffering as a result of this imperfection is not God's design as punishment for sinning or as an inducement to repent.

Two sets of laws govern the universe—physical and moral. The physical order is autonomous and apparently self-governing. But humans can learn to control some of its destructive capabilities or can exacerbate them by mishandling its laws. In both instances, the effect on humans follows directly from the natural cause, and not as a willful reward or punishment.

Still, the ineluctable effects of good and bad deeds leave room for the thesis that "God's ways are just, the righteous will abide by them, and the sinners will stumble over them" (Hosea 14, 10). Kaplan does not attribute the suffering of the righteous and the prosperity of the wicked to God's will. Instead, he concludes that correction of imbalances is possible by learning the laws of interaction and applying them wisely. Behavior often has dire consequences, but experience suggests that the latter cannot be forestalled by following the traditional formula of repenting, praying, and giving charity. The uncertainty of divine Providence distresses supernaturalists. However, Kaplan's theology asks only for faith that further knowledge about the physical and moral law will add to our ability to lessen the measure of our pain and sorrow and maximize our fulfillment. Kaplan asks for no guarantees.

As I indicated, theological confusion stems from treating transcendent and supernatural as identical. It is impossible for theologians to avoid two basic questions. If God cannot be material—because of the limitations of matter in the face of divine eternity and freedom—how can we explain the abyss between spirit and the creation of matter? And if God is omnipotent and all-good, how can natural evil come to be? Cosmological evil and divine justice are the axes on which all serious theology rests. To be honest, no theology, including the proposals of Kook and Kaplan, has yet supplied a decisive answer to the problem. Each response raises questions that cannot be answered within its purview. Whoever argues for creatio ex nihilo (the creation of the world out of nothing) has no answer to the presence of cosmic evil. If one sees evil as inherent in reality, one can have nothing to say about the genesis of existence. In the last analysis, theological preference reflects the personality of the thinker. Persons who are not bothered by paradox can accept the dilemma of a good and powerful God who created a defective and often evil world. They do not question God's goodness and accept their fate as somehow justifiable in the context of a moral economy whose complexities God alone can fathom. Other theologians, like Kaplan, reject a God-idea that lamely justifies evil on the grounds that mortals are incapable of knowing what it is. Since God will do no wrong, say such theologians, it is human judgment that is deficient.

In view of the limitations of both theological styles, we can now better understand the advantages and disadvantages of the ways in which Kook and Kaplan use the term "God." For Kook, material nature is the immanent expression of a spiritual God who Himself stands over and above it. Since God is wholly Other, Kook is not called upon to provide explanations for the inconsistencies of existence. God is beyond our reach. But this view has its disadvantage. Kook cannot enable us to perceive how a perfect, spiritual God can be immanent in a material, flawed universe of His own making. Nor does he have at his disposal anything except dogmatic assertion to prove historical revelation or miracles. Finally, God's justice remains a mystery.

Naturalistic theology also lacks some answers. Kaplan cannot satisfy the person who wants to be certain that the cosmos is no accident but was created wisely and operates according to a well-defined blueprint. Kaplan's bracketing of the problem is scant comfort to a mind that seeks certainty. Kaplan's Process requires a sophistication in prayer that relatively few persons are currently capable of exhibiting. Kaplan was conscious of these difficulties, which he sought to overcome by a revision of the naturalist approach that he termed "transnaturalism." In one formulation, he writes:

> Transnaturalism is that extension of naturalism which takes into account much that mechanistic or materialistic or positivistic science is incapable of dealing with. Transnaturalism reaches into the domain where mind, personality, purpose, ideals, values and meanings dwell. It treats of the good and the true . . . it . . . has a language of its own, the language of simile, metaphor and poetry. That is the language of symbol, myth, and drama. In that universe of discourse, belief in God spells trust in life and man, as capable of transcending the potentialities for evil that inhere in his animal ancestry, in his social heritage, and in the conditions of his environment. Transnaturalist religion beholds God in the fulfillment of human nature and not in the suspension of the natural order. Its function is not to help man overcome the hazards of nature, but to enable him to bring under control his inhumanity to his fellowman.[39]

Thus, the terms "God" and "man" are correlatives. In the context of human salvation, this fact helps us to understand "why, with the changes in our conception of human personality, we necessarily change our conception of God."[40]

Kaplan suggests that we define the soul as the process of self-fulfillment or its opposite, frustration. The soul is not apart from man but is more than he is at any moment of his life. The soul is immanent in man but transcends his present being. Kaplan asks, "Does the awareness of God depend upon our conceiving God as a personal being, or may God be conceived in other ways, and yet be the subject of our awareness, or the object of our worship?"[41] He suggests that we are best advised to think of God "*as the cosmic process that makes for man's life abundant or salvation.*"[42] (Italics, MMK) In one sense, God is the immanent cosmic process of the natural order—as the soul is the development of man. But He is also transcendent, insofar as cosmic laws provide the framework of all possible phenomena. This transcendent realm is no less real than the immanent activity of the cosmos. Transcendence is broader than immanent existence but is not separate from the latter and does not determine its direction. Still, the cosmos is conditioned by this transcendent reality or, if you will, by God.

Modern men and women, Jew or non-Jew, have to choose between two theologies. One is the tradition of an eternal, supernatural God who breaks into time and can revolutionize existence as He sees fit—as He has done in the past. This God has disclosed His will to Israel and its prophets. The alternative view is that humankind's function is to explore the universe in which the human race has emerged, to formulate values by which life can be sustained, and to ascertain, as well as possible, whether human values meet the requirements of the cosmic order. The second choice ranges from atheistic pessimism to a realistic or optimistic theism. The latter bespeaks the faith that existence is capable of satisfying human needs and legitimate purposes.

Judaism has room for both theological views. My own preference is for the one that offers us no eternal life and no loving Father or Mother with whom we can dialogue as we do with our earthly parents or to whom we can pray in the literal sense. In response to these seeming drawbacks, Kaplan offers an intellectually honest confrontation with reality. He enables us to have a God who is not responsible for natural or moral evil. He frees us from having to justify intellectual and moral claims that have patently been outgrown. He opens doors to creative thought and to broad education, His idea of God is assured of further refinement as knowledge expands. Kaplan also makes it likely that Jewish theology will continue to exert its influence on the world's religions. This brand of theology undoubtedly appears dangerous to those who fear contact with foreign cultures. But for Jews who feel duty-bound to turn to all reasonable sources of religious inspiration, it seems to me to be the preferable route.

NOTES

1. Orot, p. 119 (Hebrew edition).
2. Ibid.
3. Ibid.

4. Ibid., p. 120.

5. Ibid.

6. *Hilkhot Yesodei HaTorah* 2:2. We should expect that the path to God for a halakhically loyal Jew would be through the study of Torah. One strand in Jewish tradition holds that anyone who interrupts his study to enjoy the beauties of nature distances himself from salvation. But there is an opposite trend, already manifest in the Bible. "How great are your works, O God, your thoughts are very profound" (Ps. 92, 6). The Psalmist might not have sought God in the wonders of nature, but he was undoubtedly enthralled by them and discovered in them the hand of God. More than a millennium later, when the revival of Greek philosophy threatened belief in God and when leading thinkers saw the need to prove His existence by logical demonstration, Maimonides proclaimed that the way to God is through introspection about "His great deeds and creatures."

7. *Orot,* p. 119 (Hebrew edition).

8. Ibid., pp. 124–125. Yosef Ben-Shelomo describes Kook's efforts to escape the dilemma brought on by his two conflicting aims. In the first, he wants to become one with God. This departure from pure reason can easily lead to an idolatrous conception of God. In the second aim, Kook has to have recourse to reason. This inclination is "apt to bring forth a dry and barren monotheism" (*Shirat Hayyim,* p. 29). Kook never resolved this dilemma because he saw something positive in man's strong desire to experience God in nature. It is this passion that leads to progress in the unmasking of the secrets of existence.

9. The classic statement of this view is the remark of Ben Bag Bag: "Turn it [the Torah] and turn it over again, for everything is in it" *(Pirke Avot—Sayings of the Fathers,* 5:25).

10. *Sabbath Prayer Book* (New York: Jewish Reconstructionist Foundation, 1962, pp. 342, 344, 346).

11. *Diaries,* August 14, 1932.

12. Kaplan also starts from the premise that "unless we contemplate man against a cosmic background, his life becomes too unimportant to try to improve it" (*Diaries,* August 14, 1932) In opposition to this opinion, it is worthwhile to refer once again to Kaplan's observation: "Habituate yourself to the idea that it is no more possible to be aware of the whole of God in any single experience than it is to sense all of electricity in a single shock. The fallacy of identifying any one experience or even a cluster of experiences as the revelation of Deity in his fullness gives rise to idolatry" (*Diaries,* July 13, 1936).

13. JWS, p. 26.

14. JC, pp. 135–136.

15. JWS, pp. 26–27. Kaplan often declares that God is unknowable and that all our concepts of Him fail to describe the reality to which the word "God" points.

16. JC, p. 436.

17. Ibid.

18. FAJ, p. 185. In this passage, Kaplan refers to the Jewish religious school in the United States. But he believed that the cultivation of the virtues mentioned is the function of all education.

19. Ibid., p. 171.

20. OR, Vol. 1, pp. 379–380.

21. See Kaplan's discussion on thanksgiving in FAJ, pp. 303–313.

22. *Hilkhot Yesodei HaTorah*, 6:1.

23. Ibid., 6:2.

24. OR, Vol. 1, p.46.

25. Ibid., p. 47.

26. See the excellent discussion by Harold Schulweis, "The Unity of Adonai and Elohim," in *The Reconstructionist*, Vol. 59, No.1, Spring 1994.

27. OR, Vol. 1, p. 47.

28. *Eruvin*, 13a.

29. *Diaries*, August 8, 1940.

30. QJA, p. 131.

31. *Judaism Without Supernaturalism* (henceforth, JWS) (New York: Reconstructionist Press, 1958, p. 23). Kook, too, acknowledges humanity's rise from a more primitive condition. He writes: "In ancient times, humanity was less developed, and human will was more primitive. The vision of God was then directed to thrusting aside this rebellious reason, which in most of society was subject to animal desires. Belief in God was then a rejection of the natural longings which were driven toward ugliness and sin. The beautification of the world in the course of time came about through the exalted revelation of God in Israel, the experience of time, the broadening of social relations and the advance of science. All these combined to purify the human spirit. Even though man is not fully perfected, many of his thoughts and aspirations are now directed to divine good" (OR, Vol. 2, p. 545). Kook's remarks seem to compromise his supernaturalist theology, but there is no denying the kabbalism and revelationism in his thought. Kook pictures the universe and humankind as the fruits of a long process of cosmic deterioration and recovery. This dialectic is well documented in the evolution of Judaism. The ideal state of the universe preceded its material formation. With the latter, and especially after the sin of Adam and Eve, humans became defective. But the seed of perfection was transmitted through selected

individuals until the birth of Jacob. Through him and his offspring, Jews were endowed with this divine quality and with the responsibility to repair the cosmic deficiency. Unfortunately, Israel, like the rest of humankind, retains the tendency to fall. Therefore, redemption depends on the struggles of the Jewish people to live up to its calling.

32. *Religion of Ethical Nationalism* (henceforth, REN) (New York: Macmillan, 1970, p. 50).

33. This verse is usually interpreted as referring to different fates for body and soul. The material body disintegrates into lifelessness, while the soul rises to enjoy God's presence forever. But the clear meaning is that man is restored to his prenatal state. Just as he had no consciousness before God breathed into him the breath of life, so, at death, God reclaims the soul without its retaining any of the experiences it accumulated while it was related to the body.

34. See *Perek Helek* (Rambam's commentary on the last chapter of the talmudic tradate, Sanhedrin).

35. Kook portrays human fulfillment as occurring only when the process of *tikkun* reaches its end. But he draws no conclusions about God from his knowledge of man. (See OK, Vol. 2, p. 531 and the entire section, "The Rise of the Cosmos.")

36. REN, p. 21.

37. Ibid., p. 25.

38. *Shirat Hayyim*, pp. 42–43.

39. See the interesting commentary of the Malbim on this verse.

40. JWS, p. 10. Also helpful is the analysis of transnaturalism by William Kaufman in his essay, "Mordecai M. Kaplan's Transnaturalism and American Naturalism," in *The American Journal of Theology and Philosophy,* Vol. 2, No. 1, January 1990.

41. FAJ, p. 171.

42. Ibid., pp. 182–183.

6
Prayer

PARTICIPANTS in public worship are unlikely to concentrate uninterruptedly on the content and intent of their prayers. They are
often disturbed by worries; by some distracting idea, object, or
person; or by nearby conversations. Even in the midst of sincere
devotion, they may encounter a familiar word or phrase in the
prayer book that sets off a train of thought which destroys their
concentration on the prayer being recited. Perhaps most disturbing is the monotony of repetitive recitation of the same text—
whether the traditional one or any of the revisions.

Kaplan differentiates between praying and "davening," that is,
mindless recitation of the prescribed text. Whether one repeats a
fixed liturgical text alone or with a congregation, a tremendous
effort is required to concentrate on the meaning of the words. Of
course, there are precious moments when the prayer speaks to the
heart, but they are few. For Kaplan one such moment occurred
during the *Shivah*, the week of mourning, following the death of
his first wife. While leading the service, he read from one of his
original prayers. The worshipers were transfixed by the deep
emotion with which Kaplan prayed, particularly when he came
to the following section:

> God is in the faith
> By which we overcome
> The fear of loneliness, of helplessness,
> Of failure and of death.
> God is in the hope
> Which, like a shaft of light,
> Cleaves the dark abysms
> Of sin, of suffering and of despair.
>
> God is in the love
> Which creates, protects, forgives.
> His is the spirit

Which broods on the chaos men have wrought,
Disturbing its static wrongs,
And stirring into life the formless beginnings
Of the new and better world.[1]

At the end of the service, one of Kaplan's colleagues, known to disagree with his views, said to him, "When I heard you recite your prayer, I was tempted to become one of your followers."

Thus, this was a special moment for both Kaplan and those attending the service. In his *Diaries*, Kaplan constantly complains about the boredom of communal worship and of his failure to achieve *kavvanah* (devotion) for himself and his congregants.

Kook is equally forceful about the need to make prayer sincere and profound. To the best of my knowledge, however, he saw no reason to tamper with the content of the liturgy as a step toward increasing devotion. Kook was confident that he could attain the desired mood within the traditional framework. Nonetheless, as I shall try to demonstrate, there is some doubt as to whether this confidence was warranted in the light of some elements in his philosophy of prayer.

Both thinkers agree that *kavvanah* must be based on coordination between reason and emotion. But Kook contradicts himself. On the one hand, he states, "Prayer is not intended to effect any change in God, who is eternally changeless."[2] To emphasize the point, he adds, "It is essential that prayer be devoid of any thought of causing change or emotion in the Holy One, blessed be He."[3] At the same time, he describes prayer as "speaking to God, as to a flexible ruler, to a father willing to change his mind, or to a generous, righteous person who might be induced to increase his charitable contribution—all at the bidding of another soul. . . ."[4] Kook distinguishes between a person's emotional drives and the philosophical presupposition that no prayer can alter anything in God. Humans cannot be satisfied with cognition alone. They want to feel that their appeal has been heard and will be answered.[5] The contradiction, it turns out, is only apparent. The act of turning to a listening ear expresses the realization that one is subject to forces beyond one's control, whereas awareness that God cannot be changed by prayer is a realistic appraisal resulting from human experience. Honest prayer is an effort to steer a course between these two realities.

Kook regards emotion and reason as supplementary forms of behavior. When men and women perceive that a need is not being satisfied, they want to be assured of two things—that their wants are not arbitrary but are inherent aspects of their essence as creatures of God and that reality is such that the satisfaction of those wants is possible. Yet experience teaches them that their hopes cannot always be fulfilled and that they must learn to accept disappointment with equanimity. They then realize that God is not to be used as an instrument for carrying out the demands of the human will. Rather, God is to be conceived as a saving force to be pursued and to be relied upon, but never to be fully grasped. Nor should God be expected to grant humankind's every wish. Reason's function is not to subdue human urges or emotional drives but to temper them with a sense of realism. An awareness of life's blessings and pitfalls, as well as of one's mental prowess and limitations, is the catalyst of honest prayer.

Kook was not the first pious thinker to confront the dilemma of praying to a God who does not change. I have already commented that Yehudah Halevi rejected Aristotelian philosophy because it left no room for prayer. Paradoxically, however, he also acknowledged that the philosophic position of God's unchangeability was correct.[6] This is a classic example of how the emotional need to feel God's saving power takes precedence over the rational sense that prayers of petition meant to overturn natural order have no foundation.

Although mysticism prevails in Kook's mentality, we must not underestimate the degree of rationalism in his system. Conversely, we should be open to the mystical elements in Kaplan's rationalism. Critics charge that he lacks emotion and that his prayer is devoid of feeling and therefore shallow or even untrue. There is no basis for this criticism. Consider, for example, Kaplan's interpretation of *Shemini Atzeret* as a holy day meant to imprint on the Jewish mind the need for prayer. Kaplan emphasizes that religion as a whole and prayer in particular cannot be satisfied with reason alone.

> For God must not be held merely as idea; He must be felt as a presence if we want not only to know about God but to know God. "Taste and see

that the Lord is good," says the Psalmist (34, 9). Religious souls
have never been satisfied with an awareness of God merely as an
intellectual concept. They always crave a religious experience in
which the reality of God would be brought home to them with
. . . immediacy. . . ."[7] (Italics, MMK)

To escape this dilemma, Kaplan goes beyond Kook in rejecting
the notion that God literally listens to prayer. The response to
prayer has to be conceived as an activity of the worshiper. This is
borne out in the reflexive form of the Hebrew word for praying—*hithpalel*. For rationalists, then, who want to feel that they
are praying to God and not to themselves, true prayer cannot be
monodirectional. Somehow it must be a dialogue between the
person and God. Therefore, Kaplan, too, has to wrestle with the
status of feeling and the sense that human needs can be identified
and fulfilled.

Thus far, we have noted the similarities between the two men.
We turn now to their illuminating differences.

KOOK ON PRAYER

Kook's commentary on the *Siddur* is replete with paradigms intended to assist us in revitalizing prayers, many of which have
become sterile. But we shall have to reconcile some of Kook's
theologically and philosophically daring treatments of prayer with
his strict adherence to the form and content of halakhic liturgy.
Kook occupied two worlds but felt no need to remove their contradictions.

Kook envisaged prayer as a cosmic process that proceeds without human awareness. "The uninterrupted prayer of the soul tries
relentlessly to emerge from its hiddenness into the revealed
world."[8] The soul always prays, never ceasing to cling to its Beloved. But it is in the hour of articulated prayer that the soul
finally comes to overt expression.[9] In passing, I observe that Kook
should not be classified as a process theologian. Prayer is not one
of the orderly and autonomous movements of nature. To Kook,
nature itself is not autonomous; it is created and managed by God.
Nonetheless, Kook defines prayer as "a remarkable law which
God has enacted in order to accomplish the complete fulfillment of

His creatures, particularly their moral perfection, but which is not to be conceived as inherent in the law of God's nature, Heaven forbid."[10] (Italics, JJC) That is to say, prayer is a process, like all natural laws, but it is not an autonomous phenomenon or a necessary attribute of God such as His existence. Rather, it is a function of the free will of God and man. The soul could not pray unless it had this potentiality. Kook sees it as one of the most characteristic and important human activities, which God fashioned before Creation. However, it is up to man to bring it to actuality. Prayer is like a natural resource that has to be manipulated for human benefit. But the soul is not the terminal of the process. Prayer seeks to connect the soul with God.

Kook's emphasis on the role of prayer in the moral training of the individual bears repetition. Like the other *mitzvot*, prayer straightens "man's path and purifies his virtues and thoughts."[11] The work of prayer is in the soul and is not directed to the mind of God.

We can clarify Kook's intent by comparing prayer with repentance (*Teshuvah*). Of *Teshuvah* Kook writes:

> The currents of repentance flow. They resemble the flaming waves on the surface of the sun that burst forth and ascend in their endless conflict. They give life to many worlds and to countless creations. We are powerless to absorb the multitude of varying colors with which this giant sun of repentance illumines all the constellations— because of the profusion of their numbers, their remarkable speed and the fact that they emanate from the Source of life. . . .[12]

Teshuvah is thus not a human invention; humans use the light that is diffused like the rays of the sun throughout existence. Kook notes further: "By means of repentance all things return to God. By means of its power which prevails in all the worlds, all things return and are united with the perfect godly existence. . . ."[13] *Teshuvah* contributes to cosmic correction and to the unification of Creation with God—but only if people fulfill their duty. At its highest level, *Teshuvah* is a stage of prayer. Both stem from the source of transcendent unity, a gift to the person who is able to appreciate it. For this gift, men and women need not wait. They have only to appropriate it.

Hence, humans are partners in the prayer process. They release its force. Kook analyzes the steps that have to be taken so that people can truly pray. First, they must want to pray. This urge must come from within, such as a desire to perform a *mitzvah*. In contrast to Yeshaiah Leibowitz, who dismisses the idea that prayer is a response to spiritual needs or a means of satisfying them, and who says that a Jew must pray only because he or she is commanded to do so, Kook maintains that such an approach would make prayer a burden. Without an inner desire, no one can attain the necessary mood of supplication. However, even if this condition is fulfilled, prayer is incomplete unless it seeks to be a response to God's wish. Human purpose cannot be met unless it is also God's purpose. Prayer is a test of the purity and probity of the worshiper. It is not, or should not be, a technique only for achieving peace of mind. It can often be soul-wrenching, as when it becomes clear to a person that he or she appears before God for base, egoistic reasons. Insofar as prayer uncovers human shallowness and narrowness, it can be very depressing or exalting. The effect depends on the character of the worshiper.

We have observed that prayer is intimately connected with emotion. It is motivated by feeling. Nonetheless, Kook demands, "[R]eason should predominate over feeling, to the point where it can generate something new over and beyond the inner emotion. . . ."[14] Kook knows that many worshipers seek in prayer release from reason and logic. He, on the contrary, assigns an important role to intellect. Reason and emotion belong together in prayer, although each has a specific function. Feeling operates spontaneously, while reason is motivated by a conscious act of will. Activating reason in prayer requires special effort and great caution. Since reason requires effort, the worshiper will tend to concentrate on thoughts that are beyond the scope of spontaneous emotion. Thus, the worshiper may become so absorbed in ideas that he or she may miss the essence of prayer.

Kook fails to adequately deal with the implications of his analysis of the roles of reason and emotion in the prayer experience. He daringly remarks, "[E]motions are of little worth when compared with the exalted objective of eliciting God's will by means of prayer."[15] That is to say, the aim of prayer is not necessarily tied to the feelings that arouse a person to pray. Yet without emotion, prayer is unlikely to be generated or made significant. But is emotion only an embellishment for the essentially intellectual content of prayer? Undoubtedly, Kook, the mystic, would not entertain such an idea, for at the heart of faith is emotion. Without it, reason can easily lead us to heresy.

Kook does not attempt to resolve this conflict. What is faith? Is it a function of feeling or intellect, or both? If both, what is the contribution of each faculty? I doubt that Kook fully understood the soul-searching of the loyal Jew whose faith in God and in the divinity of the Torah has been shaken by modern science—particularly social science. Kook was certainly aware of the challenge of the new mentality, but he apparently underestimated its severity. Therefore, it is hard to grasp the implications of his insistence that it is reason, after all, which takes precedence over emotion in worship. Perhaps he meant only that the worshiper must try to apply the words of the liturgy to life's experiences, so that not only does the worshiper utter the text but also sees its relevance to life and to the world. Kook certainly did not intend to grant reason the critical function of evaluating the traditional liturgy or altering its content. Accordingly, we are not surprised that he felt constrained by the limits imposed by the *Halakhah*. But within those borders the flight of his imagination is remarkable.

I stated above that the worshiper cannot be satisfied with merely an intellectual exercise or even an emotional outpouring. He or she wants to experience God. Prayer is a preparation for receiving the abundance of the divine Spirit. As a means to an end, prayer carries its own reward, for there is no greater delight than the feeling that one is in touch with God. Kook, the mystic, cannot describe this feeling. Although he feels attachment to God, he is unable to communicate the details of the experience to others.[16] Kook's reticence is understandable. He would have to describe the appearance of God, and we refer again to God's words to Moses: "Man shall not see Me and live" (Ex. 33, 20). Kook is willing to proclaim the worshiper's ability to experience God, but his affirmation has a rationalist's restraint. Prayer is a human act, with the other side of the coin being prophecy. A serious thinker has to highlight the role of disciplined thought, which gives authority to the experience of the senses and normal consciousness. At some point the overpowering ecstatic experience has to be coordinated with the judgment of the mind.

In Kook's system, however, reason is subject to the sovereignty of the Torah. Prayer is intended to confront mundane existence with the abundant life from above, which is adumbrated in Torah. The worshiper must, as faithfully as possible, execute the demands of Torah. Since the quality of eternal life is far superior to that of normal, daily life, it is hoped that the influence of prayer will inspire the worshiper to absorb the light of Torah and conduct himself or herself accordingly. When the natural order proceeds properly, then, as Kook puts it dialectically, "The significance of miracles becomes great, indeed."[17] Kook tells us that miracles should not be defined as divine interference with the normal order of things. That order itself is the miracle and suffices to elicit in humans the sense of sublimity before all the wonders of reality. But when humans violate the laws of nature and the *mitzvot* of the Torah, mundane existence becomes impoverished, and appeals for miracles become an annoyance imposed on Heaven. When this happens, prayer loses much of its educational value and humans lose their capacity for self-fulfillment. Instead of praising God, the worshiper appears before Him whining and pleading to be saved from his or her weaknesses and suffering.

According to Kook's vision, prayer is much more than a petition. While it is true that prayer is directed from below to above, this does not necessarily mean an appeal for supernatural help. Quite the contrary. Through prayer, worshipers purify the image of God within them, refine their inherent holiness, and raise their souls toward their destined heights. By means of prayer, worshipers learn that in order to reach this spiritual goal, they must develop their minds and perfect their virtues. This recognition brings Jews to the study of Torah, the true means of uniting the two worlds of mundane existence and eternal life. In this way, divine wisdom is appropriated by human reason, and Jews thereby strengthen their essential nature. As Kook states:

> The Torah stirs man to new conceptions and truths that constantly flow from it and which exist eternally in the Source of eternal life. Prayer does not announce new knowledge or enrich man's intellect with its truths; it takes some of the well-known, established knowledge and deepens the moral stature of the soul by impressing its message on the emotions.[18]

For prayer to implant the desired effect into the soul, the Jew must first study and learn Torah, for only by doing so can reason acquire absolute truth. Prayer adds emotional power to the revelations of reason.

We are in a closed circle. Reason cannot be allowed to fly off in all directions. If we want a firm anchor for our lives, we must turn to Torah; this is the mind's proper field of activity. No other intellectual profession can raise us to the realm of eternal life. Although prayer is a separate discipline, it is closely related to Torah. In Kook's eyes, legitimate human wants are not identical with what we feel at any time. It is true that the soul prays incessantly, but only in the traditional liturgy are our real needs articulated. Even then, their disclosure depends upon our knowledge of Torah. The more Torah a person knows, the more successful will be his or her prayer. For the traditional liturgy is the emotional expression of toraitic reason. Ultimately, Kook could not handle the awful tension between his awareness of the modern world and its open-mindedness and his loyalty to Torah as God's Word. His only outlet was his ceaseless effort to discover the secrets of Torah. He believed that buried in them is the answer to the contradictions and conflicts between autonomous experience and what is implicit in accepting the full authority of Torah.

The roles of emotion and reason in prayer require careful delineation. Prayer has to translate rational concepts into feelings that will have a moral and spiritual impact on the soul and subsequently on the will. Thus, the force of will depends on the breadth and depth of knowledge that is refracted through the emotions. In this manner, Kook explains that reason plays an important role in prayer.

However, we should not expect Kook to support a modern conception of prayer that is based on scientific knowledge and the latest insights into human nature. I repeat one example of what Kook means by "well-known, established knowledge" and the resultant strengthening of the soul through prayer. Apparently, he sensed the spiritual difficulty in the disparate blessings that men and women recite each morning. A man is expected to thank God for not having made him a woman. The usual interpretation is that the male Jew is blessed with the duty to perform many *mitzvot*, from which women, because of their household obligations and physiological structure, are exempt. (In traditional terms, women are not obligated to perform *mitzvot* that are subject to barriers of time.) This interpretation, particularly the part relating to social convention, did not satisfy Kook. Social habit is subject to radical alteration. Therefore, he interpreted the benediction differently:

> Souls are destined to be divided into categories of active and receptive, of affecting life and existence in all their splendor or being affected by them. This is the essential difference between the active, legislating, conquering and subjugating soul of the male and that of the woman, which is recorded, acted and engraved upon, and conquered and subjugated by the authority of the male.[19]

Instead of rewording the benediction recited by Jewish men to take into account the best available information about the physiology, psychology, and sociology of women, Kook prefers to justify the traditional formulation. His apology restates kabbalistic imagination without attempting to relate to fact or logic. In defending the wisdom of the benediction recited by women, which thanks God for having made them according to His will, Kook says,

> Despite the advantage of the active male, whose deeds make a notable impression on life and on the universe, the passive woman also benefits from her status. The fact that she is made to receive impressions rather than initiate them gives her an advantage over a male. As a consequence of his independence, his deeds and enthusiastic activism, the male discovers his physical and spiritual limits. This condition sometimes diverts him from supernal, godly purposes. The passive woman is not confronted by such a possibility.[20]

Kook's openness is restricted to the halakhically defined area. It is doubtful whether the most conclusive scientific disproof of Kook's thesis would convince him to change the morning blessings. He would, instead, come up with another excuse for leaving the text untouched. To the best of my knowledge, no traditionalist has ever suggested that it is precisely the woman's blessing—"who has made me according to His will"—which is the benediction with the more profound and uplifting sentiment.

Humans can easily become victims of their bodily and spiritual urges. Only the Torah can arrange these urges in the order of their validity or indicate whether they are divinely implanted needs. Moreover, it is not only the *yetzer hara* (the evil inclination) that lies in wait to mislead all of us; we can also be distracted by the difficulty of balancing legitimate needs. Truthful prayer can give direction to our emotions. Hence, again, the precondition for prayer has to be Torah-study or, as Kook writes:

> The physical, beastly wants of man require the limitation and or-
> dering of Torah. Thus, the person who does not listen to Torah will
> note that his physical feelings will become abominable. [Moreover]
> without the circumscription of divine, rational guidance, his prayer,
> even though directed upwards, can be turned upside down, spoil,
> and become a stumbling block. . . . Therefore, it is unwise for a
> person to interrupt study in order to pray.[21]

Reason has to be subject to toraitic discipline. Sometimes, how-ever, it exaggerates the accuracy of its insights, overestimates the range of its autonomy, and, as a result, misleads.

Yet Kook shows many flashes of realism. Although he believes that the *Halakhah* offers a method of thinking and a way of life suitable to most Jews, he admits that only a select number are capable of eliciting its moral message by means of reason alone. R. Simeon b. Yohai and his students, whose profession was said to be the study of Torah, were exempt from prayer. All others had to have recourse to prayer in order to convert theory into practice. Without the feeling generated in worship, knowledge remains an abstraction. Nevertheless, the reference to bar Yohai, recorded in Shabbat lla, raises the question as to why he and his disciples were so unique that they were freed from the duty to pray. Attempts to answer this question are all conjecture. How-ever, I think that we shall not stray far from the truth if we say that Kook does not credit all forms of Torah study with that authority. Erudition alone cannot ensure good deeds and meritorious be-havior. Only study that is aimed at and successful in revealing toraitic secrets can lay claim to such status. It is the joining of reason and emotion, of intellect and imagination, that might, on rare occasions, render prayer superfluous. Kook may have tried to scale this height, perhaps in the wee hours around midnight, when he was accustomed to pen many of his thoughts. Judging by his emotion-laden writing, he was inspired by his deep meditation on words of Torah. However, his humility deterred him from refraining from statutory prayer. Apparently, he did not regard himself as qualified to emulate the likes of bar Yohai.

Despite this distinction between the prayer of scholars and that of most others, the prayer of the latter still has its own merit. Kook states that when the soul pours forth the sincere yearnings of a contrite heart, these supplications will prove acceptable to God. This is not an intellectual judgment; it is an expression of Kook's traditional and humanistic spirit and his profound love of Israel and humanity. When all is said and done, communal prayer is meant to join together all the knowledge, pain, joy, and aspirations of the Jewish people and to place them in one basket before the bench of divine judgment. While it is only the individual who prays, his or her prayer is joined to that of the people as a whole. In the end, although the individual's prayer is absorbed into the supplications of the congregation, the divine response reaches each worshiper as if he or she stood alone in the synagogue. In prayer, too, the insight of Karl Marx applies: "From each according to his ability to each according to his needs." Kook phrases the idea in his own way. "The intent of the individual, which is expressed in his interpretation of the liturgical words, is an essential of prayer, while that of the whole group, directed to Heaven, represents the complete thrust. And that completeness is already found, essentially, in the *kavvanah* of the individual."[22] The individual prays for the fulfillment of his or her own needs and receives in return what the group is capable of providing. It is God, of course, who mediates the answer.

For Kook the prayer of the individual is what he or she utters in the ecclesia of Israel, while that of Israel is the expression of Jewish nationalism. The individual Jew can easily be tempted to think that "[t]he national sentiment in each Jew prepares his heart to worship God and enables him to appreciate the worth of the *mitzvot* and to observe them lovingly."[23] But that is not so. Nationalism is subordinate to Torah and public prayer. While nationalism may strengthen the ties between Jews, there is a goal beyond social and national objectives. If not intent upon God, prayer loses its true purpose. Nationalism is no substitute for worship of God.

According to Kook, whoever can pray will recite the daily

morning, afternoon, and evening liturgies in the spirit of performing a *mitzvah* in pure happiness. Habit must not diminish the sincerity of the supplications or deprive reason of its right to doubt
or to introduce new ideas into worship. Prayer will always challenge worshipers to improve themselves and spur them to seek
communion with God. But if they are honest and open to their
environment, worshipers will receive little peace of mind from
prayer. They will always be aware of the gap between their desire
for unity and the variegated reality.

In summing up Kook's vision of prayer, let us refer to one of
his heartfelt expressions:

> The supernal God, whom we long to reach, in Whom we wish
> to be absorbed, into whose light we want to be gathered—all in
> vain—descends of His own accord into the midst of the world. We
> discover Him and delight in His love and find rest and peace in His
> place of serenity. Sometimes, He visits us through His lofty light
> with a flash of inspiration beyond all our ability to imagine.[24]

Kook's philosophy of prayer belongs to the classic tradition on
the subject. It deserves the careful attention of mystics and rationalists alike, for it has insights that should interest both mindsets.
But he left many fields fallow. Either he could not or he preferred
not to plow certain problematic areas. To find a serious attempt
to address some of these untouched issues, we have to turn to
Kaplan.

KAPLAN ON PRAYER

Kaplan, like Kook, sought communion with God. But when a
rationalist uses a term that smacks of mysticism, we become concerned. Is the experience of God about which he speaks identical
to that at which Kook aimed? Kook knew that "God transcends
all ideas or feelings of His existence that might enter our consciousness."[25] Nonetheless, Kook seriously sought actual union
with God. Kaplan, on the other hand, entertained no such hope.
He looked in two other directions, which were more realistic but
just as deeply felt and which emanated from a natural mysticism.
He wanted, first, to feel God, not only to conceive Him.[26] He

understood that God is perceived by men and women in many different ways according to their capacities and education. These perceptions are all the more reason for faith in God's existence and in His saving power. Such faith is a precondition for any religious outlook on life.

The second component of Kaplan's religious aspirations can be found in the following lines:

> In our various interpretations of God as the Power that makes for certain desirable goals, there is one point that is not taken into account, and that is that we accept these goals, without identifying the Power, that makes for them, as God, as the Spirit that so possesses us as to compel our adoration and worship.[27]

The experience of God resides in the intellectual and emotional confidence that we are capable of detecting traces of God's workings during our earthly existence. This same confidence, it must be added, also carries the seeds of serious mistakes and even heresy. Like Kook, Kaplan realized that the certainty of the moment is bound to evaporate at some point. Yet without it, we cannot function constructively. Therefore, it is better for a person to take the leap of faith rather than to refrain from acting on the assumption of an orderly universe.

Since prayer is a religious act par excellence, it should be conducted according to the highest standards of morality and intellectual honesty. Although prayer does not engage only the intellect, it must at least try to lend its power to the search for truth. We are unable to discover absolute truth, but we are capable of differentiating between fact and fiction and between a reasonable idea and one that cannot stand up to criticism. Therefore, Kaplan argues that one of the functions of prayer must be to offer the worshipers the intellectual and moral foundations on which to build their lives and to which to give their full devotion.

Kaplan's consistency leads him to draw conclusions that are implicit in his philosophy of prayer. The *Siddur* must be a living text expressing the spirit of the age. The creativity of the intellect must not be limited to additions to the liturgy. It also has to act as a critic, filter, reformer, and seeker of new insights into the broad range of human knowledge. True, the traditional prayer book is itself a resource for locating original spiritual insights. Kaplan insisted that sincere efforts be made to revitalize its contents while preserving as much of its form as possible. But employing the principle that the Torah, including the *Siddur*, contains all the information and inspiration that Jews need for their fulfillment is bound to limit the effectiveness of prayer. Such an approach will becloud the path to God and convert prayer into an exercise in erudition and commentary. It will repress self-expression and the responsibility of each generation to correct the errors of the past. Nevertheless, the other side of the coin is the tie with Jewish heritage. The need to uproot, correct, improve, and add neither detracts from the great achievement of tradition nor weakens our love for it. The structure of the *Siddur* took centuries to compose. The creative process never ceases. In the past, creativity in prayer was mostly confined to the addition of *piyyutim*, that is, commentary and melodic renditions. Some Jewish communities developed their own wording of the liturgy, but the halakhists were reluctant to alter its statutory content and form. Nor did they see the need for such action. All Jews were free to probe the meaning of the liturgy or to pour out their hearts in a personal way. There was no reason to change the prayer tradition.

Rabbi Joseph Hertz epitomized the ancestral Jewish spirit in his commentary on the *Siddur*. For example, in justifying retention of the prayer for the restoration of the Temple and the sacrificial system, he quotes the opinion of M. Friedlander, the head of Jews College in London at the end of the nineteenth century. Friedlander notes that many Jews were uncomfortable with such a petition, but he says,

> Let him whose heart is not with his fellow worshippers in any of their supplications, silently substitute his own prayers for them; but let him not interfere with the devotion of those to whom "the statutes of the Lord are right, rejoicing the heart; the commandments of the Lord right, enlightening the eyes; the judgments true and righteous altogether" [Ps. 19, 9–10], and who yearn for the opportunity of fulfilling Divine commandments which they cannot observe at present.[28]

It is reasonable to assume that Jews can be found in Orthodox synagogues who are intellectually troubled by certain prayers. To remain within the synagogue, these Jews have to resort to stratagems like those of Hertz and Friedlander, that ignore the plain intent of the prayers or, like Kook, that seek out some supposed secret in their contents.

Kaplan tried never to speak a word of prayer to which he could not grant his mind's wholehearted assent. He sought to express in prayer the beliefs and commitments that were most precious to him as a human being and as a Jew. Kaplan maintained, "[T]he content of the prayer must correspond with the particular conception of God to which we can wholeheartedly ascribe [sic]."[29] He added, "Religious prayer is the utterance of those thoughts that imply either the actual awareness of God or the desire to attain such awareness."[30] In this spirit, Kaplan attempted to rework the Jewish liturgy. He and his colleagues worked assiduously on the wording of the prayers, sifting, amending, and supplementing them in accordance with carefully formulated criteria of morality, spirituality, and esthetics. They tried to avoid arbitrariness, as is evident in the following examples.

Kaplan and his co-editors removed prayers enunciating the election of Israel. Kaplan strongly objected to apologetical efforts to mitigate the sense of Israel's superiority that is apparent in praise of God for having "raised us above all tongues," "distinguished between the holy and the profane, between light and darkness, between Israel and the nations,"[31] and "chosen us from all the nations in giving us the Torah." No doubt, our ancestors viewed Israel's election as a call to Israel to assume responsibility for the moral and spiritual education of the rest of humankind. But even this God-appointed vocation of noblesse oblige is marked by a comparison of the favored with the less fortunate. Kaplan wanted Israel to be an ethical nation, but he felt this same obligation devolved on all peoples.

A second example stems from Kaplan's preference for a realistic and courageous spirituality, fashioned after the Bible. In keeping with this conviction, he rejected what he considered to be the vain hope for resurrection of the dead and urged a return to the this-worldly emphasis of biblical theology. Praying for bodily restoration encourages the worshiper to flee from reality.

Despite the picture we have painted thus far, Kaplan greatly appreciated the poetic elements in prayer and he himself experienced the emotional force of the ancient liturgy. But he was not satisfied with simply preserving the statutory words. He wanted his revised prayer books to include religious poetry, meditations, and other prayers or inspirational selections from the length and breadth of Jewish creativity. All these forms of expression, whatever their emotional overtones, also communicate ideas. Therefore, Kaplan argued that the poetry of prayer should bring before God sentiments and notions that can be rationally defended. Although no person can be absolutely consistent, the worshiper should aim for that goal. Honesty eventually finds verbal expression, and the worshiper who wishes to sanctify life in his or her prayers must speak the truth. Therefore, Kaplan rejected the claim that the traditional liturgy should remain untouched because the sanctity and emotional power of its age outweigh any consideration of intellectual probity. Traditionalists counter that since the text of the *Siddur* is suffused with the sufferings and the joys, the wisdom and the righteousness of our ancestors, no one has the right to tarnish the memories of these pious forebears. If the latter found the prayers inspiring, and if their ancestors and posterity were ready to sacrifice their lives for its values, how can Kaplan and others of his persuasion dare to tamper with its sanctity? Kaplan's forthright answer is that prayer must come from the heart and mind of the worshiper and not only from the souls of past generations.

Kaplan argues thus:

> Excessive prayer . . . often represents the verbalization of interests that should express themselves in deeds, not in words. Preoccupation with the sense of sin may result in such self-contempt as to emphasize rather than heal the breach between the crude appetites of men and their deeper, more stable and more significant social emotions. The masochism of self-mortification leads inevitably to the sadism of masochism.[32]

The balance of enlightened religion is always in need of readjustment. Kaplan deduced that the worshiper has to blend reason and emotion, the fixed and the novel, the needs and values of the group, and the impulses of the individual ego. Reverence for the past should be an aid, not a hindrance, to the creation of the future.

Kook, in his own way, found adequate flexibility and inspiration in the dynamism of the traditional liturgy. Kaplan called for the use in the synagogue of classical sources that had been ignored, as well as the whole range of Jewish spiritual expression, from its earliest days to modern times. Whereas Kook thought it was legitimate to interpolate original ideas into traditional words whose actual meaning is opposed or unrelated to the new concepts, Kaplan substituted readings and prayers befitting the unprecedented new currents of thought.

Both thinkers have a problem stemming from the fact that a person is often motivated to pray by an impulse to overcome some moral or spiritual weakness. To whom should the plea for help be addressed? Traditional Jews look to the God of Israel who hears their supplication. However, as we recall, Kook writes that prayer is meant to have an impact on the worshiper and not to cause God to change any intentions He might have. God is not to be conceived as an instrument to be used by humans for their egoistic purposes. I see no way for Kook to sidestep his dilemma. In his view, God cannot be simply an autonomous process of cosmic law; He has to be able to create, legislate, and judge. He is not merely contained in Creation, law, and judgment. He has to be more than spiritual and moral ideals; it is He who determines the norms by which humans must live and rewards and punishes them according to their deeds. If God determines human behavior, what is the point in praying to Him? If He leaves loopholes, should not the worshiper try to affect His response?

Kaplan's problem is no less acute. If God is a process and not a Being, what is the aim of prayer? This is an ancient issue. Many of the Sages fought anthropomorphism. They expressed their concern about describing God in human terms in the oft-used *kiveyakhol* (as it were) or "the Torah speaks in human language." God's incorporeity is one of the thirteen principles of Jewish belief formulated by Rambam. Yet Kaplan, as we have seen, sought to experience God directly through prayer. What does he mean by direct experience of a non-corporeal existent? He can give us only a hint. Man, he writes repeatedly, is impelled by the cosmic orderly process of which he is a part to seek fulfillment. His ambition is not only to live but to live abundantly. Prayer, then, is one of the ways by which he tries to expand his horizons, to locate the meaning of his destiny and the sources of his salvation, and to gain the confidence and courage to continue his struggle to implement these hopes. Prayer is one of the best ways for men to match wants and needs—to ensure that they want what they should and not merely what they fancy. In prayer, man employs transcendent criteria by which he learns to judge the sanctity and the moral worth of his behavior. At this point, Kaplan warns against the propensity of some thinkers to identify ideals themselves as God. He cautions against this propensity, which is manifest, for example, in John Dewey's *A Common Faith*. Kaplan states:

> The purpose in the various attempts to reinterpret the God idea is not to resolve [sic] the god idea into ethics. It is to identify those experiences which should represent for us the actual working of what we understand by the conception of God. Without the actual awareness of His presence, experienced as beatitude and inner illumination, we are likely to be content with the humanistic interpretation of life. But this interpretation is inadequate, because it fails to express and to foster the feeling that man's ethical aspirations are part of a cosmic urge, by obeying which man makes himself at home in the universe.[33]

Kaplan seeks to avoid subjectivity. Postulating that man's salvation is conditioned by cosmic forces which he did not create but which, to some extent he can control and appropriate, Kaplan searches for the best ways of identifying the constructive and destructive elements among them. But objective identification of these forces can never be absolute. Man must always sharpen his power of perception and his ability to understand. In prayer, man affirms what to him appears certain and acceptable as expressions of transcendent truth. Therefore, when science and advanced thinking alter man's image of nature and of himself, honesty requires that the affirmations of prayer be brought into line. Thus, most of the work of reason in worship should be done before the congregation gathers to pray. In order for the worshiper to experience God, he or she must be able to believe sincerely in the intellectual content and truth of the prayers and to implement their message. If they bespeak ideas or values that fail to match humankind's values or conception of life, the worshipers will be unable to find the satisfaction they seek.

Why does an individual need congregational worship? In the light of what has been said, would it not be more logical for the worshiper to pray alone and articulate his or her own beliefs? Kaplan replies: "There are people who in the strength of their ego-consciousness are loath to submit to the experience of being depersonalized or deindividualized. . . ."[34] However, to feel God's presence, a person has to transcend his or her limited consciousness. Personal religion is part of the rhythm of life, but if a person exaggerates his or her self-isolation, that individual will eventually succumb to "pessimism and world-weariness."[35] Group worship, on the other hand, connects people with their neighbors and their spiritual horizons and deters them from stationing themselves at the center of the universe. Furthermore, communal worship adds to the experience of all persons. They can relate to the wisdom of their ancestors and acquire the distilled values and aspirations of generations of collective search.

Kook and Kaplan argued that public and group expression of religious sentiments is a human need, especially of mentally mature persons. As Kaplan phrased it, "The greater one's mental development, the more subject one is to contradictory tendencies, and the more susceptible to mutually exclusive influences. The more intelligent a man is, the more likely is he to be engaged continually in making peace between reason and impulse."[36] No one is exempt from this complex. However, most people adopt the accepted ideas and values of their society and only occasionally are challenged to choose between conflicting notions. On those occasions, says Kaplan,

> [it] should not be difficult for us to understand . . . how public worship acts as an antidote to the strain of self-consciousness, how it recharges, as it were, the spent energies of the world-weary and depressed. It resolves the conflict between reason and impulse by enabling us so to identify ourselves with those with whom we worship in common that we absorb their experiences, their needs and their interests. This tends to restore our mental balance, because it necessarily weakens the onset of our selfish urges. *To be united with a community in a spirit of religious devotion is to be united with it in a spirit of love.*[37] (Italics, MMK)

Moreover, it is human nature to have others share our sorrows and joys. While we know that others cannot feel the same pain

that we do, we are comforted by their empathy. Similarly, although we do not expect others to be joyous in the same way
that we are at certain moments, we often prefer not to relish our
happiness alone. We need to share it with loved ones. This is one
of the characteristics of group worship. The *minyan* (quorum) for
prayer is composed of persons whose moods vary. Even if the
group is brought together by accident, each person knows that he
or she needs others to carry out the *mitzvah* of Jewish worship.
At the same time, each one is conscious that other worshipers,
whose moods vary, look to him or her for support. Communal
prayer, then, is seen by both men and women as an excellent
means of broadening human perspectives while also attending to
individual needs.

Kaplan concludes that prayer alone cannot raise our moral state.
Prayer has to be preceded by preparation of the heart and followed by implementation of its dictates.

> No notion has been so prevalent and so misleading as the one that
> the mere act of worship has a spiritualizing effect on the human
> being. Before worship can have any genuine spiritual influence
> upon us, before it can reveal God to us, we must qualify ourselves
> by an arduous discipline in deeds of self-control, honesty, courage
> and kindness. When we come to the synagogue, after having tried
> our utmost to deal fairly with our neighbor, to suppress our evil
> impulses, and have made an effort to meet our responsibilities as
> human beings, then worship can yield its measure of spiritual
> strength and give us a sense of inward peace. Communion with
> God is a reward of holy and righteous living.[38]

CONCLUSION

The trauma suffered by our ancestors when the Temple was destroyed lasted for hundreds of years. Most of our people, in the
course of time, adjusted to the new situation and found a substitute for the sacrificial system. Nonetheless, the nation as a whole
continued to mourn the destruction. To this day, there are Jews
who pray seriously for the rebuilding of the Temple and the restoration of its cult. But for most Jews, including those who still
utter the prayers of restoration, the petition is merely a symbol of

past glory. They do not intend to replace the "prayer of the heart" with animal sacrifices.

We have reached a crossroads. Jews who regularly worship in the synagogue are a small minority. The crowded sanctuaries on the Days of Awe indicate only that many Jews want to retain contact with the tradition and with other Jews. They do not deem prayer to be an essential part of their lives. In this, Jews are no different from the communicants of other religions who have accepted the foundations of modern culture. Only a few thinkers of the caliber of Kook and Kaplan have had the ability to see the issue of prayer in its full complexity—theological, emotional, psychological, intellectual, and esthetic. They not only want to preserve the tradition but also to prevent it from becoming mindless, lacking feeling and enthusiasm, and blind to the dynamism of life. At this point, Kook and Kaplan part company. Whereas Kook did not contemplate adjusting the liturgy to the new realities, Kaplan made every effort to achieve coherence between what a contemporary Jew believes and should believe and the words he or she utters in prayer. Both men succeeded in attracting thousands of disciples and in passing their ideas on to the next generation, but this represents only a small minority of Jews. Among that minority are to be found disciples to whom the words of their teacher have become mere habit.

One thing is certain. To survive the current crisis in prayer, the Jewish people, like all others, will have to be led by men and women of faith and spirituality, who will have the courage to speak out. Equally as important as their philosophies were the personal examples set by Kook and Kaplan. To them prayer was a challenge they could not ignore. It will be left to future generations to decide which of the two ways of thinking and behaving will capture the hearts of the people. Until the die is cast, it behooves all of us to study both visions carefully.

NOTES

1. *Sabbath Prayerbook* (New York: Society for the Advancement of Judaism, 5726, p. 391).

2. OR, Vol. 1, Introduction, p. 15. Kook wrestles with the problem

of divine attributes. In one astounding passage, he writes: "There is no harm in denying will to God, because it is a limited attribute. But necessity is even more restricted or at least not less so than the will. Therefore, we should seek an attribute that is superior to each of these and is, by its nature, ineffable. Similarly, there is no harm in renouncing God's intention. But accident surely is not an aspect of divinity; it is insignificant and weak, as compared with will and intention. Obviously, though, we find intense interest in the combined concepts of accident and purpose, because they together cause the activity of being, which is necessarily revealed by God" (AT, p. 30).

3. OR, Vol. 1, p. 15.

4. Ibid. See also AT, 75–76. "The prayer of the righteous converts God's anger to His attribute of mercy. Philosophy cannot grasp the lack of change in God's will. It cannot rise to the level of explanation of how God contains in His essence all the changes in His will, so to speak. All these metamorphoses are implanted in the very essence of God's unity, in eternal contrast to the active will of man as he turns to God. . . ."

5. Here Kook expresses the common Rabbinic strategy of "as if." See the essay by Gilbert S. Rosenthal, "As-If Theology and Liberal Judaism," *Conservative Judaism*, Vol. 39, No. 1, Fall 1986, pp. 34–35.

6. *The Kozari*, Essay 1:2.

7. MG, p. 244.

8. OR, Vol. 1, "Matters of Prayer," p. 11.

9. Ibid.

10. Ibid., p. 15.

11. Ibid., p. 251

12. *Orot Teshuvah—Lights of Return* (henceforth, OT), with commentary and notes by Yaakov Halevi Filver (Jerusalem, 5737, 4:1, p. 20).

13. Ibid., 4:2, pp. 22–23.

14. OR, Vol. 1, p. 15. Still, Kook does not fully penetrate the dynamic relationship between reason and emotion. Let us ask ourselves why we need these two components of consciousness in prayer. The impulse to pray can come from either or both sources. Most frequently, private prayer is motivated by a personal, emotion-filled experience. The person is happy, sad, worried, angry, afraid, and so forth, and he or she must bare his or her soul before God. On such occasions, a person wants to avoid having emotion result in an irrational reaction, like self-pity, self-importance, or other forms of ill-advised self-perception. Similarly, the honest worshiper wants to avoid feelings of hate or envy. A reasonable person will not permit blind emotion to dictate his or her conduct. The worshiper wants to tie his or her emotions to worthy purposes that can be justified, morally, spiritually, and psychologically.

15. Ibid.

16. Jacob B. Agus writes: "In common with nearly all other great mystics, he insists that the mystical experience is unique and ineffable, so radically different from the normal course of events as not to be expressible in the medium of common speech. Silence alone does justice to the sacred intensity of mystical ecstasy" (*Banner of Jerusalem*, p. 129). Nonetheless, Kook is certain that the mystical calls he hears come from the realm of God's transcendence.

17. OR, Vol. 1, p. 19.

18. Ibid., p. 20.

19. Ibid., p. 71.

20. Ibid., pp. 71–72.

21. Ibid., p. 21.

22. Ibid., p. 28.

23. Ibid., p. 30.

24. *Orot*, p. 120.

25. Ibid., p. 119. See the passage cited above from MG, p. 244. I also recommend the article by David Blumenthal, "On Being a Rationalist and a Mystic," in *The Reconstructionist*, September 1987. Blumenthal demonstrates that Maimonides' rationalism contained a goodly measure of mysticism. He declares that we have to rid our minds of the dichotomy between spirit and reason. Kaplan is often accused of being a dry rationalist, but, says Blumenthal, a person's dedication to reason does not necessarily imply that he is uninterested in or assigns no importance to spirituality.

26. MG, 244. Similarly, Kook writes: "[I]t is our great duty to seek out the holy aspects of our various experiences in life. . . ."(cited in MR, p. 412).

27. MG, p. 33.

28. *Sabbath Prayerbook* (New York: Bloch, 1948, pp. 532–533).

29. MG, p. 33.

30. Ibid.

31. My friend, Rabbi Harold Schulweis, who rejects the doctrine of Israel's election, nevertheless tries to provide a sophisticated justification for retaining the phrase "between Israel and the nations" in the *Havdalah* prayer. Differences between peoples are natural and positive. "Israel and the nations are not the same; the attempt to reduce them to one sameness is a disservice to each. Israel and the nations have chosen to enter different, at times overlapping, covenants, each with wisdom and truths, each blessed by God. . . . *Havdalah*-wisdom separates in order to unite. Without separation there can be no true integration" ("*Havdalah:* the Jewish Wisdom of Separation," *The Reconstructionist*, September–

October 1989, p. 20). Schulweis is correct in pointing to the variety and uniqueness that characterize the phenomena of existence and make them so interesting. But between this natural separation and the idea of election—which involves a conscious act of God—there is an abyss. See the chapter on election.

32. MG, pp. 55–56. In truth, the will of God, as Kaplan sees it, is the inexhaustible number of possibilities in the conduct of the cosmos. A sick person, for example, can live or die, but the determination of the outcome is made not by an arbitrary or unknown decision of a supernatural power, but by a combination of orderly natural circumstances, the knowledge and skills or lack of them of doctors, the availability of medicines, the psychic state of the person, and the like. A prayer for health should be designed to strengthen the will of all who are involved in the treatment of an illness to contribute their share to the proper and complete use of the curative forces in nature and in man. If the patient dies despite sincere effort, all parties should understand that the outcome is not a manifestation of divine judgment or the desire of God to cause suffering or sorrow. I remind the reader that the choice is between the immanent supernatural God of Kook and the immanent-transcendent God of Kaplan. The first is willful, punishing, or favoring with grace, often in ways that seem arbitrary to man. The second appears in the transcendent order in which the affairs of the cosmos take place. This alternative is a rejection of God as a conscious, thinking Being, but it renders unnecessary the need to try and justify natural evil.

33. Ibid., pp. 244–245.

34. Ibid., p. 251.

35. Ibid., p. 252.

36. Ibid., p. 255.

37. Ibid., p. 256.

38. Ibid., p. 252.

7
Teshuvah

FASCINATION with time leaves people no rest. They want to explore its roots in their past, in that of their families, and in the history of their people. Nor can they escape the vicissitudes and challenges of the present or relinquish the urge to fulfill aspirations for the future. There are those who are tied to the past, as if the present and future are irrelevant; others are mired in the present and are oblivious to the past and future. Still others face forward but have no interest in the influence of the past and present on the days to come.

TESHUVAH AND COSMIC REPAIR

The Ari, the Kabbalist Isaac Luria, taught that the cosmic process began with God's self-contraction, continued with the "breaking of the vessels," and will conclude with the successful outcome of *tikkun* (repair) and the restoration of God's unity. "By means of *teshuvah* (repentance), everything returns to God; by virtue of the power of *teshuvah* that reigns in all the galaxies, everything reconnects with the full, divine reality."[1] This is the kabbalistic basis of Kook's dialectical outlook. The human race is obligated to mend that which was distorted by God's free and ineffable decision to create the universe out of Himself. Humans can delay or facilitate the process of repair. In this perspective, return is a complicated act. It is not merely the expression of regret for past sins. Kook, who sensed the complications, acknowledges that while the subject consumed him for many years, he procrastinated in publishing his ideas. In the opening remarks to *Lights of Return*, he testifies that he struggled with his conscience, asking himself whether he was worthy enough to speak about the subject. In the end, the force of his concern and his inner urge and confidence that he had something important to say overcame his reticence.

Kook presents an unusual phenomenology of *teshuvah* as a cosmic process. He suggests that there are three aspects or types of *teshuvah*—natural; that which has its roots in religious consciousness; and intellectual or rational. This division is based on Kook's assumption that return is a universal phenomenon, a part of the process of cosmic repair.[2]

Teshuvah typifies the ideal movement of the cosmos; instead of a creative thrust forward toward an uncharted future, it glances backward toward a primeval perfection. This vision applies not only to mending the universe at large but also to restoring humanity, which has disobeyed the laws of nature that cause bodily and psychic illness. *Teshuvah* is essential to health, and Kook calls this type of return physical or natural. He considers the violation of physical laws to be no less sinful than the suborning of moral law. Both are sins against God as well as against man.

While natural *teshuvah* is inherent in humans as creatures of God,[3] the second type, which Kook calls *emunit*, is founded on religious sensibility. Such repentance supplements natural return, for, as the Sages believed, he who performs a *mitzvah* concerning which he has been commanded is superior to him who does so for its own sake or for some spiritual or moral satisfaction or relief. This *teshuvah* has been introduced to humankind by Jewish religious tradition.

The third and highest type of *teshuvah* is rational. A person repents when he or she understands its inherent value—in the spirit of serving the Master without expectation of reward. In this context, a person behaves out of a "clear understanding that stems from a complete philosophy of life and that comes to the fore after the natural and the religious forms of *teshuvah* have left their imprint."[4] Kook's distinction between rational and religious *teshuvah* is somewhat ambiguous. Religious repentance is performed for the sake of doing a *mitzvah*. Is this repentance not for its own sake? Rational repentance is done when a man or woman sees the inherent worth of his or her act. Here, too, is a *mitzvah lishmah*, for its own sake. But this blurring should not deflect us from Kook's main point, which is that no return is possible without the strenuous engagement of the entire expertise of the soul.

Kook addresses the differences in the speed of repentance. Sometimes people have a sudden urge to do *teshuvah*. At times, they can complete all the steps of return in a fraction of a second. In a flash, they discover their sins, confess them, behave as they should, and vow never to repeat their misdeeds. Generally, however, repentance occurs much more gradually. These diverse reactions characterize both individuals and groups. There are many paths in *teshuvah,* some of which are difficult or hazardous. Frequently, we hide the sin or sins for which we must repent by defensive repression or simply by unawareness. Of course, repentance is easier when we know our sins, but every person has moments when "his mind is sealed, when he wanders away from the straight path into undesirable behavior . . . his intellect becomes coarse, his feeling becomes melancholy, and he thirsts for that which only arouses spiritual nausea. His soul withers; he realises that there is no God within him."[5]

Thus, sometimes return has to be undertaken without realizing the nature of our guilt. However, pinpointing the sin is not the major consideration. More important is the determination to return to Torah and honest faith. It is this return that enables us to overcome our depression.[6] We then feel that all our misdeeds, even those we have been unable to identify, have been erased. We are new beings. Kook has hit upon a psychological fact; we need not recall all our mistakes or sins to live positively, but we must have an ever alert conscience. If *teshuvah* can accomplish this purpose, it should be cultivated.

As stated, Kook believes that atonement even operates subconsciously, pushing the entire cosmos toward God. Kook calls this process of overcoming natural faults and evils *general teshuvah,* as opposed to *private return.* The latter includes the need to atone for both individual sins and the sins of society as a whole. All human culture requires and is subject to the impact of the cosmic spirit of holinesss that impels it toward unity. But in addition to the underlying movement of existence, repentance has to involve each individual's active will for goodness. This will sprouts from each person's knowledge of the ways of nature and history. The subjectivity of the will must be tempered by a sense of reality. Only in the context of a respect for fact can repentance be successful. Willingness to accept this authority "supplies a necessary supplement to man's complete freedom. Man is so free that he is able to subject himself wherever necessary and become a slave, when that slavery is the true freedom."[7] "The force and depth of emotion empower necessity over desire. Only that desire, which is exalted and noble and possesses the qualities of necessity, is complete and steadfast. Therefore, it must step beyond necessity."[8] The human will does not function in a vacuum. Consequently, it behooves each person to choose his or her actions on the basis of the knowledge of fact, or, as Kook states, necessity. *Teshuvah*, as an act of choice, must also be founded on knowledge and not on the emotionally driven will.

When an individual does *teshuvah*, he or she joins and strengthens a cosmic process of fixed order and contributes to the repair and return of the All. This organic approach befits Kook's nationalistic ideology. Israel's vocation is to effectuate universal *tikkun*. Each Jew, therefore, must see himself or herself as a link in the chain that binds the Jewish people, humankind, and the entire universe. Each person's act is decisive in the process of cosmic redemption or damnation.

Return is accomplished through cooperation between body and mind, on the order of "a sound mind in a healthy body."[9] However, physical and mental perfection is never static. The world is always in flux, and the body and mind constantly face new and disrupting challenges. There is always a need for self-correction. *Teshuvah* helps us to avoid being swept along by the stream of habit, which, for Kook, often carries the flotsam and jetsam of error and sin. These are the inevitable consequences of a departure from the way of Torah. Is not the fear of the Lord evidence of the pure and stable soul (Ps. 19, 10)? Nonetheless, Kook dares to indicate a serious impediment that can sometimes block the road to *teshuvah*:

> The world does not stand still; it continues to develop. . . . Stubborn adherence to a sinful habit, either in idea or practice, is a disease bordering on tortuous slavery, which prevents the light of return from shining brightly. For *teshuvah* aims at full and unique freedom, that of God, in which there is no enslavement.[10]

Kook embraces the two worlds as if they were one. He accepts evolution but finds its roots already embedded in Torah and, most particularly, in toraitic secrets.[11] Loyal Jews know how to adjust to a changing world, even as they remain steadfast in the halakhic realm. Kook's originality as a halakhist lies in the broad perspective through which he observes the world. Anyone who accepts his premises will have no difficulty in seeing the need for constant *teshuvah*. Not so Jews who stubbornly reject what they consider to be outmoded ideas or practices of the Jewish heritage. They will not agree that they are blindly obstinate or insolent, or that they hold firmly to "the ropes of sin." They look upon Kook and other halakhists as incapable of adjusting Judaism to the new reality.

Despite Kook's declaration that *teshuvah* is universal and innate in man, he attributes to the soul and heritage of the Jewish people qualities that are unknown or less potent in other nations. "The moral world of Israel is broader and attached to the 613 *mitzvot*."[12] Non-Jews have been given only the seven Noahide laws, the laws given to the sons of Noah. As a result, they feel neither the moral burden nor the impulse and need to study and engage in *teshuvah* in depth. Furthermore, Israel's strong sense of responsibility paradoxically increases the number of temptations that are apt to boost the destructive influence of the Evil Impulse and to lure the people away from the path of Torah. If it were not for the special quality of the Jewish soul, the outcome of the struggle would be disastrous. But Israel's bent for morality can never be ended. Such is the nature of its soul. For this reason, the door of return is never locked to the Jewish people. In the end, the "holy nation" will accomplish its mission and bring all creatures to complete repentance and harmony. While the wicked are lost in confusion and frustration, Israel's strong will, functioning with the power of Jewish morality, will remove the distortions in thought and deed of all people. Jewish repentence, individually and collectively, has significance for the entire cosmos.

The great asset, *teshuvah*, exacts a price. Although every healthy human being fears sin, the sensitivity of the people of Israel is greater. Other peoples avoid sin and do penance mainly out of fear of punishment. Jews are concerned principally with evil itself and the need to uproot it from their character. It is no wonder, then, that the fear of sin among Jews parallels the details about it contained in the Torah, as set forth in the long lists of misdeeds to which humans are prone. "An ignorant person cannot be sin-fearing" (M. Avot, 2:6). Ignorant here means lacking knowledge of Torah, for the Torah instructs us as to the permitted and forbidden. In summary, Jewish return is conditioned by a combination of genetic inheritance and inherited culture.

Nonetheless, Israel's election cannot hide the fact that there are disturbances "in the tents of Shem" (in Jewish ranks). Kook's discerning eyes observe the faults that need correction. "It is impossible for anyone to be attached to the truth of Israel's nationhood unless his soul has been purified through *teshuvah* of his deplorable sins and unworthy qualities, or unless his soul was pure from the outset."[13] Israel's pure soul is always potentially available, but it is often soiled by the sins of many Jewish men and women. Therefore, *teshuvah* must become widespread and elicit the spiritual truth that is buried in Jewish nationhood. Kook sees this truth in Israel's devotion to God and its ethic of justice, which differentiate it from all other nations. It is in Israel alone that

> [t]he proclamation of God . . . as the Lord of the universe, the preserver of the Covenant and loving-kindness and all the paths of justice (all of which are God's attributes) becomes the foundation of its national life and the prerequisite for the establishment of its government on its land. . . . Therefore, whoever, in theory and more so in practice, weakens the idea that sustains the nation, is a traitor. . . . No other nation in the world is by its nature tied to a total faith in the knowledge that God is in its midst.[14]

Such a passage enables us to understand why Kook was opposed to denuding Zionism of religious content and why he was so exacting in his demands for return. Despite his chauvinistic theory, he did not regard Jews as paragons of virtue. Jewish sinners are legion.

Kook tries to exact a measure of good even from evil.[15] He is unable, however, to explain how we can distinguish between good and evil, except where that distinction is set forth in traditional law or, in many instances, where it is self-evident. Where the law is ambiguous, Kook undoubtedly relies on halakhic debate to resolve the issue. In any case, the penitent must never surrender to influences that might weaken his or her resolve to fight against sin.

Sin destroys harmony and completeness and "sunders the ideal unity."[16] The soul operates both actively and passively, and sin interferes with both operations. It prevents the soul from perceiving divine inspiration and undermines its intellectual faculty. Until *teshuvah* has done its work, Jews cannot grasp the harmony that awaits disclosure and repair. The kabbalistic myth of contraction and *tikkun* takes on a moral emphasis. Through *teshuvah*, Jews bring closer the redemption that inheres in the pristine cosmic unity and harmony. For the traditional Jew, this means the observance of the *mitzvot*, but this is too simplistic for Kook. *Teshuvah* demands a strong intellectual effort as well. For example, penitents sometimes lack understanding about the essence of good and evil. Or, when they are capable of determining their distinctive qualities, they do not know what they must do to overcome evil and achieve good. Therefore, they have to expend greater effort to define good and evil, strengthen their resolve in the face of all the barriers in their way, and/or search more assiduously for the means to implement their determination. In Kook's view, the worship of the Days of Awe, and particularly in that of Yom Kippur, is an attempt to sharpen all of these forms of action. He declares that penitents can become spiritually enervated and unable to act as a result of the effort they have to put into *teshuvah*. In the holiday of *Sukkot*, the Jewish calendar provides an escape-hatch from this danger. This Feast of Tabernacles comes to repair the debilitating effects of Rosh Hashanah and Yom Kippur on the Jewish soul. While these days exert a strong, electrifying influence by eliminating the poison that has eaten away at the Jewish soul, they also weaken its healthy vitality.[17] Sukkot, the season of joy, restores this vitality and strengthens resolve. Only then can *teshuvah* be fully enacted.

Return involves knowing the actions that a person must avoid and those that should be adopted. This involves emotion, not intellect alone. Kook speaks in turgid tones of "the spiritual satisfaction and the rational enlightenment of lofty perceptions and the clarity and powerful sanctity of a pure imagination that array the supernal understanding and embrace all of life's activities."[18]

However, when reason is absent, one tends to rely on emotional certainty. After all, the choice of values is subjective. But one can also think organically, relying on experience and observing the way that values interact and affect the solution of problems. Emotion sustains the spiritual health of the individual and the group as they examine the complex relationship between values.

Reason, on the other hand, contributes to *teshuvah* through its unending attempts to peel away layer after layer of human nature. For instance, is violence innate in humans, or is it learned? If it is genetic, what can be done to restrain it? Clearly, when *teshuvah* is undertaken with careful attention to scientific understanding of the psyche, it is different from what it is when viewed through the lenses of tradition. Kook's awareness of reality does not lead him to adopt a scientific approach to repentance, but he asserts, "[I]f the world would busy itself with Torah to the extent that would enable it to see the connection between the whole and its parts, *teshuvah* and *tikkun* would be effectuated."[19] If we interpret Torah to mean involving the exercise of all our faculties, we approach what is meant by the use of reason. In this connection, we cannot avoid the problem of the interaction between reason and morality. Is an immoral person thereby also faulty in intellect? Is a person of limited intellect capable of doing complete *teshuvah*? Kook discusses this issue thoroughly, but his most important statements on the subject are to be found in the introduction to his commentary on the *Siddur*. There he concludes that success in prayer depends on complete cooperation between reason and conscience. In Kook's dialectic, the very determination to return is itself *teshuvah*. Confession of sin is an indication of a healthy mind. Nonetheless, the whole discipline of return has to be completed before we can be certain that the partnership of reason and morality is permanent.

We mentioned above that *teshuvah* contributes to cosmic repair and the return of the All to God. In Kook's hands, his kabbalistic myth becomes a profound educational venture. *Teshuvah* is the decisive move toward *tikkun*, overcoming the fear of death and leading to ultimate union with God. By returning, the individual enters "into the general essence of the nation . . . and is absorbed from there into the overall existence of the universe. In the supernal reality, he finds his happiness—in the divine splendor, power, illumination, delight and abundant life that gush forth from eternal existence."[20] This poetic recipe undoubtedly attracts those who are convinced that the myth of *tzimtzum* is a cosmological fact and that the behavior of the individual Jew is the cornerstone of *tikkun*. Jews thus come to associate their salvation with that of the Jewish people, in keeping with the biblical vision. Salvation, in turn, is a decisive step in the direction of reversing contraction and reconstructing the absolute unity of God. In such a cosmology, the death of the individual loses its sting.[21]

Teshuvah is an endless series of thoughts and actions. Judaism, in general, attaches less importance to good intentions than it does to good deeds. The latter can be performed without intent and still elicit the reward that is attached to exemplary behavior.[22] In this spirit, Kook declares that insignificant thoughts and deeds combine to effectuate *teshuvah* because together they raise humankind to a higher and more illuminating level. This is in keeping with the idea of return as a collective enterprise. Because each person plays a role in the total configuration of *teshuvah*, he or she must not be deterred either by the smallness of the act (feeling that his or her sin is too insignificant to count) or its magnitude (arousing concern that repentance is beyond reach). *Teshuvah* is not a one-time act. Therefore, a person must seek to repair any failings observed.

Among the educational facets of *teshuvah* is the duty of the people to foster a mood of reverence, probity, truth, and wisdom, within which the will can be trained as an instrument for life and goodness. Or, in Kook's words:

> Pure intellectual integrity declares that the entire enterprise of knowledge must be directed to the ideal foundation of imparting to the will the purest countenance appropriate to it, refining, strengthening, sanctifying and purifying it by means of various educative disciplines, so that its aspirations should always be lofty and exalted. The areas of knowledge should occupy themselves with how to bring forth from the potential to the actual all the particulars toward which the upright and virtuous wills prevailing in the world strive. These particulars are the necessary components of a decent, material and spiritual life.[23]

Kook's words present a serious challenge for the modern university. Institutions of higher learning have often failed to live up to their educational responsibility. In Germany, doctors, judges, physicists, and other university graduates willingly carried out Hitler's satanic designs. Elsewhere in the world, universities deny that they bear responsibility for training morally good men and women as well as informed scientists and literate persons. They refuse to acknowledge that their obligation extends to the moral maturation of their students. In many instances when the universities do accept a moral function, the tools of implementation have not been sharpened. Kook's theory of *teshuvah* deserves a serious hearing within academic halls.

KAPLAN ON *TESHUVAH*

Like Kook, but from a rationalistic rather than a mystical point of departure, Kaplan regards *teshuvah* as a ceaseless process. He writes, "Repentance stands for nothing less than the continual remaking of human nature."[24] This sentence alone already indicates the similar foci of the two thinkers. However, whereas Kook defines *teshuvah* as a return to cosmic unity and harmony, Kaplan's vision is more modest. Return has no preordained goal. Return involves a strenuous, continuous effort at self-transformation. The change is mainly a moral one, the transformation of the penitent to a "*beriah hadashah,* a new creature, a regenerate peronality."[25] Kook and Kaplan differ in their interpretation of *beriah hadashah*. Kook conceives of the new person as one who has been restored to man's pure, pristine state. Kaplan thinks in terms of the penitent's becoming a new and hopefully better person than he or she had ever been in the past.

Kook and Kaplan agree on the question of reconciliation. Kaplan states his view as follows: "Translated into action, the doctrine of the unity of God calls for the integration of all life's purposes into a consistent pattern of thought and conduct."[26] He continues, "Religious teachers have been wont to classify sins in three categories: sins against oneself, sins against one's neighbors, and sins against God. This is all wrong. Every sin is at the same time a sin against ourselves, a sin against neighbors, and a sin against God."[27] Thus, the objective of repentance is to establish harmony among human beings and to overcome as much as possible the adverse effects of the discontinuities in nature. The situation is paradoxical. The cosmic laws that underlie natural processes supply the conditions for their order and disorder. At the same time, people must learn to apply these laws if they are to have any hope of mitigating the evils inherent in existence. Unity and disunity seem to be endemic to reality, although it is possible that humans can weight the balance in favor of unity—at least insofar as expanding the borders of their fulfillment is concerned. Humans are creatures and subject to natural forces, but they can use the regularity of these forces to their advantage. Harmony between persons is in their hands. For Kaplan, the potential for universal concord is a manifestation of God's existence. The cosmos is not just a collection of accidents. All people who violate its laws sin against themselves, their fellows, and God.

Teshuvah follows an individual's recognition of his or her share in the degree of disorder that characterizes the evolution of the cosmos. Just as people are impelled to study nature and ameliorate its ills wherever they can, so they are driven to correct their sins, their departures from physical and moral law. Kook regards Jewish tradition as adequately detailing the nature and content of sin. Kaplan, on the other hand, has to deal with two opponents—those who today speak of trespasses, blemishes, and mistakes, but not of sin, and those, like Kook, who continue to regard sin as a sacramental category.

Kaplan faces a problem of folk psychology. Modernists who worship in the synagogue do not take literally the refrain in the *Mahzor* of the Days of Awe, "Prayer, repentance and charity avert the evil decree." Most are also convinced that the annual repetition of the prayers, the confessions, the pleas for forgiveness, and the recollection of the atonement through sacrifice of Temple days produce little or no change in the character and behavior of the worshipers. Yet they are not motivated to bring the liturgy into line with their theological convictions. In liberal circles, changes are introduced, but the theological gap remains in their treatment of *teshuvah*. This psychological condition testifies to the power of traditional customs. "Such practices had the psychological effect of exorcising the dread of the terrible consequences which might have followed from some involuntary or unconscious transgression."[28] In no way does Kaplan underestimate the psychological value of cult in stimulating individuals to alter their behavior, but he maintains that attention must be paid in *teshuvah* to our new insights into human nature.

"In earliest times," Kaplan claims, "sin and repentance un-doubtedly . . . were part of the thought pattern in which holiness was conceived as the experience of a presence which called forth awe, terror, fascination, wonder and devotion."[29] In that universe of discourse, people tended to attribute to natural phenomena and important objects qualities of personality similar to their own. To make certain that these forces would work to their benefit, the ancients invented methods of conciliation.

> From generation to generation there grew by continual accretion a mass of law and precept defining which behavior was permissible and which prohibited in the presence of the holy object. To violate these laws and precepts was to offend the deity that was regarded as having enjoined them. This constituted sin.[30]

Our ancestors lived in this atmosphere for a long time. Vestiges of that era remain in the Bible, particularly in the laws of ritual purity and impurity associated with the sacrificial cult. The priests had to be extremely cautious to ensure that they and the masses who frequented the Temple precincts would be free of all blem-ish. Impurity might drive away the *Shekhinah*, God's Presence, and cause punishment to descend on priests and laity alike. To this day, the elaborate ritual of purification is recited annually on Yom Kippur, in the impressive *Avodah* service. Despite the de-struction of the Temple and the abandonment of animal sacrifices, the *Avodah* bears witness to the belief of many Jews that they must continue to adhere to the laws of ritual purity.

> The sacramental character of the atonement, i.e., its potency to nullify the effect of Israel's sinfulness through the putative influence of its ritual on God rather than through their influence on Israel directly, is evidenced in the fact that the purification of the sanctu-ary and of those who minister to it is the immediate object of the Yom Kippur ritual.[31]

In describing biblical *teshuvah* as an integral part of the Temple cult, Kaplan does not intend to cast aspersion on our Israelite ancestors. Their stage of knowledge was such that they related the evils that befell them to causes which today we would deem irrelevant. To their credit, however, even with their limited un-derstanding, they emphasized the ethical factor in repentance. Is-rael's prophets gave their people new insight into the meaning of divine holiness. Kaplan writes: *"The fear of offending God by transgressions of the moral law supplemented, and* eventually tended to supersede, the fear of offending Him by transgressions of ritual taboos. The sacramental ritual then came to be interpreted symbolically."*[32] (Italics, MMK)

In almost all spiritual transitions, the break between past and current customs and patterns of thought is not absolute. The prophets, for instance, did not call for the elimination of the Temple cult; they demanded that the cult be filled with ethical purpose. The talmudic Sages, in turn, frequently interpreted the ritual and cultic *mitzvot* as ethical symbols. "They were to be obeyed because of the influence which their observance was expected to have on one's moral attitudes; the perfunctory performance of them, without an awareness of their moral meaning, was regarded as inadequate."[33] However, precisely because of this revised view of sin as mainly a moral rather than a ritual deficiency, Yom Kippur's emphasis on atoning for sins against God more than for those against one's fellows is paradoxical. Atonement for the latter can be accomplished only when reconciliation has taken place directly between the offender and the offended. The paradox is apparent only if we remember Kaplan's assertion that sins against oneself and the other are equally sins against God. Therefore, by seeking atonement with God, we are also aiming at self-transformation. *"If the desire for absolution and restored serenity which lay behind the rites of atonement can be keenly experienced by us and symbolically expressed in a stirring ritual, it may function as an impulse to reconstruct our lives in accordance with our highest ideals."*[34] (Italics, MMK)

On the other hand, Kaplan warns against foisting moral intent on cultic practices to whose sacramental purposes it is too easy to return. There is no reason to suppose that prayers for the rebuilding of the Temple and the restoration of the sacrifices are aimed at ethical advance. No doubt, these prayers are uttered by worshipers who pay scant attention to their intent. But the effect of such mindless recitation is to distract the worshiper from what ought to be a central concern of his or her prayers—strengthening the determination to become a better person. Thus, argues Kaplan, the modern Jew should extricate the concept of sin from its age-old supernaturalistic setting. As long as sin is conceived as rebellion against a supernatural God, repentance will require that the penitent obey "revealed" laws and practices that sometimes offend his or her moral, spiritual, or esthetic sensibilities. Kaplan says:

> It is obvious, that from the point of view of ethical religion, the terms "sin" and "atonement" cannot have the same meaning as from the point of view of revelational religion. Sin can no longer mean the provocation of God's wrath through disobedience of the revealed law, nor can atonement mean the restoration to His grace by a pledge of future obedience, however sincere.[35]

Nonetheless, Kaplan believes that concepts like "sin" and *teshuvah* in their traditional sense point to human needs that have to be identified and satisfied even today. For example, the fast of the Day of Atonement symbolizes the need to retain a sense of proportion between the satisfaction of one's needs and the gratification of one's greed. When a person permits the need for food to lead to the obsession of overeating, he or she does damage to himself or herself and possibly to those who must suffer the effects of these irrational desires. The sin of the individual becomes a social blight. Sin destroys the harmony projected by human ideals that are

> the expression of life's tendency to organize itself. Life seeks to make of every organism, whether individual or social, a perfect pattern in which every part contributes to the perpetuation and enhancement of the whole, while the whole energizes every part. *This effort of life to achieve and express unity, harmony and integrity is what makes life holy; this is the evidence of the divine; whatever thwarts this tendency is sin.*[36] (Italics, MMK)

Among human needs, Kaplan gives an honored place to freedom, particularly freedom of choice. Although he acknowledges the problematic nature of such freedom, he is convinced that peace and justice are impossible unless men and women are held responsible for their decisions and actions and unless they are capable of understanding the connection between cause and effect and between an act and its consequences. Education for values should enable an individual to use his or her free intellect effectively. This implies that values should not be transmitted as fiats which the learner is expected to absorb without an opportunity for critical appraisal of their premises. A free soul is the desired product of honest, open-minded teaching. Only an extraordinary personality can stand courageously against authoritarian educators. Freedom and responsibility are unalterably tied to one another. One cannot exist without the other. A sense of responsibility leads a free person to repent for his or her misdeeds. As long as there is awareness of the destructive results of misbehavior, the desire for self-purification will increase. The circle is closed. A sense of responsibility of a free soul is an important aspect of a God-consciousness. Only one who believes that freedom and responsibility are essential links in the cosmic chain will be capable of understanding their significance and the duties they impose.

Kaplan refuses to rely on *Halakhah* alone as the basis for the distinction between good and evil conduct and its bearing on sin and repentance. Up-to-date and verified knowledge is imperative for religion, because it supplies new insights into the reasons for our actions and improved ways of doing *teshuvah*. We can no longer rely on the too facile pleas to choose life over death, blessing over curse, and good over evil, as if all of these concepts denote situations or eternal values that are clear to all of us. We have to know—or try honestly to learn—why we behave in certain ways. Before we assume the right to exact punishment from an evil doer, we have to know whether or not that person acted in full freedom and responsibility. We must also reflect on what effect punishment might have on his or her character. It follows that to remold human nature "in the interest of unity, harmony and integrity one must apply both introspection and that objective knowledge of human behavior which constitutes the science of psychology. The one without the other is doomed to failure."[37]

The human personality is not an isolated entity. It is formed out of many genetic factors and life experiences, such as family and neighborly relations, vocational involvements, economic standing, the religious and social institutions in which the individual is active, and national identity. If a person's character develops a flaw, it is clear that its correction is dependent, to some extent, on a sober appraisal and adjustment of the relevant environmental factors. For example, an alcoholic who is sincerely determined to overcome his or her weakness knows that he or she cannot succeed without medical or psychological assistance and without a radical change in lifestyle. Resolve alone is insufficient.

Despite his insistence that the latest findings of the physical and behavioral sciences be applied to religion, Kaplan gives full credence to many of the insights of ancestral tradition. Like Kook, although not to the same extent, he quotes from many classic sources and extrapolates the psychosocial wisdom from them. Effective return calls for the integration of science, which informs us as to what *can* be done, and the distilled wisdom of the humanities and religion, which instructs us as to what *should* be done to make us fully human. So that the *ought* is more than unfounded imagination, we have to unlearn our past mistakes before we can use advanced knowledge effectively.

By this time, the reader will have realized that Kook and Kaplan share areas of agreement in their perceptions of sin and repentance, despite their sharp theological conflict. This agreement stems from the common traditional roots and humanistic purposes of their thinking. Still, their differences are very significant. They present two plausible but ultimately conflicting alternatives for the contemporary Jew. Kook stakes everything on his belief that the study of Torah can reveal the full meaning of sin and how to cope with it. Kaplan calls upon Jews to expand the borders of their knowledge and competence by reaching out to every source of information available, traditional or otherwise. The quality of *teshuvah* will, of course, depend upon which of these two directions is followed. In the first instance, the path is fairly well delineated. In the second, each circumstance of penance presents a new challenge. Not only must we evaluate our deeds and misdeeds, but we must search for new ethical horizons that bespeak a hope for increasing the quantity of good in the world.[38] Thus, the distance between Kook and Kaplan regarding their hopes for a better humankind is short, but the paths of *teshuvah* that they recommend for achieving these hopes are divergent.

NOTES

1. OT, 4:2, p. 23.
2. *Teshuvah* is one of the phenomena that , according to tradition,

was prepared by God prior to the act of Creation. As Kook states, "*Teshuvah* resides in the depths of existential life, because it preceded the world. Even before sin arose, *teshuvah* was ready to deal with it" (ibid., p. 40; see also p. 44). (The translations from *Lights of Return* are my own, but I have borrowed a few phrases from the competent translation of Alter B. Z. Metzger [New York: Yeshiva University Press, 1978]. Page references are to the Hebrew edition.)

3. Ibid., p. 10. Note the sources that Filber provides to clarify Kook's analysis. His many citations, some parallel to the body of the text, are very helpful to any reader who wishes to study Kook in depth.

4. Ibid., 5:6, p. 36. Kook states that "*teshuvah* is natural to man," a thought repeated a number of times in his works.

5. Ibid., p. 18.

6. Ibid., pp. 18–19.

7. Needless to say, this statement is a double-edged sword, especially in regard to spiritual and moral issues. How does one identify the Absolute?

8. *Haggadah of Pesah* (Jerusalem: Mosad HaRav Kook, 1863, p. 25).

9. OT, 5:1, p. 33.

10. Ibid., pp. 34–36.

11. Ibid., 10:1, p. 72. "Truly perfect repentance requires exalted contemplation, ascent to the splendid world abounding in truth and holiness. This is possible only by means of preoccupation with the profundities of Torah and the divine wisdom of the esoteric universe." From this thought, we learn that Kook, like Maimonides, encouraged reflection beyond the limits of Torah. But Kook believed that the cosmic secrets are mainly to be sought in the Torah itself. God's wisdom is revealed in the pages of the Bible and in the halakhic enterprise. Reflections on nature and reality are aids in plumbing the depths of Torah. It is true that Kook emphasized that repentance cannot be complete without knowledge that necessarily extends beyond the tradition. At times, he sounded as if he believed that these extraneous sources contribute uniquely and independently to the requisite knowledge. Yet he made no effort to draw the logical conclusions from these instances. For example, he could not agree that human reason has at least as much authority as Torah. In OT 10:5, p. 75, he identifies the tools that enable humans to reach the highest realms. They are as follows: "The Torah, faith, ancestral customs, general agreement and inner probity." All these approaches and natural law are simply different ways of explaining the method and content of Torah. In Kook's conception, there can be no contradiction between the Torah and what can be gleaned with the aid of all of the foregoing instruments.

12. Ibid., 6:3, p. 42.

13. Ibid., 13:1, p. 101.

14. *Iggerot Hareiyah* (*Letters of HaRav Kook*, henceforth, KL) (Jerusalem: Mosad HaRav Kook, 5722, Vol. 1, p. 20).

15. OT, 9:5, p. 67.

16. Ibid., 9:6, p. 68.

17. Ibid., 9:10, p. 71.

18. Ibid., 10:2, p. 73.

19. AT, p. 1.

20. OT, 11:3, pp. 93–94. There are many scattered passages in which Kook discusses the universal vocation of Israel, but note OT, pp. 102–103, 120.

21. It is well to remind those who regard this mystical conception as too abstract and unconvincing that rationalism, too, has its limitations. To illustrate, Rambam's notion that it is the human race and not the individual that survives offers little comfort to the person who wants life eternal. As far as the immortality of the race is concerned, that, too, is subject to serious doubt.

22. Note the dispute on this subject in *Y. Peah* 1:16, Col. 2.

23. OT, 15:2, p. 135.

24. MG, p. 178.

25. Ibid., p. 149. Kaplan cites two sources for the idea of a new being—*Vayikra Rabbah* 29:12 and *Y. Rosh Hashanah* 3:8, p. 59, Col. 3.

26. Ibid., p. 172. For some reason, this passage was not translated by Avraham Regelson and does not appear in the Hebrew version published by Mass, Jerusalem, 1938.

27. Ibid.

28. Ibid., p. 151.

29. Ibid., p. 150.

30. Ibid., p. 151.

31. Ibid., p. 153.

32. Ibid., p. 155.

33. Ibid., p. 158.

34. Ibid., pp. 157–158.

35. Ibid., p. 161.

36. Ibid., p. 167.

37. Ibid., p. 169.

38. Compare Kook's assertion that "[a]ll thought of repentance binds the past to the future, and the future arises as the will rises in love" (AT, p. 41). I believe that the point of conflict between Kook and Kaplan is that while Kook wants the cosmos to return to its state before Creation, Kaplan wants a future of endless growth and expanding horizons.

8
Values

MUCH INK has been spilled over the discussion of values. Each dictionary has a sizable list of definitions for the word "value," a sure sign that disagreement is bound to occur when any attempt is made to determine its place in human affairs. For instance, the reputable *Chambers Twentieth Century Dictionary* lists, among others, the following definitions: "worth; fair equivalent; intrinsic worth or goodness; recognition of such worth; that which renders anything useful or estimable; relative worth; high worth; esteem; excellence; precise meaning."[1] The term is open to different and opposite interpretations. Yet it is unimaginable that people could live without values or that a society could exist without common criteria of behavior for all its members.

The matter becomes more complicated when we deal with so-called *Jewish* values. Is it legitimate to speak of Jewish values? Is it possible to speak of a Jewish expression for universal values? Do values lose their universality when they are said to express the spirit of a particular society? Do we have the right to speak of values that are uniquely Jewish or that are found in greater measure among Jews than among other peoples?

Kook and Kaplan took these questions seriously. Their dispute should cast light on the sharpness of the debate among Jews about values in general and Jewish values in particular. In this short treatment, it is impossible to touch on the many values considered by the two men. Thus, I have chosen to concentrate only on their reflections on holiness, love, and justice. The choice is somewhat arbitrary, although these values are undoubtedly central concerns in the thinking of both men.

HOLINESS

In his great work, *Orot Hakodesh (Lights of Holiness)*, Kook writes:

There are a profane world and one of holiness, secular worlds and holy worlds. These worlds contradict one another. Naturally, the contradiction is subjective. Man's limited grasp cannot explain the difference between the holy and the profane or soften their contradictions that are resolved only in the supernal world, in the abode of the Holy of Holies.[2]

Profane and holy are conceived relatively. The one objective holiness is that of God, which human beings can grasp only to a limited extent. If Kook were to rest his case here, his thinking would be threatening to Orthodoxy. However, he does not define holiness as that which is declared such by humans. The holy is to be found in the many *mitzvot* that are set forth in the Written and Oral Law; in the Sabbath and other holy days; in the study of the Bible, Talmud, and other classic texts; in the sanctification of God's Name; and in the laws of family purity and of diet. These and their like belong to the realm of holiness. Subjectivity might enter in regard to the details of interpretation or observance, but in and of themselves, the *mitzvot* express God's will and the truth of His revelation. Nevertheless, despite the sanctity of the words of Scripture, which are particularly defined in the *Halakhah*, Kook asserts that there is another realm of sacred meaning in the esoteric aspects of Torah. Holiness, so to speak, expands and deepens as a person approaches closer to union with God. In this connection, Kook obviously distinguishes between the perception of holiness on the part of the masses and "the ascent in discernment of talented men of spirit."[3] Holiness is thus a positive, objective category. People need holiness, which is the collection of transcendent values beyond the material world.[4] Sanctity, in turn, is in need of people. The universe suffers from the damage caused by God's contraction and the consequent dispersion of the destructive sparks. People, and particularly the Jewish people, must bring about "a reversal of everything to complete, absolute holiness by means of gradual, uninterrupted acts of loving-kindness, peace, judgment, truth and mercy."[5] Kook called these works the lofty vocation of the soul. Despite his mystical approach, Kook is realistic. He avoids simplistic inferences. He even warns:

> Let us not lose sight of the great need to provide a firm foundation for the proper organisation of body and soul; that is to say, the divine, noble, ideal, supernal holiness must have some connection with profane spirituality. The latter, in turn, must relate to bodily

principles. The unification of all the forces is the foundation of the entire structure.[6]

Kook emphasizes this dialectical approach in his effort to establish a bridge between the sacred and the profane, between spirit and matter, between soul and body. It is evident in his encouragement of spiritual adventure.

> Whoever does not range over vast spaces and does not search sincerely for truth and goodness, suffers no spiritual disturbances; but neither does he engage in independent ventures. He takes cover in the shadow of natural structures, like rabbits who find shelter beneath the rocks. But one who has the soul of a real man, who does not cease his diligent efforts, seeks protection only in what his own spirit has built.[7]

Kook's observation requires explanation. Undoubtedly, his remark angers Jewish Fundamentalists who believe that the instruments of the Torah suffice to fashion the character of the devoted Jew. What does Kook mean by ranging over wide areas? Where should a daring person search? What are the borders of permissible reflection? What is to be the fate of conclusions that challenge basic principles of the *Halakhah*? How can danger be avoided if the chains that link the Jew to the "natural structures" of Torah are loosened? And what will the independent structures of the seeker look like? These questions concern those on Kook's left and right. Conceivably, his daring approach could lead one far from the halakhic path. At the same time, reformers might ask why Kook stops at the border of such a conclusion. Why is his writing so ambivalent? Is he convinced that his adventurism is no threat to the halakhically accepted notion of holiness? Does Kook believe that as long as a person observes the physical world honestly and piercingly, it will appear clothed with sanctity? Does an honest look at reality lead to the *Halakhah*?

Kook was protected from the disturbing implications of his position by his belief in the perfect light and goodness of the Torah. He was confident of his intellect's ability to navigate safely through the waters of the tradition, for they are the channels to transcendent truth.[8] The toraitic sea is broad and deep and lends itself to many different routes of travel. The breadth and profundity of Kook's journey were amazing. However, when Kook called on his fellows to build "independent structures," despite the risk of such ventures, he was thinking only of initiatives within the Torah itself and not beyond its precincts. He identified intellectual and moral integrity with obedience to God's word. In such honesty, there is no room for skepticism about the literal truth of the Torah. Kook did not budge from the premise that neither God nor the devoted Jew would ever revise the sacred Law (lo yamir dato). Holiness is not subject to human evaluation except in regard to its application to life situations. And such steps have to be taken according to directives of the divine Oral Law. Holiness begins with the acceptance of "the heavenly burden," the authority of Torah. Acceptance has to be spelled out in observance of the mitzvot. Logic, despite its importance for an ordered life, has its place only in this toraitic setting. Persons like Kook undoubtedly find peace in this type of holiness and reject any action that would breach its borders.

Kaplan, of course, sees holiness differently. For him, conferring the designation "holy" on any phenomenon is a human act of a peculiar kind. He argues:

> Ratiocination plays a minor part in collective religion; emotion and collation practically monopolize the whole of it. The God-idea in every collective religion functions not as an intellectual assent to a proposition, but as an organic acceptance of certain elements in the life and environment of the group, or of reality as a whole in its relation to the group, as contributing to one's self-fulfillment or salvation. Such organic acceptance is articulated in the adjective "holy" which is applied to whatever object is accepted in this spirit.[9]

Thus, holiness is viewed as a quality of social existence. Although it is designated by the individual, it is conditioned by the cultural development of each people.

Kaplan turns to anthropology and psychology as aids in formulating his idea of holiness. According to him, before people developed conceptions of God, they identified inanimate objects and living things, places, and persons in their environment that were instrumental in satisfying their needs. They attributed to these phenomena power that could be harnessed if they adhered to certain forms of action. Today, we call these acts magic. In the course of time, the acts became group customs and traditions, and the people related to them in awe. With this development, "the notion of godhood began to emerge, for *psychologically, the notion of godhood is the precipitate of the notion of holiness.*"[10] (Italics, MMK) Later, the "holy" was expanded to include laws, social relations, truths, and ideals.

Kaplan disagrees that the national sancta are gifts from God, but he nonetheless attributes a degree of objectivity to them, even though they are human inventions. The identification of certain forces as life-serving is based on accumulated human experience in assessing causes and effects. The differences between modern science and the certainties and theories of the past can largely be explained by the greater information available to later generations. For this reason, objectivity is never certain. Rather, it is an intellectual mood that posits the inability of mortals to achieve knowledge of absolute truth; human experience and reach are too limited. Nevertheless, human beings are obligated to reject ideas they cannot believe and practices they deplore. Kaplan maintains, "[T]here are moments in every person's life, no matter how prosaic or matter of fact, when 'holy' is the only word that can adequately express what he feels about certain persons, things or ideals."[11] Life is a continuum on which the term "holy," as we have said, is applied to the cosmic force or forces that are thought to make human redemption possible. However, since we are the measures of that power or those powers, the definitions of the "holy" must always have a high degree of subjectivity. This should neither surprise us nor cause us to eliminate it as an important category of our consciousness. Whether we define the "holy" as a reference to a supernatural God or as an immanent process of some kind, the "holy" symbolizes the fact that our redemption must ultimately be conditioned by forces we must obey.

Ever since people began to perceive the connection between the holy and God, they have envisaged the former as any act that reduces the distance between themselves and Deity. Jewish tradition sees the cultic and moral *mitzvot* as the way of holiness. This was the thrust of the command that Israel be a holy people and a priestly commonwealth. Despite Kaplan's opposition to the idea that the *mitzvot* are divinely revealed and his rejection of

Israel's election, he pleads, no less than does Kook, for a moral national vocation. Our people, which was the first to dedicate itself to seeking the knowledge of God and to implementing God's purpose for the human race, must respond willingly to the ancestral call to always live according to the highest norms of law and justice. The content of these values is likely to change over time, but the tendency will remain to judge phenomena in terms of their importance for the maturation of humankind.

Kook does not pursue his view that the sacred and the profane are relative to our limited understanding to its logical conclusion that Jewish tradition might not hold the only key to God's will or to the identification of the holy. Kaplan agrees that the holy is rooted in an orderly, commanding reality, but he denies that the apprehension of this holiness has been perfectly achieved in the toraitic heritage. By all means, he says, let us examine all of the classic texts; but not all that is holy is to be found in them, and not all that they disclose is to be considered holy. Fundamentalists deem this position to be heresy. However, Kaplan accepts only those aspects of rabbinic thought and practice that accord with universally approved standards of intellect and moral judgment. Many such standards have accumulated since the heyday of the Tannaim and Amoraim and their scholarly successors. The current debate in the Jewish world is between two schools. The school of which Kook is a leading figure argues that there is no need to alter any of the principles underlying halakhic Judaism. The second, composed of Kaplan and all his followers, believes that the continuity and spiritual integrity of the Jewish people can be maintained only in the midst of constant and sometimes radical change.

Despite the abyss between himself and Orthodoxy, Kaplan sought to find a basis for Jewish unity in pluralism. He believed that there is enough in the constellation of Jewish sancta to preserve a high degree of Jewish commonality. Like other peoples, the Jews are bound by their common recognition of heroes, objects, places, and historic events as epitomizing important and sacred values. Jews sense that they share with other Jews a rich heritage of sancta. It might be that they do not regard some of these sancta as compelling, but they are nonetheless part of the Jewish consciousness. As long as a goodly number of Jews find a common language of holiness, their disagreements about its meaning will be for "the sake of heaven." Certainly, this is true in regard to the meaning and content of Jewish dedication to a national ethic of justice.

LOVE

Kook and Kaplan were great lovers—of God, Israel, Torah, and humankind. All of these loves stem from the feeling that we cannot live alone. We must be realistic and recognize our limitations as mortal individuals, whose fulfillment is dependent on cosmic support and the loving help of others who wish us well. In contrast to the popular Christian opinion that persisted for many centuries, which highlighted Christianity's advocacy of love as opposed to Judaism's conception of a stern God of retributive justice, Judaism has clearly regarded love as one of the cardinal values of religious faith. Kook and Kaplan thoroughly agree on this value.

Jewish tradition is replete with efforts to resolve the question as to whether God should be worshiped out of awe and fear or out of love. Rambam, for instance, summarizes Rabbinic views and states that both motivations in worship are commanded (*Hilkhot Yesodei Hatorah* 2:1). All lives contain moments of sublimity, awe, fear, helplessness, or loneliness, during which we experience a sense of utter inadequacy and unworthiness before the mighty power that guides the universe and defines the parameters of mortal destiny. At such moments, we are filled with awe or fear of God. And it is precisely then that we are called upon to transcend our psychological state and turn to God in love. On the other hand, we all have moments of joy and satisfaction when we see everything in a positive light. We tend to internalize the cosmos, as if we are the knowers, the known, and the act of knowing. We often forget that we do not control existence, and we thus render ourselves incapable of coping with the stark and dark reality that also appears before us from time to time. Hence, when we are joyful, when our hearts are filled with love of God, we are told to fear and stand in awe of Him.

Of the two *mitzvot*, tradition prefers worship of God out of love. Our mortality and the evils that befall us force us to scale spiritual heights in order to maintain our faith in the face of such challenges to our ability to love. When we succeed, we have risen to the highest stage of spirituality. Love of God marks our surrender to the hidden power and wisdom of God and indicates our willingness to obey God's laws. When we worship out of love, hope of reward is superfluous. The lover is satisfied with whatever the beloved gives and values it as eminently worthwhile. Only such a lover can transcend the many disappointments that are bound to occur in life. This spiritual level is a step higher than the grudging acceptance of life that was expressed by the majority in the previously mentioned debate between the schools of Hillel and Shammai. Those who worship God out of love affirm life unreservedly, without regard to their fulfillment.

In describing this self-effacing love, Kaplan associates it with the wish for fulfillment that drives everyone. In his opinion, man's "capacity to repent, or to remake himself, is the source of his continuing to believe in the ultimate achievement of his destiny, despite his repeated frustrations."[12] Repentance is one side of the coin of decent human relations, with forgiveness being the other side. Both virtues assume the existence of a transcendent force on whom or on which one must rely for fulfillment. If forgiveness is a quality of God, then it is our duty to imitate the Deity and forgive those who hurt us, for, "[i]n contrast with man's cardinal sin, which consists in playing the god, man's cardinal virtue consists in being Godlike. *To be Godlike is to exercise that redemptive love which expresses itself as forgiveness in such a way as to elicit penitence from the sinner.*"[13] (Italics, MMK)

Kaplan differentiates between redemptive love and erotic and possessive loves. Erotic love is part of our biological inheritance and requires no outside command. But because of its spontaneity, it has to be supervised, limited, and subject to moral and esthetic restraints. Possessive love, on the other hand, is no more than the satisfaction that a person attains from the beloved; that is to say, it is a relationship in which the other is used to satisfy a lustful passion or some other egoistic desire of the lover. Only redemptive love is true love. It is the only kind that is not spontaneous. "Though we must assume its presence deep down in our nature at its best, we have to exert our powers of mind and will to bring it forth. That is why it is the subject of divine command."[14] Just when we are angry at someone who has harmed us, we hear the warning from above: "You shall not take vengeance, or bear a grudge against any fellow Jew. You shall love your neighbor as yourself; I am the Lord, your God" (Lev. 19, 18).

Kaplan addresses the ambivalence in Jewish tradition about whether one should forgive an offender before he or she has done *teshuvah* or only after the offender has proven himself or herself. In contrast to the famous verse from Leviticus, just quoted, we note that R. Yohanan says in the name of R. Simeon ben Yehozadak, "Any scholar who does not take vengeance and does not hold a grudge is not a (true) scholar" (Yoma 23b). At the same time, the Sages seem to agree regarding revenge. They say, "Those who are insulted or shamed and do not retort in kind do so out of love and bear their pains with joy" (Yoma 23b).[15] Redemptive love is not always rewarded, but it is the only love worthy of being called Godly. Kaplan realizes how hard it is for us to refrain from avenging a hurt that has been done to us, but he argues that our ability to love is diminished whenever we succumb to hatred. The sentiment, "as He is merciful, so must you be," is what raises us above the beasts. Love of others, no less than love of God, is a stringent commandment. Without it, there can be no Kingdom of God. Kaplan writes that the redemptive power of our love "should be able to penetrate to the hidden springs of goodness beneath the hard and repellent exterior of man's selfishness, pettiness and moral insensitiveness, and by forgiveness and kindness bring that goodness to the surface."[16]

Kook broadens the area of forgiveness and adds a new, problematic note to the issue of love and hate. He writes:

> Even though love of man sometimes embraces the wicked, this in no way excludes hatred of wickedness. On the contrary, love strengthens this antipathy, for evil comes into the embrace of love by virtue of that element of the good which resides in it. Since we separate out the good for our love, our hatred is then directed toward the completely hollow wickedness that remains.[17]

This distinction between the wicked who have good in them and those who deserve our hatred is an important test of character. Similarly, redemptive love, whether of the individual or the group as a whole, is constantly being tested. Sometimes, we are disappointed at the behavior of others, even of those closest to us. We are tempted to erupt in anger and hatred. We must then be reminded that the repair of the universe depends on our ability to persist in our faith in others—when it is so easy to despair of their goodness. "I said in my *haste,* all men deceive" (Ps. 116, 11). (Italics, JJC)

In addition to intellectual preparation, we need to cultivate the virtues of kindness and empathy before we can show a capacity for redemptive love. Kaplan further states that the entire people must learn how to behave in this spirit. He knows that the act of love in international relations can be dangerous for the ingroup. If the enemy is bent on our destruction and persists in feeling hatred for us, responding with a policy of love is difficult. Is it even conceivable that any civilized nation could deal kindly with the Nazis? Applied to international relations, love becomes possible only when the nations involved share a broad base of values. Still, are hatred and animosity the only alternatives when love is impossible? Is there no middle way? Moreover, the absence of love does not imply the presence of dislike or hatred. Kaplan's analysis calls for clarification.

Both thinkers deal with love in all its manifestations as personal and collective and as national and universal. But it is faith in God that confers on love its life-giving force. R. Akiva regarded the "Song of Songs" as the most exalted expression of the love between God and Israel. In relating to this view, Kook states that only one who, at the time he breathes his last, is able in love to prolong the recital of God's unity ("Hear O Israel, the Lord is our God, the Lord is One.") is capable of "appreciating the true value of pure and natural personal love. He alone can arrange in their proper order pure, natural love, enlightened patriotism and the sacred, splendid love of God."[18] Here is how Kook describes the arrangement:

> The love of the All comes first, then love of man followed by love of Israel. The latter love embraces the All, since it is Israel's mission, in the future, to perfect all that happens. All these loves are active, to love so as to act for the good and exaltation of all. The love of God is the greatest of all loves, for it is always active and never loses

any of its essence. The heart that is filled with love of God enjoys supreme bliss.[19]

It is love of God that empowers us to love in a saving way. For Kook, as for Kaplan, love is organic; one cannot truly love except when each act of love is part of a cosmic perspective and when cosmic love is spelled out in specific relationships.

It is hard to conceive of humans without love. Kook realizes that some people are indifferent to one or more of the loves I have mentioned. They become mired in the dark areas of life. Kook regards such persons as abnormal. Healthy persons must love, for thus they were created. Nevertheless, although Kook argues that love is a cosmic process in which all individuals and nations participate, Israel is endowed with the extra love of God's gift of Torah and the *mitzvot*. Kaplan also relates the Jew's love of Torah to his or her love of the Jewish people. But these loves can be attributed to the fact that Israel and its traditions stem from life experiences. It is natural for a person to love what belongs to him or her. Kook admits that Israel has faults that have to be uprooted, but he asserts that Israel's greater capacity for love is its biological inheritance. Kaplan sees love as learned, rather than genetic. Whereas Kook cannot understand how some Jews can love the heritage without conforming to all its minutiae, Kaplan compares their reaction to that of children toward their parents. Sons and daughters can love their parents deeply without adopting their lifestyle. Similarly, love of God is consonant with rejection of certain practices and the adoption of a nontraditional set of values. Kook evidently sees *amor dei* and walking in the way of the fathers as identical, or at least as interdependent. Kaplan regards love of nation as better fostered when later generations are free from irrational restraints imposed by the elders. He advises the older generations to encourage the enrichment of Torah not only by addition but by critical reevaluation, correction, and elimination of outmoded ideas and practices. True love includes the mutual openness to criticism of both the lover and the beloved.

Because there are so many ways to love, it is not surprising that Kook should look favorably on Jews who try in their own way to implement their love of God. He mentions two main directions of love of God among Jews. One is that of the medieval

philosopher Bahya ibn Pakudah, whom Kook cites as arguing that
love of God stems from the intellectual encounter between the
divine soul of man and Torah.[20] A second direction is set in motion by what he calls the "wisdom of feeling."[21] This love, too, is
grounded with Torah, with the emphasis here being placed on
the study of *Aggadah*, which arouses the heart and its emotions.
The ways of intellect and emotion are in constant tension. However, according to Kook, both are appropriate expressions of love
of God, because they manifest complete faith in the truth of
Torah as God's Word.

No one can doubt Kook's love of God when, after reading a
passage from the Torah, he would recite the traditional words,
"Blessed are You, Eternal, our God, who has given us a Torah of
truth and implanted in us eternal life." Is it possible not to love
the One who has taught us Truth? But how does one describe
Kaplan's love of God and Torah? He, after all, sees Torah as an
evolving, changing phenomenon, as conveying only partial truth,
as often mistaken in its moral and spiritual conceptions and mis-
leading in its perceptions of reality. Here we encounter the distinction between traditionalism or orthodoxy and modernism. A
person who views the cosmos as ever-changing, developing, and
creating must regard love, too, as a process of maturation. A relationship between parents and children, which does not keep pace
with the growth of the son or daughter, the aging of the father
and mother, and the metamorphoses that normally occur in life,
is deficient in wisdom and likely to become psychologically
harmful to parents and children alike. Similarly, love of Torah is
an expression of a person who regards the ancestral legacy as a
part of his or her personality and identity. But this internalization
of tradition must not freeze one's mentality. Moreover, one must
be able to transmit the heritage to one's children with greater
understanding of its positive and negative features than that to
which one is heir. Such a person learns to love Torah as a ceaseless
search for and occasional revelation or discovery of important
truths about human destiny. Kook and Kaplan represent two different ways of approaching cosmic love.

Kook and Kaplan share a common antipathy to chauvinism,
while holding disparate views of Jewish nationalism. Kook proclaims forthrightly:

Only on a soul rich in love of man and all creatures can love of nation rest in all its nobility and grand spirituality. The narrowness which sees everything beyond the borders of the unique nation of Israel as ugly and impure is one of the terrible blights that can ruin the entire structure of spiritual goodness for whose illumination all sensitive souls eagerly strive.[22]

Philosophically, it appears that Kook is inconsistent, since he repeatedly claims that Israel has received from on high unique spiritual talents and moral virtues. He also supports the Rabbinic opinion concerning the holiness of Eretz Yisrael and the impurity of all foreign lands. Nonetheless, the fact remains that his inconsistency does not affect his humane moral nature. Everyone can rise above his abstract philosophy and transcend his blind patriotism and love for his people. Kook had no psychological difficulty in affirming his universalism without losing one iota of his nationalistic vision. This was the outcome of his profound love of all humankind.[23]

The similarity of the views of our thinkers regarding love should encourage us to have faith that dialogue between the intellectual extremes in Judaism is possible. Honest rationalists and mystics must realize the limitations of their respective outlooks and open their minds to the possibilities in the opposing position. The mystery of the universe requires every reasonable person to believe in the reality and power of all kinds of love but to beware of their excesses. The mystic and rationalist alike are called upon to prevent their love from blinding them to the faults in the objects of their attachment. A godly people can only be built on honest love. Love draws men and women together; honesty enables them to admit their respective shortcomings and to cooperate in trying to correct them.

JUSTICE

On the surface, Kook rarely seems to write about justice, but his works breathe the spirit of this value. In keeping with his *Kabbalism*, he prefers to speak of *tikkun* (repair). Everyone is expected to participate in this process. Although man's reach is short, Kook insists:

When a man can do some good, he should not be negligent but should give the matter thought. However, he should not dwell uselessly on what he knows is beyond his capacity to correct. He should remove his mind from worry that is apt to be deeply disturbing but rather refine his soul and busy himself, as best he can and with intellectual clarity, in repairing the world.[24]

Ultimately, however, Kook was skeptical about man's ability to effect very much in the way of redemption. Without Torah and divine assistance, many men and women seem to lack the ability to improve themselves.

Kook was a practical mystic. As we have noted, he believed that the observance of the *mitzvot* by all Jews would cleanse the world of wickedness and reconstruct the cosmic oneness. Justice is not an end in itself, but a means to the final redemption. However, since justice concerns the ways in which humans react to one another, its attainment is restricted by virtue of man's mortality and his limited knowledge. Earthly justice can never be absolute or eternal.

Kook usually identifies justice with goodness. Justice is mediated by good and pious individuals. The prerequisite for devotion to God is carrying out the *mitzvot*. Absent from Kook's thought is the fact that justice involves a choice between two or more options, each of which might be good in its own right. It seems to me that this problem escaped him, because he regarded justice, as he did goodness, as an absolute. It is hard to find the tension of complex moral decision-making in Kook's works. The *Halakhah* occasionally oversimplifies or ignores the moral issues that underlie some of its concerns. Consider, for example, the halakhic handling of the "ownership" of Eretz Yisrael and the relationship between Jews and Arabs. For halakhists, it is all set forth in the classics of Jewish law.[25] Kook lived before articulation of Palestinian identity, but even in those pre-State days the issue of Arab rights in Palestine was on the Zionist agenda. Nonetheless, for Kook the moral tension was not a major worry. He fully accepted the myth that God had divided the earth among all the nations prior to Creation. Since Eretz Yisrael was allotted to the seed of Abraham, there was no basis for concern about the claims of any other people. Paternalistically, Kook totally supported guarding the human rights of Arabs, but to him there was no moral question about what national possession of the land entails.

Kook founds justice on goodness; Kaplan, on equality. Kaplan declares:

> The ideal of justice is based on the assumption that human beings are intrinsically equal, notwithstanding their apparent inequality in all possible respects of ability, character and fortune. Justice is the antithesis of discrimination either in favor or against. As discrimination is based on that which actually or supposedly makes men unequal, so is justice based on the belief that what makes them unequal is either secondary or illusory.[26]

Acceptance of the principle of equality is the prerequisite of all pursuit of justice. Equality transcends all conceptions of justice but does enter into all of them; for justice attempts to overcome the inequalities that pervade the existing world. Kaplan illustrates the point by referring to the distribution of food in times of austerity. Under conditions of short supply, the plight of a sick person is direr than that of a healthy person. It would be just to reduce this inequality by providing the unhealthy man or woman with an extra measure of food. The enlightened human being seems to be driven to rise up against inequality. Kaplan writes: "It is the purpose of all laws and institutions, insofar as they are just, not to maintain . . . disparity, but to ignore it in the interest of a higher law than that of unconscious nature, the law of human equality, which is the law of God."[27]

Kaplan forces us to turn our attention to equality. The pursuit of justice is a *mitzvah*, because it often requires us to oppose nature. "The truth is," Kaplan says, "that, in nature, equality and liberty may be contradictory, but in God, they are complementary."[28] Humans are born unequal, and nature as a whole also plays favorites. Therefore, in order for justice to triumph, spiritual power has to be arrayed against the natural process and applied "so changing the conditions of human life that all men shall be fit to survive."[29]

Kaplan maintains that much of post-prophetic Jewish tradition did not emulate the Prophets' passion for equality. Instead, Rabbinic Judaism adopted a generally passive attitude of making the best of existing inequalities. The rich should view their status as one of noblesse oblige and treat the poor and other unfortunates with kindness and generosity. The tradition did not demand any social upheaval aimed at equalizing the conditions of life of the various socioeconomic classes. Paternalism guided Jewish social attitudes for many generations. This is not to say that our ancestors deemed inequality to be just or justifed. They viewed it as a fact of life. The poor will not disappear from the earth.

However, quality is not just a socioeconomic matter; it is a spiritual problem as well. The self-esteem of every person and the moral character of every society require a sense of equality in all areas of life that are not determined by genetic causes. Every movement toward equality heightens a person's faith in the possibility of God's salvation. Only when people are free to choose the paths of their lives can they be said to be equal. And equality exists among men and women who feel that they are free to choose to act in responsible ways and who respect one another as free and responsible agents. For equality to prevail, people need not have the same talents. It is just to deny an unskilled person the right to be a surgeon. Since justice is a social value, all persons should want to contribute to the good of the group by not assuming roles for which they are unfit. At the same time, everyone has the right to demand that society provide access to the available resources that are necessary for the satisfaction of physical, psychic, and spiritual needs. It follows that the apprehension of justice implies that the happiness of a rational person depends on his or her ability to employ all his or her faculties and positive dispositions and not seek to emulate the capabilities of others. Envy is a destructive bent of mind.

In the course of his reflections on justice and equality, Kaplan recommends that

> we seek self-fulfillment by developing our powers for creation and not for destruction or domination; that all men should be encouraged to use their creative powers to the utmost; that, in seeking to advance the interest of our nation, our race, our class, or any other social unit to which we belong, we insist on their behaving in their collective capacity as moral agencies, on their respecting the personal dignity of their constituent individuals, and on their seeking cooperation with, and not domination of, similar societal groups; that, finally, the universal right of all men to seek commu-

nion with God and the spiritual security of sharing in His omni-
present and eternal life, by reverencing their loyalties in those
traditions and institutions through which they have experienced
God, and by not permitting the hegemony of any one tradition
over others.[30]

Justice is a by-product of the acceptance of pluralism and the
multicoloration of the human race, along with the protection of
the right of every individual to fulfill his or her unique potential.
This conception is both realistic and idealistic. It is realistic in that
it addresses the inequality that is intrinsic in nature. It is idealistic
insofar as it encourages the pursuit of equality for the future of
humankind.

Whoever looks for absolute justice will not find it in Kaplan's
outlook. Those who seek a clear analysis of justice and plausible
suggestions for its implementation will not derive much satisfaction from Kook. On the other hand, anyone whose heart is open
to the call, "Justice, justice shall you pursue" (Deut. 16, 20), will
benefit from a careful reading of both men.

THE VALUE OF VALUES

Kook and Kaplan found that Israel's uniqueness stems from its
desire to become a priestly and holy people. Both men were conscious of the fact that the implementation of ideals cannot be a
duty exclusive to Jews. The purpose of all peoples should be to
unite in a common effort to create an international society of
concord and decency. While such a purpose should engage all
rational beings, in fact the discrimination between values of
greater or lesser importance to human salvation is far from self-
evident. Values have a different valence under different circumstances. In the face of tyranny, for instance, loyal Jews tend to
treat all the *mitzvot* as equally significant, whereas under freedom
many Jews often discard the values underlying them. Nonetheless,
Kook and Kaplan hoped that the observance of the *mitzvot* in the
spirit of the values they symbolize would raise the spiritual and
moral levels of their practitioners. The ultimate value of the commandments lies in the contribution that their observance can
make to the education of humankind.

Kook and Kaplan disagreed about the meaning of "value." As a halakhist, Kook was certain as to the definition and implementation of the concept. The problem of values could arise for him only in a halakhic context, such as could happen during a talmudic discussion when varied opinions are expressed. For the most part, true values were not a subject for independent thought or debate between autonomous schools of ethical theory. If Jews and Arabs disagree about the right to Eretz Yisrael or Falastin, this is a halakhic and not a moral issue. The restrictions that the *Halakhah* imposes on alien residents (in which category all non-Jews are placed under the *Halakhah*) have a legal warrant. The morality of such legislation might trouble sensitive halakhists, but the problem has to be resolved by deciding what is halakhically possible and not by a compromise or by determining what is morally proper. I do not dispute the fact that Kook constantly refers to the moral concerns of the rabbis and his own endeavors to formulate morally defensible halakhic opinions. Indeed, even a superficial glance at *Beer Eliyahu,* Kook's commentary on the study by the Vilna Gaon of the laws of judges, will prove the profundity of the Rav's moral theorizing. However, as I have tried to show, the path of Kook's thought follows the rules and the principles of the *Halakhah*—manmade values are subservient to halakhic dictates. Of course, there is nothing unusual about this. All legal systems are characterized by tensions between their machinery and moral considerations. But the question that has to be asked is this: Would Kook have been prepared to acknowledge that Jewish law should be open to nullification, amendment, or correction that might be influenced by non-Jewish ethical sources or by non-halakhic Jewish moral insights? Would he have been willing to search for new and improved moral standards in the thought of non-Jewish theologians or moral theorists? If Kook were convinced of the moral rectitude of these extra-halakhic sources, would he have been willing to revamp the *Halakhah* in favor of a more up-to-date ethos? The answer is No! A good illustration of his position is the changing status of women, which we shall consider in Chapter 14.

Kaplan never expected to find in Judaism the full expression of God's will. He denied that a single culture could reveal, invent, or discover all the universal values that define the ideal man or woman or that its entire value system could be free of mistaken notions. The people of Israel, like other peoples, must always be receptive to legitimate criticism and convincing innovations from within and without. The Torah and its values must be our "life and the length of our days," both for the truths it embodies and for its capacity for growth along with the maturation and expanding horizons of the Jewish people. Kaplan's works are replete with suggested excisions or revisions of traditional concepts and practices—the Chosen People doctrine, other-worldliness, resurrection, the status of women, the halakhic method, and many other long-standing ideas and social habits. During his more than fifty-year teaching career at the Jewish Theological Seminary of America, he was often criticized by his colleagues for his attempts to democratize the *Halakhah* and transpose the Jewish religion into the key of naturalism.

In the end, Kaplan's pioneering led the way to new horizons. Many of his "radical" steps are now commonplace among non-Orthodox Jews. The revolution in the role of women, the constant publication of new versions of the Pesah *Haggadah,* the openness to liturgical change, the concern for intellectual honesty in the interpretation of Judaism—these developments can be attributed to a great extent to the thinking that Kaplan galvanized.

All this should help us to grasp the attitudes of Kook and Kaplan toward war. As expected, Kook's point of departure is halakhic. One illustration is contained in a letter he wrote to his parents during World War I, in which he considers the duties of a soldier in compulsory and voluntary wars.[31] For instance, he distinguishes between the soldier's obligation to risk his life with his fellows during an assault on a dangerous enemy or on a people resisting Jewish settlement in Eretz Yisrael and his duty when confronting a lone enemy soldier. In the latter case, he may use his judgment as to how to apply the toraitic rule that the observance of the *mitzvot* is meant to enhance life—"you shall live by them."

Similarly, in one of his responsa Kook discusses the question of the status of Egypt, if it were to be conquered in an attack launched by the Jews. Would the annexation of the conquered area make it halakhically a part of Eretz Yisrael?[32] Kook's answer is irrelevant for our purpose. What is of interest is the halakhic background of his decision. The moral perspective is subordinate to the halakhic consideration. Kook does not question the morality of a war initiated to expand the borders of Eretz Yisrael. In his response to the question raised by his interlocutor, Rabbi Menashe Grossberg, he had to relate to the specific issue of Egypt's status under Jewish conquest. But the student has the right to inquire why Kook chose to make a reply devoid of reference to the ethics of aggression.

Kaplan's treatment of war is worlds apart from the halakhic approach. Paramount in his mind is the curse of war. Humankind must unite to remove this moral scourge from the face of the earth. The issue is not to argue the merits of wars to fill out or expand the borders of Eretz Yisrael, or defensive or aggressive wars, but how to prevent wars altogether, no matter what their justification. Kaplan thought hard about pacifism, but he could not accept it. He felt that armed defense against attack is often the only possible way for a people to ensure its survival or any kind of meaningful life. At such moments, the moral problem is bracketed. If one's life is threatened by an enemy, the enemy's blood has no more sanctity than one's own. However, even in self-defense, a people's army must behave, to the best of its ability, in accordance with universal moral standards. But the very fact that occasions arise when nations are forced to choose between their annihilation and engaging in the immoral act of violence is indicative of our continuing primitivism. Kaplan calls for an all-out, cooperative effort of all peoples to find alternative ways of solving international conflicts.

Kaplan's detestation of violence led him to recommend that the sin of war be highlighted in the prayers, meditations, and sermons of Yom Kippur. He urged that the day be devoted to arousing the Jewish people to dedicate itself totally to the elimination of armed conflict as part of its spiritual vocation. It is true that war sometimes does have positive outcomes—reconciliation between enemies and inventions stimulated by the needs of the hour—but Kaplan could not have written the following lines that Kook composed during World War I:

> When a great war occurs in the world, the power of the Messiah appears. The season of the nightingale arrives, the nightingale of

wicked tyrants; the evil ones are wiped out, the world becomes sweet-smelling, and the sound of the turtle-dove is heard in our land. The unjust death of multitudes, that results from the upheavals of battle, should be seen in some sense as the redeeming influence of the death of the righteous. They rise to heaven, to the source of life, and their worthy lives cause goodness and blessing to descend on the cosmic structure, in all its meanings and values. Later, after the war, the world is renewed in a new spirit, and the feet of the Messiah are revealed. The anticipation of the Messiah is great or weak in accordance with the magnitude and quality of the war.[33]

Kook's faith leads him to seek the good in evil. The omnipotent, good God has created a world in which everything has a purpose, although it sometimes appears to us to be absolute evil. In Kook's case, his idealism triumphed over his realism. Kaplan was no less eager than Kook to bring about the days of the Messiah, but he believed that wicked means could not effect that end. Still, people can learn from their mistakes and avoid them in the future. On this assumption Kaplan rested his hope for peace and his plea for a concentrated attack on the problem of war. Kook placed his reliance on the God of hosts who would not lead His creatures astray.

Kook believed that all values were determined from the beginning of time and were given to Israel to foster and carry out. But our ancestors sinned, and so we suffer. Because of the sin of the golden calf, strangers occupied our land for two millennia. During this period, the Jewish people lived as a peaceful nation. In the light of what was happening in the world during the war between Germany and the Allies, the sin of the golden calf would be erased, and Israel would return to its land "to conduct its commonwealth on foundations of goodness, wisdom, probity and clear, divine illumination."[34] That is to say, Israel's history is designed according to God's Providence. If the era of Jewish suffering was long, evidently it had to be so, for thus God decreed. But Kook's main interest was to create a better future, and for this he turned to the *Halakhah*.

For Kaplan, values were more complex. Not only did their meaning and referents change from generation to generation, but their future implementation will require greater skill than can be acquired solely from Jewish tradition. War might be interpreted

as God's punishment for our sins, but these sins stem from surrender to our baser instincts as well as from mental deficiency. To
end violence and war, we must be able to locate and diagnose the
reasons and motivations for our mistakes and sins of the past. We
must also seek new ways to implement our idealistic purposes. In
this process, values have to be reevaluated, so that they can better
illuminate the road on which we travel in our quest for God's
will.

NOTES

1. *Chambers Twentieth Century Dictionary,* 1991.

2. OK, Vol. 2, p. 311. Note also Kook's view on the relativism of
the sacred and the profane, in our chapter on education.

3. Ibid., p. 307.

4. Ibid., p. 317.

5. Ibid., p. 314.

6. Ibid., p. 313.

7. Ibid., p. 314.

8. *Musar Avikha* (henceforth, MA) (Jerusalem: Mosad HaRav Kook,
1979, p. 45).

9. JC, p. 317.

10. Ibid., p. 318.

11. Ibid.

12. FAJ, p. 331.

13. Ibid.

14. Ibid.

15. See my remarks on the God of vengeance in "Neepad Nekamah:
Reflections on Divine and Human Attributes," in *Siah Mesharim,* No.
21, Tishri, 5751, pp. 26–27.

16. FAJ, p. 333.

17. MA, p. 95.

18. *Haggadah Shel Pesah* (Jerusalem: Mosad HaRav Kook, 1963, p. 6).

19. MA, p. 92.

20. KL, Vol. 3, L. 693, p. 68.

21. Ibid.

22. Ibid., p. 96.

23. Naturally, Kook himself saw no contradiction between the lofty
divine status of Israel and the universalism of Jewish morality. This was
God's doing. He chose the Jews. "Israel is suffused with the light of

divine power and splendor, the consciousness of which is filled with the life of eternal wisdom, the life of grace and love of all creatures. . . ." (*Orot,* p. 18).

24. MA, p. 151.
25. See, for example, Rashi's well-known interpretation of Creation.
26. FAJ, p. 313.
27. Ibid., p. 314.
28. Ibid., p. 323.
29. Ibid., p. 316.
30. Ibid., p. 327.
31. KL, Vol. 3, L. 944, pp. 458–459.
32. MK, R. 145, pp. 348–350.
33. *Orot,* p. 13.
34. Ibid., p. 14.

9

Jewish Identity and Character

ENDLESS DEBATE takes place in Israel over the propriety and implications of the Law of Return and the question of who is a Jew. These issues of Jewish identity are both spiritual and political and evoke deep emotions. This is not the place to probe the political aspects of the debate. Kook died before the political implications dominated the public mind—not only in Israel but in the Diaspora as well—and Kaplan died before any political resolution was in sight. Nevertheless, their views on the nature of Jewish peoplehood are of both historical and practical interest. What they had to say can help shed light on the current disputes on the "whoness" (identity) and the "whatness" (character) of the Jewish people.

WHO IS A JEW?

At first glance, the determination of who is a Jew is simple. For almost two millennia, a Jew has been defined as a male or female who is born to a Jewish mother or undergoes a halakhic conversion. (I do not intend to analyze the complicated issue of what is entailed in a halakhic conversion.) However, a careful reading of Jewish history strongly suggests that the definition of a Jew will continue to be a matter of religious and anthropological controversy for a long time to come.

Human identity is an ongoing process, conditioned by both internal impulses and external forces. Sometimes, the role of the external factors is minor, as, for example, during the many centuries when the advancement of science was slow and intellectual currents flowed within fairly narrow banks. In such an era, the consensus concerning the social and ideological roots of revealed religions remains stable. It is then easy to believe that the popular norm for defining identity is final. Indeed, this is what happened to the halakhic enterprise. It was taken as self-evident, and the question of who is a Jew did not become a subject for controversy. Today, the Jewish people faces the possibility of a greater split than that which ensued from the conflict between the Rabbanites and the Karaites twelve centuries ago. In the long run, the differences of opinion concerning who is a Jew are more significant for Jewish continuity than those that are involved in the formation of a new government in the State of Israel.

Now that the conditions of life change so rapidly and radically for all peoples, it is important to broaden our understanding of the cumbersome route of Jewish national identity. There can be no doubt that the halakhic designation can no longer operate without fundamental change. At the same time, no alternative has yet been offered that is likely to gain the overwhelming agreement of Jews throughout the world. Despite this lack of consensus, I believe that the circumstances to be taken into account and the available options are clear.

Both Kook and Kaplan grasped the significance of the dynamic relationship between the whole and the part, between the national entity and the individual. They understood that the communal whole is an abstraction. Yet its cultural embodiment is responsible for the personality of the individual. As Kook stated very well,

> Healthy common sense recognizes that the whole in itself does not really exist. It is a generality whose reality and purpose are in its capacity to confer on all its parts some measure of the common good. The individual can attain the good only insofar as he is part of a collective. . . .[1]

The individual owes his entire being, even his life, to the group. Kook says to each person, "You are duty-bound to participate in the work of your people and to contribute to its self-perfection. . . ."[2] This duty will be fulfilled to the extent that the individual loves his people. "We note that love of nation is greater even than love of one's children and of one's own life. . . ."[3]

In one of his early essays, Kaplan expresses an opposite point of view. Relying on the social science of that time (1915), he wrote that a human society must be seen not only as a collection of individuals but as a physical entity in its own right, more real than the brains of the persons of whom it is composed.[4] Although he later abandoned this notion, his initial intuition guided him through all the adjustments in his thinking—society sets the borders of individual development, but the individual plays a reciprocal role in the framing of society. The relationship between the whole and the part is organic and mutual. A society gives its members language, mental and behavioral habits, and a sense of values that make them into the kinds of human beings they become.[5] On the other hand, although individuals are motivated by their desire for self-fulfillment, they will achieve that purpose only if they are devoted to the maturation of their people.[6]

Both Kook and Kaplan assert that no description of Jewish identity can overlook the continuous interaction between Jewry as a whole and the Jewish individual. It is impossible to define the identity of the people without considering the uniqueness of every Jew, man or woman. Nor can the identity of the individual Jew be grasped outside the context of his or her involvement in the struggle for Jewish survival and the effort to vitalize Jewish culture. However, no matter how important is the concept of Jewish identity, Kook and Kaplan realize that the whatness, the purpose and content of Jewish life, is the main question with which the Jewish people must wrestle. This problem is less acute for Kook, for the obvious reason that he needs only to devote himself more fully to strengthening the *Halakhah*. Kaplan has to formulate new guidelines both for the continuity of the Jewish people and for the structuring of Jewish unity. Thus, while he wants to revolutionize the method and content of the *Halakhah*, Kaplan is also concerned about Jewish unity. This concern means that he must be willing to compromise in order to leave the door open to the participation of traditionalists. For example, if the latter were willing to accept democratic decision-making, liberal Jews should be willing to accept a halakhic ruling if it could gain majority support. Kaplan feels that there are some issues, particularly matters of marriage and divorce, about which even liberals opposed to the halakhic rulings should compromise for the sake of communal peace. To preserve an orderly society, Kaplan believes it is necessary, at least for a limited time, to impose legislation on a resistant minority, no matter how large. The question of who is a Jew is one of those issues that requires both legislation and compromise. The fact is that until now, the majority of Jews, particularly in Israel, who appear to have lost much of their respect for many halakhic conceptions of marriage and divorce, have passively accepted Orthodox rabbinical authority, for the reason just cited. But time is running out, and this emphasis on Jewish unity is giving way to denominational departures, antinomianism, and considerable anarchy. This is especially true in the Diaspora, where Jews are now less prone than in the past to adhere to the dictates of the halakhic rabbinate in regard to laws of personal status. Any resolution of this problem will require a measure of patience and tolerance that will tax the Jewish mind and soul. Kaplan called for this spirit, but it does not seem to be in the offing.

WHAT IS A JEW?

The question of *what* is a Jew is another matter. It touches at the roots of the Jewish vocation. Jewish identity is a formal question, whereas the quality of Jewish life is a judgmental concern that can have no single or decisive answer. Undoubtedly, the two questions are intertwined. Jewish identity is more than a genetic or sociological concern. The otherness or distinctiveness of the Jewish people is not merely a question of birth or formal conversion of individuals. The otherness of the Jews also involves a set of purposes that transform them from passive individuals into subjects who choose their identity because of their love for the Jewish culture and way of life. In our day, the Jewish lifestyle and the goals of Jewish existence have become critical problems. The voluntarism of the pluralistic society constitutes an unprecedented problem for Jewish survivalists. The degree of uniformity wanted by Kook, as would be expected from an Orthodox Jew, is no longer possible; nor, I believe, would it be desirable. Israel was the first nation to proclaim the ideal of national freedom, but it has lagged behind others in its insights about the meaning of individual liberty.[7] Furthermore, even in regard to national freedom, we Jews have yet to explore its meaning fully. For two thousand years, we have been able to experience the problem of freedom only from within the perspective of our powerlessness.

Values have to be studied both in their abstract meaning and in the way in which they are embodied in the character of the individual and the group. Kook's tolerance is illustrated in an incident depicting how even ideological rigidity can give way to extraordinary tolerance. According to the story, a kibbutznik from a secular settlement came one *Tish'ah B'Av*, a fast day, to consult with Kook on some matter. Realizing that the man had traveled a long distance in hot weather and was not accustomed to fasting, Kook summoned his wife and asked her to prepare some food and drink for the guest. This unusual tolerance on the part of the Chief Rabbi shows that as important as ideology is, collective Jewish life must be grounded in love of other Jews, a willingness to compromise, and a readiness to allow others the freedom to observe or not to observe traditional practices.

On another occasion, in correspondence with Rabbi Menahem Porush, Kook explained his tolerance toward "free thinkers":

> When I examine my deeds and test my ways, it occurs to me that my critics are right. Perhaps I am too tolerant toward the open minded and my attitude toward the unobservant too forbearing. My conscience is pricked. However, when I realise that I also bear no rancour toward my pious opponents and try with all my strength to help them, and when I feel great affection even for those who hurt or vex me, this provides me with inner succour and proves that all my actions are for the sake of Heaven. All my tolerant ways stem from love of Israel . . . and from my tendency to seek that which is good in the other. [8]

These incidents indicate that ideological controversy need not end in social fission. The precondition for coexistence is widespread tolerance of the kind Kook exhibited. But what is apt to happen when spiritual and communal leaders, who hold Kook's ideology, lack this virtue? They will consider someone like Kook to be a rebel against the essence of Judaism.

The issue of coexistence looks different when one examines Kaplan's character. I did not have the privilege of meeting Kook. I know him only from his writings and the testimony of several persons who had been in his company. On the other hand, I knew Kaplan from close contact as a student and as a coworker for many years. He always tried to live up to the moral and spiritual ideals of his philosophy, but he had to battle his impatience. He was incapable of engaging in small talk or of associating with anyone who was intellectually dishonest or immoral. However, he was magnanimous toward opponents whose criticism was expressed respectfully and cogently, and he apologized to those whom he was too quick to criticize. He was less pleased with supporters who were unable to formulate their ideas logically and clearly. Kaplan was not a neutral personality, but no one, as far as I know, ever doubted the virtues that made him as charismatic as he was—his intellectual honesty and moral courage.

In assessing Kaplan's contribution to the content of Judaism, we have to address his program for Jewish life. Its application would lead to a tolerant and open society. This conclusion follows from what Kaplan writes about the current condition of Jewish religion. For reasons of realism and idealism, Kaplan postulates that pluralism in faith and practice is justified and should be considered a permanent condition of Jewish life. Even if something is to be said for a version that would limit Judaism to

> a specific system of belief and regimen of conduct, departure from which constitutes a departure from the norm, is sufficient to condemn such a version of Judaism as unworkable. The expectation of getting all Jews to submit to one code of law and doctrine is, under modern conditions, nothing less than chimerical. The variety of ideas which obtain in Jewish life is a replica of that which exists in the world at large.[9]

To expect a single type of religion to unite all Jews is as futile as to expect all humankind to subscribe to one universal religion. In the same passage, Kaplan asserts, "Judaism must be so construed as to grant to the individual Jew the right to regard as his religion whatever he conscientiously accepts as such."

Kook offers us a single, authentic Judaism, which should be enforced as much as possible through gentle persuasion. Kaplan calls for a multicolored culture that eschews coercion and any attempt to impose uniformity. Both thinkers agree that Judaism changed in the past and that it should continue to do so in the future. Anyone who claims that the *Halakhah* has been, is, or should be static does not understand its spirit. Every page in the Mishnah and *Gemara*, in the codes, and in the responsa literature testifies to the uninterrupted process of adaptation to the needs of the hour. What divides the halakhists of all ages is the question of how far is it permissible to stretch halakhic hermeneutics (methods of interpretation) or to tread on untried paths.

Since Kook is limited by the *Halakhah*, he obviously has less room to maneuver than does Kaplan. But even in this more confined space, there is plenty of room for serious differences of opinion between liberals and conservatives, between the lenient and the strict. It is hard to place Kook in any of these categories when it comes to his halakhic decisions. The law stands above all, and Kook tries to render decisions that seem to be clearly implicit in halakhic precedent and logic. Nevertheless, even in this relatively narrow halakhic perspective, as compared to that of the open society, the degrees of liberality and strict constructionism vary. For instance, we sense Kook's liberalism in his notes on and analysis of the Vilna Gaon's commentary on the laws of judges. For example, in his discussion of the qualities to be expected of a judge, as listed in the *Shulhan Arukh*[10] and in the commentary of the Gaon, Kook first cites their description: "In a court of three [judges], each one must possess seven qualities—wisdom, humility, reverence, disdain of money, love of truth, love of all creatures and good reputation." Then, among his comments, Kook writes:

> A good name—reputation—is conferred on a man not only because of some personal good deeds but because it is clear that goodness and integrity have become ingrained in his character and essence. A reputation points to a person's true quality and is marked by a fixed strength of character. . . . These virtues, when they become dominant in a-person, define his reputation, which is his crowning achievement.[11]

Later on, in his treatment of reverence, Kook comments that a judge

> should not overdo reverence to the extent that fear would deprive him of a perspective on life and cause him to pervert justice or

possibly lead to the total disappearance of judgment and to the destruction of the world. Reverence has to be accompanied by much courage, so that in keeping to the right path, one does not stumble in it.[12]

Kook repeatedly argues that the *Halakhah* loses its raison d'être if it ceases to strive for the training of moral human beings.

Kaplan's conception of Israel's vocation offers a similar view. Basing his belief on the command that Abraham's descendants "shall keep the way of the Lord to do righteousness and justice" (Gen. 18, 19), Kaplan emphasizes that the main thrust of this charge is to contribute to the elimination of violence. Resorting to violence is "a perversion of what should be man's way of life."[13] As a result of humankind's failure to live peacefully, God had to appoint Abraham to head a nation that would carry out this vision of peace and justice. This is the essence of Torah.

> Whether the Prophets antedated or followed the Torah of tradition, there can be no question that, by the time they came upon the scene, all Israel had assumed that they were covenanted to God by means of Torah, or the way of life based on justice and loving kindness.[14]

Both Kook and Kaplan conceive the essence of Judaism to be a program for implementing universal moral values. However, they do not rest with this narrow definition. As we noted above, Kook calls upon Jews not only to be reverent but to take full advantage of the life force. Kook's intent is unclear, but he indicates that Jews, like all people, undergo an array of physical, social, and spiritual experiences that influence the formation of their souls and force them to choose between varieties of behavior. The Torah does not always supply a ready-made recommendation; or, if it does have a directive, the individual is often unable to decipher it with sufficient ease and speed. Therefore, Kook argues, a person should not flee from the arena of life. Judaism embraces life in all its fullness, and none of its forms may ignore any aspect of existence. The terms "life" and "civilization," as used by Kook and Kaplan, respectively, are very close in meaning. In both instances, Judaism is defined as a vital, changing culture and not as a collection of precious stones to be transmitted from generation to generation for the passive enjoyment of the heirs.

Kook regards the Torah as more than a container. It is a method for effecting change and dictating its spirit, but it is also a body of ideational dogmas, such as divine revelation, the world-to-come, and reward and punishment. The Written Law is true and not to be uprooted in any way. It is to be the central principle of education, and its study is to be the main preoccupation of the Jew. Adjustment of the *mitzvot* or their enrichment is the sole prerogative of halakhic masters. From the inception of the halakhic system, its authority has been open to all qualified men and is uniquely aristocratic. The decisions of this aristocracy are never considered departures from tradition, since they are held to be implicit in the *Halakhah*, merely awaiting the proper time for their determination.

However, one aspect of Kook's thought extends beyond devout Judaism and stirs the ire of Fundamentalists. I refer to the hints in Kook's ideas and conduct of a world that lies beyond rabbinic Judaism. For example, he often displays an openness that is not intrinsic to the Torah itself. This trait is manifest in his tolerance toward sinners—and anyone who knowingly disobeys a toraitic command or denies a basic principle of the tradition is a sinner. Kook's dialectical thinking, which offers secular nationalists and religious reformers a function in the scheme of redemption, also goads the extremists. Of course, in his theory Kook is neither a pluralist nor a person who tolerates deviation from the halakhic norm. Only the "kasher" Jew is Kook's ideal. Yet by highlighting the popular notion that "a Jew who sins is nonetheless a Jew" (Sanhedran 44a), Kook finds a place in the Jewish community for the non-Orthodox. He believes that they, too, contribute to a vital Judaism by building the land and increasing awareness of the need to adjust Jewish life to new circumstances. Kook assumes that the presence of such Jews will eventually spur halakhic Jews to more creatively apply the *Halakhah* to life. In the end, the deviants will repent and return to authentic Judaism.

Kook's Judaism is inner-directed. He respected science, technology, and general creative thought, but he did not evaluate them objectively in their own terms. He was more interested in how the *Halakhah* might use them for its own purposes. His more right-wing opponents severely attacked him for opening this narrow slit to the light of modernism. On the other hand, anyone who looks to Kook as a partner in the application of such general enlightenment to further Judaism is doomed to disappointment. For Kook, it is Judaism that casts its light outward. Only that outside light which can strengthen its existing foundations is permitted to pass into its midst. Within the historic tradition, Kook gives ardent approval to theologians and philosophers of all persuasions who tapped non-Jewish wisdom for what they could contribute to buttressing the walls of Judaism. Perhaps Kook did not realize the extent of the change that these thinkers made in the actual essence of Judaism, but he understood that the Jewish people has to live in a world of interaction between cultures and between systems of thinking. Kook respected both the logical probing of Saadiah Gaon, Maimonides, and other like-minded individuals and those who cautioned about the limits of rationalism and gave their support to the cogency of historical revelation. In Kook's eyes, they all enunciated the Word of God. Tradition and reason are partners.

In the same spirit, Kook values *midrash* and *aggadah* (homiletical and philosophical exegesis and interpretation of biblical texts), even as he devotes much of his energy to the furtherance of the *Halakhah*. He concludes, "The spiritual aspect of sacred faith resides in the *mitzvah* of rational knowing, which connects the Torah directly to the divine human soul."[15] Similarly, "[how] does one come to love the Lord? By studying *Aggadah*. For thus one comes to identify the Creator and to adhere to his ways."[16] Enlightened Judaism, according to Kook, has to be constructed out of continuous and expanding wisdom. This blueprint for a glorified Judaism can be accomplished within the tradition. Despite what has been said above about Kook's awareness of the interdependence of cultures, he was also concerned about foreign influences on halakhic Judaism. Hence, the less Jews have to do with the gentile world, the better off they are and the greater will be the likelihood of an authentic Jewish culture. Moreover, he proclaims that Israel must be loyal to the Torah and its commandments "for the sake of mankind and its moral progress; for human fate depends on the direction of our existence. . . ."[17] The Jewish mission is universal, but its implementation is, so to speak, one-directional. The Jewish people is equipped with all the tools necessary for the salvation of humankind.[18]

Kaplan bestrides two worlds. He regards Judaism as unique and endowed with universal qualities. Nevertheless, he does not infer from this perception the election or the superiority of Israel. All peoples have their peculiar individuality, and they must respect the uniqueness of other groups and learn for their own advantage what the others have to impart. Therefore, Kaplan advocates constant and open interaction between nations. Such contacts constitute a challenge to the ability of each group to survive the inevitable competition of cultures. Many benefits for growth inhere in intercultural exchange.

Particularity and Universal Redemption

A gap of vision and temperament exists between Kaplan and Kook. Kook strives for the unity and redemption of all peoples; their salvation will result from the conduct of the Jews. All peoples will bow before God if the Jews fulfill their role faithfully. This is a kind of paternalistic exclusivism.

Kaplan, on the other hand, claims that human redemption does not require the homogenization of cultures. In his opinion, each nation can express its nature in a unique lifestyle that need not conflict with that of other peoples. The light of the universe is refracted into all the colors of the rainbow. Some of the colors will remain primary; others will blend. A people filled with the zest for life and a passion for survival will want to preserve as much of its native coloration as possible.

On the basis of this conception, Kaplan concludes:

> The modern challenge to Judaism differs radically from the one which the Jewish People encountered in the past. That challenge emanates from the spirit of this-worldliness, or secularism, which permeates contemporary human life. The transfer of the center of gravity of human existence from the other world to this world is both the cause and the effect of modern man's passionate desire to acquire mastery over the forces of nature and his growing ability to render the world he lives in more habitable.[19]

This revolution opens the door wide to the sin of pride. It entices people to believe that they have the power to do anything they wish in the natural order. But potential hubris is not confined to this vision alone. It seeks to entrap any man or woman who is absolutely certain about the truth and validity of his or her conceptions and values. This potential hubris not only endangers naturalists but can be a stumbling block for supernaturalists as well. Thus, although HaRav Kook was a humble man, his humility did not save him from serious errors in his perception of reality and in his evaluation of the spiritual and moral levels of Jewry and other nations.

Kaplan's humanism should not be construed as an attack on theism. Like Kook, he held that theism and humanism are a team and not rivals. However, the two men differed about the essence of each concept. They started from the same point, namely, that men and women are the subjects of the world into which they are born, but as Kaplan saw it, God does not rule that world like a king over his subjects, but as a law that both binds and frees. He argued that this naturalistic theology is demanded by virtue of what we now know about our cosmic home and ourselves. Our current knowledge empowers us to deal with some of the disorders of nature more maturely than our ancestors could have hoped to do. This maturity should lead us to disown conceptions about this world and the afterlife that have persisted for many centuries but have now lost their cogency.

> Formerly, the evils in the world, both natural and social, presented an impregnable wall, against which man seemed to dash himself in vain. Hence the more aware of his helplessness man grew, the more he found it necessary to look to another world than this one for the meaning of his existence. This led him to conclude that affliction and misery were part of the divine plan as means of rendering man worthy of the bliss in the hereafter. . . . But once man realized what power he possessed to make the world more habitable by manipulating the forces of nature, he tended to abandon the idea that all of life's evils were inevitable. He began to think of eliminating those evils instead of trying to find some plausible explanation for them.[20]

Kaplan's analysis depicts a Judaism whose spirit is close to that of biblical religion. In his view, biblical man looked for his salvation in this world. He wanted to experience God's blessings from the confines of his flesh. Kaplan in no way believed that it is possible to eradicate all natural and moral evil. Only an omnipotent Power can do that. But our success in playing our cosmic role should not be judged by the standards of perfection, which in any case are beyond human comprehension. Instead, we should measure ourselves by the degree to which we do or do not put to intelligent use the instruments we hold in our hands. As our knowledge increases, the image of evil changes before our eyes. Our responsibility to combat evil grows. It is the fight against evil, not its complete elimination, that constitutes the fulfillment of human destiny.

In summary, Kaplan sees the Jewish essence in the obligation of Jews to learn about and contribute to the enhancement of human goodness and international amity. This stand against isolationism increases the burden that Jews must carry. While visiting in the tents of Ham and Japhet, Jews have to continue to respect the universal elements in their own heritage. It is easy to be loyal to "Jewish values" when one is surrounded solely by Jews. It is tempting, when one lives in a physical and spiritual ghetto, to hold that one's heritage stands above all others, as there is no challenge to one's presuppositions. Kaplan could never entertain such a thought. Along with Kook, he opposed a society that behaved as if nothing had happened in the world in the last two hundred or three hundred years. But whereas Kook refused to believe that the events of this period necessitate any fundamental alteration of the basics of Judaism, Kaplan felt that such changes are peremptory, even though many of them cannot be extrapolated from the classic texts.[21]

How can we explain this discrepancy in the views of two men who equally devote themselves to the creative survival of their people, the strengthening of its religion, the broadening of its culture, and the building of its land? The question is complicated and does not lend itself to an easy answer. One fact, however, stands out. As far as Kook is concerned, Judaism is a precious object given to Israel for use and safekeeping, in exchange for the reward inherent in that privilege. Israel is responsible for any damage done to this precious commodity. Therefore, every effort has to be made to restore the bond between the Jewish people and its sacred heritage. To solve today's problems we must look backward. "Remember the days of old / Consider the years of past ages; / Ask your father, he will inform you, / Your elders, they will tell you" (Deut. 32, 7).

As Kaplan sees it, the character of the Jew is composed of religious or spiritual nationalism and a culture that is founded on truth, goodness, and beauty.[22] But whereas Kook's perception of Judaism is that of a slow and reluctantly changing culture, Kaplan's vision is that of a conscious, dynamic adaptation to a topsy-turvy environment. The daily discoveries about humans and nature that are made in scientific laboratories throughout the world and the rethinking about human nature that develops in the minds of trained social scientists are major components of the air that Kaplan breathes. This constant flow of knowledge is bound to frustrate men and women who want their lives to stand on firm, certain intellectual grounds. Moreover, the social fluidity of the modern world has opened the floodgates to mixed marriage, assimilation, and deculturation, along with opportunities for deepening loyalties and for enriching native cultures. Kaplan confronts the challenge head-on. To survive, Judaism not only has to be passed *on*; it has to be *passed* on—evaluated anew, amended, and energized.[23]

Despite my preference for the Kaplanian view, I have to respond to Kook's loyalty to the halakhic tradition by acknowledging the need to look for an anchor in this chapter of our heritage. In the midst of change, there must be a balancing force. Hence, the dispute between Kook and Kaplan is "for the sake of heaven." They both want the Jewish people to continue its extraordinary odyssey, but they lead us in different directions. We need not repeat what has already been said about their differences. One more distinction can be added, however—their grasp of Judaism under Jewish autonomy. Through the years halakhic Judaism adapted itself to many types of polity, in which the Jewish people was always a minority. Kook foresaw no radical challenge to halakhic principles when a Jewish state would come into existence. Sovereignty would simply activate the halakhic institutions and legislative and judicial procedures that had lain dormant for many centuries. As for the Jewish lifestyle, it would have to include those enterprises essential to the building of a country; but these would be mere additions to the tradition, in no way antithetical to its spirit or content. Jews throughout the world would continue to be bound by halakhic observance. After the ingathering of all the exiles, the *Halakhah* would identify their Jewishness.

When Kook depicted the return to Zion as the beginning of redemption, he meant that in Eretz Yisrael the Jewish people would finally use the halakhic tools at its disposal to establish a humane society for itself and for the non-Jews who would come under Jewish sovereignty. He offered no hint that he would have supported the establishment of a democratic state. Now that history has overtaken his vision, the following questions remain to be asked: Which aspects of Kook's conception of Jewish identity and its content might be helpful today in the administration of the state and in the inner life of Jewry? What, aside from the call for the ingathering of the exiles, would Kook have to say to Jews in the Diaspora about their identity as Jews and as citizens of the countries in which they reside? Such questions would be difficult for him. For Kook, nothing would have changed concerning the identity or character of the Jewish people. The answer of returning to tradition is clear and decisive. But is it cogent and convincing?

In regard to Jewish identity, the perspectives of Kook and Kaplan present further complexities. The traditional Jewish community, in which halakhic authority was universally accepted, no longer exists, except for a small minority. Survivalist Jews such as Kaplan and other modernists shun efforts to restore the halakhic system. Instead, they put their energies into revising the Jewish identity and forms of polity under freedom according to the special conditions in Israel and the Diaspora. This is a problem that cannot be solved by discourse alone. The Jewish people might be able to survive without a practical solution to its identity crisis, despite the frustration that it generates. All segments of Jewish society discuss the problem incessantly, but no serious effort has been made to bring the groups together for a persistent dialogue designed to effect some basic changes in Jewish polity. Without a willingness to engage in such cooperative soul-searching, it is unlikely that a rational solution can be found to the identity issue. The only other response, which may or may not be constructive, is to continue the current policy of laissez faire and hope for the best.

If the followers of Kook and Kaplan are loyal to the spirit of the two teachers, they will want to hear each other out and try to reach a practical compromise. Their leadership could have a constructive influence on the other open-minded elements among the people. Kaplan himself envisaged an approach to Jewish identity that is worth quoting here:

> To be a Jew should mean to be identified with a group which until recently knew itself, and was known by the rest of the world, as a nation, and which must continue as such, if it is to survive at all.
>
> By reason, however, of its dispersion among other nations and of the entire character of the past, the Jewish nation cannot be one in the same sense as other nations of the world. Nationhood in its case cannot be synonymous with statehood or with the machinery of government, but with a specific civilization. This cultural conception of nationhood, though at present represented only by the Jews, will have to be adopted by the rest of the world, since it is the only conception consonant with the hope that the nations will ultimately be federated into a world commonwealth.[24]

NOTES

1. "Afikim Banegev," in *HaPeles*, 5663, p. 508. In a similar vein, Kook writes: "When we are by ourselves and recite 'Hear, O Israel,' it is not the individual or partisan Jew we have in mind, but catholic Israel, the whole Jewish people" (*HaTor*, Vol. 1, No. 2).

2. "Teudat Yisrael U'leumiyutah," *HaPeles*, 5661, p. 60.

3. Ibid., p. 227.

4. "What Is Judaism?" *Menorah Journal*, December 1915, p. 315.

5. JWS, p. 52.

6. MG, p. 53.

7. See, for example, Kook's observation, "We cannot possibly love a Jew who contemptuously disobeys the laws of our sacred Torah, sealed on our heart, through which alone we recognize the fountainhead of our national life" ("Teudat Yisrael U'leumiyutah," *HaPeles*, 5661, p. 49).

8. Quoted in *Moadei Reiyah*, collected by Moshe Zvi Neriah (Jerusalem: Moriah, 5740, p. 279).

9. JC, p. 303.

10. *Hoshen Hamishpat*, Laws of Judges, 7:11.

11. *Beer Eliyahu* (Jerusalem: Mosad HaRav Kook, 5733, p. 83).

12. Ibid., p. 86.

13. FAJ, p. 466.

14. Ibid., pp. 466–467.

15. KL, Vol. 3, L. 793, p. 68.

16. Ibid.

17. "Teudat Yisrael U'Leumiyutah," *HaPeles*, 5661, p. 46.

18. "Israel is to teach the nations the pure concept of God, because
. . . we have to know that human progress depends on the desire of each
sensitive person to carry out this mission to the best of his ability. According to the part one plays in general life, so should be one's duty to
mankind. The entire human race must live as a family. Each person
should be concerned about the welfare of his neighbor, without regard
to race or nation" (Ibid., p. 82). These positive qualities, it seems, are
native only to Israel, which is obligated to transmit them to the other
nations. "This is Judaism's vocation: To impress on Israel the seal of
God's Unity and Providence, so that this remarkable people will truly
be God's people and be able to know this clear truth that can bring
blessing to the whole world" (Ibid., p. 83). Kook vacillated between the
notion that divine truth is genetic in the Jewish character and the idea
that the Jewish people has this talent because it has the Torah.

19. *The Greater Judaism in the Making* (henceforth, GJM) (New York:
Reconstructionist Press, 1960, p. 150).

20. Ibid., p. 151.

21. Compare the attitude of Efraim Shmueli: "Once again, people do
not seek an answer to the cosmic questions about God, human actions
and destiny, that are found in Scriptures. The entire conception of onto-
logical reality of our generations does not permit drawing conclusions
about existence, and particularly precludes offering comfort or promises
of salvation on the basis of previous cultures" (*Hayahadut bein Samkhut
L'hashraah—Judaism—Between Authority and Inspiration* [Tel Aviv: Sifriat
HaPoalim, 1988, p. 102]).

22. Kaplan defines Judaism as an evolving religious civilization, with
religion being the fulcrum on which every aspect of the Jewish people's
culture rests. In his book, *A History of Jewish Thought in the 20th Century*,
Eliezer Schweid distinguishes between civilization and culture, the first
being "the material enterprise of man" and the latter, "the activity of
man on himself, the expression and refinement, the elevation and sophistication of his sentiments, thought, personal qualities and behavioral
values. . . . The term 'culture,' in contrast to 'civilization' refers to the
internalized and subjective aspect of man. . . ." (pp. 214–215). This
semantic excursion points to the fact that Kook, Kaplan, and Schweid
place different emphases on the interplay between matter and spirit. Schweid's effort to produce exact denotations of the two terms helps us to

understand his usage. However, words like civilization and culture are idiosyncratic, and the reader has to judge each thinker in terms of his special usage.

23. JT, p. 34.
24. Ibid., p. 49.

10

Chosenness and Responsibility

No CONCEPT is more germane to the essence of traditional Judaism than chosenness. Hardly a biblical verse having to do with the nature and vocation of the Jewish people can be understood outside the context of Israel's election. The persistent faith in Israel's special role in the divine scheme helps to explain the Jewish people's remarkable will to live in the face of centuries of suffering. The soul of the Jew was always directed to the future, when God's promise would be fulfilled. Paradoxically, Israel's election was interpreted as a justification for its persecution. From one perspective, Israel's sorry lot seemed to be arbitrary and incomprehensible, for its source was in God's mysterious omnipotence. But since God's choice of Israel was tied to the latter's loyalty to the moral and spiritual vocation that it adopted early in its existence, the nation had no right to complain. The Jews knew how to justify their lot. The long Exile was the punishment for their sins. Only when they had paid the full price would the return to Zion take place and Israel could then play out its role as the spiritual teacher of humankind.

Kook, of course, accepted the Chosen People doctrine without question. But this assertion is too facile to describe his interpretation of such a complex idea. We shall first have to list a few of the ways in which election has been understood in the evolution of Jewish thought.

1. Chosenness is a theological concept. It is always composed of a chooser, a chosen one or electee, and a mission that the electee is expected to carry out in well-defined ways. In Judaism, the chooser is God. The electee is Israel, whose mission is to be a light to the nations and to bring them to God. Obedience to the Torah is the means for achieving this end.

2. Each element in the doctrine of chosenness involves a host

of questions, the responses to which have, over the ages, resulted in the assignment of new and sometimes contradictory meanings. One classic example is the paradoxical way in which the Prophets sought to establish God's power and justice. At a time when other nations found the truth of their gods in their ability to assure military victory, the Prophets taught the Hebrews to see their defeat in war as a punishment meted out to them for their rebellion against God's dictates. "You only have I known of all the families of the earth; / Therefore I will visit upon you all your iniquities" (Amos 3, 2). When depression overtook the people as their conditions worsened, the profound vision of Amos and the similar messages of other Prophets restored their morale and their faith that God had indeed chosen them. This conclusion was implicit in the prophetic teaching that Israel's election gives it no advantage if it fails to live up to its moral responsibility.

Another illustration of the doctrine's complexity is found in *The Kozari* of Yehudah Halevi. The king, who serves as Halevi's spokesman in the book, asks the following question: "Why was the Torah not given directly to all men? Would this not have been a more worthy demonstration of divine wisdom?"[1] Why, in other words, did God choose an intermediary who would teach His path to the rest of humankind? The response of the Jewish Sage is twofold. On one hand, mortal man cannot answer this question. One might as well ask why all animals were not endowed with the faculty of speech. On the other hand, the Sage says, Israel was chosen because of its natural qualities. That is to say, Israel deserved to be chosen by virtue of its biological superiority. This strand in the thread of election is part of the fabric of Habad Hasidism and other philosophies of contemporary Judaism. One hears it often from the mouths of many Jews who speak of "the Jewish brain."

3. From the beginning, Jewish chosenness included the ownership of Eretz Yisrael. Without the Land, the people could not fulfill its charge, and without devotion to its mission, possession of the Land would be imperiled. The connection between Israel and the Land of Israel is unlike that between other nations and their lands. Eretz Yisrael is chosen, no less than Israel, and is endowed with supernatural qualities.

4. Election has no meaning without Torah. Israel was chosen

to live the life of Torah and to bring its light to all people. But it is also the instrument that ensures Jewish survival. There is only one divine law, and it belongs to Israel.

5. As mentioned above, Israel's election is attributed to its moral and spiritual excellence. Others, however, claim that the receipt of the Torah is what defines the election—as is evident in the traditional blessing recited by Jews when called to the reading of the Torah in the synagogue. "Blessed are you, O God, our lord, King of the universe, who has chosen us from among all the nations by giving us His Torah. . . ." The noted Zionist theoretician, Hayyim Greenberg, comments that the selection of Israel is not an indication of racial superiority but of the possession of a higher faith that will some day become the universal property of man.[2] In other words, universal redemption will be achieved when all nations accept the Torah.

6. Some say that election is reciprocal. God chooses Israel and Israel chooses God, as is enunciated in the liturgy of Yom Kippur, "We have chosen You, and You have chosen us." David Ben-Gurion was wont to declare that it is Israel who chooses God in a one-sided action.

7. Through all the strands of chosenness, the comparative mood is dominant—"who has raised us above all tongues," "separated us from the mistaken ones," "who has set us off as the holy from the profane."[3] At times, the comparison is meant to state a fact; on other occasions, the design is to emphasize noblesse oblige or to indicate Israel's superiority. In the future, Israel will be the head and not the tail; the nations will bring their wealth to Israel and bow to Israel's monarchs.

8. The feeling of election is commonplace among many peoples, perhaps among all, and is apparently rooted in deep impulses in the human psyche. In building up our self-esteem, many of us tend to exaggerate our own qualities while minimizing those of others. This habit is equally characteristic of nations in their search for morale.

9. Those who wish to dodge the theological difficulties of election frequently take refuge in love. Love is thought to justify actions that defy rational analysis and that cannot and must not be subjected to the canons of logic. By proclaiming the love relationship between God and Israel, chosenness requires no further sub-

stantiation on the part of its adherents. Even if Israel were to be unworthy of God's love, God's own affection for Israel would still be understandable. Is it not common for parents to continue to love a son or daughter who is an evil person? The fact that Israel is stiff-necked and at times rebellious does not diminish God's affection for His people. If He has chosen Israel to be His beloved, why should anyone deny this cosmic "fact"?

KOOK ON ELECTION

Kook constructed a massive theological structure to house his views on God's love of Israel and the need for all Jews to love one another. These loves are built into the composition of the universe. "Love of Israel and the defense of the Jewish people and each individual Jew is not only an emotional expression; it is a major, multi-faceted enterprise of Torah, of broad and profound wisdom, illumined by the lustrous light of loving kindness."[4] The love of Israel that burned in Kook was not a blind passion that lacked all logic. It demanded of the Jew profound understanding of the responsibility for acting out the love that is the meaning of Israel's election. Each Jew has to be an honest defense attorney for all fellow Jews.

Kook calls out against "[r]etreat from the acknowledgment of our superiority, denial of 'You have chosen us' and that we are different from all other peoples, with a special history unmatched by any nation. When we recognise that we are greater than and excel other peoples, we know ourselves. If we forget our greatness, we forget ourselves. A people that loses its self-knowledge is indeed of low stature."[5] Israel is worthy of its station by virtue of its inherent nature, but even more so because it has a divine culture.

> The vitality of Israel's soul comes from its sacred source. We were born in the path of truth and faith, and we continue to grow by following it. Our values are not separate from one another; unity dwells within us, and the light of the one living God shines in our midst. Our laws, the laws of Torah and of the living God, mark us off from all other nations. Holiness works within us; our aspirations are directed toward the sacred. There are drops of holiness among

all peoples, but the totality of life's values do not sprout from them. . . . Not so, Israel. The quest for God . . . remains a special Jewish quality, which is revealed in its divine, all-embracing and eternal nature and shines forth in Eretz Yisrael, in the land of its possession, the place where the light of the holy treasure shines. [6]

Kook knows that "[t]he world in its fullness waits for Israel, for the light it casts on the glorious Name of God, for this people whom God created to utter His praise, for the knowledge that stems from the blessing of Abraham, for the 'blessed be the supernal God who created heaven and earth,' for the people that dwells alone and is not counted among the nations, for the people whom God leads and who has no alien deity, for the people that cleanses the entire world of its impurities. . . ."[7] This breathtaking hubris also characterizes Kook's description of the nations.

The gentile world is thus constructed: it is divided, has no unity of body and soul, has no inner sense of connection and harmony with the materiality and spirituality of the world, has no inner relatedness between thoughts and deeds. Cooperation is, at the present time, something to strive for, when Israel's power will dawn. . . . How much power remains to be exerted in order to redeem the lights from the dark places into which they have fallen!—They will be redeemed forever with the redemption of the holy people.[8]

Kook adopts the popular ploy of contrasting the best in Israel with the worst in other nations. In addition, he attributes a hidden spiritual power to the Jewish people, while denying such a capability to all non-Jewish groups. A statement such as the following appears time and again throughout Kook's writings: "We excel in a way no other people can duplicate."[9] This claim is common to many of those who believe in Israel's chosenness, including some secularists who assert that the Jewish people has a yearning for excellence beyond that of other nations.

Israel's faults help to put into bold relief the one-sidedness of election. It is true that the doctrine also stresses Israel's responsibility for its moral vocation. It has to agree to the terms of its responsibility. Israel is a partner in the process of election, but it is a junior partner, really a silent one. God determines the terms of Israel's election—their content, their implications for the rest of humankind, their reward, and their punishment. Israel, like all other nations, is a tool in God's hands, although it has the advantage of God's love and that love is expressed in the special responsibility God has conferred upon Israel and in its capacity to correct the deficiencies of the cosmos. In this way was the doctrine expanded, a step that was necessary to overcome God's arbitrariness in the original formulation. God's love has to extend to all of His creatures, but if it can be shown that the Jewish people has superior qualities or talents, its election can somehow be justified—if only in its own eyes. The argument, it seems to me, is quite specious, but it explains why Jewish spiritual leaders continue to search for qualities of the Jewish mind and spirit that could substantiate the propriety of God's choice.

We should expect that Kook will caution us against the arrogant claim that Israel has been given a monopoly on spirituality, and he does not fail us. Long ago it was stated that "[a] gentile who studies Torah is comparable to a High Priest."[10] Kook declares, "Regarding exceptional persons, we do not distinguish one nation from another . . . but what we claim for Israel is the special divine quality of the soul of the people as a whole, which is naturally imparted to each individual in a unique way. . . ."[11] Although Kook acknowledges that which is common to all humans, he cannot free himself from the aura of chosenness. Undoubtedly, he says, there are intellectual and moral virtuosi among all peoples, but only the Jewish collective has a native talent for godliness.[12] Moreover, Kook's attitude toward non-Jews is ambivalent. In contrast to his statements about the merit of a gentile who studies Torah, Kook says that to engage in "the pure matters of Torah requires preparation . . . but sinners will stumble against them. Therefore, it is forbidden to teach Torah to a non-Jew. If an exception comes along, and the Torah has influenced him for the good, one should not draw any general conclusions from his example. General rules cover the majority norm, and only expert scholars are authorized to permit exceptions as a temporary expedient."[13] Thus, Israel's mission is to inspire the gentiles to live in God's light. Non-Jews need Israel's guidance, for "[h]igher knowledge is absent from the heart of the nations, although not necessarily from the heart of certain individuals among them."[14]

In the light of Israel's election, Kook questions why so many young Jews abandon not only the *Halakhah* but Judaism in its entirety—when their greatness is so evident. He answers:

> Most of the youth who depart do so because they seek the foundation of absolute justice, which is unattainable. They lack a proper cosmic perspective. They do not realize that the defect [in Judaism] is not in our inner spirit but in the lack of means, the land and the sovereignty that we lost. Now that we have returned to the correct path, it is proper that they rejoin us.[15]

The abandonment of Judaism should be attributed to *galut*, exile, and not to any inherent deficiency in the Jews or in Judaism. The return to Zion will correct everything.

Kook's confidence in the salutary effects of the reconstitution of Israel's national sovereignty is a logical derivative of his utter faith in Israel's election. He does not hesitate to acknowledge Israel's imperfections, but he knows that they will be corrected during the rebuilding. Therefore, he need not reexamine Israel's national principles or the basis of its polity in the light of advances made throughout the civilized world. To Kook, the Jews remain a people apart and are not required to attend to the concepts of state and society that are promulgated elsewhere. The destiny and aspirations of the Jews are independent of natural historical processes. "The Torah of God is perfect" (Ps. 19, 8) and needs no alteration.

The price of certainty is to be found in Kook's lack of historical sense. Not that he ignored what was happening in the world, but, as we have stated, he adopted the view held by important Jewish thinkers that Israel stands above history. He explains:

> When our great inner strength is aroused and clarified, we shall not fear heresy or despair. We shall extract effectively from all things the good and the true that already inhere in the inner being of the ecclesia of Israel. This is the eternal life implanted in us by the Torah of truth. . . . We know God not from or by means of the world, but from our inner soul, from our godly disposition. We begin with this trait, join it to the totality of this nation, purify its historical light, and when we are fully armed, we go out to learn about the broad world.[16]

But it is precisely the historical light that is missing. Nothing in the evolution of Judaism is ever new. Each change is an uncovering of what was contained in the Torah from the moment of its revelation at Mt. Sinai. This, I believe, is a high price to pay for certainty about the truth of the Torah. Any reading of the history of Judaism must encounter its weaknesses and errors. Refusal to acknowledge these limitations endangers the Jewish future. Whoever eschews learning from reliable sources of information and spiritual and moral insight cannot compete with the creative forces among those who are transforming the human landscape.

Since Kook affirms that all men influence the course of civilization, why should there be such emphasis on being a nation that chooses to live alone? Why this isolationism? Kook replies that only the Jews clearly know human worth. As compared with us, Kook writes, "the rest of the world is far, indeed, from this understanding. Everyone else believes that man is passive toward existence, that he is influenced but does not himself influence. But this derogation is untrue. . . . And this is one of the ways in which Israel excels. Israel's spiritual maturation, expressed in its impact on existence, is its special characteristic."[17] Israel alone has a creative soul; other nations can picture only what is already present. Hence, not only is chosenness a moral and spiritual duty, but it is also a native wisdom. This natural, biological trait is an oft-repeated theme in Kook's thought. True, Kook does not believe that this endowment entitles Israel to dominion over other nations, inasmuch as the purpose of its election is to enable it to educate the rest of humankind in God's ways. He states forthrightly:

> The nature of Israel's collective soul is godly. It is not its election that confers on it its divine advantage; nor is its high station a reward for its good deeds, its righteousness or its integrity. Its racial, physical and spiritual make-up have endowed it with its divine strength. Election did not cause this trait, and no defect in the scheme of chosenness can take it away.[18]

Two dangers are inherent in this type of national self-image: (1) the misguided assumption that the chosen people has virtues and excellence that are denied to other groups; and (2) the tendency to attribute to other peoples undesirable traits or weaknesses that they are powerless to overcome. Kook is explicit:

> The mood of depression and disintegration that was cast upon Christian Europe, and not much less in Moslem Asia, *and which*

cannot be alleviated, could not exist side by side with social renewal replete with a strong zest for life. To bring the latter to perfect expression, it is necessary that a people have the light of the true God in its collective soul. Only Israel has this trait now, as it did at the outset of its career. The separation of religion and society suits the nations but harms us. We have to illuminate the gloom and explain what divides one religion from another, what entitles one religion to be called such because of its greatness and originality and another which is virtually obliterated and able to survive only by virtue of what it can steal and wrest from the source.[19] (Italics, JJC)

This is not the place to dispute Kook's assumption that the separation of religion and people (including the state) is a bad thing. However, it is pertinent to note what Kook sees as a weakness of Christianity and Islam but not of Judaism. Communicants of these religions are devoid of God's light and therefore are unable to correct their defects.[20]

We can argue about the relative spiritual and moral levels of this religion or that. We can assume that, according to criteria accepted by all parties to a dispute, one religion, at a given time, might surpass another in its godliness. Kook, however, makes no effort to prove; instead, he proclaims. According to him, gentile religions cannot mature, whereas Judaism has already achieved a higher level. The individual Jew must only recognize this fact and act accordingly. The example Kook offers is instructive. It is the ultimate question of today: Can a non-Jew hope to achieve equality in a Jewish state? Or is it only the Jewish majority that can attain full rights? More profoundly, when we speak about separation of religion and state, do we mean separation between the whole body politic and spirituality, or, as is customary in enlightened states, between the state and a religious *establishment* of any kind? Danger to freedom lurks in the efforts of one religion or religious lobby to control the instruments of government of a pluralistic state. Kook did not comprehend this danger because he did not conceive of a democratic and pluralistic Jewish state, or in the case of the Diaspora, of a pluralistic Jewish community.

We have already touched upon Kook's attitude toward Eretz Yisrael, and we shall elaborate on the subject in another chapter. Here, I add a few comments that bear on the doctrine of chosenness. As might be expected, Kook contrasts the purity of Eretz Yisrael with the impurity of all other lands. There are two ways to look at Kook's image of the country. One can regard Israel's love of its homeland as an example of true and eternal love. The Land of Israel is poor in natural resources, yet the Jewish people loves it profoundly. Better stated, we should say that because of its poverty, the Land has evoked Israel's devotion. Only it has been able to arouse fully the desire for a national life. Every Zionist will agree to this notion of an unmoved mover. But Kook finds Eretz Yisrael to be an active force. It rewards those who merit its love and punishes those who provoke it.[21] Thus, Eretz Yisrael does not belong to the category of natural territory. It is the land of *supernatural redemption.* Just as Israel alone possesses the Torah of salvation, so does it own the land of divine salvation. The national redemption that will spring forth out of the Land will embrace all humankind and not only Israel.

Furthermore, Eretz Yisrael is not to be thought of as a tool to attract Jews to the *mitzvot,* especially those that are applicable only in the Land itself. It is inherently holy, and settlement in it is the essence of its holiness.[22] Israel's election is incomplete without Eretz Yisrael, and the holiness of its land cannot be fulfilled unless Israel occupies and builds on it. Nothing that is done by other peoples on and with their lands has any spiritual significance or contributes to their sanctity. As far as Jewry is concerned, its holiness in the lands of the impure dispersion cannot be compared in any way to its profound reality in Eretz Yisrael.[23] Kook is not at all interested in giving a psycho-sociological analysis of the difference between settlement in the countries of the Dispersion and dwelling in Eretz Yisrael. His intention is to show that only a theologically grounded description can explain the nature of Israel's relationship to its homeland. Only such a faith can substantiate Kook's optimism that the rebuilding of Eretz Yisrael will cleanse the Jewish people of its sins.

Kook's love of Israel was so all-consuming that he could even find merit in its defects. For example, despite his ceaseless struggle against deviations from the Torah, he could say, "Jewish heresy is full of faith and holiness, even more than the faith of all the nations."[24] In Kook's philosophy, we find one of the most forthright statements of the chosen people doctrine as a mixture of particularism and universalism. We shall examine this point further after a summary of Kaplan's critique of the concept.

KAPLAN'S CRITIQUE

Throughout his career Kaplan was obsessed with the doctrine of election. Although he regarded it as the key to an understanding of the Bible, he came gradually to see it as a stumbling block to spiritual maturation. At the outset of his teaching career at the Teachers Institute and the Rabbinical School of the Jewish Theological Seminary of America, he tried to interpret the doctrine and its traditional formulations in ways that would enable him to feel comfortable with the idea. In an article on the centrality of Torah, which appeared in 1914 in the *Students' Annual* of the Seminary, Kaplan treated chosenness in much the same way as did Kook. Like the latter, his point of departure was his love of the Jewish people.

> After all, our love for Judaism depends upon the intensity with which we entertain the desire to be at one with Israel. If that desire, which may be called the Jewish social will-to-live, burns within us not as a smouldering spark but with the white heat of an ardent soul, we are bound to love and cherish the institutions through which the life of our people has found its highest and most self-conscious expression.[25]

At this stage of his life, Kaplan had lost his belief in the literal historicity of the theophany at Mt. Sinai. Nevertheless, he thought it possible to reinterpret revelation so as to shore up the authority of the Torah. He writes:

> The discovery of natural law in the physical world has not banished God from men's thoughts. Why, then, should the study of the Bible from a rational standpoint interfere with the notion of revelation which is writ large on every page, in whatever way we read it? . . . As Jews, it is not enough for us to have faith in the reality of revelation. We must go further and believe that Israel has been the chief instrument of that revelation.[26]

Kaplan then proclaims, "Such a claim for Israel is by no means unsupported by a proper reading of history and human experience."[27] He concludes:

[T]he dominating purpose which has molded the Torah into a consistent whole has been to define Israel's function in the world as a divinely chosen people. With this in mind, every incident that is recorded in the Torah, every law that it commands, every character that is made to pass before us and every poem, prayer or prophecy that is included in it, will be found in some way related to the divinely appointed destiny for which Israel was chosen.[28]

Thus, the idea of Israel's election was so important to Kaplan that it took an emotional as well as intellectual upheaval on his part before he could abandon his efforts at reinterpretation and seek an alternative to the concept.

Early on, Kaplan had recognized the difference between the Jewish and Calvinistic versions of election. He declared:

The individual does not thank God because he happens to be of those whom God for some reason known to himself has selected for divine favor; he thanks God that through the national civilization at his disposal he is given the opportunity of experiencing God's election. The election is contingent upon his living the civilization of his people, upon his utilizing the nationhood of his people as the sanction of his purposes and the directing principle of their achievement.[29]

Here election is conceived as the force that drives a Jew to elicit from Judaism whatever it has to offer for the fashioning of positive personalities. Chosenness is a means to an exalted end—to create a people that can be, individually and collectively, a blessing to all humankind. In this formulation of the early 1930s, Kaplan was still trying to reinterpret chosenness and to retain the traditional wording.

Kaplan considers nationhood to be an asset in human life, but his eyes are open to the damage it can cause in its exaggerated form of chauvinism. He never tires of denouncing such a distortion of the national spirit. Nationalism became the focus of civilization for the Jews. They instinctively sensed its ideal potential, and they pictured Israel as the unique nation. This faith, in turn, was validated by the additional belief that their God is the only true God.[30] The ancient Jews traced the source of their loyalty to the supreme Deity, not to themselves or their initiative but to the will of that very same Power. Kaplan finds in the attitude of the patriarchs a conception that can be of help to us today. "The belief that God chose Israel held in latent form the generalization that the possession of true nationhood qualified a people to achieve its highest potentialities."[31] The election of Israel, in its biblical formulation, attempted to steer the Israelites between a natural feeling of privilege at being God's chosen ones and the sense of responsibility that this role imposed on them. Kaplan quotes the verse from Amos that we cited above, as well as Deut. 7, 7, "The Lord did not set His love on you nor choose you, because you are more numerous than any people, for you are the fewest of all people." This modesty lends a moral tone to election, but it does not eliminate the feeling of superiority, as we shall explain below.

Another positive feature of chosenness is described by Kaplan. During the centuries of exile,

> the Jewish consciousness was always employed in the contempla-
> tion of the future. This national self-consciousness inhered in every
> individual Jew who was humanized and spiritualized through the
> enlarged mental horizon as he could never have been otherwise.
> This result was achieved for him by his intense nationhood, al-
> though he was incapable of isolating and naming the sense of na-
> tionhood itself. Feeling its power, however, he used the only term
> by which he could identify and explain it: Israel, the chosen of
> God.[32]

Nevertheless, argues Kaplan, we have to overcome the inertia that chains us to an outmoded type of thinking.

> The modern man who is used to thinking in terms of humanity as
> a whole can no longer reconcile himself to the notion of any peo-
> ple, or body of believers, constituting a type of society which may
> be described as belonging to a supernatural order. This is conse-
> quently what the doctrine of "election" has hitherto implied. As a
> psychological defense to counteract the humiliation to which the
> Jewish people was subjected, the doctrine of "election" had its
> value. As an expression of the sense of spiritual achievement in the
> past, it had some justification in fact. But nowadays, when only
> present achievement tends to satisfy the human spirit, the doctrine
> of Israel's election, in its traditional sense, cannot be expected to
> make the slightest difference in the behavior or outlook of the
> Jew.[33]

By "the modern man," Kaplan means those persons who find their satisfaction in the act of living without having to compare themselves to others. Kaplan realizes that most men and women need the psychological support that comes from a feeling like that of election or of being graced by a special talent, but he came to believe that the loss resulting from such a psychological anodyne is greater than the gain. Probing the nature of this loss occupied him without end.

As a theological concept, election is an expression of supernaturalistic theology. There has to be a cosmic chooser, and He, of course, is, by definition, beyond nature and in control of it. It is true, and Kaplan was aware of the fact, that many persons do have a sense of being chosen. He quotes with approval the statement of Rudolf Otto, the famous Christian mystic:

> The recipient of divine grace feels and knows ever more and more surely, as he looks back on his past, that he has not grown into his present self through any achievement or effort of his own, and that, apart from his own will and power, grace was imparted to him, grasped him, impelled him, and led him.[34]

However, there is nothing in this state of mind to prove that behind it is a choosing God. Moreover, when an individual or an entire people proclaim election, they have to identify the chooser. If they point to the God of the cosmos, they thereby declare their superiority. For no one is chosen for a crucial assignment unless he or she possesses special talents or is granted them in order to fulfill the charge. Why did God not spread responsibility for implementing His will equally among peoples and nations? How can we prove that the feeling of election is, indeed, warranted? And if the "chosen ones" declare apologetically that everyone is chosen—every person has his or her own capabilities—how can they defend the horrible lot of the multitudes of human beings who are born with deformed bodies and minds and of nations whose circumstances limit the possibilities of civilized growth? Are they, too, chosen? Among creatures are the handicapped and the unfortunate. No good God would want such asymmetry. The psychological argument for the sense of election is theologically monstrous.

The first reference to chosenness in the Bible is the command to Avram to travel to Canaan. From that moment on, Eretz Yis-rael has been an ineluctable element in the doctrine. Chronologi-cally, the choice of Canaan as the homeland of the Jewish people antedated the Hebrew *aliyah*. According to the Bible, the decision was God's. From a historical perspective, the settlement of the Hebrews in Canaan spanned centuries of nomadic wandering in the region of the Fertile Crescent. A clear reference to this process is the verse, "And Terah took his son, Avram, and Lot, the son of his son, Haran, and Sarai, the wife of Avram and with them left Ur Kasdim and headed for Canaan. When they reached Haran, they sojourned there" (Gen. 11, 31). Thus, Avraham, as he came to be known, apparently fulfilled a family plan to emigrate to Canaan.

This is the historical root of the biblical account, except that the biblical authors incorporated the history in a theological vi-sion. The story of the wandering shepherd tribes becomes the drama of the evolution of a nation in its promised land. Israel's chosenness was a perception of the folk imagination, but from the moment it was invented, the myth took on a life of its own. Henceforth, the Jewish people was destined to follow a unique historical path. Kaplan became convinced that election has to be treated in the context of the understanding of Jewish history, the relation of Jewry to the rest of humankind, and its theological, psychological, and moral implications.

As long as it was possible to believe wholeheartedly that the Torah was revealed at Sinai, chosenness was credible. But what happens when this belief no longer burns in the heart of the ma-jority of Jews and when the talmudic discussions of the rabbis are no longer considered to contain the intent of Moses at the time of the theophany?[35] If the Torah, instead, is the collective wisdom of the Jewish people as it endeavored to solve the problems of its national life—as Kaplan believed—then the doctrine of election by a supernatural God has no basis. Kaplan writes:

> [T]he possession of the Torah proves that we are chosen, only if we also accept the idea that the Torah is the one doctrine, or way of life, that expresses God's will and gives assurance of God's grace and salvation. . . . Unless we believe that God has revealed only to Jews the way of life which expresses the divine goal of human evolution, we cannot honestly affirm belief in the Chosen People idea.[36]

But from the moment we maintain that the Torah is not only true but is the only proper way of life, we cannot deny that election implies superiority. There is a great difference between thanking God "who has drawn us to His service" and blessing Him "who has raised us above all other tongues" (benedictions in the Jewish prayer book). The first formula applies to all, the second only to the chosen ones.

Many efforts have been made throughout the generations to refine the doctrine of election as an instrument for Jewish survival. All are deficient in one way or another—logically, spiritually, or morally.[37] The worst interpretations, however, are those that advance the notion of Israel's superiority. Kaplan analyzes three of them.[38]

The first interpretation claims that Israel is exclusively endowed with certain superior characteristics. Even if Jews did not always live up to the saying, "Three qualities mark this people: They are merciful, modest and perform acts of loving-kindness,"[39] they at least set noble standards for themselves. But there is a great difference between discovering meritorious ideals and conduct among Jews and the view of chosenness of the Reform theologian, Kaufmann Kohler. Kohler argued that the Jewish people has a special talent for ethical monotheism. This apologetic is nothing less than racism—not in its virulent form, but certainly a questionable declaration of Israel's biological excellence and superiority.

A second interpretation maintains that the Jews were the first people to enunciate the values that would bring about universal salvation. Kaplan regards this claim as conceit. Other peoples and individuals throughout the world have also contributed to the ideals and standards that are so essential to the making of fine human character. However, even if the Jews have pioneered in many areas of ethical living, this is no justification for according Israel a divine role that is denied to other nations. Our ancestors' success should not be attributed to the arbitrary will of God to play favorites—far better for our people to be modest and self-critical.

A third group of interpreters claims that only the Jews possess religious and moral ideals. They believe that Jewish teachings are eternally correct. Jews are the discoverers or receivers and transmitters of these divine ideals. Again, there can be no question that the Jewish contribution to the spiritual and moral progress of humankind has been considerable. At the same time, this fact does not authenticate the claim that the Jewish role is the outcome of Israel's election as the sole agent for bringing God's grace to humanity. By definition, universal ideals and values are transmittable from one group to another. Moreover, throughout history, they have sprouted in the soils of many peoples. To cite one instance, the democratic ethos is composed of strands that were woven in the cultures of Israel, Greece, England, France, and the United States—to name just a few of the national contributors. In the light of this historical testimony, there is no basis for the claim that only the Jews are capable of discovering universal, divine truth. Once again we are confronted with a form of racism and a shaky theology. The omnipotent God is seen as scattering talents unequally among His creatures.

In another aspect of his analysis, Kaplan refers to the determined opposition of the Jewish people to missionary activity. Those Jews who articulate the third interpretation of election believe that they are called to save humankind by being loyal to the one divine religion, their own. Jewish apologists distinguish between their path and that of the representatives of other religions. They believe that the proper way to persuade non-Jews of the truths of Judaism is to make certain that all Jews live up to their heritage. They also point with pride to the fact that Judaism grants a place in the world-to-come to the righteous of all nations, provided they observe the universal Noahide laws. However, even this measure of openness loses much of its commendability when we realize that, according to Maimonides, the fulfillment of non-Jews is limited to those "who obey the laws because [they believe that] God commanded them in the Torah, that He communicated them to mankind through Moses, our Teacher, and that the sons of Noah had previously been commanded concerning them. But if the non-Jews observe the laws out of their own reasoning, they are not to have the status of resident aliens or be considered as among the righteous gentiles or their wise men."[40] Thus, this religious liberalism turns out to be spiritual imperialism. Kaplan concludes that the Jewish mission, as depicted in the doctrine of chosenness, depends on the willingness of the non-Jews to agree to the idea that the Jewish people is the channel leading to universal salvation. Hidden in Rambam's presentation is the thought that while God's commands might be deduced by the human intellect, this was not God's intent. Remember that the Jew, too, will not achieve the rewards of the afterlife, if he or she does not confess to the truth of the Torah and to its being God's revelation.[41]

Different diagrams can be drawn to illustrate the connection among the various strands of Judaism. For example, a well-known triangle links together the three corners of God, Israel, and Torah. Since the latter two corners are the work of God, they are totally dependent upon His will. Using the same triangle, we might conceive of another type of relationship among the three factors. Let us assume for the sake of argument that control is in the hands of the Jewish people. In this case, however, there is no basis for the election hypothesis. Chosenness is founded on the conception of a supernatural God. Then, too, we might imagine an organically structured triangle of God, Eretz Yisrael, and the Jewish people. Once more, in the context of election, God is the pinnacle of the triangle; the other two points would lack all reality without God's action.

If the chosen people doctrine were to mean no more than the idea that all peoples are selected to perform certain tasks, we should not have witnessed the manifold effects that it caused in the stream of Jewish history. But it was accompanied by the idea that Israel stands at the vortex of human history. Kaplan writes:

> History throughout the Bible is God-centered, in that it is a history of God's activity and self-manifestation. It is in a sense, however, also man-centered, in that man is represented as the purpose of creation and the chief occasion for God's self-manifestation. On the other hand, of all the descendants of Adam, only Israel is considered capable of fulfilling God's purpose in having created man.[42]

In the Talmud and Midrash, "Israel . . . is declared to be not only the purpose of creation, but also the source of the world's stability."[43] It is argued that the fate of the cosmos depends on the behavior of the Jews. This sort of national egocentrism ill befits the interdependent world in which we live. No nation alone can bring salvation to other peoples. No blueprint can be devised that would enable one nation to build the structure of world peace and amity. All peoples can and must contribute their share to such a venture. Instead of relying on its election, each nation is called upon to examine its own situation and to conduct itself as it would wish other nations to behave if they were governed by the same set of circumstances.

If this is what is demanded by human progress toward the fulfillment of the dream of God's kingdom on earth, how is Israel supposed to view its Torah? We have already noted that election is epitomized in the granting of the Torah, and we pointed out that this vital thread in the election complex is articulated in the blessing recited by every person who is called to the reading of the Torah in the synagogue. Kaplan's problem is to preserve among Jews love for and loyalty to the Torah without the psychological support of chosenness. He suggests that we try to communicate to each Jew the awareness that one's own fulfillment as a human being can be accomplished through participation in the life of the Jewish people and its culture. In this spirit, Kaplan describes Torah as symbol, content, and process. "As a covenant, the Torah is a symbol, representing the truth that a nation becomes such not through the accident of common ancestry or physical propinquity, but through the consent of those who constitute it to live together and to make their common past the inspiration for a common future."[44] The overpowering will of the Jewish people to survive is, to a great extent, a result of the spiritual power of Torah.

As content, "the Torah emphasizes the important truth that a nation is not a fighting unit but a cultural group, united not by the instincts that keep together wolf-packs for purposes of offense and defense, but by the urge to develop those human differentia and potentialities which only collective life can bring forth."[45]

As process, Torah is expressed in education. Ideally, in Kaplan's view, the entire social fabric, including the political structure, should be subservient to education. Torah's purpose should be to develop the skills of every individual. If the society does not direct its activities to that end, it blocks human progress.

Finally,

[i]f what makes them [the Jews] a nation is the Torah and all that it represents as symbol, as content and as process, it is their duty to

uphold their nationhood, even as their ancestors had it uphold the unity of God, to the point of martyrdom. The division of mankind into nations derives from laws of human nature and geography that cannot be defied. Cosmopolitanism is a vain delusion, and in the mouths of Jews who deny their nationhood, it often goes together, paradoxically enough, with an obstreperous patriotism for the countries of which they are citizens. When not disciplined and brought under the control of a moral standard such as represented by the Torah of Israel, nationhood is sure to run amuck, and, driven by the wild impulses of greed and vanity, is bound to wreak ruin upon all who come in its path.[46]

It follows that to secure for itself a nationalism that is spiritually and morally universal, a people must divest itself of the sense of chosenness. Rather, says Kaplan, "[a] far nobler motive than the assertion of a claim to spiritual superiority is the need for a people always to strive to outdo itself, always to keep on growing in moral and spiritual capacity."[47] This declaration is a substitute for the idea of election. Whoever truly strives to repair the world must be grateful for spiritual achievement wherever it occurs. Every people is called upon to care for its own vineyard.

Concluding Remarks

I have tried to present Kook's views on chosenness in the best possible light. His goal was to contribute to the moral and spiritual perfection of all people. But I cannot escape the conclusion that his world consists of two compartments, one occupied by the Jewish people and the other by the rest of the human race. Kook sees no lack of taste in the feeling of noblesse oblige, because for him the status of the Jews as chosen is a fact and not a matter of conjecture.[48]

Kaplan, on the other hand, finds two faults with this orientation. In the first place, if election is considered to be the natural outcome of racial superiority, the pernicious implications of chosenness are obvious. Cultural differences, stemming from historical, geographical, and other circumstances that condition the growth of every people, are part of human evolution. However, while there are undoubtedly moments of superior achievement in the history of many nations, the retention of such lofty status is not a genetic trait of any group. Achievement and failure are common to all human endeavors. Second, the evaluation of so-called Jewish values cannot be undertaken within the system of election itself. The criteria of judgment concerning the Jewish contribution have to be established by universal consensus. In that light, there is ample evidence that Jewish claims to the possession of God's commands are sometimes unwarranted.

Kaplan's position conflicts with long-standing notions that have scarcely been challenged. Surrender of such ideas involves a radical change in folk mentality. Psychological resistance to revolutionary change is bound to be strong. Even after most Jews no longer hold to the historicity of revelation, they continue unthinkingly to recite the traditional formulae praising God for having chosen us from among the nations and given us the Torah, for having raised us above all tongues, and for having separated us from the perverse ones. A large proportion of Jews remain indifferent to the need for rethinking the rationale for Jewish commitment. It is easier to follow centuries-old intellectual habits. Secular Jews identify election with uniqueness, with which they have no difficulty. They take refuge in Israel's longevity, in its unusual history, its high culture, and even here and there in the thought that Jews pursue excellence in greater measure than other peoples But this secularization of election deprives it of its true meaning. Without the Chooser, the doctrine loses its historical and logical basis. Many Jews are too insecure to abandon the belief that their people has been assigned or is fated to play a preordained role in the fashioning of human history. Otherwise, why be a Jew? Kaplan's critique thus runs afoul of this psychological conservatism. Until we Jews emancipate ourselves from this psychological urge to feel important as compared with other nations and to feel that our qualities are unmatched, we shall not be moved by logic or theological exactitude to surrender the notion of election.

NOTES

1. *The Kozari*, Hebrew translation by Yehudah Even-Shmuel (Tel-Aviv: Dvir, 1972, 1:102).

2. "The Universalism of the Chosen People," in *The Inner Eye* (New York: Jewish Frontier Association, 1953, p. 56).

3. Kook, for instance, declares, "The difference between Israel and the nations is not one of gradation. It is nothing less than the difference between light and darkness" (*Shemuot Reivah*, pp. 88–89).

4. *Orot*, p. 148.

5. "Derekh Hatehiyah," in *HaNir*, 1909, p. 3.

6. *Orot*, pp. 20–21.

7. Ibid., p. 22. "The ecclesia of Israel is the highest spiritual manifestation of human existence" (AT, p. 14).

8. Ibid., p. 23.

9. KL, Vol. 1, L. 50, pp. 58–59.

10. Bava Kama, 38a.

11. "Derekh Hatehiyah," p. 2.

12. KL, Vol. 1, L. 64, pp. 70–71.

13. KL, Vol. 3, L. 89, p. 99. See Kook's letter to Rabbi Shmuel Alexandrov (Ibid., L. 140, p. 178): "There is no other nation in the entire world, aside from Israel, in whose soul is stored up, as its very essence, the precious treasure of the highest illumination. There are pious and wise individuals, but there is on earth no 'righteous people,' except for Israel. And this foundation is spread to each Jew." In another place, Kook comments, "The plenitude of the holy spirit, which is unique in Israel, is much greater in height and uniqueness than all types of holy spirit which all humans earn according to their deeds" (OK, Vol. 1, p. 29).

14. KL, Vol. 1, p. 135.

15. The pendulum swings back and forth. "I have never claimed that men are denied access to knowledge of divine things. If these were lacking in nature, we should have no way of raising men to the level of bliss that we wish for them. But there is insufficient vitality in the nationalisms of the nations to grasp the many worlds of the divine realm. Nor do they possess God's love as their inner nature" (KL, Vol. 1, L. 110, p. 135).

16. Ibid., L. 140, p. 178.

17. KL, L. 44, p. 45. "All gentiles are subservient to the powerful control of the flow of natural forces. They have no higher aspiration other than to fulfil their natural desires. This is not the fate of Jacob. His inner urge is to conquer himself. His soul's desire is to secure eternal life for all. individuals and collective entities and movements alike. [He longs] to raise them all to that level of life's meaning as is to be found in the supernal Eden of creative wisdom, in which the real purpose of existence is immersed" (OK, Vol. 3, pp. 33–34). Kook might have given

thought to the audacity of attributing spiritual exclusivity to his people. He often refers to the holiness that is to be found in the human race in general. However, each time he does so, he feels it necessary to note the special qualities of the chosen people. Here is a typical example: "It is proper that the content of holiness should be understood initially as applying to all mankind. For the sacred is discerned as universal, and the relationship of man to God transcends any single people. But afterwards, it takes on new garb in Israel. However, world-wide moral deterioration resulted in mankind's forgetting its holy origin. A new creation came into being in Israel, and now all thought about holiness starts from Jewry" (OK, Vol. 2, p. 299). Mostly, however, Kook feels no reason for apologetics or explanations. He repeatedly points out the qualities that entitle Israel to its election. "We are called upon to unite the world, but before we do so, we are expected to disclose the plan for spiritual unity which is our secret self. This exalted plan, which has never been imparted to other nations, is intrinsic to our intellect and our morality, to the nature of our soul and to our individual heredity. It has pulsed through our remarkable history, in our blood and our physical structure. . . ." (KL, Vol. 3, L. 748, pp. 13–14).

18. OK, Vol. 3, p. 77.

19. *Shabbat Haaretz* (henceforth, SH) (Jerusalem: Mosad HaRav Kook, 5739, Introduction, p. 7).

20. KL, Vol. 1, L. 164, pp. 214–215.

21. See OT, p. 101, and particularly Filver's note: "Among other nations, the relationship of the individual to the nation as a whole is not bound up with morality or religious life. Hence, separation of religion and state is possible, and the individual can still remain patriotic, even if he takes exception to the religious consensus. This cannot occur in Israel. The basis of Jewish nationalism is in carrying out the Torah. Whoever cuts himself off from Jewish religion will sooner or later find himself fenced off from national values, such as homeland, avoidance of mixed marriage, and the like."

22. "Because of the weakness of the national soul, the land will not perform its characteristic function" (SH, Introduction, p. 11).

23. SH, p. 62.

24. Ibid., p. 30.

25. MA, p. 100.

26. This essay was reprinted fifty years after it first appeared. *The Reconstructionist*, Vol. 30, No. 7, 1964, p. 13.

27. Ibid., p. 11.

28. Ibid.

29. Ibid., p. 17.

30. JC, p. 258.

31. Ibid., p. 257.

32. Ibid., pp. 262–263.

33. Ibid., p. 43. When Kaplan writes that only current achievement can satisfy the human spirit, he does not mean to turn his back on the accomplishments of the past. He wants only to emphasize that for the past to gain the approval of the current generation, it has to prove that it is in accord with the best standards prevailing today.

34. Quoted in JC, note on p. 539.

35. *Menahot* 29b.

36. QJA, p. 205.

37. See, for example, *Sifre*, Haazinu, 312. "Whence does God recognize His lot—from Jacob, as is written, 'For God has chosen Israel for Himself, / Jacob for His treasure' (Ps. 135, 4). And it says further that His people Jacob is God's lot and inheritance. The matter is still uncertain: we do not know whether God chose Israel as His treasure or whether Israel chose the Holy One, blessed be He. But we are taught, 'The Lord, your God, has chosen you' (Deut. 7, 6). How do we know that Jacob also chose God? It is written, 'Not like these is the portion of Jacob; / For He is the shaper of all things, / And Israel is the tribe of His inheritance; / The Lord of hosts is His name' (Jer. 10, 17)." This homiletical interpretation is seen to be forced when taken in the context of the biblical thrust of election. However, even if we concede that the initiative of the human individual and the nation is an essential feature of God's choosing, there is still no comparison between the choice of Israel from among all the nations and obedience on Israel's part (or by any other people) to the one God. Accepting God's rule is not identical with being elected. The casuistry fails.

38. FAJ, p. 215.

39. *Yevamot* 79a.

40. *Mishneh Torah*, Laws of Kings 8:11.

41. There seems to be occasional contradictions between Maimonides as the halakhic scholar and as the philosopher. While the halakhist expects unquestioning obedience to the *mitzvot*, the philosopher offers real salvation only to those who can rise to metaphysical heights. This is the case despite the danger for simple faith and for submission to authority that lies in philosophical speculation.

42. GJM, p. 35.

43. Ibid. An error in footnote 18 (p. 518) makes it difficult to determine to which midrash Kaplan refers when he or the printer sends the reader to *Yevamot* 38a. The error, however, does not detract from the significance of his observation. A good example of his intent can be

found in *Tanhuma*, Terumah 9: "for were it not for them [Israel], rain would never fall. It is for their sake that the Holy One, blessed be He, causes light to shine in this world. . . ."

44. JC, pp. 258–259.

45. Ibid., p. 259.

46. Ibid., pp. 159–260.

47. FAJ, p. 226.

48. Kook follows Yehudah Halevi as if there has been no change in man's understanding of the course of natural events since the twelfth century. Kook could easily have written these words of Halevi: "Even if we acknowledge that other peoples have followed Him and worshiped Him, either from hearsay or tradition, where do we find that God accepted them, clung to them, was satisfied with their worship and was angered by their rebellion? We observe that they are abandoned to nature and accident to which they owe success or failure and not to divine Providence. That is clear to all" (*The Kozari*, 4:3). It suffices to ask, What is so clear?

11

Exile and Redemption: The Role of Eretz Yisrael

SOPHISTICATED THINKERS try not to base their entire intellectual system on a single factor. Nonetheless, they cannot avoid emphasizing one or two points that are viewed as more salient than the others. If we want to get at the heart of Kook's and Kaplan's outlooks, there is no better way than to examine their treatment of the role of Eretz Yisrael in Jewish life. That examination is best conducted after a brief review of the thinking of Halevi, Rambam, and Maharal on the subject.

Throughout the centuries, ceaseless efforts have been made to define the essence of the romance of Israel and its land. Jews have never been satisfied with the biblical claim that God willed this marriage. One of the most impressive attempts to probe deeply into the people-land relationship was that of Yehudah Halevi in the twelfth century. He tried to demonstrate that Eretz Yisrael is graced with qualities that raise it above all other lands. Not only does Eretz Yisrael have the natural resources of all lands, but it is also endowed with supernatural gifts. Only in this land can prophecy emerge, "for Eretz Yisrael—its air, soil and sky—is distinguished by its ability to foster prophecy, as long as this trait is complemented by proper preparation and tilling of the soil for the raising of plant species."[1] Halevi claims, "Everyone who prophesied did so in this land or in its behalf."[2] The relationship between Israel and its land is so special that only here can the people carry out its prophetic assignments. True, national redemption cannot be guaranteed merely by dwelling in this land. The people must build and tend it to benefit from its blessings. There is also a negative side of the coin. Only in Eretz Yisrael can the people fulfill itself; in the Diaspora, there is no chance for national redemption.

The Maharal (R. Yehudah Loew b. Bezalel) (c.1525–1609)

maintained that Israel's right to the Land of Israel is based on the assumption that every nation has been accorded its own natural homeland; only there can it live normally and fully. Israel's exile is unnatural and must therefore come to an end. The theses of Halevi and Maharal are powerful, once one accepts their supernatural foundation. But when one inspects the real geographical condition of Eretz Yisrael and its geopolitical status and tries to understand why this particular stretch of land has aroused the love of the Jewish people, the door can be opened to a more objective analysis.

The rationalist Maimonides (1135–1204) also highlighted the central role of Eretz Yisrael in the creative survival of the Jewish people. His position is well delineated in several laws found in the Laws of Kings, in his massive code *Mishneh Torah*. Taking into account both the objective and the subjective factors of the exile, Rambam decrees that perpetual residence outside of Eretz Yisrael is absolutely forbidden, although temporary domicile, except in Egypt, is permitted. Citing a few of his *halakhot* from chapter five of the Laws of Kings captures the mood of Rambam's thinking on the subject:

> It is always forbidden to leave Eretz Yisrael, except in order to study Torah, to get married, to prevent idolatry, and on condition that one will return (halakhah 9); The great scholars would kiss the borders and stones of Eretz Yisrael and roll around on its soil (halakhah 10); Whoever dwells in Eretz Yisrael has his sins forgiven. . . . Even if he walks only four cubits (in the Land), he merits a place in the world-to-come (halakhah 11). It is always preferable for a person to dwell in Eretz Yisrael, even in a city where most of the inhabitants are idolaters, than to dwell outside of the Land in a place where there is a majority of Jews. For leaving Eretz Yisrael is tantamount to idolatry (halakhah 12).

Only through utter devotion to Eretz Yisrael can the Jewish people continue its creative development and, then, only through protecting and building it. Love galvanizes a people to turn its potentiality into the reality demanded by its ideals and circumstances. The image of scholars kissing the soil and rolling in it indicates Rambam's awareness that love of the homeland has to find expression in physical contact with the soil. In Rambam's moments of mystical rationalism, we find the basis for his belief that occupying the Land can bring about redemption from the national sins of the Jewish people and fulfillment for the individual Jew.

The source of these visions lies in the supernaturalism that Yehudah Halevi fully adopted and from which Rambam strayed significantly but not completely. As I have said, the traditional Jewish claim to Eretz Yisrael is theological. Ownership of the Land is an integral part of the Chosen People doctrine. It is, I believe, the fulcrum on which the idea of Jewish election rests. In the Bible, the gift of the Land antedates the revelation of the Torah. Halevi and Rambam differ in their views on Eretz Yisrael only as regards its inherent nature. Halevi stresses the supernatural qualities of the Land, whereas Maimonides attributes its creative power to God's decision to betroth it to Israel. Let us now see how Kook and Kaplan portray the role of Eretz Yisrael in Jewish life.

KOOK ON ERETZ YISRAEL

In Kook's love for God, Eretz Yisrael, the Jewish people, and the Torah, it is God who is paramount. But the four objects—or more accurately, subjects—of Kook's love are bound together inseparably. To love God is to love His people; to love Israel is to love its homeland, while to love Eretz Yisrael is to love the Torah that was designed for it and that grows in its soil. Eretz Yisrael without God and Israel is like a body without a soul.

Kook's Zionism is an integral element in his theology, which culminates in a political. program for the Jewish people. Redemption will not come solely from the side of God. The Jews must be actively involved in the process. Political activism must be of the kind that will reveal to all men and women Israel's love for God.

> We all feel within us our total nation. Its striving for absolute good, the good of all, is a goal for which it is worthwhile to establish a commonwealth and engage in politics. We see from our flesh that absolute good is the eternal divine good in all of existence, and we yearn constantly to trace its tracks in the national and universal

sense. Therefore, love of God and cleaving to Him are of our very essence and cannot be erased or altered.[3]

Kook poses the idea that the universe is both unified and split. Since God is One, so must His Creation be one. But Kook embraces the kabbalistic notion of the fissionization of the cosmos. Only Israel was granted the ability to understand the secret of God's unity and to apply it to everyday life. Unfortunately, stumbling blocks are in the way of repairing the damage that accompanied Creation. One of the main obstacles is the exile. As long as Israel is

> in the impure territory of the nations, it is impossible for the united world outlook to be revealed. Divisiveness currently rules the universe. Splintered and alienated, individual opinions dominate life's arenas. All effort to breathe Israelite air and to grasp the secret of the unified world is foiled by the atmosphere of foreign lands. The impure soil outside of Eretz Yisrael is full of the stench of idolatry, and Israel on foreign soil practices idolatry, even though it might itself be pure. There is no way to eliminate this idolatry except by having all Jews gather in Eretz Yisrael. . . .[4]

A straight line passes from the talmudic Sages to Halevi, Rambam, Maharal, and HaRav Kook. They all point to the negative impact of the lands of exile. As contrasted with the vacuousness of the lands of exile, "[t]he air of Eretz Yisrael makes wise. It illumines the soul as to the basis of the unified world. In Eretz Yisrael, we draw sustenance from the light of Israelite wisdom, from the special spiritual quality of Israel's life, from Israel's philosophy of life and of the universe, which is basically the triumph of the united over the fragmented world."[5]

Therefore, the return to Eretz Yisrael and the establishment there of a vital Jewry are necessary to put Israel's inherent traits to work.[6] Israel has a special sensitivity to God's unity; and it is only the Jewish people who can restore cosmic unity to its original state.[7] This sensitivity is only one factor, but a vital one, in Israel's godly character. Kook writes:

> The world of idol worship and of heresy knows only itself, its crass, materialistic pleasures. Even its spiritual enjoyments are self-seeking. That which is more base and ugly and that which is united in

egocentric interests are too deeply rooted in this world. All this has
no place in Jacob. . . .[8]

Kook continues:

Love of God is intrinsic to the Jewish character. as is love of Eretz
Yisrael. Our relationship to Eretz Yisrael is not incidental, but
rather a divine connection that is part of our nature. All our essential being is tied to the precious land, and our being distanced from
it, as a result of our sins, did not cause any change in our essential
attitude. . . .[9]

The exile is powerless to do any damage to our national character,
but it can affect our ability to use it to the best advantage. Israel
was born with a predisposition for loving-kindness that is lacking
in other nations; to activate this trait, however, it must return to
its homeland.

Nevertheless, Israel's divine salvation, like the completion of
Creation, necessitates the participation of the entire Jewish people. In keeping with the Zeitgeist, Kook articulates a view of
nation-building similar to that of Aaron David Gordon's philosophy of work. Kook maintains that the first step in the renewal of
Jewish nationhood must be its physical rehabilitation. Jews must
engage in all the enterprises of a normal, sovereign society—in
agriculture, industry, education, literature, building, health, and
so on. Only then will the land be able to exercise its constructive
powers.

The soul is organically connected to the body. This outlook
explains Kook's respect for the nonreligious and even antireligious halutzim. Their fructification of the soil and their social in-
ventiveness played an important role in the process of
redemption. Kook hoped and expected that these pioneers would
ultimately find their way back to a halakhic lifestyle. He castigated
the excessive pietists who viewed with disrespect those engaged
in the reconstruction of the land and regarded any physical or
intellectual labor outside the Beit Hamidrash (house of study) as
an interference with Israel's sole mission—the study of Torah.

Kook's basic philosophy was tied to past centuries, but he also
wanted to establish a society and a state that would aim at development in all areas of life. He saw no contradiction between this

aspiration and the traditional ideological and practical means of achieving it. He pegged the entire process on the election of Israel. This interpretation of chosenness has a humanistic and universal purpose—the unification of all humanity and the inculcation of the love of God in all human beings. We can dissent from Kook's paternalism, but his aim indicates his love of all people and hope for their brotherhood. He believed:

> Love of Israel requires us to love every man. If love of Israel generates hatred of any section of mankind, this is an indication that our soul has not yet been purified of its defilement and is unable to participate in the paradise of supernal love.[10]

Kook's supernatural anthropology and his notions about physiology, psychology, and social development are mostly unfounded.[11] Even his tolerance of the kibbutz humanists never reached the level of acceptance of their new vision of humanity and work. He admired and loved these idealistic workers, but he rejected all positions in Judaism that departed from belief in the theophany at Sinai and divinely revealed Torah. Zion's return would be complete only with the reinstatement of the *Halakhah* in the life of all Jews. Belonging to the chosen people means to live according to the Torah, to study it, and to obey its dictates. Outside of this framework, no Jew can be considered "kasher," even if he or she makes a noteworthy contribution to rebuilding Eretz Yisrael. The Return demands full implementation of classic Judaism.

THE STATUS OF NON-JEWS IN ERETZ YISRAEL AND IN THE STATE OF ISRAEL

All peoples espouse a greater or lesser number of universal moral values. But creativity occurs in the moral sphere no less than in other areas of human activity. Therefore, it is likely that new developments will sometimes stand in opposition to ancestral conceptions or expand our understanding of long-held moral norms. Values such as quality, intimacy (and I do not refer to sexual intimacy), intellectual honesty, human rights, freedom of science, religion, and culture, along with other ideals of modernity, expand the horizons of enlightened societies. We should not expect to find in Jewish tradition all of the values that we need to solve the problems of Jewish life in the State of Israel and in the lands of our dispersion.

The above observation is unacceptable to many Jews. They prefer to believe that the tradition, more exactly, the *Halakhah*, is able to adapt efficiently to the changing circumstances of life. They tend to select and emphasize traditional values that appeal to them and to ignore those that have lost their salience. At times, they interpolate into the tradition certain values that are actually foreign to it but which they claim are part of the historical heritage. This is not the place to analyze such an approach, but it seems to me that the kind of apologetics which would try to demonstrate that traditional Judaism calls for a democratic polity dishonors both Judaism and democracy. It makes both of them what they are not.

Everyone can quote verses, laws, and *aggadot* (homiletical statements, tales, parables, and the like) that testify to the goodness of our ancestors and their warm feelings for non-Jews, but honesty requires us to admit that not every source expresses a complete universalism. No doubt, the biblical attitude toward the alien was a marked advance in the treatment of the stranger, but when seen in the light of today's ethical standards, it was then, and is now, a paternalistic approach. It cannot serve as a model for the treatment of minorities in a modern state.

On the other hand, the negation of an inherited value should be done with a sense of history and by the employment of historical tools of criticism. We should judge the values of the past in the light of the social and religious circumstances of their age and not in terms of today's norms. That is to say, while we must at times reject the ideas and ideals of our forebears, we must also cultivate empathy for them in their struggle to advance to a higher level of ethical achievement. A law like the ban on selling land to a gentile in Eretz Yisrael or the practice of applying the term "man" to a Jew but not to a non-Jew is certainly unacceptable to a democratic mind. Nevertheless, in turning our back on such views, we must see ourselves as heirs to the struggle of our ancestors against implacable enemies. Our mental health depends upon our ability to criticize our past without apologetics but also without contempt. Civilization progresses slowly, and each generation has to learn from the mistakes of previous ones. To function morally, we must all reckon with the fact that the best of people are sometimes morally obtuse.

When we hypostatize terms such as "Judaism," "*Halakhah,*" "Torah," "Jewish thought," and the like, we erect a roadblock to moral progress, because these terms are identified with the norms of the past. Any deviation is viewed as inauthentic. A modern, enlightened Jewish society would be deemed a contradiction in terms. This danger is adumbrated in Kook's thought and his halakhic rulings regarding the status of non-Jews under Jewish sovereignty. Despite Kook's celebrated humaneness and his belief that Jews are destined to repair the world, his philosophy has been used to support several political positions that contravene what would seem to inhere in his character and moral purpose. Where does Kook's halakhic thinking lead us in determining the status of Arabs and other non-Jews in Eretz Yisrael?

In a letter written in 1911, Kook criticizes Rabbi Meir Berlin for publishing in his Zionist journal an article that was harshly critical of Arabs. The author of the article called the Arabs "the enemy." Kook maintained that such terms, as applied to Arabs,

> [w]hen they appear in a Hebrew organ . . . can be infinitely poisonous. How much ammunition is placed in the hands of our many enemies who scratch out and survey every syllable we utter, in order to find grounds for libelling us. You are undoubtedly aware of the fact that there are Arabs who read and write Hebrew. They translate into Turkish and send to the capital and to the highest and most dangerous officials any expression of hatred of the native population or any slight suspicion of revolutionary intent. . . . On the contrary, we ought to describe pleasant moments of peaceful relations and brotherhood which we actually experience in the contacts between leading dignitaries of the *Yishuv* and Arab inhabitants of the land—naturally, the best of them.[12]

Kook's humanity was sprinkled with the pragmatism of the ancient Sage, Avtalyon, who warned his fellow scholars to guard their language (M. Avot 1:11). Kook understood that the tongue is a double-edged sword in politics and statesmanship. One has to avoid offensive rhetoric. Kook's reference to positive relations with Arabs was a true expression of the outer-directedness of his love of Israel, which demands love of all people. However, Kook spared no criticism of the gentiles. Scattered throughout his writings are strong attacks on Christianity and Islam. Nevertheless, he tried to deal with issues and avoided the language of hate and derision.

Kook tried to influence his colleagues and those engaged in building the country to act with decency toward Arabs, but he could not escape the constraints imposed by the *Halakhah*. Therefore, he could offer the Arabs and other minority groups only an inferior status in Eretz Yisrael.

There is little point to asking what Kook would have said had he lived to witness the establishment of the State of Israel. He could not have altered the halakhic requirements, and it is unlikely that he would have changed his political views either. Eretz Yisrael belongs to a single people. Even if their ancestors have dwelt in the land for many generations, non-Jews may continue to live there only on sufferance.

Kook knew that Eretz Yisrael attracted many non-Jews and that one such group claimed title to it. Nonetheless, he stubbornly clung to his opinion that longing for the land is an essential trait only of the Jewish people. He writes: "The Sages said that the verse in the *tohekhah* [chastisement], 'And your enemies who dwell in it [the land] shall be astonished' [at its barrenness], turns out to be a good thing for Israel. For while strangers can find no satisfaction in Eretz Yisrael . . . this curse becomes a blessing for Israel."[13]

Still, Kook has to address the problem of Arab status in more than a homiletic fashion. He asserts: "It has to be said that the Ishmaelites [Arabs] are not idolaters. They are to be regarded as *gerei toshav* [resident aliens], and it is permissible for them to own land."[14] This is the case at least to the extent that they can retain possession of land already belonging to them. Selling new plots to non-Jews is another question. Kook stresses the distance of the Arabs from idolatry and attests to their trustworthiness as agents in the legal fictions of selling *matzot* to non-Jews for the week of Pesah and selling the whole of Eretz Yisrael to a non-Jew during the Shemittah year. (This legal fiction enables Jews to satisfy biblical and halakhic prohibitions of possession of unleavened foods during Pesah and of tilling Jewish-owned soil during the sabbatical year, while at the same time avoiding the financial difficulties that applying the law would involve.)

If someone were to ask why the Sages, in their day, did not permit the sale of land to gentiles, Kook had a ready reponse: "In their time, it was difficult to find a non-Jew who was not an idolater. Therefore, we must obey the toraitic prohibition against such sale."[15] Thus, implicit in Kook's halakhic interpretation, it is no longer a matter of principle that one cannot sell land to a non-Jew, contrary to conditions that prevailed in mishnaic times. Non-Jews are now presumed to be free of idolatry.

Nevertheless, Kook sticks to the *Halakhah*, which declares that it is advisable to restrict as much as possible the permanent settlement of non-Jews (including, of course, Arabs), on the soil of Eretz Yisrael. He cites Rambam ("Laws of Idolatry" 10:4): "Why should we not sell soil to them [non-Jews]? Because it is said: And you shall not permit them to encamp—do not give them a resting place, for if they have no soil of their own, their stay will be temporary." Kook adds:

> That is to say, lack of land lessens the chance of their permanent settlement. This is the main objective—to prevent their permanent residence on the land. Nevertheless, since some of them already are permanent residents, by virtue of their owning soil, the Torah restriction does not apply—only a question of how much additional acreage to permit. . . . And as to the difficulty posed by my learned friend,[16] "Why should the law, You shall not let them encamp, apply to the seven Canaanite nations, seeing that they already owned territory?" I reply: How did they acquire it? Since Israel subdued them, the land of Israel came into its possession by right of conquest . . . and even though individual Canaanites remained, the land as a whole was acquired by the conquerors.[17]

Halakhic principles concerning real estate still hold in our day, Kook asserted. Thus, the rights of non-Jews are limited in this regard, something that cannot be countenanced in an enlightened society. A further expansion of the picture shows that the status of gentiles under the *Halakhah* is discriminatory in other ways as well, with gentiles largely dependent on the paternalism of the Jewish authorities. Thus, despite his loving nature, Kook, had he lived, would have been unable to equalize the right of non-Jews to own property with that of Jews in the Jewish state. The non-

Jew, under the *Halakhah*, can hope to attain only the status of a *ger toshav*, a resident alien.

The problem of equality for Israel's Arabs is not confined to the halakhic perspective. Much soul-searching is being done by liberal, democratic-minded Jews who are confused about how to preserve the Jewish character of the State of Israel while granting full equality to Arab citizens. The issue is not simply one of individual rights, as is the case in Western democracies. In Israel, Arabs wish to foster their national identity, but neither they nor the Jewish majority has thought through the complexities of the relationship between two independent peoples in a common democratic state. The outcome of the peace process is bound to affect the status of Israel's Arab population; but if Kook's philosophy were to guide Israel's government, Arab citizens would be denied full equality.

The *Halakhah* is sometimes depicted as a democratic instrument. I find this claim to be specious. *Halakhah* and democracy are contradictory in crucial ways, among them their conceptions of authority, sources and methods of legislation, and certain ethical assumptions. Nor is democracy itself to be viewed uncritically as a perfect form of polity. Therefore, its proponents within Judaism must keep an open mind to elements in traditional Jewish law that deserve to be incorporated in the new dispensation. In choosing between the two polities, a policy of passivity is apt to be disastrous. But as long as the State of Israel continues to function as a democracy, it must not only foster Jewish culture but also encourage Arabs to feel that they are living on their own soil and are free to cultivate a high Arab culture. A change of mentality has to take place among the Arabs as well, for they have to develop a positive attitude toward their status as a free minority in a pluralistic, democratic state.

Is it possible to have a Jewish state in Eretz Yisrael, in which the rights of minorities would not be compromised and in whose administration they would have a fair share? This complicated issue cannot be explored here. But it can be said that Israel will have to carefully define the dividing line between those areas of life that come under the jurisdiction of state law and those that belong rightfully to the preferences of individuals, congregations, and other voluntary groups. According to this outlook, which is intrinsic to the democratic ideal and incompatible with Kook's vision of Jewish society, life in Israel would follow three paths. One would be the road of Jewish voluntarism, which would require the formation of a new type of community unknown in Jewish history. A second course would involve non-Jewish citizens, most notably Arabs. It is likely that many of the non-Jews would also divide along religious lines but would be united by national attachments. The third path would be traveled by both Jews and non-Jews, as they endeavor to strengthen the ties that bind them in the furtherance of their common democracy in Israel. But as long as Jews remain the majority, it stands to reason that their influence in the shaping of Israel's culture will be decisive. However, when we recall that much of what Jews identify as specifically Jewish was the product of a pre-State Jewish minority, we should be able to look more soberly at the extent to which cultural creativity needs government regulation or support.

Ralph Barton Perry, the American historian, distinguishes between political and social democracy.[18] Of course, without majority rule and the willingness of minorities to abide by majority decision, no democratic society could survive. But if the human and civil rights of the individual are not strictly protected, no democracy can be considered enlightened. Social democracy implies such ideals as liberty, equality, fraternity, and pluralism.

The road to social democracy in Eretz Yisrael stretches out before us. We need only glance at Israel's state symbols to understand how far we are from giving non-Jews the feeling that citizenship in the state is a mark of equality. The national hymn, "Hatikvah," and the state flag are both Jewish symbols, and they can hardly be said to represent all of Israel's citizens. Can Israel's Arab citizens be expected to express their loyalty to Israel by singing a hymn glorifying the role of Eretz Yisrael in the Jewish soul? Other democracies are similarly identified in one way or another with majority cultures—Christian symbols play at least a ceremonial role in England and other European countries, and efforts are constantly under way in the United States to restore them to official status. But how would American Jewry react to replacing "The Star Spangled Banner" with "Onward Christian Soldiers" or to mounting a cross on the Capitol? Pragmatically, one must take account of the historical and psychological background to contemporary conceptions of state symbols. In Israel they cannot be easily exchanged for more neutral representations of the spirit of the state—certainly not during the generations that experienced the horrors of Nazism and the disabilities of life under Arab and Moslem rule. But while history might explain why people behave the way they do, it cannot always justify that behavior. Until Israelis of varied ethnic backgrounds understand what is entailed in social democracy, they will be unable to capture the heart of the country's minorities.

The obstacle to maximum equality for all Israelis is readily seen. Despite the peace process, security has yet to be guaranteed. Even if current hopes are fulfilled and all Arab states agree to diplomatic ties with Israel, animosity against the State and against Jews is likely to persist among Arab and Islamic extremists for a long time to come. Some Israel Arabs will also find it difficult to divest themselves of their long-held prejudices. Of greater concern is the gap in political conceptions between Orthodox Islam and the modern political culture that the State of Israel represents. It is questionable whether ardent Moslems will soon accept the right of Jews to have their own sovereignty in the Middle East. Fanatical nationalism is also characteristic of many Christian Arabs, who are motivated not by Christian ideals but by their need to match the patriotism of their Moslem fellow Arabs. Both sets of extremists provide the manpower for Arab terrorism. Terrorism, in turn, adds fuel to the claim of many Jews that Eretz Yisrael must remain an exclusive enterprise of the Jewish people. It will take time and enormous patience before the Jewish majority in Israel will be able to accept that a modern state must be founded on equal opportunity for all. Majorities have the decision-making right, but minorities must have the protection of the law and the opportunity to participate in all affairs of common concern. This problem will be further aggravated as Israel's Arabs continue to climb the ladder of education and enlightenment. Moreover, since Arabs in the surrounding states are also heading in this direction, it would be dangerous for Israel not to take the steps now to convince the Arab peoples that it regards them as partners in the furtherance of an advanced civilization in the Middle East and adapts its internal legislation accordingly.

I add here a few theological notes on the ownership of land.

Theological arguments to prove the right of any people to the possession of a particular territory are likely to convince only the true believers. If two peoples dispute proprietary rights to a land, and each claims exclusive ownership by virtue of divine warrant, the argument usually culminates in violence. A people that insists its land is a gift from God has only this assertion on which to rely. I believe that a theist ought to be convinced that no peoples have a God-given, exclusive right to any piece of earth. All peoples should consider their occupancy of a land to be in the nature of tenancy. They are entitled to occupancy as long as they care for the natural resources of that land and erect upon it a humane society. How does a people acquire the right of tenancy?[19] I feel that the argument of God's gift raises serious doubts. We have seen that even Kook finds this argument to be inadequate, for he adds that it was the conquest of Canaan that deprived its native peoples of their lien and transferred it to Israel. But although conquest determines possession, it does not prove its legality.

Kook often refrained from carrying his ideas to their logical conclusion. His human warmth and tolerance put a brake on some of his extreme views. As I have indicated, we cannot profess to know the political position Kook would have taken if he were alive today. His son, Zvi Yehudah Kook, did follow the extreme track, but it is possible that his father's personality, if not his philosophy, might have set up a barrier between himself and the political radicals who carry to its extreme the claim that Eretz Yisrael belongs exclusively to the Jewish people. Even so, HaRav Kook was in full accord with the tradition that God arranged the marriage of Israel and Eretz Yisrael before the Creation. Consequently, he believed that Israel could not relinquish its responsibility toward and for the Land. Israel has to live in it and fulfill its mission within all its borders.

Kook paints a beautiful picture of the romantic relationship between the Jewish people and Eretz Yisrael. But his portrayal does not help us understand how the meeting with the Land stirs the people to creative endeavors. To understand this, we have to turn to Kaplan.

The preceding reflections are only the beginning of a theological and moral analysis of Israel's sovereignty in Eretz Yisrael. The State of Israel has every right to exist, but it must ensure equal status for its non-Jewish citizens. One important aspect of this type of analysis is to answer these basic questions: What are the obligations of the Jewish majority in a democratic Jewish state? How can Arabs and other non-Jewish minorities be convinced that they can achieve a rich and fulfilling life, even though they are minorities? Our answers to these questions will reveal our true moral values.

KAPLAN ON ERETZ YISRAEL

Because Kook's and Kaplan's views on Eretz Yisrael differ so greatly, it is desirable to indicate the points they have in common. They are both motivated by their unending love of the Jewish people. Although they cannot explain the basis of that love, it is not a blind emotion. Both men know the faults of the Jews, and they call attention to them as the first step in their correction through redemptive love. Second, they both emphasize the moral thrust of the Torah and the centrality of the Pentateuch to Israel's distinctiveness. In this context, Kook sees the Written Law as the governing authority of Judaism in its entirety, whereas Kaplan regards it as one of the principal sources for the continuity of Jewish culture. Third, both in the divinely revealed *Halakhah* of Kook and in the evolving democratic *Halakhah* of Kaplan, the resettlement of the Jews in Eretz Yisrael is a precondition for a vital Judaism. Fourth, both men regard the Land not only as a means to the reconstruction of the nation but as an end in itself, albeit in different degrees, to be cherished unconditionally. Fifth, only Eretz Yisrael has the power to evoke creative abilities in the Jewish people in all areas of life.

Despite these points of agreement, Kaplan journeys far from Kook in the way he perceives the Jewish people and its religious civilization. As a Zionist, Kaplan has the following problems: Why is a land necessary for Jewish survival? Why does this land have to be Eretz Yisrael? What entitles the Jewish people to regard Eretz Yisrael as its own? In relying on the doctrine of election as the sanction for the relation between a people and its land, Kook, on the other hand, could have sidestepped these questions. However, he was too alert to modern conceptions and too aware of the ethical difficulties of state nationalism to avoid the moral issues of the return to Zion. Nor could he be blind to the plain fact that Arabs live on and work the soil and stake their own claim to Palestine. In the end, he resorts to the dogmatic, theological argument mentioned previously. At the same time, Kook relates to other factors in the relationship between people and land. He rejects a purely spiritual grounding for a vital Judaism, insisting on the unity of matter and spirit. Without land, the people cannot cultivate a living culture. Then, by arguing that only the Jewish people is capable of fructifying Eretz Yisrael, Kook seems to hint that chosenness is insufficient and that the ecology of a land can be protected only by the conscious effort of a people who love it. The right to a land has to be decided, at least to some extent, by the way in which rival suitors respond to its challenge.

In one of many passages on the role of land in the evolution of Judaism, Kaplan states his position:

Judaism could neither have arisen nor continued to exist apart from the land that gave it birth . . . A common country moulds an aggregate of human beings into a people. It serves as the physical basis of a people's life and civilization. Mere physical propinquity is sufficient to give rise to common interests which in turn find expression in a social framework, a common language, common customs, laws, forms of worship, ethical standards and social aspirations. What soil is to a tree, a land is to the civilization of a people.[20]

How does Kaplan deal with the question as to why, after courageous survival in exile for two millennia under the oppressive rule of foreign nations, the Jewish people, in order to continue its existence, must return to its ancient homeland? First, he examines the factors in the past that accounted for survival.

No matter where Jews lived, culturally and spiritually they moved in a Palestinian milieu. Even the climate and other physical conditions of the countries they lived in did not seem to interest them. We do not find that they prayed for rain or dew for the countries of their dispersion. It did not matter to them that Palestine was in the possession of Bedouin or Turks; the petition that her crops might prosper went up three times daily, as though the Jews lived there in undisturbed possession. After each meal, the Jew gave thanks for the land as though he were still living in it and enjoying its produce. The memory of having once lived in Palestine and the certainty of occupying it again, could not be considered the equivalent of actually living there, but they were at least effective anodynes for his *Heimweh* [homesickness]. The Jew remembered that he was in exile and bitterly deplored his condition.[21]

In other words, the Jews were successful alchemists who converted the dross of the exile into the gold of Jerusalem every time they dreamed of the return to Zion. They learned the art of survival even though they were uprooted from their soil.

Kaplan explains that the passion for Jewish revival in Eretz Yisrael engendered a sense of unity among Jews more powerful than that achieved by other peoples living undisturbed on their own soil. This unity found dramatic expression in the uninterrupted persistence of scholarly Jews in studying and elaborating on the laws pertaining to the practice of the tradition in Eretz Yisrael. Simultaneously, the masses continued to pray in the synagogue and at every meal for redemption in the Land.

Historical recollections and analysis of past connections of Israel with its land cannot suffice to establish the legal and moral basis of ownership or sovereignty. Why, after the emancipation, does Israel need the Land? Part of the answer is self-explanatory. Emancipation for Jews is far from complete in many lands. Only in some democratic states have Jews attained full human and civic rights. Yet even in these enlightened countries, disturbing outbreaks of anti-Semitism have occurred. Kaplan accepts the General Zionist view that only in their own state can Jews produce effective antidotes to the poison of anti-Semitism. Nonetheless, such reasoning still falls short of explaining the need for and justification of a Jewish commonwealth in Eretz Yisrael. In the face of anti-Semitism, Jewish unity and survival are conceivable as a natural response to the threat to the nation's right to exist unconditionally. But under freedom, the will to live requires other motivations. Kaplan writes:

> The Zionist movement is . . . thus not merely the outcome of the need of Jews for a haven of refuge from persecution or discrimination. It is principally a response of the Jewish People to its inner drive to metamorphose itself into a new corporate entity, by transposing its spiritual heritage into the key of naturalistic and this-worldly salvation.[22]

For Kaplan, the fate of the Jewish people is guided by all the laws of history that rule the passage of all other nations through time. This naturalistic way of looking at Jewish history in no way precludes seeing the uniqueness of the Jewish struggle for survival. It merely denies the need to go beyond normal canons of historical explanation. By and large, those who want to celebrate the power of the supernatural God who determines their people's history point to its special God-given genius. They do not attribute national faults or weaknesses to God's action. Kaplan never denied the uniqueness of the Jewish epic, but he accounted for it by referring to the concatenation of the natural factors that condition the life of every people—geographical, demographic, and historical circumstances; cultural heritage; opportunities and skills; the impact of neighbors; and the like. It is in this context that Kaplan sets the Jewish need for a land. Judaism, says Kaplan, did not spring into existence at a single moment, as would be the case with a religion that begins with the revelatory experience of a Moses, Jesus, or Mohammed. Instead, Kaplan regards Judaism as a civilization, "the product of social interaction of a group commonly known as a nation, whose life is rooted in a specific part of the earth."[23] He continues, "Each civilization has its own landscape which it conceptualizes and thus makes an object of consciousness. Those who are identified with the civilization share the psychological values of that landscape, even if they be far removed from it."[24] When Kaplan wrote these lines in 1934, he asked himself a question that is pertinent even today: Is it possible for Eretz Yisrael to continue to function in the Jewish mind, as it has for two thousand years, without being settled by a large sovereign Jewish community?

Kaplan's answer can be summarized in his reasoning that "the basis of Jewish unity can no longer be merely a tradition which served mainly to qualify all who lived by it for bliss in the hereafter. What Jews need now is a living collective experience that they can share in common."[25] Only in a sovereign state in a land deemed by the nation to be its own can this experience come to full fruition. The conditions of life for minority groups in free states are not conducive to long-lasting ethnic survival. There is little basis for assuming that minorities, who lack the inspiration of a creative national center, can achieve the kind of collective consciousness that can assure the creative continuity of their cultures.

Up to this point, Kaplan fits in with the Zionist consensus. However, he departs from the norm when he rejects the conclusion of *shelilat hagolah*, the negation of the Diaspora. According to this view, Jewish life outside of Eretz Yisrael is doomed to extinction—and in the thinking of some negators, deservedly so. Kaplan, on the other hand, adopts the position taken by the late Israel educator, Eliezer Rieger, among others: "Eretz Yisrael and the *Gola* are mutually indispensable. Without the *Gola* to encompass it, Eretz Yisrael will become parochial; and without Eretz Yisrael as its center the *Gola* is apt to deteriorate."[26] The land, says Kaplan, is necessary to elicit the civilization-building power of the Jewish people. Nevertheless, despite its glorious and central role in Jewish survival, Eretz Yisrael cannot carry the whole burden of the future alone. Therefore, it is necessary to devise a theory of Jewish identity and a strategy for Jewish continuity in the homeland and the Diaspora, according to standards of democracy and pluralism.

Kaplan places great emphasis on the psychology of Western Jews. He maintains that Ahad HaAm, who came out of an atmosphere of East European tyranny and who felt that Jews owed nothing to the lands of their domicile, did not seem to realize that Jews living in free countries "could not possibly allow their love for the Jewish People to monopolize their affections, that they had also to find a place in their souls for the nations whose citizens they were."[27] The psychology of patriotism and love of one's people in today's Diaspora is different in the setting of democratic pluralism from what it was in the lands of exile in the past. The free states of the West have opened the doors of self-fulfillment to all their Jewish citizens and have communicated to them the sense of belonging to lands that are no less theirs than they are other native or immigrant citizens'. All this, without diminishing their love for and devotion to Eretz Yisrael!

Obviously, the matter is not so simple. Conflicts of interest and dual loyalty arise. However, Kaplan insists that as the spirit of democratic freedom expands, it becomes possible for men and women to love more than one country, each in a unique way. Tension will nonetheless continue to trouble Jews who see as a genuine choice either *aliyah* to the ancient homeland of their Jewish heritage or continued domicile in the beloved land of their birth or residence. The need to choose is disturbing and pathetic, as is illustrated in a paragraph that Kaplan wrote in Hebrew while traveling to Palestine for a sabbatical:

> I still ask whether I delude myself when I think that there is hope for a future for Judaism in this country [United States]. Should I not be convinced that this country is a desert and wasteland that devours and destroys every vestige of our heritage? I think that eventually . . . I shall have to draw the conclusion that if I want to find satisfaction in my life, I shall have to devote my remaining powers to our people in Eretz Yisrael. Only there is there hope for our future. Is it not better to cast in one's lot with those who are destined to survive and not with those who are doomed to annihilation. If I were in my youth, I would undoubtedly move to Eretz Yisrael. But now, it is almost too late.[28]

One must assess a reflection of this kind carefully. Kaplan never budged from his conviction that the Judaism of the future will be created under freedom. There can be no guarantee of success; nor can we rely on the assumption that love will conquer all. Jews in the free Diaspora know that they must travel between resistance to a continuing anti-Semitism and the seductive attraction of a liberal and accepting environment. The fight against anti-Semitism causes no ideological strain. All that is needed is to plan strategies of defense and counterattack. But the spread of freedom creates a complicated situation. Although Jews in the democratic Diaspora no longer feel that they are strangers in a hostile world, the struggle against the magnetic power of assimilation becomes pronounced. One form of self-defense is to help prepare a sanctuary in Eretz Yisrael that can be a refuge from both recurring hatred and the ravages of deculturation. In addition, however, loyal Jews in the Dispersion want a strategy for survival where they can express themselves freely and openly. Kaplan pondered deeply about this dual problem. It was in the challenge of freedom that he saw why, despite growing emancipation, a national homeland had become indispensable to Jewish continuity. Modern Jews need a land of their own in order to stir their imagination and to provide an outlet for their creative energy as Jews.

Kaplan understood from the outset that the formation of an autonomous Jewish community in Eretz Yisrael would not only occupy those engaged daily and at firsthand in the process, but would also establish for Jews outside the land an agenda of supporting activities, dialogue, and mutual criticism that would fire their interest in creating a vital Judaism of their own. In this process, the creative accomplishments of the *Yishuv* would supply much of the raw material which diaspora Jews could adapt for their own needs.

Despite his criticism of Ahad HaAm, Kaplan writes about himself, "Through the impact of both Zionism and Ahad HaAm's writings, I became aware of the essential character of the Jewish universe of discourse."[29] The emphases that Ahad HaAm placed upon cultural Zionism, naturalistic Judaism, and Jewish morality were close to Kaplan's heart, even though he took exception to some of the famous essayist's formulations. For instance, Kaplan reworked Ahad HaAm's idea of Eretz Yisrael as a "spiritual center." Kaplan thought that Ahad HaAm had not made clear that the influence of the *Yishuv* would not be that of an active force working on a passive and receptive body, but instead would inspire diaspora Jews to undertake their own form of nation-building. Mere passivity would lead to cultural atrophy. However, Kaplan believed that the will of Jews to live in the free world would be strong enough to stir them to match Zionist creativity with their own brand of activism. He declared:

> Even Ahad Ha'Am was convinced that it was impossible for Judaism to take root in the Diaspora. His assumption that Eretz Yisrael would serve as a spiritual center sustaining Jewish life in the Diaspora referred to a transitional period preparatory to the ultimate ingathering of all Jews in Zion. It is true that he expected the interim period to last a long time. He did not expect the Jews to be fully prepared for national autonomy before a number of generations had passed. But that a permanent Diaspora could be part of the destiny of the Jewish People never entered his mind.[30]

Kaplan has been accused of sociolatry (worship of a group) and of overemphasizing the role played by the Jewish people in Judaism. The criticism is unfounded. First, Kaplan comments:

> With all due deference to Ahad HaAm, one cannot help but regard as chimerical and unpsychologic his effort to bring about the rena-

scence of the Jewish people by urging the substitution of loyalty
and devotion to the Jewish national being in place of the individu-
alistic yearning for personal salvation. He contends that such complete identification of the individual with the group existed before
other-worldly motivation was introduced into Judaism, and could
therefore again become the characteristic of Jewish consciousness.
This contention overlooks the progressive self-assertion of the individual which may almost be formulated into a law of human history. Once men have learned to reckon with the individual as an
end rather than as a means in appraising the value of any social ideal
or program, it is reactionary to ask the individual to sink back into
his former subservience.[31]

Thus, the nation is not an end in itself. It is composed of individuals, each of whom has the right to expect support from his or her
people in the quest for salvation.

However, Kaplan maintains that it is naïve to think that the
fulfillment of the Jewish individual can be secured totally within
a secularist perspective. He notes:

With the exception of Buber, most of the thinkers including Ahad
HaAm developed a definitely secular notion of Jewish nationalism,
which was, at best, to find collective expression in some ethical or
social system of values. Though these secularist thinkers would
have been the first to deplore conversion to a non-Jewish religion
as apostasy, they never took the trouble to explain why, on the one
hand, they relegated religion to the private discretion, or conscience, of the individual, and on the other, condemned him, if he
used that right to become a Christian or a Moslem.[32]

Kaplan thinks that Ahad HaAm did not understand the historical development of religion and was unaware of the fact that

[t]he interplay of people and land is more responsible for the individuality of the Jewish People and its contribution to civilization
than any other factor in its life. . . . That interplay of land and
people is without parallel in human history; a fact that has been
accepted as fundamental to religion and which has made Eretz Yisrael a Holy Land for half of mankind. The effort to resume the
interaction of the Jewish People cannot succeed if it ignores this.[33]

The return to Zion, according to Kaplan, is a religious act, for
the revitalization of the Jewish religion is largely dependent on

what is done by the autonomous Jewish people in its land to create an enlightened society and to educate individuals of high moral standards.

The question remains: Why does this land have to be Eretz Yisael? The *traditional* view is self-explanatory—the combination of Israel and Eretz Yisrael was formed in the divine laboratory. Authentic Judaism can only be developed by following the rules of this chemistry. Kaplan looks for a *naturalistic* explanation. He traces the origins, evolution, and metamorphoses of the Jewish people and its romance with Eretz Yisrael, all the time resorting to experiences communicable to all men and women. When people settle in a certain land, establish an economy and a polity, and become attached to its landscape, they acquire a sense of "we-ness" and of owning the land as its national prerogative. That emotion is related exclusively to the land in which it sprouts.

If people are uprooted and forced into exile, one of two things can happen. They can either disintegrate, which has been the fate of most nations that have been driven from their land, or the people can invent a strategy of survival, which has been the particular genius of the Jewish people. In the case of the Jews, the passion for Eretz Yisrael never abated and was one of the main reasons why they retained their unity and extraordinary will to live. Nevertheless, unanswered questions still abound. Assuming, as Kaplan does, that the story of Abraham is a mythic reflection on the wanderings of the Hebrew nomads, why did these tribes not remain in Mesopotamia? Then, too, why did they choose Canaan as their permanent residence? How is it that no other people who settled in Canaan was ever able to exhibit the creative energy that the Hebrews demonstrated there? How is it that the land is still capable of generating that energy in Jews who live there and of strengthening the attachment to it of Jews residing in the Dispersion?

Questions such as these fuel Kaplan's Zionist thought. To some of them, there can be only one answer—every love contains elements of mystery, arbitrariness, and ineffability. Moreover, since a people's tie to a land is a love relationship, little can be added to that fact. However, love, like any other human emotion, neither needs nor is subject to supernatural explanation. Kaplan argues that the Jewish people needs Eretz Yisrael because it is the one land that can stir it to collective creativity. The following excerpt from a reading prepared by Kaplan and his colleagues should enable us to see their understanding of the role of Eretz Yisrael in the redemption of the Jewish people:

> Not as a gift is a homeland acquired, nor through claims
>   based on statutes and charters;
> It cannot be bought for gold, nor taken by force.
> By the sweat of pioneers, by the toil of workers with brawn
>   and brain is it built,
> By men and women armed with invincible will, and
>   prepared to link their destiny to a sublime purpose.
> A homeland is a creation, the collective achievement of a
>   people,
> The fruit of its physical, mental and moral labors for many
>   ages.[34]

This reading was collected and arranged from the ideas of Jewish thinkers concerning what its homeland should mean to the Jewish people. Again, only Eretz Yisrael can make such a vision a reality for the Jews. Before the rise of the State of Israel, Kaplan and his fellow editors prepared another collection of thoughts by Hebrew writers about the Land and the people. Here are some typical lines:

> Whenever some memory of the Land is kindled in the heart
>   of the Jew, his blood flows more exultantly; all his being is
>   aroused to new heroism, new fortitude, a new thirst for
>   God.
> Every contact with the Land works a complete revolution in
>   his outlook on life, an uplift which is a return to God, a
>   veritable redemption.
> Every contact with the Land heals the soul of the people and
>   brings to life all the good that is latent in the hidden
>   recesses of its spirit.
> The great joy of creation now throbs through the arteries of
>   all Jewry, the creation of a people risen to full stature,
>   vigorous, thriving, responsible.[35]

These lines, perhaps too bombastic, are a reasonable substitute for chosenness as an explanation of the Jewish attitude toward the Land and as a spur to the reactivation of Jewish national creativity. By concentrating on the natural behavior of a people in its territorial setting, Kaplan renders unnecessary the dilemma of belief in a God of universal loving-kindness, who nonetheless plays favorites. Not that all peoples relate to their lands as the Jews have done in regard to Eretz Yisrael. The point is that deep love and mere flirtation or passing affection are forms of this-worldly, common human behavior.

One major question remains. How does Kaplan justify the Jewish claim to Eretz Yisrael, in view of the counterclaim of the Arabs? Kaplan's premises offer only a partial justification. The truth is that from a naturalistic and humanistic outlook, the claims of all nations that they hold writs of ownership on their lands have only tentative validity. Every such claim is relative to historical accident and to the needs of humankind as a whole. Kaplan tries to buttress his apologia by recourse to Jewish history, the needs of the Jewish people, and the human rights to which the Jews are as much entitled as any other nation. This argument, however, does not exhibit sufficient empathy for the plight of the Palestinian Arabs whose sentiments toward Falastin are similar to those of the Jews. They have also suffered from international power plays, from the inner and destructive conflicts of their fellow Arabs, and not least from the dynamic thrust of Jewish and Western culture into their own dormant civilization.

Kaplan's analysis stops short of an appreciation of the emerging Palestinian consciousness. He does mention the mistakes of the *Yishuv* in its treatment of the Arabs in pre-State days. The following is a typical remark:

> Jews should have realized that they have to live with the Arabs, and should not have attempted to build a Jewish economy by discouraging employment of Arabs. They should have tried to develop a single high-level economy in which exploitation of both Arab and Jewish labor would have been precluded. No effort or ingenuity should have been spared in devising ways and means of effecting a *modus vivendi* that would have been satisfactory to all who have a significant interest in the land.[36]

However, Kaplan did not foresee the enormous complexity of the problem, although he, more than Kook, knew that it could not be solved paternalistically. Even now, in the midst of the peace process, it is evident that the Jewish majority in the State of Israel will have to accord Arab citizens a more honorable role than has been the case to date. However, the Arabs, too, have a long road to travel before being able to fashion a proper role for themselves within Israel's democracy.

ERETZ YISRAEL AND THE FUTURE OF JEWISH NATIONALISM?

Kook and Kaplan stand at opposite ends of the Jewish consensus regarding the Jewish future in Eretz Yisrael. This consensus is founded on one basic point of agreement, namely, that the future of Judaism depends on the success of Jewish settlement in Eretz Yisrael and the quality of the Jewish state. Kook and Kaplan were united in their love of the land, in their determination that Jewish roots should once again be sunk into its soil, in their conviction that only this land could generate a renewed and creative Jewish nationalism, and in their vision that this nationalism must lead to a high morality. Kook paints a model of a people and its land held together by God's election. Kaplan proposes a unity of land and people based on historic ties, human needs, social reality, and the will to survive. Kook's vision has the attraction of romantic poetry, but is it poetry to be believed in? Kaplan is more prosaic, but he opens the doors to ethical inquiry into the possibilities and dangers of modern nationalism.

NOTES

1. *The Kozari*, IV:17, p. 175.
2. Ibid., II:14, p. 53.
3. *Orot*, p. 52.
4. OK, Vol. 2, pp. 423–424. Kook repeats this theme several times. See, for example, KL, Vol. 1, L. 96, pp. 112–113.
5. OK, Vol. 2, p. 423.
6. Early in his career, Kook had already articulated his conviction that Eretz Yisrael is the key to a full Jewish life and to the fulfillment of the national mission. For example, he wrote, "[T]here is no doubt that we cannot carry out our overall mission unless we are a nation dwelling in Eretz Yisrael on sacred soil. For only there can the national spirit

develop and become a light to the world" ("Teudat Yisrael U'leumiyuto"—"Israel's Mission and Its Nationalism," *HaPeles*, 5661, p. 89).

7. "How fortunate we are in our lot, that we were chosen to restore to the world the great and simple truth, which is intertwined with the renewal of the [divine] light for the entire world. We have this talent in our very essence, individually and collectively, in the form of our history, in the nature of our flesh, in the climate of our country, in the souls of our great ancestors" (OK, Vol. 1, p. 4).

8. OR, Vol. 2, p. 264.

9. Ibid., p. 265.

10. *Orot*, p. 149. Similarly, "I love everyone. I cannot but love all creatures, all peoples. . . . My love of Israel is more intense, more profound, but my inner desire spreads with its powerful love literally to everyone. I do not have to activate this love. It flows automatically from the depths of the sacred wisdom of the divine soul" (AT, p. 31).

11. We have already noted, for example, his benighted views on the essence of men and women. See OR, Vol. 1, pp. 71–72.

12. KL, Vol. 2, L. 398, p. 56.

13. KL, Vol. 1, L. 229, p. 288.

14. MK, R. 58, p. 122.

15. Ibid.

16. The letter concerns the fictitious sale to a non-Jew of land for the *Shemittah* (sabbatical year), similar to the custom of selling leavened food for the week of Pesah.

17. MK, R. 68, pp. 138–139.

18. Ralph Barton Perry, *Puritanism and Democracy* (New York: Vanguard, 1044, pp. 438–439).

19. *Sabbath Prayerbook* (New York: Jewish Reconstructionist Foundation, 1945, pp. 475–479).

20. JC, p. 186. We often forget that before the establishment of the State of Israel, Eretz Yisrael in the areas allocated to the British mandate was designated in English even by Zionists as Palestine.

21. Ibid., p. 288.

22. *The New Zionism* (henceforth, NZ) (New York: Herzl Press, 1959, p. 71).

23. JC, p. 186.

24. Ibid.

25. NZ, p. 71.

26. Quoted by Kaplan, Ibid., p. 96.

27. GJM, p. 423.

28. *Diaries*, August 22, 1935.

29. *Mordecai M. Kaplan: An Evaluation*, ed. by Ira Eisenstein and Eu-

gene Kohn (New York: Jewish Reconstructionist Foundation, 1952, p. 298).

30. NZ, p. 75.
31. JC, p. 282.
32. NZ, p. 77.
33. Ibid., p. 139.
34. *Sabbath Prayerbook*, p. 479.
35. Ibid., p. 483.
36. FAJ, p. 136.

12

Jewish Education

THE BEST WAY to capture the spirit and utility of a philosophy is to examine its educational implications. In effect, both Kook and Kaplan can be looked upon as thinkers who tried to improve the quality of Jewish education.

A NEO-TRADITIONAL PHILOSOPHY OF EDUCATION

Kook's educational philosophy might be easily but too facilely described as a normal embodiment of traditional piety. Education is synonymous with the study of Torah and with acquiring knowledge of the classic literature of the Bible, Mishnah, the Jerusalem and Babylonian Talmuds, Midrash, Commentaries, Responsa, Codes, and the philosophies of Judaism. This ideal was well represented by Kook. However, there are many gates to Torah study, and Kook opened one all his own.

Talmud Torah (the study of Jewish texts) is considered to be as important as all the other *mitzvot* combined. Kook could have been satisfied with this maxim and preached the continuation, without change, of the traditional halakhic system of education. However, his thinking was too advanced to allow him to follow this customary path. He believed that education must initiate as well as preserve. The school had to contribute to the broadening of tradition and to the unification of the people. Illustrative of Kook's spirit is the title page of the first copy of *Ittur Sofrim*, a short-lived journal that he inaugurated in his youth. He writes that the purpose of this scholarly collection is "[t]o enlarge and glorify Torah, to increase the measure of reverence for the great scholars and men of wisdom, to bind together the divisions in Israel in peace and brotherly love."[1] We find here the roots of Kook's dream of a new type of *yeshivah*, which would broaden the horizons of *Talmud Torah* to include the proper application of the findings of scientific methods of research. Kook was convinced that a faithful Jew would not be harmed by honest confrontation with modern research. On the contrary, unless Jewish Sages act in a spirit appropriate to each period, the *Halakhah* would become fossilized and future generations would leave the vineyard of Torah. However, Kook erected a protective wall against a broad acceptance of scientific research. He deemed it inconceivable to allow modern scholarship to uncover faults or contradictions in the tradition, and, of course, it had no authority to undermine the foundations of the *Halakhah*. Any education that would cast doubt on traditional principles is to be disregarded. Hence, Kook insisted that teachers of Judaism must be pious and observant.

However, Kook's realism leads him to draw some surprising conclusions. He states:

> Some persons fall into bad ways, because, in their methods of study and spiritual maturation, they have rebelled against their true character. Thus, one individual might be qualified for *Aggadah* and ill-disposed to busy himself regularly with halakhic matters. But he might lack self-understanding and steep himself in the customary practice of halakhic study, thereby developing an antipathy to that which is not in keeping with his nature. However, if he could find and fulfil his real vocation and busy himself with that aspect of Torah for which he is fit, he would perceive immediately that his dislike of halakhic issues is not caused by any lack in these sacred, essential studies. He would know that his soul needs another area of Torah for his constant attention. He would then remain supremely devoted to the holiness of the Torah and succeed in that aspect of it in which he has special talent. Through him, those who are strong in *Halakhah* would be helped to sweeten it with the charm of the *Aggadah*.[2]

The above passage is entirely in keeping with traditional Torah study but contains the potential for broadening its conception. We can assume that when making his comment, Kook was thinking of the interesting discussion on educational method in *Avodah Zarah* 19a. There, the Rabbis are in general agreement that teachers are best advised to take their students' interests into account and to allow them to study the text that most attracts them at the moment. Kook reiterated his conviction that personal preference would lead students to lifelong specialization in certain areas of Torah.

Kook regarded the study of Torah as a collective enterprise; that is, we must not expect all students to be capable of encompassing the whole toraitic tradition or of understanding it with the same depth or exactitude as some of their peers. It is not only a person's interest in certain texts that determines success in study or research; native abilities are important as well. All students have to know themselves and not try to master subjects beyond their capacity. Vain effort can easily end in mistakes that can be damaging to the students and the community. Therefore, Kook envisaged an educational institution that would be a community of teachers, students, and researchers who would pool their learning. Judaism should be a product of group cooperation. It is against this background that we are able to see the difference between the "Old Yeshivah" and the new type that he wanted to develop. Whereas in the former all students study the same texts in the same way, in Kook's ideal school, the subjects to be studied would cover a vast field, with many opportunities for specialization and individual research. Kook's modernism is clearly delineated in this aspect of his educational theory.

Nonetheless, Kook stressed that the concentration of a student on one or more subjects has to be confined to the toraitic framework. Otherwise, Kook's contention that the road to God passes through all human experiences might lead us to believe that we can approach God more effectively through these experiences than through pages of the classic halakhic literature. Immediately after his progressive remarks, he writes:

> Although the entire universe and all thought and emotion are flooded with divine light and the holiness of supernal life, and despite the fact that righteous men enjoy God's sweetness by constantly visiting His Temple, nonetheless the fount of the basic illumination is hidden in the Torah. When one walks along the road, reflecting on Torah and interrupts his meditation and declares "how beautiful is this tree or how lovely this field," Scriptures regard him as forfeiting his soul. Even though this forfeiture of life is merely figurative, once a person has risen to the level of contemplating God, he is nonetheless regarded as having abandoned true existence.[3]

Kook's hesitation stands out. On the one hand, he believes that man, as a creature made in God's image, has the power to discern signs of Him in the phenomena of nature and in human behavior. On the other hand, as a believer in the revelation at Mt. Sinai, Kook has to protect the priority of Torah study over all experiential methods of seeking God. Consequently, although he respects science, he trusts "only the scientific knowledge that comes from the experience of direct and keen sense perception, whether it be the sense of smell or of taste. In this case we can rely on them [the scientists] on the assumption that an artisan will do nothing to damage the reputation of his craftsmanship."[4] We have already referred to this attitude.[5] The only reliable source for the knowledge of God's truth that is within the range of human capability is the Torah. However, Kook contradicts himself. He first rejects, or at least casts doubt on, scientific hypotheses that are not based on sense perception; yet he accepts some of the foundations of evolutionary theory and applies them to his own belief in the constant rise of the profane to the holy. This is evident in the following passage:

> The theory of evolution, which is now gaining favor in the world, befits the secret lore of the *Kabbalah* more than any other philosophical system. Evolution, which heads in the direction of transcendence, makes for optimism in the world. For we cannot be pessimistic when we see that everything is developing and being uplifted.[6]

Kook places evolution in the category of philosophy rather than science. He adopts the theory but not on the testimony of the senses. The scope of sense perception is very narrow when compared to the enormous cosmic process and the advancement of humankind. Yet because the belief in evolution supports the idea that man can rise to a state of holiness, he deems true a theory (whether philosophical or scientific is of little consequence) that he would reject out of hand if it were to contradict anything in the Torah. Kook's inconsistency in regard to abstract theory is further manifest in his response to the challenge of modern astronomy to traditional cosmology. In his opinion, "The new universal spirit resulting from the scientific extension of the sensual image of physical being has to cause a similar new and broader understanding among the masses of the spiritual world and its ideational connections. All this requires profound study concerning how to see all this afresh in the scheme of tikkun."[7]

Thus, Kook emerges as a modern thinker who is aware of the need to adjust hallowed ideas to the most advanced knowledge and well-informed theory. However, he does not consider science to be as authoritative as accepted tradition. He tells us that much research and thought have to be invested by pious halakhic masters who are best qualified to coordinate the new knowledge with "all the good that is stored up in the pure form of the old."[8]

Whether Kook fully grasped the mood of the intellectuals is doubtful. He could not fathom their enthusiastic endorsement of scientific method, but he perceived the danger that the new mentality posed to the halakhic system. It is important to note that a devoted traditionalist nonetheless understood that Torah study has to relate seriously to the universe as portrayed by science. Unfortunately, he merely called attention to the problem and urged his fellow scholars to try and solve it without making any radical adjustment in the fundamentals of halakhic Judaism.

THE SPIRIT OF KOOK'S PHILOSOPHY OF EDUCATION

Kook's letters and other writings paint a picture of his modern Orthodox theory of education. His demand for the teaching of all aspects of the *Halakhah* and for the inculcation of total loyalty to its spirit and letter testifies to his unrelenting traditionalism. His modernism comes to the fore in his rather radical approach to methods of research and instruction. He recommends turning to the sciences as an aid to a deeper understanding of the classic texts—albeit with constant vigilance against any departure from the halakhic limits. Briefly, Kook wants Jewish education to be both strictly traditional and enlightened. He wants to induce in the learners faithfulness to the halakhic heritage, while enabling them to cope with the changing world. The tension between these objectives will persist, but Kook is unafraid. The Torah will remain the final and absolute source of truth.

Occasionally, Kook's writings suggest his doubt that the enlightened Orthodox education he espouses is sufficient. His efforts to give secular science a voice, even in the restricted form he recommends, still arouse the wrath of the Fundamentalists. Against their vigorous attacks, Kook finds refuge in Rambam, who, eight hundred years ago, had set an example for future generations of enlightened intellectuals. Rambam had made the science of his time and the thought of the great gentile philosophers an essential part of Torah and its study. Kook brings this approach up-to-date, but he also drops hints about an even more radical perspective on the education of Jews. What follows is what I consider to be one of Kook's most remarkable efforts to deal with the tension between tradition and change and its bearing on education.

Kook is explicit about the tension in which he lives:

> He who enters the halakhic precincts from the broad expanse of pure intellection interspersed with feeling and beautiful, magnificent poetry is greatly tortured. For the *Halakhah*'s beauty is as black as the raven, and its sacred strength is designed to rule the world that is filled with darkness, filth and mass upheavals. But a person with a glorious soul, sensitive to the splendor of holiness, feels his terrible suffering, all the pains of confinement, as he goes from one study to another.[9]

It is hard to find in the limited scope of human conceptions and halakhic decisions an appropriate description of the divine light. Kook wants to throw off the chains of time and place, but he also senses that this aspiration can be hazardous. Nevertheless, whereas in his halakhic writings, there is hardly a trace of this tension, in his philosophical writings and correspondence, he asks far-reaching questions.

Let us refer again to Kook's statement that spiritual stability can be achieved only in a godly context.

> If a man aspires to anything less than this high estate, he is immediately tossed around like a ship foundering at sea. . . . But God transcends all reality from which we hope to glean some feeling or idea about Him. Whatever is beyond our reach is worth nothing, and whatever is worthless cannot be a resting place for the mind. Therefore, scholars in search of God are generally weary and worn of spirit. When the soul is activated by the brightest light, it cannot be satisfied with the light of justice of the finest deeds of goodness,

with the light of truth that is found in the clearest learning, or with beauty in its most magnificent representations.[10]

Kook empathizes with the pain of all those who demand of themselves and the world a perfection that reality cannot grant them. As a result, only through prayer can humankind gain a feeling of completion and be able to judge Creation positively.[11] However, this is not the end of the road. Kook, like Moses, wants to see God's glory and to know Him.

> Faith in God indicates the great daring of fully developed human consciousness and will. Of course, clarification comes about only with complete knowledge of all reality, according to the best of our ability. The rule always holds that knowledge of God comes from knowledge of His acts. Faith embraces all items of knowledge and frames them into an ordered whole, thereby giving life to all who are blessed with its light; it vitalizes morality, individual and social life. . . .[12]

Kook wants to free reason to do its job. He has to do this within the halakhic mood, but one that he modifies radically. He struggles against a reliance on revelation that ignores verified knowledge of reality. He asks:

> And how can man conjecture about God's greatness, in a manner which will expand and not blur the essential splendor of the soul, if not by increasing the power of his knowledge, emancipating his imagination and the horizons of his thought, by his understanding of the universe and of life, and by the richness of his feeling about the whole of being? In all this, man has to engage in all branches of wisdom, in all studies of life, and in all the religious and moral insights of different national cultures.[13]

A Startling Approach to Torah Education

Kook stakes out two approaches. One emphasizes intense study of classic texts; the other offers a universe of expanding experience. In the second world, students who are distracted from Torah by the wonder and beauty of nature do not forfeit their lives. Instead, perceiving and appreciating the tree and the field is the very method by which they proceed to the divine gate.

However, Kook is not merely a follower of Maimonides, who suggested that love of God is derived from observing the wonder and beauty of nature and the sublimity of Creation. Kook not only walks along this path, which opens wide the door to the esthetic sphere that had been just slightly ajar in Jewish religion, but also steps off into some interesting byways. One example appears under the title *Shir Vasiah,* the meaning of which will emerge in the following discussion.

The Tanna (scholar of the mishnaic period), Ben Azzai, said: "Despise no man and carp at nothing; for there is no man who does not have his hour, and there is no thing that does not have its place"(M. Avot IV:3). Using this statement as a basis, Kook makes his well-known declaration, "The difference between sacred and secular things is relative, in accordance with our limited perspective."[14] Kook believes that life proceeds toward greater perfection and unity. This involves the fulfillment of human destiny and the attainment by all things of their allotted place. But how can man be enabled to "picture with inner insight the place of all things"[15] and of man's holiness? Kook answers his own question, as he says,"[b]y carefully cultivating the method for differentiating between good and evil."[16] The person who walks along this path is capable of incorporating everything into the good, thereby overcoming the relative and experiencing life in its fullness. We have to turn to Kook's philosophy of education to understand what is behind this vagueness.

In three short paragraphs, Kook articulates a profoundly suggestive theory. The secret of education is contained in three terms, whose source is in Ps. 105, 2. "Sing (*shiru*) to Him, sing praises (*zamru*) to Him; / Speak (*sihu*) of all His marvelous works." Kook arranges the three terms, all of which have to do with vocal expression, in order of priority. *Zemer,* or tune, is at the bottom of the ladder; then comes *shir,* or verbal song; at the top of the order is *siah,* or verbalization. In the Hebrew, all these words have three-letter roots. Together they represent three components of a distinctive educational method. Despite the order of preference, Kook undoubtedly intends for all of these methods to be included in the Jewish educational system. Of greatest interest, however, is Kook's conception of the role of *siah.*

Kook describes the three educational methods as follows:

The principle of *siah*, the attribute of Isaac, stands above that of *shir*, which is the basis of the revelation of Israel's holiness, *shir el* [in Hebrew, a play on the letters Y-I-S-R-A-E-L], God's song—reason, power of implementation and will. [Again, a play on the Hebrew letters of *shir*, shin, yod, resh.] *Shir* is a step above *zemer*, which embraces only the lingering melody but not the original force of the song. Instead of reason comes memory; in place of active implementation comes thought; instead of powerful will filled with the light of reason and the power of complete effectuation, there eventuates a weak will. This will survives feebly with the help of memory of the past and by reflection on the practical ideals that one would like to carry out but cannot do.

But even the will is only a small branch of the tree of life. The future progresses toward the fulfillment of life, as all that is profane rises to the sacred, all that is of little value to what is exalted and uplifted. Now I have given you Torah; in the future, I shall grant you life. This is the principle of *siah*-reason, the power of implementation and life. . . .[17]

A reader of these lines cannot help but marvel at Kook's imagination, at his profundity, and at the wealth of suggestive references at his disposal. One returns to this passage again and again and finds new meanings in it, all the while uncertain about whether Kook's intent has been correctly grasped. I suspect that Kook himself might have had trouble explaining everything that went through his mind as he wrote this piece. Nor is it beyond the realm of possibility that he repressed thoughts that were even more daring than those he committed to paper.

It is interesting to note that Kook did not assign any patriarchal symbolism to *zemer* as he did to *shir* and *siah*. *Siah*, symbolizing Isaac, is derived by Kook from Gen. 24, 63: "And Isaac went out at eventide to walk (*lasuah*) in the field. . . ." The popular midrashic interpretation of *lasuah* is that Isaac went to meditate or pray. This gives Kook room for his imaginative reading. *Shir*, by virtue of Kook's word play, is read as the song of Israel, the name given to Jacob after wrestling with the angel and which Kook takes as symbolizing the spiritual qualities of Jacob. The Rabbis presumed that this supposedly guileless son of Jacob transmitted his genetic virtues to his progeny, the Jewish people. Kook saw in *zemer* an allusion to Torah, which links Israel to God. Such symbolism might have seemed to Kook to require no patriarchal reference.[18] The three concepts provide the scaffolding for Kook's structure of Jewish study.

It might be that Kook's method of using traditional nomenclature and concepts was a poetic ploy that enabled him to drop hints to strong-minded readers without upsetting the weak, who would not fathom his true intent. Or, it might be that we have an example of a pious preacher who found an interesting text that he used imaginatively without having any extraneous aim in mind. Thus, if we adopt the second interpretation of *Shir Vasiah*, the lack of a patriarchal referent for *zemer* is unimportant, whereas the symbolism of using Isaac and Jacob to represent the search for God and recognition of the holiness of Israel is in keeping with the rather forced traditional commentaries.

Although we can dismiss Kook's sermonic ornamentation, we have to take seriously the implications of his three concepts. *Zemer*—memory, thought, and weak will—represents a critique of traditional education, particularly of the yeshivah. Memory, by which Kook means the accumulation of traditional learning, particularly the contents of the halakhic literature, is a necessary component of Jewish study. However, the accepted traditional method of study puts thought to work on extracting from only a limited field of knowledge. Kook apparently feels that this type of erudition (*lamdanut*) cannot lead to the kind of vigorous Judaism for which he strove. Reason can elicit from the classic texts only a weak form of behavior. Such study cannot change the human condition, because it is an inadequate means of implementing the messages of the Torah itself. Students of this mindset lack the courage and the ability to transcend the past. Some of them might sense the need to advance into a new age, but they can do nothing to act upon that feeling by enriching their study habits.[19]

The mood of *shir* is different. Reason, harnessed to practical ability, leads to a strong will and vigorous endeavor. This combination impels us from theory to practice and from thought to action. Reason extends beyond abstraction and guides us in choosing between right and wrong.[20] *Shir* designates strong and qualified people who are able to convert their ideas into reality. Such people do not hesitate to act on what they think is needed or proper. They read about the past without stopping at its literal meaning. Instead, they study and apply it as they believe the Sages of old would expect them to do today.

By placing *shir* above *zemer*, Kook favors the sort of study engaged in by the scholars whom Rambam describes in his *Perek Helek*: "Those men who grasp the greatness and intelligence of our Sages of blessed memory, whose words all touch on true and worthwhile subjects. [The Rabbis] discovered truth, avoided the impossible and affirmed that which has to be." It follows that the protagonist of *shir* is the modern halakhist who dares to broaden the four cubits of the Law to include truths that have only been uncovered in our era. Kook's hints, however, are insufficient to enable us to be certain about the significance of the conative stage of *shir*. He tells us that the way to the loftiest height of human experience is through the ability to distinguish between good and evil. But how can we be sure that our reason and power of effectuation will produce a will that is not only strong but good? We cannot, but we can be certain that Kook believes that erudition and unimaginative thinking are inadequate to the cultivation of a creative will.

Had Kook stopped at this point, he would still have carried Torah education into modern times. But he was enticed into the mood of *siah*—reason, implementation, and life. This halakhic man exclaims, "Now I give you *Torah*; in the future, I shall give you *life*." (Italics, JJC) As his proof-text, Kook quotes Ps. 119, 99: "I understand more than all my teachers; / For Thy testimonies are my meditation (*siha li*)." God's testimonies transcend everything that can be taught by mortal instructors. As we have already indicated, divine knowledge is to be found in the phenomena of nature and in human behavior—in brief, in the life process. We are thus told to speak of the Torah not only as our life but of life as Torah abundant. In Kook's eyes, there is no contradiction between the two visions. He remains the pious Jew who never fears that experiencing the fullness of life will cause him to deny the truth of Torah. Nevertheless, the road to God requires more than the study of the Oral and Written Law. Life as a whole is the Teacher, and there is nothing in life that is not potentially a subject for Jewish study.[21]

The concept "life" requires clarification, especially in Kook's penetrating but convoluted thinking. In a striking paragraph, he writes:

> The Creator, blessed be He, imbued all living things with love of life. For life is good . . . inasmuch as the good God chose it for the benefit of his creatures. The essence of life is the awareness of its reality. The more a person senses that there is something beyond him greater in amount and in quality, the more life he has. The basic point of life is the sense of reality, but it becomes greater and loftier to the extent one realises how much quantity and quality exist beyond oneself. Thus, the more one experiences of significant phenomena, the greater life becomes.[22]

Kook portrays life as a process that man can experience for only a brief moment. Reality is that moment. But the essence of life is the demand that man try to extend the moment to an experience of greater significance, that is to say, to transcend both what has been learned from the past and what is experienced in the present. He has to reach out to horizons beyond those immediately before him. As life streams by, reality will change in ways that the wildest imagination cannot contemplate—in Kook's language, the profane will rise to the state of holiness. It seems to me that in thoughts like these, Kook introduces an element of adventure into Judaism and Jewish education. He knows that erudition does not suffice to improve the measure of goodness in the world. His own proposal is also of limited value, but at least it challenges our complacency. He tells us that life has to and can be better than it is.

Note that *siah* lacks three components that we find in *shir* and *zemer*—memory, thought, and will or ambition. Apparently, although Kook prized a strong will to achieve, which powers man's moral responsibility, he wanted devotion to goodness to become intrinsic to human nature. Man would then live truth, beauty, and goodness in a way that would unite reason and deeds. Choice would be unnecessary. Kook looked forward eagerly to a human condition in which "materiality and spirituality, the laws of nature and reason, the laws of morality and justice and those of the soul are woven together—a condition in which past, present and future are surveyed as one and all come from the one omnipotent God."[23] Thus, the life referred to in *siah* is both the product of the imaginative activation of reason and the catalyst for such adventurous thought. Education that ignores the experiences of life and is confined to textual study cannot help humans to achieve their potential.

As I have stated, Kook might have hesitated to follow the logic of his ideas, hiding their consequences from his readers and from himself. However, it is unnecessary and unfair to rest a case on suspicion. All I wish to do is to examine what Kook has written and see where he leads us. He emerges as an extremely pious educator who sought to broaden Judaism by applying to it every positive asset that can be drawn from modern life, provided that it will not undermine any principle of the Torah. But this approach seems to be self-contradictory. How can a tradition be enriched without removing some of the dross that inevitably collects in the course of time? As Eliezer Schweid declares, "If Israel has a narrow range of mundane life, its renewed Oral Law will also be limited; if its life is broad, then its Oral Law will follow suit. In Israel . . . there will have to be an *Halakhah* that befits all these enterprises."[24] Kook's vision is all the more daring when we realize how tied he is to traditionalism.[25] Now, sixty years after Kook's death, many Jewish educators have yet to take up the challenge he laid down, perhaps fearing that they will have to tread a dangerous path.

Kaplan's View of the Educational Challenge

In 1909, Solomon Schechter, then president of the Jewish Theological Seminary of America, located in New York City, invited Mordecai Kaplan to found and become the first principal of the Seminary's Teachers Institute. Kaplan accepted the offer, even though he was aware of the difficulties he would face. This turning point in his career occurred at a crucial period in his intellectual development. He felt that as a result of the heterodox views he had begun to espouse, he no longer had the right to serve the Orthodox congregation in which he was employed. Schechter's request was thus a godsend. Almost fifty years after Kaplan began his rabbinical career, he asked himself,

How . . . was it possible for me in that turbulent state of mind to accept a pulpit and to organize educational courses for young and old? Two factors contributed to my being accepted by the Orthodox congregation and to my own ability to accept the situation. One was my conformity to Jewish ritual practice to which, despite my doubts and questionings, I strictly adhered. That was due, no doubt, to the pious home in which I had been brought up, and to the Seminary where I had by that time spent nine years. The other factor was the abundance of Jewish teaching and preaching material available which was informative and edifying, and which did not necessitate one's becoming involved in any of the basic theological problems.[26]

Quickly, however, Kaplan was forced to deal with those very problems. He had to confront the spiritual and theological issues that disturbed him and apply them to the mundane concerns of the living Jewish people. For instance, he tells about delivering a sermon at a *Kol Nidrei* service, in which he urged the members of the congregation who worked on Shabbat—and in those days there were many, even in Orthodox synagogues, who did so—to try at least to observe Friday evening and to preserve in their homes as much of the Sabbath spirit as they could. This approach aroused the anger of the more pious in the congregation, who accused Kaplan of authorizing violation of the Sabbath. This charge resembled the Fundamentalist opposition to Kook's support of the *halutzim*, who, despite their abandonment of ritual tradition, were leaders in carrying out the duty to rebuild the homeland. Kook hoped that the kibbutnikim would eventually return to halakhic tradition, but the pietists were uncompromising. However, whereas Kook held that the pioneers were nonetheless sinners against the truth of Torah, Kaplan argued that the process of reconstructing Jewish life had to be two-directional. The deviants had to be convinced of the worth of many of the aspects of the heritage that they had abandoned, but, at the same time, the tradition needed some radical revisions. As long as the literal belief in historical revelation remained the basis of Torah study, it would be impossible to harmonize Judaism and the new world of group interaction and advanced thought.

Kaplan fought against assimilation, the danger of which he saw at the outset of his professional career. He knew that he had to find a substitute for belief in the absolute truth of Torah that could serve as a convincing rationale for Jewish survival. Unless a cure could be found for the blow of deculturation, a disaster worse than the destruction of the Temple and the loss of independence would occur—certainly for diaspora Jewry. Still, Kaplan believed in the power of the traditional resources for the cultivation of a vital, humane culture. To his mind, every national culture has the potential of training men and women to become fully human. A culture binds an individual to a group that unites the generations, the living and the dead and those yet to be born. A tradition converts the members of a people from being isolated, purposeless individuals to men and women who seek to rise above their physical and mental limitations and who learn the meaning of loyalty. Kaplan writes: "Since it is tradition that elicits such traits as loyalty and social responsibility, it is folly to think of dispensing with it in any education of which character development is an objective."[27] Therefore, the main problem of education is to determine the criteria according to which we should select those traditional and environmental resources that are truly life-enhancing.

We have reached the point at which Kook and Kaplan part company. For Kaplan, reason is supreme, at least when revelation contradicts currently accepted intellectual and moral standards. He cannot accept the compromise of Rambam and other medieval philosophers, namely, that reason, revelation, and tradition differ theoretically but not in practice, for "[w]here there is a conflict between them, we do not discard our rational conviction to conform to revelation, but we change the meaning of revelation by a process of allegorical interpretation to conform to the conclusions of reason."[28] The Maimonidean compromise displeases Kaplan because, having acquired a sense of history and an understanding of the evolution of thought, it is inappropriate for anyone to interpolate into classic texts ideas that clearly belong to another universe of discourse. We must teach the past without apologetics as it developed and not as we should like it to have been. But, if we lose faith in the divine origin of our heritage, how can we continue to be inspired by it and find it to be relevant? Kaplan considered this question to be crucial, because without the Bible, and particularly the Pentateuch, an authoritative, Jewish identity becomes extremely problematic. Therefore, he proceeded to tackle the full gamut of problems that arose from his rejection of supernaturalism. His intuition led him to focus on Jewish peoplehood as his point of departure. Loyalty to the Jewish people and the determination to contribute to its creative survival became the organizing principles of his educational philosophy. It was within that context that Kaplan conducted his quest for God and Judaism's adjustment to the evolving world.

When Kaplan took up the reins of the Teachers Institute, he knew that the interpretation and teaching of the Bible would be the greatest difficulty. As long as the Bible was considered to be the word of God, its place in the curriculum was indisputable, whether or not it aroused the interest of children or adults. But when this simple faith was weakened, many Jews no longer related to the text or, even when their attachment to Judaism remained vital, they ceased to regard it as a determining factor in their lives. Kaplan tried to restore the Bible to its central place in the self-identity of Jews. He was convinced that despite the drastic changes that had taken place in the mentality of most Jews, the biblical text could still speak forcefully to the human condition and to the Jewish mind. He believed that it possesses an appeal "for a mature and well informed mind that is capable of reconstructing in imagination the life situations of which the Biblical literature is the record and commentary."[29] Kaplan argued that common sense should make it apparent that a people desirous of strengthening the foundations of its being and its culture could hardly ignore the account of its formative years. The Bible is unmatched as a record of the historical, cultural, and spiritual evolution of the Jews for over a thousand years. However, for that account to be useful today, it would be necessary to correct some of the common misinterpretations of its authority.

Kaplan himself had to change his view about the Bible as God's revelation to the Jews. His 1914 essay, referred to above, focused on the centrality of the Pentateuch as the main source of authority in Judaism. By retaining this perception of the Pentateuch, Israel would be able to continue to be a vehicle of divine revelation. That is to say, the Bible should be seen not as a fount of religious information but as an inspiring and commanding force. The Bible, Kaplan thought then, speaks to us with the voice of God and the spirit of our people. It has borne and validated the hopes of our nation for the centuries of its composition and the subsequent centuries down to the present. As a unifying and authoritative document, the Torah offers a powerful rationale for Jewish survival.[30]

In this essay, Kaplan touched on the problematic nature of belief in revelation, but he had not yet clarified for himself the difference between historical revelation, such as the theophany at Sinai, and the knowledge of God as perceived in gradual revelation. Thirty years later, he wrote quite differently. *"Spiritual religion affirms that it is unnecessary to resort to supernatural revelation for experiencing the reality of God. Man's experience of God is as real as his experience of his own personality."*[31] (Italics, MMK) In other words, the experience of both God and man is rooted in the native consciousness of human beings. In both instances, man is often prone to mistaken notions. If today we know—or think we know—more about God than ever before, this is a result of growing knowledge about nature and about ourselves. Revelation is thus interpreted as the most warranted and compelling knowledge of reality that we can attain at any given moment.

The Torah can retain its authority only among survivalist Jews. However, they have to realize that while the Bible is the link to their ancestors and the point of departure for their future as Jews, it cannot be accepted uncritically. Kaplan, for instance, cannot agree with the assessment of Nachmanides, who comments: "For to you [Israel] alone does He give His Torah and the *mitzvot* that are dear to Him."[32] Nor is the Bible to be read as an accurate record of early Jewish history. It is founded on well authenticated historical recollections and data that point to ancient events, figures, and cultural developments in Israel's proto-history and national origins. However, for what today passes as a reasonably accurate account of actual events and actors, we have to be highly selective and tentative about our judgments concerning much of the biblical era. We also have to rely on extraneous sources. For Kaplan, the very fact, apparent in the biblical text and supported by modern research, that Israel's early history was not one of unity and cultural stability can enhance the Bible's educational value. The portrayal of the patriarchs, their deeds and misdeeds and their vision of a great posterity; the views of man and God that were spoken of in song, prophecy, prayer, and meditation; the cultic creativity and the moral concern—all these compose a magnificent panorama of the past that illumines our own lives as Jews and as individuals. Wrestling with this heritage is an essential part of being Jews and of becoming more fully human.

What has been said in regard to the Torah in the narrow sense of the term applies equally to Torah in its broader meaning—that is, all of the Jewish tradition that developed after the biblical era. "Studying Torah can no longer mean what it formerly meant to the Jew—reliving the experience of divine revelation."[33] Kaplan acknowledges that traditional Torah study can make a contribution to experiencing and learning about God, but he maintains that our knowledge of reality has expanded too far to permit blind belief in the reliability of the biblical messages. Nonetheless, every generation has to keep in touch with the past. For the Jews, the Torah has provided insight into the ceaseless opening of new vistas that stimulated their ancestors to creative adaptation to the vicissitudes of their national existence. If we were to try to freeze Jewish tradition, we could not succeed. Life forces men and their cultures to change. However, Kaplan goes a step further when he argues that change must, as far as possible, be planned and, at times, be at variance with or in opposition or addition to the teachings of our forebears.

The resemblance between the conceptions of Torah of Kaplan and Maimonides should be noted. Kook, too, was influenced by Rambam's insistence that Torah had to be a life-enhancing teaching and not merely a collection of formal wisdom. However, Kook halted at the threshold of the salon, into which the medieval philosopher had entered. Despite the limited intellectual tools available in his day, Maimonides had broadened the content of Torah. He made metaphysics and the sciences—astronomy, physics, mathematics, and other fields of learning and investigation—mandatory subjects of study. This annexation of so-called secular knowledge broke down the wall separating the study of Judaism and extraneous learning. Anything that is necessary to enable Jews to become better and wiser men and women would henceforth have to be brought within the purview of Jewish education. Kook, however, turned to the new knowledge to strengthen tradition. Kaplan, like Maimonides, identified as Torah every study that could help the Jewish people advance morally and fulfill its spiritual and cultural potential.[34]

Every ideology of national or cultural survival has to come to grips with the impact of time. Existence has a history and a present, and survival is directed to the future. Philosophies of life are differentiated by the ways in which they conceive the dynamics of cultural development in the passage of time. Kook, for example, who hoped for the elevation of the Jewish people and all humankind to the level of holiness, saw the future as the fulfillment of the past or at least of what was potentially there. He faced the present realistically and fearlessly, while recognizing the fact that the majority of Jews had traveled far from what he considered to be the sacred foundations of the Halakhah. This condition, however, was to be overcome, not by looking for and correcting mistakes in the tradition and encouraging the fashioning of a more adequate future, but by a more intense mining of the accumulated wisdom of the past for treasures yet to be revealed.

In contrast, although he considered the study of the past to be essential, Kaplan argued that it has to be done with the latest tools of investigation. He knew that the problems of the present could not be solved without studying their roots in the evolution of Jewish civilization and without an accurate picture of the current Jewish condition. The combined knowledge of past and present would, he felt, enable today's Jewish educators to ask the right questions. Only thus could the heritage be seen objectively and plans for the future be imaginatively but responsibly formulated.

Kaplan thus saw his efforts as centering on education. The educator he wanted to train would be very different from Kook's ideal. Both men declared that a teacher at any level has to be erudite, but then they parted company. As we have noted, Kook looked for teachers who knew how to apply the latest knowledge to broaden the tradition, validate it, and sweeten it for all Jews. For Kaplan, the interpretation of the past was problematic. He thought that teachers of Judaism should be aware of that fact so that they could inspire their pupils and students to love it even as they viewed it with occasional disagreement. Obviously, this was and is a difficult assignment.

One of the foundation stones of Kaplan's educational philosophy is his assumption that man yearns "to find himself in a universe that is friendly to his highest purpose, to fulfill the most valued potentialities of his nature and to achieve a social order that is founded on justice and peace."[35] This is not to say that Kaplan identified human aspirations with God's will. Only those human purposes that are actually in keeping with those of God will be rewarded by the cosmos. Men and women have to pay the price of their inevitable mistakes, and they must never cease searching for what is truly desirable. As long as they try to correct their mistakes and improve their conduct, as long as they are in a state of repentance, even for sins of which they are unaware, they preserve their humanity and have acquired one of the major qualifications for the right to teach.

This understanding, Kaplan says, radically changes the aim of education and the meaning of *Torah lishmah* ("Torah for its own sake") as popularly accepted up to now. Generally, it is thought that the study of Torah is an objective in itself. The student of Torah, it is true, merits many rewards, as R. Meir declared,[36] but the learner's heart is set on the process of study and not on any benefit that might accrue from it. Kaplan acknowledges that mastering a great tradition has a built-in spiritual reward that inheres in the knowledge of any grand cultural creation. But a person of Kaplan's mentality can no longer take for granted the unblemished worth of every word of the classic texts. The saying of Ben Bag Bag, "Turn it over, turn it over, for it contains everything,"[37] provides the psychological basis for studying the Torah for its own sake. But as soon as one reckons that the Torah can be mistaken and also mislead, then one has both to study it in its own terms and rethink its relevance for today. This is no longer *Torah lishmah*.

"It must be remembered," Kaplan writes, "that we are not dealing with questions of fact. To interpret the past functionally does not mean to follow in the footsteps of the traditional harmonizers who tried to prove that the Scriptures had anticipated every recently discovered scientific fact."[38] Therefore, the aim of studying and teaching the Bible and halakhic literature should be to help us understand how our ancestors tried to raise themselves and to educate their children to a fuller life than had been achieved by previous generations of Jews and of humankind in general. We do not have to agree with our forebears' conception of the full life, but we should respect their seriousness and profundity and apply as much of their thinking as we can to our own lives.

Kaplan suggests what he calls a functional method of interpreting the classical heritage. It is based on three premises. First, Jewish tradition in general and Jewish religion in particular are capable of instilling in us a number of valuable states of mind, like faith, hope, and courage, and to inspire us to become positive people. There is no reason to think that the living heritage has lost this power. Second, it is permissible and necessary to reexamine the tradition with the best instruments at our disposal. Third, we have to emancipate ourselves from the idea that morality and spirituality must be rooted in theurgic theology.

It might be asked: What is the point of all this commentary on the meaning of the past? Why not simply begin with new standards and values unconnected with what we have rejected out of hand? Kaplan's answer is that men naturally tend to feel "that there is some objective truth to the course which human history has taken. If all that man achieved of culture and religion should turn out to be illusory, what meaning can human life have, as a whole?[39] Undoubtedly we share with the ancients some common notions about what contributes to human progress. This fact encourages our faith in humankind. *"The advantage of utilizing traditional concepts is that they carry with them the accumulated momentum and emotional drive of man's previous efforts to attain greater spiritual power."*[40] (Italics, MMK)

On the basis of the preceding assumptions, Kaplan suggests the following system of interpretation:

1. With the development of the so-called scientific study of history, most Jews, with the possible exception of rigid traditionalists, have come to believe that Judaism should be viewed as the cultural and spiritual creation of the Jewish people's grappling with its problems throughout the ages. Judaism is subject to the same natural laws and inevitable metamorphosis as any other cultural entity. Yet I think it is fair to state that Jewish educators have not coped with what this means for the authority and relevance of the Bible. Kaplan raised this issue eighty years ago, but in 5742 (1981/1982), we find three biblical scholars at the liberal Orthodox Bar-Ilan University dramatically presenting the trauma suf-

fered by modern scholars when they have to come to terms with the educational implications of their own scientific method of biblical research.[41] In a three-article symposium, the scholars agree on the need for biblical criticism. One proclaims proudly, "Bar Ilan University is the only Orthodox institution in the world that deals with the Bible on a research level."[42] Another writes: "If we acknowledge the legitimacy in Judaism of *peshat* [seeking the simple meaning of the text]—and we cannot help but do so—and if, further, we attend to the essential features of this method. . . . we are forced to agree that the only way to advance our apprehension of the simple meaning is to use the scientific method."[43] However, after this affirmation, one of the participants in the symposium, Uriel Simon, states: "[W]ithin the Bible Department, we stop short of conducting systematic scientific research into the Pentateuch because of the *educational danger* attached to it. We are restrained by the *special sanctity of the Torah* and by the relative newness of this branch of biblical research based on Jewish-religious axiomatics. We see clearly that our abstinence is very problematic, particularly as regards *intellectual honesty*. Nonetheless, we are convinced that this is the right path for us to follow at this time." [44] (Italics, JJC). Thus, many decades after Kaplan and others recognized the essential role of scientific research not only in disclosing accurately the intent of the biblical authors but also in putting the *Halakhah* into a historical perspective, Jewish intellectuals, including many that are non-Orthodox, still hesitate to deal with the consequences of their research. This reaction, although disappointing, is not surprising. Rabbinic Judaism, for all its history of adjustment to changing needs, is tied to the Written Law as its final authority. Any threat to that authority is bound to endanger the whole halakhic structure. Therefore, Kaplan comments, so long as Jewish law is dependent on the written word of the Torah, "any attempt to study the Bible from the historical point of view will be considered a blow to the very vitals of Jewish religion."[45] Kaplan should have written the Pentateuch rather than Torah. The last two sections of the Bible are, as Simon and his colleagues attest, easier for Orthodox scholars to handle scientifically. Be that as it may, Kaplan quickly took up the challenge.[46]

2. Kaplan states: "It is only in retrospect as we review the consequences in thought and action of any tradition that we begin to

sense its full significance."[47] That is to say, only after the fact are we able, with the help of psychology and the other human and social sciences, to learn how an idea came to be and what in it might have lasting value.

3. Kaplan argues that the Jewish religion should be formulated as the attempt to implement the ineluctable values of all worthy human aspiration. He says, "These values are the product not of any single religious philosophy, or ethical tendency, but of the various social and intellectual forces that have entered into the shaping of any modern civilization. In reinterpreting the traditional values of a spiritual heritage or civilization, we are conserving accumulated energy that would otherwise go to waste."[48]

4. Kaplan distinguishes between two methods of interpretation. The first, which typifies halakhic Judaism, is dubbed by Kaplan as transvaluation or "ascribing meanings to the traditional content of a religion or social heritage, which could neither have been contemplated nor implied by the authors of that content."[49] This kind of interpretation is presumably legitimized by the sense of group continuity and by faith in the revealed character of the Written and Oral Torah. All the Jew has to do is to reveal the secret truths embodied in the sacred words. In fact, the significance of the interpretive process escapes most Jews. In the first place, changes in intellectual and moral perceptions take place that are nonetheless deemed to be continuations or new applications of eternal ideas or values. Second, to justify the new thoughts or actions, the commentators look for supporting biblical verses or for the statements or legal opinions of their predecessors. Third, to effect this technique, they take verses out of context and attribute forced meanings to them. Kaplan cites a number of examples to indicate why he calls for a new type of interpretation of the classic texts. I cite only a few.

He mentions the well-known transformation undergone in the *lex talionis*—an eye for an eye, a tooth for a tooth, etc.—whereby monetary compensation replaces physical retribution. Whether the more humane punishment was practiced in the biblical period or was an invention of the rabbis is immaterial. The point is that we have an example of how a text can be deliberately given a meaning that was not implicit in it. On the first verse of Genesis, R. Yonah asks in the name of R. Levi: "Why was the world created with the letter *beth*? Just as *beth* is closed on three sides and open on its forward side, so you may not state what is below or above, what lies ahead and what occurred before Creation. You may ask only concerning what has already been created and its aftermath." (Gen, R. I:10) This is surely not what was meant or implied by the author of the Creation story.

The medieval philosophers had to undertake a similar apologetic to justify their preoccupation with metaphysics. An earlier version of the philosophical resort to transvaluation is Philo's allegories. For example, he interprets the four rivers flowing from the Garden of Eden as symbols of virtues—Pishon for piety, Hidekel for loving-kindess, Gihon for courage, and Perat for resistance to temptation.[50]

5. In place of the above method of interpolation, Kaplan recommends what he calls *revaluation,* or an attempt to disengage "from *the traditional content those elements in it which answer permanent Postulates of human nature, and in integrating them into our own ideology.* When we revaluate, we analyze or break up the traditional values into their implications, and single out for acceptance those implications which can help us to meet our own moral and spiritual needs; the rest may be relegated to archeology."[51] (Italics, MMK)

It is doubtful whether the classical authors could have recognized the disparity between the two methods of interpretation. We, however, by using our broader knowledge objectively, must try to draw warranted conclusions from the views and behavior of our ancestors. This means that we must courageously reject traditional conceptions that do not accord with our best understanding of what is true and good. Kaplan admits that there is no unanimity concerning truth and goodness. Therefore, there must be room in education for differences of opinion. Teachers and students alike must be free to decide for themselves the principles on which they wish to base their way of life. This does not exempt all concerned in the educational process from the responsibility of substantiating their positions according to standards of intellectual honesty and respect for facts.

The educational philosophies of Kook and Kaplan are hewn out of wide-ranging, imaginative, and organic visions of reality. Both see the world as changing and progressing, however slowly and unevenly. Both advocate pleasantness, tolerance, and appeal to reason. Yet if their disciples were to try to establish a common school or formulate a joint curriculum, they would be over-whelmed by the disparity in their educational theories.

These differences are manifest when we examine the recom-mendations of the two men as to the character of the key institu-tions of Jewish nationalism and higher learning. The educational enterprise in every society is largely conditioned by what happens on the higher levels of research and study. In Jewish life, this means, first of all, the general colleges and universities and their broad curricula of arts and sciences, research and technology. Par-allel to these institutions are yeshivot and training schools for rab-bis, teachers, and other community workers. The ideals of these institutions more or less determine the objectives and procedures of elementary and secondary Jewish schools. Much has been writ-ten about the impact of Kook's model yeshivah on education in Israel, but to better understand its advantages and limitations, we should turn to Kaplan's proposal for a university of Judaism.

Kaplan stressed the need for studying and recapturing the tradi-tion in all its facets and trying to uncover treasures that previous generations had overlooked. However, the future cannot be built on the past alone. Its usefulness is truncated, if it is presented uncritically. The reworking of the past must be done responsibly by sympathetic and up-to-date scholarship. This, together with the need to find proper Jewish forms in which to express the treasures of the human spirit, whatever their origins, obviously calls for a new type of educational leadership.

The different educational conceptions of Kook and Kaplan can be illustrated by reference to the windows in the Temple of Solo-mon. They were "broad within and narrow without" (I Kings 6, 4). Rashi comments that they were not like other windows which have an opposite shape in order to admit more light. The Temple had God's light and needed none from the outside. Kook believes that the Torah generates light not only for the Jews but for the other nations as well. Jewish education has all the resources it needs within Judaism. If, nonetheless, Kook added foreign lan-guages and the application of scientific instruments to Torah study, this is indicative of his awareness of the world around him, not of his belief that these tools have to be used to produce necessary changes in Judaism.

Kaplan wanted windows through which light can flow in both directions. They must be wide and transparent, admitting light from the outside and projecting it from within. Jews must appreciate the light in their own tradition but never lose sight of the rays of knowledge and wisdom from the outside. The light in both directions is to be judged by universal standards of purity. The life of every nation should be both independent and interdependent, with all that is implicit in this way of looking at one's own culture and those of other peoples.

It is important to bear in mind that while Kook focused his attention on the future of Judaism in Eretz Yisrael, he believed his thought also to be relevant to the Diaspora. Kaplan devoted himself to strengthening Jewish life in the free Diaspora, but he thought that the Jews could not survive in that world unless they constructed a Zionist Judaism. Both men stressed the oneness of the Jewish people. Kook looked to Jewish education to motivate the ingathering of the exiles, for this is God's wish. Kaplan preached Zionist Judaism and the centrality of Eretz Yisrael, but he doubted the practicality of the total ingathering. Jewish education, therefore, has to help prepare the ground for creative and pluralistic Jewish survival in both the homeland and the Dispersion.

One of the steps in this direction, according to Kaplan, is to foster adult Jewish education beyond the training of Jewish professionals and academics. A Judaism consisting only of academic experts will have no future. A creative people will not emerge from the yeshivot or the universities of soulless academic scholarship. A live Judaism requires an informed laity who will feel their Jewish knowledge to be an essential part of their fulfillment as human beings.

TOWARD A UNIVERSITY OF JUDAISM

To educate such a laity, Kaplan argued, we must create a cadre of rabbis, teachers, community and group workers, psychologists, professional fund-raisers, and the like, whose commitment to the

Jewish people will be fortified by learning. Such leadership is essential for Jewish continuity under freedom. Therefore, Kaplan called for the establishment of "a University of Judaism in which not merely rabbis and teachers but all types of professional and lay leaders would be trained to meet the demand created by the functional differentiation of Jewish activity."[52] This university would also be meant for men and women who wish to serve as volunteers or who plan to study for their own enlightenment and for the Jewish quality of their homes. The curriculum of the school would range between the most elementary and the most advanced levels.

Unlike Kook, Kaplan viewed denominational pluralism as a positive phenomenon in Jewish life. The university should be structured so as to give free rein to competing interpretations of and programs for Judaism and, at the same time, foster commonality and cooperation. Kaplan set forth the following four principles for his university:

1. Strict adherence to modern academic standards. Traditional texts must be researched, taught, and studied in their historical context. Kaplan maintains, "[T]he true meaning of any text cannot be derived from the contemplation of the text itself apart from the social, economic, psychological and intellectual setting to which it belongs."[53]

2. Emphasis on the Hebraic base of the curriculum. Kaplan had a troubled romance with the Hebrew language, which he loved but never mastered to his satisfaction. He wanted to make Hebrew the second language of diaspora Jews. Its knowledge, he believed, is a precondition of a strong Jewish consciousness. He insisted on Hebrew instruction at the Teachers Institute of the Jewish Theological Seminary, whereas in the Rabbinical School, over whose faculty he had no control, most courses were taught in English, at least until several years after the establishment of the State of Israel.[54]

3. Plenitude, that is, the abundance of hours of study and of Jewish experiences. Even Jews living in Eretz Yisrael are subject to foreign influences, despite the Jewish ambience and Hebrew surroundings. They cannot escape the impact of other cultures that flood the radio waves, television and movie screens, stages and concert halls, and literature, to say nothing of the daily con-

tacts with local Arabs and endless tourists. Only the scholar who is consciously isolated from these and other influences can escape their challenge. The problem for diaspora educators is more severe. Their charges have to fulfill their obligations as citizens of their respective states, in addition to carving out a Jewish lifestyle. Therefore, Kaplan urged, "Be a Jew to the maximum degree compatible with the legitimate claims of the non-Jewish national civilization."[55] He was convinced that it is possible for Jews in the free Diaspora, even as a minute minority, to develop a variegated Judaism. Jewish culture must not be limited to ideas of God and man. "Judaism must be lived with all the senses and not merely subscribed to by our common sense."[56] In the Diaspora, the observance of rituals has national as well as spiritual import. It is incumbent on the University of Judaism to cultivate a rich and colorful set of Jewish experiences that befit a free environment.

4. Confidence that the United States (and, by inference, other liberal democracies) will be hospitable to and respectful of subcultures. Cultures need not be exclusive—indeed, in a free world they cannot be. Exclusivism, which is one of the components of the negation of the Diaspora, is, in Kaplan's opinion, a negative attitude. It contributes nothing to *aliyah*, which Kaplan favored, and harms the morale of those who want a Judaism compatible with democratic freedom and cultural interaction. The university must encourage Jews to live in two civilizations, both of which are hopefully founded on enlightened values.

Kaplan's vision was partly fulfilled with the establishment in Los Angeles of the University of Judaism, under the auspices of the Conservative Jewish Theological Seminary of America. The Seminary adopted Kaplan's conception of its scope but not his dream of an interdenominational institution. As might have been expected, the Hebrew Union College soon formed its own parallel school, also in Los Angeles.

When Kaplan first proposed his university idea in the mid-1940s, he recommended that its curriculum cover the following fields: religion, education, social services, the arts, democracy in its application to Jewish polity and spiritual ideals, and social research. If he were alive today, he would undoubtedly revise his concept and reorganize the structure and content of Jewish higher education, but insofar as the American scene is concerned, the training of rabbis and teachers would retain its primacy. The current function of the rabbi deserves special attention, as a means of distinguishing the difference between Kaplan's university and Kook's yeshivah. The disparity is not merely the distinction between an Orthodox and a non-Orthodox brand of education. Kaplan's vision was no less revolutionary in regard to the Reform and Conservative conceptions of training professional Jewish leadership. For today, rabbis, teachers, and practitioners in other services must be at home both in the tradition and its interpretation and in the nature of the individual and the social environment. The professional school has to be a school for coping with a broad range of life experiences.

Kaplan is unusual among Jewish thinkers in his regard for the arts. Kook, too, is of this stripe, but he insists that artists must subject themselves to halakhic restraints. For instance, in a letter to the pioneering artistic institution, Bezalel, Kook remarks:

> Through this important profession—art—beauty can be a blessing and open the gates to a livelihood for many families of our brethren living on our holy soil. . . . It will also arouse the feeling of beauty and purity, for which the children of Zion are eminently suited. It will bring cheer to many depressed souls by enlightening them about the splendor and dignity of life, nature, work and diligence.[57]

Kook explains his stand as a continuation of the eternal struggle against idolatry.

> When our ancient people was born, it found mankind in the swaddling bands of savagery. Man's sense of beauty was wild, lacking purity and delicacy. His primitiveness dominated the world. Were it not for the splendor of scientific and moral truth, beauty would have become in the hands of the crude mobs a fatty roll and an intoxicating liquor.[58]

Interestingly, Kook combines truth, goodness, and beauty. He tries to ensure that the renewed interest in art—which was undoubtedly an accompaniment of Zionism and of the desire of the people to restore its national independence and normalcy— should not spill over the halakhic container. It is the *Halakhah* that defines the parameters of the full life of truth, goodness, and beauty. Therefore, he warns the Bezalel group that while ornamentation and painting are permissible for Jews, great care must be exercised not to violate the rule against sculpting a complete bust of the human countenance (R.H. 24b). Kook argues that an art such as the sculpting of icons, which opens the door to idolatry, should be despised by the ecclesia of Israel.[59]

Thus, Kook and Kaplan diverge in their assessment of the role of the arts in the Jewish national revival and of their place in education. In the first place, Kaplan regards art as a potentially unifying force in Jewish life. "The one area in which it is still possible for Jews to achieve an awareness of kind, to learn to feel their oneness not merely through being the common target for hostility, but through a common response to values that give meaning to life, is the area of the arts."[60] Music, drama, poetry, dance, painting, and sculpture can provide common enjoyment and pride for Jews who are otherwise divided in thought and lifestyle. Second, a Judaism lacking independence, originality, and creativity cannot attract the majority of our talented youth. Third, Kaplan believes that the battle against idolatry, excessive materialism, and inordinate permissiveness cannot be won by imposing arbitrary restrictions. Artificial prohibitions can never stem the free movement of healthy minds.

Artists should, of course, try to cultivate discriminating tastes; to plumb the depths of truth, beauty, and goodness; and to learn how to harmonize them in their work. In the setting of a modern university of Judaism, artists of all kinds would be able to develop their talents against the background of a vital Jewish panorama. Kaplan writes: "Each one of the five schools of the University of Judaism thus far named [rabbinical and teacher training, social work, the arts, and the school for democracy] is likely to remain static, and to fall behind in its needed adaptation to meet the changing conditions of life, unless it is in close touch with a research department."[61] In that department, accepted assumptions must be continually reexamined, unknown facts unearthed, and newer methods formulated and tested.

Kaplan sought to combine the best features of the university and the yeshivah. All Jewish schools of higher learning should unite love of God, Torah, and Israel (the hallmarks of Kook's yeshivah); intellectual breadth and honesty; free inquiry and expression; and high standards of knowledge (the ideals of the university).

Unfortunately, Jewish education in all streams of Jewish life seems likely to remain tied to accepted (but not acceptable) standards. As a result, we shall lose many of our young people. However, efforts aimed at improving the system will have to address the challenges set forth by Kook and Kaplan. Eventually, the two views will have to be brought into some form of creative tension. Where else, if not in the Jewish school, can such a confrontation take place in a harmonizing spirit?

NOTES

1. Appeared in 5648 (1887/1888).
2. *Orot Hatorah* (henceforth, OH), 5745 (1984), p. 44.
3. Ibid., p. 45.
4. DK, R. 191, p. 366.
5. See also *Hullin* 97a b and *Tosafot*, beginning *samkhinan*.
6. OK, Vol. 2, p. 537.
7. Ibid., p. 541.
8. Ibid.
9. OK, Vol. 1, p. 25.
10. *Orot*, p. 119.
11. OR, Vol. 1, p. 13.
12. OK, Vol. 3, p. 107.
13. AT, p. 46.
14. OK, Vol. 3, p. 106.
15. Ibid.
16. Ibid., p. 107.
17. Ibid., pp. 106–107.
18. This speculation relates only to the context of this paragraph. In another place, Kook says specifically that *shirah*, song, is symbolic of Torah. In one of his sermons on *Simhat Torah*, he remarks, "There is a difference between song and melody. Melody comes from without. When we begin to sing or play [an instrument], the soul awakens, along with its feelings and longings. *Shirah* is greater, for it comes from within, from an overflowing soul. The soul breaks out in song.

"Scholars do not sing [wordless melodies]; they sing [with words]. The Torah that fills their mind and heart sings joyously from out of their inner soul. Blessed are they who study Torah, for it is their song."

19. Very early in his career, Kook criticized the educational practices of extremist Jews. In his important essay, "The Path of Renewal," which

appeared in *HaNir*, in 1909, he comments that when the exiles returned from Babylonia, they felt the absence of the inspiration they had enjoyed before the destruction of the first Temple. To fill that gap, they turned to exaggerated, repetitive study. This habit has continued down to modern times. "But stubborn adherence to study alone weakens the strength of the nation." In this same essay, Kook adds: "The infusion of existential spirituality is manifest more in action than it is in educational methodology. When it is cleared of extraneous dross . . . it restores the nation's full glory by recapturing the patriarchal greatness of the princes of Israel, each of whom was marked by a lofty, personal distinction." Note, however, how Kook regards the other side of memory. "How potent are the *mitzvot* of remembering and how splendid is their ability to endow our people with glorious memory and to endear it to their hearts. They all bear the complete history of beauty and life" ("The Mission of Yisrael and Its Nationalism," *HaPeles*, First Year, p. 8).

20. We can learn more about Kook's conception of life from a sermon on Vayishlah, given in 1929: "Were it not for the sin of the tree of knowledge, we, too, should not need a written Torah. For life itself would proceed according to its laws" (SR, pp. 71–72).

21. Compare again Kaplan's observation about the functioning of the will: "A stubborn will resists, a strong will persists; a stubborn will allies itself to tradition, a strong will to purpose; a stubborn will keeps to the past, a strong will builds for the future" (*Diaries*, October 17, 1915).

22. MA, p. 66. See also Kook's comment on the rise from the faulted present to the perfect future (OR, Vol. 1, p. 435).

23. OR, Vol. 1, p. 340.

24. *Moledet V'eretz Yeludah* (*Homeland and Land of Birth*) (Tel Aviv: Am Oved, 1978, p. 191).

25. My interpretation of *Shir Vasiah* is not the only one possible. I commend to the reader the interesting commentary of Shmuel Livneh in his essay, "Chapters in Ethical Theory: A Study of Orot Hakodesh," Vol. 3 (in ZR, pp. 77–90, and particularly, pp. 78–79). Livneh stresses the kabbalistic background of the section. In his view, Kook regards the present as the spoiled period between the perfect past and future. In our time, when good and evil are intertwined, Torah leads man on the road to repair the world. Evil will not disappear; it will rise and carry out its function in the perfection of life. In that future life, man will not be torn by the tension between the two inclinations of good and evil; he will behave naturally as he did before the sin of Adam. This is *siah*, the attribute of Isaac after the *Akedah*, the binding on the altar, when his pure soul was restored. Isaac continued to live in this world with his soul of the world-to-come.

26. *Mordecai M. Kaplan: An Evaluation*, ed. by Ira Eisenstein and Eugene Kohn (New York: Jewish Reconstructionist Foundation, 1952, p. 290).

27. *Judaism in Transition* (henceforth, JT) (New York: Behrman, 1941, p. 138).

28. Ibid., pp. 193–194.

29. Ibid., p. 149.

30. "The Supremacy of the Torah," in *The Reconstructionist*, Vol. 30, No. 7, May 1964. The essay first appeared in the *Students Annual* of the Jewish Theological Seminary, in 1914.

31. FAJ, p. 192.

32. Commentary of Ramban on Deut. 26, 18.

33. JC, p. 44.

34. Eliezer Schweid is mistaken when he writes: "Whereas in Kook's teaching, the Torah is meant to include all the areas of life, in Kaplan's thought culture embraces Torah as one of its elements" (*The History of Jewish Thought in the 20th Century*, p. 259). Schweid's comment oversimplifies the intention of both thinkers. Despite Kook's rootage in the view that everything is to be found in Torah, his openness to changes and discoveries bears testimony to his awareness that the outside world has influenced the content of Torah and will continue to do so—in effect if not in theory. Schweid also misconstrues Kaplan, whose aim was to preserve the vitality of Torah. To attain this goal, the Jewish people will have to convert into Torah every discovery about the nature of the physical universe and about man, every authenticated notion that is likely to improve the spiritual and moral stature of humankind. Kaplan also dared to recommend removing from the living Torah all ideas that have been shown to be false or harmful, all values not in line with the dignity and sanctity of the individual. In brief, whatever should be our life and the length of our days should become Torah. In considering Torah as the heart of civilization, Kaplan was an heir of Rambam.

35. JC, p. 389.

36. *M. Avot* VI:1.

37. Ibid., V:25.

38. JC, p. 389.

39. Ibid., p. 386.

40. Ibid.

41. The following quotations are taken from the symposium, "Biblical Research and Instruction in an Orthodox University," which appeared in *Deot*, a journal for Orthodox academicians, No. 49, 5742. My critique of the essays, titled "Biblical Criticism and the Teaching of the Pentateuch," was published in *Shdemot*, No. 88–89, Winter 1984.

42. *Deot*, p. 231.

43. Ibid., p. 236.

44. Ibid., p. 234.

45. JC, p. 387.

46. Ibid. In a later formulation (1949), Kaplan writes: "If we want our people to make the Torah an integral part of their consciousness, we must be outspoken as to whether we regard it as a monolithic text of supernatural origin, or as a human document of composite authorship" (FAJ, p. 478).

47. JC, p. 388.

48. Ibid.

49. MG, p. 3.

50. The example from Philo is to be found in the translation of his works by F. H. Colson and G. H. Whitaker, Loeb Classics, Vol. 1, pp. 187–189.

51. MG, p. 6.

52. FAJ, p. 527.

53. Ibid., p. 528.

54. My late colleague, Rabbi Elvin Kose, told me of the following incident, which illustrates Kaplan's passion for Hebrew. Kaplan was invited to be the main speaker at a fund-raising dinner for the Histadrut Ivrit of America. As chairman of the occasion, Kose led the recitation of the grace after meals. As soon as he invited the gathering to join him in the prayer, almost everyone began to engage in conversation that grew more boisterous by the minute. After the conclusion of the catastrophic grace, Kose introduced Kaplan. The latter began his Hebrew address with an angry outburst: "Shame on you! The Hebrew words alone of the *Birkat Hamazon* should have reduced you all to silence."

55. FAJ, p. 529.

56. Ibid.

57. KL, Vol. 1, L. 158, p. 204.

58. Ibid., p. 205.

59. Ibid.

60. FAJ, p. 532.

61. Ibid., p. 534.

13

Judaism and Democracy

OUR ERA is replete with confrontations. Religion and secularism are at loggerheads in every nation. Rationalists and mystics carry on their ancient controversy. Racial and ethnic conflicts often reach murderous proportions. In the past century, the demand for women's rights has surfaced, and its full effects are, at this moment, largely unpredictable. Among Jews, there is a gnawing concern that our people is heading for a *Kulturkampf* (culture clash) between Fundamentalists and the modern majority and, among the latter, a confusing battle over the parameters of *Halakhah* and democracy. An examination of Kook's and Kaplan's views on democracy should indicate how crucial is their difference of opinion for the Jewish future.

Paradoxically, the depth of the conflict is manifest in Kook's aloofness from the whole issue. Democracy is a category that Kook rarely examines, and then only superficially. As we have seen in other connections, the traditional Jewish world is a halakhic one. Hence, for Kook, democracy is no challenge. Except for the years during World War I, particularly the short time he spent in England, Kook never experienced life in a democratic setting, and during his entire education, he never tasted the flavor of the democratic vision. Only his extraordinary awareness of the events around him brought him in touch with the spirit of democratic freedom. However, this limited contact did not convince him that something radical had occurred which might augur the advent of a new chapter in Judaism.

In contrast to Kook's aloofness, Kaplan regarded democracy as an inescapable challenge to the character of Jewish nationalism. His thought is intensely concerned with democracy as a moral and political theory and as a spiritual, even theological, faith. He remarks, "[D]emocracy is a faith; its validity is not scientifically demonstrable. It demands a priori acceptance of ideals which can be proved valid only by our committing ourselves to their realization. It is a scheme of salvation that implies belief in a Power that makes for salvation."[1]

HINTS OF DEMOCRACY IN KOOK'S THOUGHTS

Although Kook's treatment of democracy is limited, his thought is peppered with observations that provide grounds for a fruitful debate with Kaplan. We should not be misled by semantics. For example, the absence of the term "religion" from the Bible does not mean that the Bible is not a religious text. Similarly, Kook's silence with respect to the term "democracy" is no indication that he is totally oblivious to its importance. At the same time, Kook's failure to use the term excessively does suggest that he ignores or disagrees with many of its concerns. For example, over a century ago, the Zionist cause was already faced with the problem of unity and diversity. All Zionists wanted national unity, but not all were prepared then, or agree today, to grant legitimacy to ideas that are to them heretical or to practices that depart from the halakhic norm. Kook noted the growing diversity among Zionists. Many devoted themselves to the *mitzvah* of building Eretz Yisrael but departed from important traditional religious conceptions and practices. Under democracy, deviation is no reason for delegitimization. But while Kook admired the patriotic efforts of the *halutzim*,[2] he nonetheless regarded them as endangering authentic Judaism and in need of rehabilitation.

Kook tried to hold on to both ends of the rope. In a letter written in 1913, he states:

> Do not be discouraged, my friend, if it happens that, as a result of the fact that Jews have come from many regions, their styles of life differ. They should all observe their customs and traditions. And as for your concern as to how our national unity can be restored, there are two answers. First, as long as each Jew respects the tradition of the other, the difference in their teachings and customs will not mar our unity. Moreover, the multi-coloration makes for spiritual richness that is harmoniously integrated among our people.[3]

Kook understands that the ingathering of the exiles means the convergence of a variety of Jewish traditions. Therefore, he calls for mutual respect. However, his tolerance of differences does not pertain to acceptance of nonhalakhic ways of life. The religious developments that he mentions in his letter do not include Reform and Conservatism, for how could halakhic loyalists adopt such foreign notions? Indeed, Kook writes, "[W]hy should we be dissembling . . . and say that we ought to pledge allegiance to the flag of religious tolerance in order to benefit Israel? . . . In truth, there is no greater danger or potential stumbling block for our people . . . than this tolerance which diverts our eyes from that which is Israel's life and length of days." He goes on to say that backsliders who wish to repent should, of course, be warmly embraced. But "to grant a party of free thinkers the right to exist legally among our people—that cannot be! Just as not a trace of idolatry remains among us, thank God, despite the fact that, according to the testimony of Scriptures, most of the nation at times were attracted to it, so we are confident that not a hint will remain of lawlessness and denial of Torah and of the God of Israel."[4]

Kook was an optimist. He believed that when the nation returned to its soil and reconstituted itself, internal differences would disappear and uniformity would be reestablished. Later, in the aforementioned letter, he writes:

> Even though regional differences might delay the group's unification, this condition will not be forever. These differences have limited and local value, only as long as the nation has not reorganized itself and set up its external and internal institutions and their connections. But once the national structure has been completed, then the tradition itself demands that we establish for the whole people an over-all high court, in the eternal, holy center that God will choose for the people in the Temple. From there will come forth one Torah for all Israel. Then we shall abide by a living tradition which wells up in the soul of the nation and is bound up with God's Torah.[5]

Kook dreamt of the Third Temple not only as a symbol but as the lone center of spiritual authority whose teachings would unite all Jews, both in Israel and in the Diaspora. Undoubtedly, Kook wanted to reconstitute the Sanhedrin (the highest legislative body and court) and the entire halakhic system of jurisprudence.

It is true that some defectors from halakhic theory and practice have been induced to return to the fold, while others, previously ignorant, have adopted a halakhic lifestyle as a means of filling their spiritual void. These modes of conduct will undoubtedly occur in the future as well. But the overwhelming majority of Jews have committed themselves to a democratic orientation, which is not likely to accede to the certainties of the halakhic way.

Kook did, however, favor a certain degree of tolerance. Writing to Dr. Moshe Seidel, with whom he exchanged many letters, he said:

> Tolerance is life-giving. as long as it is practiced in the purity of thought and morality, that can be made apparent only in the clear recognition of the essence of our national life and spiritual development. However, when tolerance is a product of a soft heart and spiritual flabbiness, it becomes a deadly poison that will ultimately raise from the netherworld a bitter fanaticism, whose proponents will be precisely those who call for tolerance.[6]

In other words, Kook would extend tolerance only to those who understand what he deems to be the inherited, genetic spirit of the Jewish people and are loyal to it. Tolerance whose source is in a soft heart or pity for others will become a stumbling block to life, "because tolerance that weakens the ability of the nation to use its life force against all who try utterly to destroy its soul and create a spirit of chaos in its ranks resembles the forbearance of a man who sees the honor of his family trampled by every unruly and violent person but, out of weakness, remains silent."[7]

How shall we interpret this "spirit of chaos"? Does every deviation from *Halakhah* destroy the national soul? Is not an occasional departure necessary in order to purify it? Clearly, Kook opposes tolerance toward anyone who takes the slightest step beyond the halakhic border. A sin is a sin and is not to be tolerated. Nevertheless, Kook relates with kindness toward the "sinners," confident that they will eventually be won over. But this is not the kind of tolerance of difference that is demanded in a democratic society, where the very striving for uniformity is distasteful.

Kook's attitude toward tolerance enables us to understand his criticism of normative Zionism. He states:

> Zionism as a movement to reclaim the national foundation of Israel is good and proper. It offers much hope. But it can never become

the stronghold of the entire people. For it does not grasp the holy light of eternal life in the nation's soul, the spirit of the true God that resides within it. Therefore, while it will succeed in dealing with the outer concerns of national revival, it will never penetrate to the inner life, which awaits another, entirely different group of builders. They will stem from that "arid soil" of pietists who opposed Zionism in ideological honesty, fearing what would happen to God's spiritual influence on the foundation of [national] life.[8]

Thus, Kook is critical of modern secular trends within the Zionist effort. They threaten what he believes to be the authentic nationalism epitomized in the *Halakhah*. The Zionist movement tries to overcome the effects of anarchic diversity, but in a different manner from that of the *Halakhah*. The future of Judaism will and should be determined by the way in which Jews respond creatively to the vicissitudes of life and not by obedience to traditional fiats. Using this method, the people should extrapolate from the rich halakhic tradition what is worthy and relevant. In this endeavor, halakhists can be of enormous help, but they cannot have the only say. In justice to Kook, few Zionist leaders have given credit to the *Halakhah* for its contributions to a creative Jewish future. But then few halakhic authorities have been sufficiently flexible and realistic in the interpretation and application of Jewish law in a democratic, pluralistic setting.

Zionism has opened the door to a variety of ideas and to experiments that sometimes fail. Occasional failure is the price that has to be paid for the benefits of the democratic process. Kook rejects the price. He sees in the new trends the deterioration of the Jewish soul.[9] He prizes the constructive contributions of those whom he calls "*olamiyim*," worldly ones, but they must not determine the conditions of the national revival, for they

perceive only the outer splendor and beauty of modern culture, which are the false glitter of a rotten tree. We might be able to walk a few steps in this dim light, but properly, we ought to foster Israel's inner spirit through the establishment of *yeshivot* and the expansion of Torah in the broadest sense of the term. The curriculum should include all subjects, from the most minor to the greatest, so that body and soul would be knit in a manner befitting a holy people walking in light toward a vital reawakening, that includes sovereignty and statehood.[10]

Despite his single-mindedness, Kook fought against extremism. His honesty led him to seek the positive in the opinions of ideological opponents. Regarding freedom of opinion, he writes:

> Remember that plain logic is always a major factor in legal judgment, whether in theory or in actual cases. Therefore, we must always try to judge with absolute integrity. If there appears to be a contradiction between two truths, this requires renewed study before we can render a decision. Therefore, we have to ask ourselves how far freedom of opinion, which is accepted today by most thinkers in the world, can be logically permitted to extend. You cannot say, there is no limit. In the first place, there is no virtue which is unharmed when exaggerated. Secondly, the nature of the situation demands that a limit be set for free thinking; otherwise, moral norms would be abandoned to a point where a person would not know where to stop. The world would then be filled with baseness.[11]

Kook and his disciples believe that modern freedom of thought deserves consideration, inasmuch as it was practiced in halakhic debate throughout the centuries, although in a more limited way. The Jewish people has mostly resisted attempts to have dogmas foisted upon it. Even Maimonides failed to get approval for making belief in an anthropomorphic view of God heretical. However, the freedom of thought allowed in halakhic discourse is far more limited than is the case in today's free societies.

The intellectual conflict within Judaism mainly regards the range of freedom. Among the Orthodox of his day, Kook was probably more attuned to the use of rational methods than were most or all of his peers. Because logical inference plays such an important role in halakhic transaction, Kook sought criteria for the extent to which reason and openness might legitimately be used. He acknowledged the relativity of the matter, stating that placing limitations on freedom

> cannot be the same for all societies. For example, the agreement by some that no harm is done for people to walk nude in the marketplace is sinful to our way of thinking. But it is not a sin, for instance, for the natives of Guiana. Since societies differ, the disparity will not be only in one issue and will depend on a variety of circumstances.[12]

However, Kook argues, a multiplicity of views must not be made a value in itself, inasmuch as "he who by his notions, and even more so by his acts, weakens the vital national idea, is a traitor, concerning whom forgiveness is wicked."[13] Kook goes on to contrast Israel with all other nations. Israel alone focuses its attention on God. Jews who advance a thought that would cast doubt on this thesis read themselves out of the Jewish consensus. Freedom of thought has to be confined to what the *Halakhah* permits. This is not an arbitrary rule, according to Kook. It is more peremptory than the laws of nature because the Torah stands above nature.

KAPLAN'S ESPOUSAL OF DEMOCRACY

Almost all of Kaplan's words are somehow connected with democratic values. For him, democracy is not merely an electoral system and form of government, but rather a philosophy of life and a religious plan of salvation.

> The main task of democracy is to salvage the freedom of the mind, to recover the right of every human being to exercise the most divine power which he possesses, the power of reason. . . . Mankind's only hope is in the achievement of that individual and personal freedom, that freedom of mind, which spells freedom of thought and freedom of expression, untrammeled by the tyranny of the state, or by the anonymous powers which pull the strings of the state.[14]

Democracy and freedom of the individual are organically related; democracy and coercion are contradictions in terms.

Kaplan had to deal with aspects of government that did not trouble or interest Kook. He lived in a Jewish community in the United States that, despite its status as a small minority, was and is as heavily involved in all the affairs of the American government as the non-Jewish majority. American Jews, like all their brethren since the Emancipation, have had to choose between retreating to a voluntary ghetto and staying as aloof as possible from the general society and its workings or carrying out their duties as equal citizens. The choice between these alternatives is fateful. Kaplan wanted Jews to interact with their neighbors, to learn from them, to disagree openly when their conscience bids them to do so, and to try and influence non-Jews when they feel they have something valid to communicate. This approach produces frequent tension and creates problems never contemplated by our ancestors.

Modern political reality, at least in part, is characterized by the creation of democratic nations out of collections of ethnic, religious, and racial groups. Kaplan suggested four principles on which a pluralistic, democratic society should be constituted:

1. The unit of government should be a geographic group, and not a racial, historical or religious group.
2. The sovereignty of a geographic group should be vested in all adults who constitute that group.
3. The interests of the geographic group as a whole should take precedence over the interests of any other group within or without the geographic group.
4. The welfare of the geographic group demands unrestricted economic and social intercourse among its constituents.[15]

These principles of the democratic state constitute a new challenge to Jewish survival. Those who adopt them forfeit exclusivity for their own groups in certain matters. They have to aspire to the evolution of a community that will include their group but which cannot be built, ab initio, solely or even mainly on what is especially dear to it. They will have to learn the art of compromise and to live cooperatively with the rest of the population. This does not mean—and Kaplan clearly rejected this notion— that subgroups should be expected to abandon their unique cultures. On the contrary! In order for the geographic group to unify its disparate population, it will have to guarantee full rights of self-expression to everyone. The common culture will have to develop out of a broad degree of consensus, freely arrived at.

A democracy requires basic laws that are acceptable to the majority of its citizens and the willingness of all to obey them. Beyond this, the success of a democracy depends on the belief of a large majority that they are blessed with freedom and equal opportunity for self-fulfillment. The democratic game is complex. On the one hand, majority rules, even a small majority. But our Sages knew long ago that a decree which is not in keeping with the communal consensus and with the basic rights of all citizens cannot last, for the vociferous objections of a minority are often as effective as the vote of a majority. This fact applies especially to a democracy, in which laws must take into account the legitimate rights of minorities.

Democracy is thus a shattering challenge to the halakhic system. Even if we give the broadest possible interpretation to the talmudic principle, "the law of the [secular] government is law" (*Bava Kamma*, 113a), there is a difference between laws forced upon Jews by a hostile foreign regime and the concessions demanded of traditional Jewish law by a democratic Jewish government. The latter situation prevails in Israel where laws have to involve Jews and non-Jews alike, both in their promulgation and in their execution, and where legislation often has to oppose or go beyond halakhic rulings. Kaplan explains that such tension is an inevitable outcome of the fact that all peoples have to live in more than one civilization—their historical one and that of the pluralistic society that characterizes every democratic state. Democracy cannot persist if each ethnic or religious group refuses on principle to make any adjustments in its own culture to serve the legitimate needs of the total society. Obviously, Kaplan supports the right to be different, but this right does not permit any group to slow down the wheels of progress by trying to impose on the majority ideas and practices that have become anachronistic, such as opposition, in the name of religion, to medical science or to the teaching of evolutionary theory in public schools.

The above-mentioned danger to the *Halakhah* is as follows. Legal authority, both in Israel and in the Diaspora, is invested in the entire people and their elected or chosen representatives instead of in a single group of halakhic scholars. For example, issues such as defining who is a Jew, laws of public domain, kashrut, basic norms, and many others can be decided in the Knesset, at least theoretically, by votes cast by Arab delegates. Kaplan explains this strange anomaly by asserting that we Jews have not yet come to terms with the burden of democracy. We want simultaneously a state that is both Jewish and democratic; however, in a democratic polity, the majority has to surrender certain privileges and subject itself to the inconvenience of having to grant equal rights to the smallest minority. The democratic whole in Israel has to include all non-Jewish citizens and care for their interests. It stands to reason that the Jewish majority will use its numerical advantage to influence legislation and the content and quality of the evolving common culture, but, says Kaplan, Israel's Jews will have to distinguish between matters that belong totally within the Jewish community and those that belong to the populace at large. The Knesset is not a fit forum for solving internal Jewish problems, many of which also concern diaspora Jews. Kaplan pleaded for the creation of an international representative body of Jews to set standards for handling questions of Jewish identity, culture, and religion.

The Jews in Israel, like those in the Dispersion, will gradually learn that they are participants in two civilizations—Judaism and Israelism. The latter is only at the outset of its development and is thus unrecognizable at this time. Jews will discover that the State of Israel can provide opportunities for the revitalization of Judaism, but it is not *the* solution. Another step is necessary—the erection of a new, internal, and democratic structure to effect Jewish unity and "religio-cultural" creativity. This same requirement will apply to Israel's minorities, if they wish to preserve their distinctive identities.[16] This process is a threat to halakhic Judaism. The election of Arabs to the Knesset and the appointment of Arab judges, already realities, assistance to non-Jewish minorities to develop their cultures and religions, the availability of a non-Jewish public domain on Sabbaths and holidays, and the possibility of civil marriage in the future are all part of the transformation that is taking place in Jewish life in Israel as a result of the democratic revolution. Kook's writings contain only scattered hints about these problems. He was undoubtedly aware of their seriousness, but he shunted them aside as susceptible to halakhic treatment.

Kook's approach concurs with the view that the less Jews have to do with gentiles and their harmful influences, the better off they will be and the stronger the hold of tradition will become. In contrast, Kaplan gives his blessing to intercultural contacts. He claims, "Religious freedom is meaningless unless it include the recognition of cultural-religious autonomy. Cultural-religious autonomy, on the other hand, does not mean segregation or separation from the life of the rest of the population."[17] He argues that Jews now need a conception of their peoplehood that will "in-

spire them with the will to demonstrate the normality of civiliza-
tional symbiosis or living simultaneously in two civilizations, with
no less zeal than their ancestors were ready to demonstrate, at all
costs, the normality of worshipping only one God."[18] Kaplan relies on the faith that cultural pluralism "can become a blessing
instead of a curse, and that each civilization should seek not to
supplant but to supplement every other, religiously as well as culturally."[19]

Zionism has always been supported by one or both of two arguments. One is that the return to Eretz Yisrael is necessary to
free the Jewish people from the animosity of the anti-Semites or
the threat of assimilation—both of which are held to be endemic
to life in the Diaspora. The second argument, the dominant one,
also calls for dissociation from the lands of exile, in this case to
enable the Jewish people to prepare a creative, authentically Jewish response to the attractions of enlightened, modern cultures.
The first rationale has generally been characteristic of halakhic
trends; the second, of secularists and liberal survivalists. The two
groups have been united in their negation of the Diaspora.

Kaplan adopted the reasoning of neither of the arguments about
detachment from the Diaspora. He identified with the Zionist
consensus, affirming the need to rebuild the Jewish homeland in
Eretz Yisrael as the central enterprise of the Jewish people. The
Land was essential as a symbol of and instrument for the revival
of Jewish nationalism. Kaplan surmised that without a national
center upon which all diaspora Jews can focus attention, it would
be unlikely that they could preserve their unity and will to live as
Jews.[20] He cites Albert Einstein: 'Palestine will become a cultural
home for all Jews, a refuge for the worst sufferers from oppression,
a field of activity for the best among us, a unifying ideal and a
source of spiritual health for the Jews of every country." The
implementation of these hopes will depend, of course, on the
kind of society that will be formed in Eretz Yisrael. In keeping
with his democratic faith, Kaplan pinned his hopes on the adoption by the Zionists of the values of freedom, responsibility, pluralism, and the rule of law.

Events have shown that Kaplan was too optimistic in his published writings, but a careful reading of his *Diaries* indicates that
he was neither naïve nor free from serious doubts about the Jews'

readiness for democratic autonomy. The ingathering of exiles in the State of Israel has brought together Jews of varied ethnic, religious, and cultural backgrounds, who differ in their political experience as well. For many of them, the democratic game as played in the West is unfamiliar. The institutions and instruments fashioned by the founding fathers of the State have frequently been unsuitable for educating the public in Israel in the ways of democracy. Kaplan thought that progress toward religious enlightenment could and should have been made at a faster pace than was the case. Long before the proclamation of the State of Israel, he warned of the dangers of religious benightedness for the Jewry of Eretz Yisrael. He hoped, however, that the example of religious pluralism that reigned among American Jews was paradigmatic for the entire people and that the democratic spirit in Israel would encourage constructive dialogue among the proponents of the various versions of the Jewish religion. It is now evident that there is a long road ahead before the Jews of Israel will be capable of conducting a rational and reasonable interchange about Judaism in general, and religious ideas and practices in particular. Dialogue does exist, but the parties enter into it unwilling to expose themselves to the possibility that if they listen carefully to their opponents, they might have to make some changes in their own conceptions. Most are ready to absorb their rivals; few are prepared for cultural interpenetration.

POINTS OF DIFFERENCE

The Jews of Israel are not yet fully attuned to seeing democracy as a political, cultural, and spiritual regime under which every person has the right to choose between ideological, faith, and value options. In a democracy few notions are so sacred and exclusive as to defy challenge or disagreement, except those that enjoy overwhelming national consensus. Even this general agreement is apt to be time-bound and subject to alteration as knowledge expands or fundamental changes occur in the conditions of life.[21]

Kook, too, erred in his prognosis. He believed that the dross of exile would be removed once the people began to reconstruct the Land of Israel and return to Torah-true Judaism. But not only the throes of exile distance most Jews from halakhic Judaism. Human civilization changes persistently, and Judaism is no exception. Democracy might not be the final stage in a person's political or spiritual maturation, but meanwhile it has forced the historical religions to rethink their principles and institutional forms.

A good example of the democratic impact can be seen in the concepts of equality in organized religions. Although egalitarianism exists in the traditional religions, its scope is limited. This is true of Kook's halakhic version, in which democratic equality plays no role. Instead of equality, the *Halakhah* is filled with contrasts—between Israel and the nations, men and women, halakhic scholars and secular-minded literati, to name just three of the more prominent instances. The contrasts do not necessarily indicate superiority and inferiority. Sometimes they refer to differences in function. However, with the functions are associated duties and rights, honor, and the advantages of status that make for inequality. Despite his humanitarianism, Kook could not quite grasp the extent to which Jewish law sets barriers in the way of equality of opportunity for certain classes of individuals.

Kaplan was obsessed with the problem of equality. Clearly, genetic equality does not exist among humans. How, then, can one speak of equality as an ideal? Kaplan responds to the challenge realistically:

> To experience the dignity of selfhood means that every individual must be made to feel that the society in which he lives regards him not merely as a means to an end, but recognizes him as an end in himself. He must not be treated as a mere cog in the machinery of production, but must be given as much freedom of choice, in the way he earns his livelihood, and in the way he spends his leisure, as is consistent with the similar rights of others and the security of all. As long as he contributes to the productive process in accordance with his abilities, he is entitled to be treated with respect, and not be made a tool for the compulsory service of others, who take advantage of his dependence on them.[22]

People must not be divided into the supporters and the dependents. They should not have to work without experiencing satisfaction from the work itself. The fact of human inequality should not be permitted to deny anyone the right to fulfillment. Everyone must be granted the opportunity to discover his or her particular talents and to exercise them in satisfying employment. Equality of opportunity is one of the main measures for judging whether a society is fair to its members. Kaplan was a pragmatic idealist, and he knew that guaranteeing complete equality is beyond the capability of any human community. Fulfillment always lies ahead of individuals and groups, but the democratic method, Kaplan asserts, has thus far proved to be more successful than any other in enabling humankind to draw nearer to fulfilling the human potential.

In regard to democracy, our two teachers differ in their attitudes toward the religions of the world. Kook acknowledges only one divine religion—Judaism. Kaplan sees religion as a phenomenon to be found in all peoples once they have lived together for a long time, especially on a common soil. All peoples are potentially capable of creating a high culture and religion, but it cannot be denied that some nations are more qualified than others. Their religions attain a higher level than that reached by the less talented. Some religions can properly be called modern and advanced, while others are still enveloped in medievalism. Without losing sight of this reality, Kaplan stresses, "[T]he ideal of equality when conceived both as spiritual and as economic equality would mean that all human beings are entitled to experience the dignity of selfhood or personality, the moral character of society, and the reality of God."[23]

Inasmuch as equality is a social matter, its level of spirituality will depend on whether or not the society acts like a congregation. Kaplan says:

> A community might be defined as that form of organization in which the welfare of each is the concern of all, and the life of the whole is the concern of each. In such a society there would still be differences in authority, based on functional divisions. Traffic regulations would still have to be obeyed, and engineers, rather than hucksters, poets or clergymen would direct the building of bridges. But men, nevertheless, would know themselves to be equal, if each one could feel that, under no circumstances would he have to be alone, unwanted, unimportant to his fellow men, insecure and forced to fend for

himself, unaided against starvation, disease and all the natural and social ills. Under no circumstances, would he be compelled to join the pack in murdering and pillaging other societies. Under the principle of equality, such a society would have to embrace all the men and nations of the earth.[24] (Italics, MMK)

No person can exist alone. Everyone is tied organically to his or her natural and social environment. Independence is expressed, or can be, in what a person thinks, feels, and does, but even this degree of self-expression is conditioned by the culture of one's people and the phenomena of existence with which one comes into contact. Kaplan thinks that while creative powers develop in man, "[t]hey merely come to a focus, as it were, in him, but they exist in God. They function as God in man, as a soul or moral personality, and, through them, he experiences himself as being in God."[25] Thus, equality is not simply a moral invention of enlightened man. It is also a manifestation of cosmic organicity.

The disagreement between Kook and Kaplan regarding democracy focuses on its authority and that of its bearers. This issue has several facets. For Kook, authority is to be sought in the supernatural source of the Torah. Kaplan opposes this heteronomous assumption, although he, too, cautions against man's attributing to himself unlimited wisdom in the choice of the proper way of life. Nevertheless, Kaplan argues, democracy is right in claiming for man the ability and the need to rule over himself. Kaplan posits:

> According to democracy, . . . the source of authority or validation is immanent in the very nature of man in that part of his nature which we identify as personality. [For Kaplan personality and soul are virtually synonymous. He sometimes resorts to the term "personality" to avoid the aura of supernaturalism that still clings to "soul."] But personality itself is . . . not reducible to scientific categories. It is, indeed, a transcendent element in man, a manifestation of the Power in the cosmos that makes for man's salvation, or God.[26]

In Kaplan's view, the general will is the source of authority for determining the direction that society should follow. However, this authority is in constant need of reevaluation and correction. It is always threatened by the temptation to dominate, by the certainty felt by powerful people that their programs are correct for the group, by the failure to identify mistakes in the perception of reality, and by similar pitfalls. In apposition to these dangers is the hubris of the supernaturalists. If Kook or his followers were able to wield the requisite power, their certainty about the complete validity of the Torah, as a revelation of God, would render impossible the establishment in Zion of a democratic polity of equality and pluralism.

Let us summarize the consequences of the social theories of Kook and Kaplan for Jewish life.

1. Theoretically, *Halakhah* and democracy appear to be two contradictory outlooks. There are many halakhic conceptions that contain seeds of democracy—"these and these are the words of the living God" (Eruvin 13b) (pluralism); "follow the majority" (Ex. 23, 2) (rule of the majority); "you shall love the stranger" (Deut. 10, 19) or "You shall have one law among you, for the alien and the citizen alike"(Ex. 12, 49) (civil rights and equality). On closer inspection, however, these halakhic principles fall short of democratic standards not only in their original context but in their application today in the State of Israel. Majority rule under the *Halakhah* covers limited areas of public concern. Civil rights and equality do not apply to the whole legislative process. The concept of the resident alien (*ger*) is unlike the idea of citizenship in modern democratic thought. Under the *Halakhah*, the *ger* can share freely in the economic and social life of the community but cannot serve as a legislator or judge. If the Arabs of Israel— theoretically, if not always in practice—enjoy civic rights, this is due to Israel's democracy and not to the spirit of the *Halakhah*.

The present State of Israel is not the one envisioned by Kook. We cannot accuse him of lack of responsibility for not having outlined in greater detail the foundations of his ideal state. Theodor Herzl described the democratic-aristocratic ideal that he conceived for the Jewish state, but his vision was impractical. In contrast, Kook probably felt that when the state was proclaimed, the *Halakhah* would be quickly adapted to the new circumstances. Since Jewish law had sustained the nation for two millennia, Kook reasoned that it could do so in the future. We must also remember that Kook died thirteen years before the declaration of the State, at a black moment in Jewish history, when hope for

Jewish sovereignty was at a low ebb and drawing blueprints for a nonexistent Jewish state seemed to be pure fantasy.

This was not the case after November 29, 1947, when the United Nations adopted the Partition Plan for Palestine and enabled the Jewish people to establish its state. The halakhists then began to consider the role of Jewish law in the state that was soon to arise. For example, the Orthodox newspaper, *HaTzofeh*, carried a series of scholarly articles on the character of a Jewish state, including the critical question as to whether non-Jews could serve as legislators or judges. The confrontation between democracy and the *Halakhah* became real, as it continues to be today, fifty years after Israel's founding as a democracy. As liberal as he was, if Kook were alive today, his liberalism would extend only as far as the *Halakhah* permits, and that, as we have seen, does not include the rights guaranteed to all citizens of a democratic state.

Kook, no doubt, would speak softly and with all of his personal decency, love of Israel, and desire for national amity. He would expect his disciples to obey the democratic law, but not out of conviction. He would pinpoint for opposition specific legislation or administrative procedures that contradict halakhic norms.

Kaplan, on the other hand, would ardently preach the cause of democracy, not only for the State of Israel but for the inner life of the Jewish people the world over. He would not retreat from the radical adjustments that democracy demands in Jewish thinking and behavior. He attempted to preserve the word *Halakhah* in the vocabulary of Jewish life, because he valued the legal and toraitic foundations of Jewish peoplehood, including the observance of ritual, the maintenance of communal practices, and the encouragement of the leadership of scholars and spiritual personalities. He was not an antinomian, but he wanted to secure these norms by means of voluntary assent and, where needed, majority vote.

2. In Kaplan's Jewish state, freedom of religion would prevail. The search for God cannot succeed in the absence of such an atmosphere. Search itself cannot guarantee knowledge of God, but when we thrust aside honest efforts to draw near to the Source of all existence, we deprive many of our fellows of equal opportunity to gain access to God's will. Freedom of religion should "be conceived as the right of all men to seek to cultivate

in themselves, and in such free association as they may choose, the religious experience, the sense of their rapport with all that renders life worthwhile for them, as individuals, as members of a particular society or communion, and as human beings sharing in the life of the cosmos."[27]

The democratic values of freedom and equality are essential as protection against the tendency of many persons to regard as absolute truth anything that they believe has been communicated to them by divine inspiration. Every so-called religious experience is a supposition that requires the kind of proof that is not available to human beings. The line separating the awareness of God and idolatry is very thin. Who can demonstrate that one's idea of God is true? But the *Halakhah* is founded on just this claim—that it gives expression to God's will. According to its premises, freedom and equality would be confined to those areas defined by the *Halakhah* itself.

3. The above comparisons, like all such efforts, need some qualification. We have to take into account the fact that Kook and Kaplan occupied different universes of discourse. Yet in this instance the comparisons are called for. In the process of reconstructing its national life, the Jewish people can either try to refurbish the Torah solely with the tools of the Torah or adapt values and ideas from every available source, including the tradition. But the people must shore up the historical foundations of Judaism and add new sections to the ancient structure. Kook's supporters claim that the instruments of Torah are authentic Judaism, while Kaplan's critics regard his program as surrendering to foreign influences. Both of these assessments, it seems to me, are shallow. Kook did not dismiss out of hand the contribution to Judaism that can come from proper appropriation of general knowledge and wisdom; and Kaplan did not preach uncritical absorption of foreign influences. The dispute between them is, again, "for the sake of heaven," and Jews have to choose the approach they think is likely to foster creative Jewish continuity. In that choice, their judgment about the place of democracy in the Jewish future is crucial.

NOTES

1. FAJ, p. 511.
2. A typical example of Kook's idea of pluralism is a passage in AT,

p. 8. "The souls of sinners [non-observant Jews], who contribute to the coming of the Messiah by their concern for the welfare of the Jewish people, Eretz Yisrael and national revival, are finer than those of deeply pious Jews who are insensitive to these overall concerns for the good of the whole and the reconstruction of the nation and the land. But the spirit of those who revere God and keep the Torah and the *mitzvot* is much more refined." Kook is known for his warm feelings toward the *halutzim* who were engaged in rebuilding the land and the people, but he never legitimized their form of Judaism.

3. KL, Vol. 2, L. 566, p. 204.

4. "Eitzot Merahok" ("Advice from Afar"), *HaPeles*, 5662, p. 532.

5. Ibid.

6. KL, L. 871, pp. 156–157. Kook's writings have generally been printed without *matres lectiones* (*ktiv haser* or absence of vowel points). From the context, Kook means tolerance and not patience (*sovlanut* and not *savlanut*).

7. Ibid., p. 157.

8. Ibid.

9. For example, although Kook favors freedom of thought when a person is attempting to clarify ideas, he attaches no inherent merit to the value itself. "Obviously, all freedom of thought in the ordinary life of the masses is simply not understandable. The free man is only he who engages in the study of Torah" (AT, p. 12).

10. KL, Vol. 3, L. 873, p. 162. The letter was to his son, Harav Tzvi Yehudah Kook.

11. KL, Vol. 1, L. 20, p. 19. Many similar passages dot Kook's writings. I cite here only one example. "A human being has to cultivate for himself a strong, free spirit to the point where he can appreciate the greatness of active thought. He will then realise how much effort mankind has to exert in order to attain pure and holy intellection in regard to the fundamental ideas from which are derived all of life's values" (AT, p. 20).

12. KL, op. cit., p. 20.

13. Ibid.

14. FAJ, p. 500.

15. JC, p. 22.

16. For a serious treatment of the importance of Kaplan's theory of democracy, see "Passion, Social Ethics, Democracy: The Theology of Mordecai Kaplan," by S. Daniel Breslauer, in the *American Journal of Theology and Philosophy*, Vol. 2, No. 1, January 1990.

17. GJM, p. 454.

18. Ibid.

19. Ibid.

20. Ibid., p. 453.

21. See, especially, Kaplan's essay, "The Need for Normative Unity in Higher Education," in *Goals for American Education*, ed. by Lyman Bryson, Louis Finkelstein, and Robert MacIver (New York: Conference of Science, Philosophy and Religion, 1950).

22. FAJ, p. 324.

23. Ibid. The fact that a religion is born in a certain place and develops in a particular culture does not mean that it cannot be adapted to other societies. There is much transplantation of religious ideas and practices. But this phenomenon raises a host of problems that cannot be treated here.

24. Ibid., p. 325.

25. Ibid., p. 326.

26. *Goals for American Education,* op. cit., p. 326.

27. FAJ, p. 326.

14

On Women

In 1922, when Kaplan's oldest daughter, Judith, was called to the Torah as a Bat Mitzvah, he could hardly have anticipated the feminist revolution that was then in its first stages. Today, when women everywhere are demanding rights that have been denied them throughout history, Kaplan's initiative appears logical and necessary. Once again, we turn to the respective views on women of our two teachers, as a means of illustrating in blunt terms the alternatives confronting Jews as they fashion their future lifestyle.

The Traditional Views of Kook

Honesty dictates that we see the status of women in proper perspective. Admittedly, traditional Jewish law discriminates against women. This is true when we look at the issue from a modern conception of human rights and of the essential nature of men and women. However, the talmudic Sages had different facts and standards of civilized behavior at their disposal. It has to be stressed that much of the halakhic legislation was designed to protect the honor and purity of Jewish women and, indeed, of foreign women who came under Jewish control. The halakhists made a supreme effort to protect women from cruel and arbitrary treatment by males who dominated Jewish society much as they did all others. Halakhic laws were meant to strengthen the bonds of love between husband and wife, to ensure the sanctity of body and soul of all women, and to guarantee their support. To this day, masses of Jewish women seem to be happy with their lives under halakhic rules and with the roles assigned to them both in the family and in the traditional society at large.[1] The *Halakhah* may be deficient in the scope of women's rights, but it also demands that men satisfy women's needs and cherish and guard their dignity. Therefore, the debate between the *Halakhah* and modernity regarding sex roles revolves around the following questions: What is meant by the honor and dignity of women? What are the needs of women, and in what areas is it or should it be incumbent on men to provide for them? What are the obligations of husband and wife in the family? What constitutes fulfillment for a female human being? What steps are necessary to equalize the status of the sexes? Does the assignment of distinct functions for men and women in the family and in society constitute inequality? Kook and Kaplan respond to each of these questions with drastically different approaches

Kook was educated, matured, and lived in the world of Proverbs 31, 10—"A virtuous wife, who can find?" When a man finds the ideal wife, she will be a woman completely dedicated to caring selflessly for him and their children. That devotion enabled many generations of men to concentrate undisturbed on the study of Torah, while their exemplary wives and mothers found fulfillment and happiness in carrying out their countless household and economic duties. There is no question that in the society of Proverbs, Chapter 31, women who performed their role faithfully earned the love and respect of their families. Seldom do we find any bitterness recorded on the part of women about the role that was assigned to them. (I qualify this statement with the comment that a number of recent studies have uncovered signs that many women in the past were deeply dissatisfied with their lot. This advancement in scholarship will undoubtedly force us to look anew at so-called feminine passivity in previous centuries.) It is hard to know whether this relative silence was due to the genuine satisfaction that women derived from their status, their fear of voicing their feelings, or the belief that they had no other options or that this was the way of the world. In any case, HaRav Kook, who would have been astonished if anyone had accused him of mistreating his wife, regarded the halakhic attitude toward women as God's will and as what is in accord with human nature. Men and women, he believed, are born as creatures endowed with different natural qualities and faculties and therefore are meant to serve separate functions. His opinion is best stated in his commentary on the benediction recited each morning by men at the outset of the prayer service. I now complete Kook's commentary, which I alluded to above.

Kook explains:

Souls are divided by their nature into those that are active and those
that are passive, those that leave the imprint of their lives on all
their precious achievements and those that are imprinted upon by
the active ones. This is the essential difference between the active,
legislative, conquering and subduing soul of the male and that of
the woman. The latter is imprinted and etched upon, influenced,
conquered and subdued under the leadership of the male. How
many good and exalted virtues, how much latitude and rapture is
there in this endowment of the active male soul, that creates and
magnifies thoughts and deeds, by virtue of its inherent essence and
holy plans! Such is the superiority of the shaping soul of the male
over that of woman. It resembles the relationship between matter
and form.[2]

This interpretation is especially revealing because it demonstrates Kook's desire to provide a natural explanation for the halakhic distinction between the *mitzvot* imposed upon males and
those required of women. Traditionally, women are exempt from
observances that are time-bound and would presumably impose
an unreasonable burden on them. Hence, according to this interpretation, males thank God for the privilege that has been accorded them in having to carry out more *mitzvot* than are
required of women. This view, however, seems to depend on
arbitrary social conventions. So Kook attempts to trace the distinction to the physiological constitution of the two sexes. Unfortunately, Kook's conception founders on the findings of modern
physiology and psychology—including what was already current
during his lifetime. Of course, males and females have important
and obvious physiological differences that affect their functions
and their functioning. However, there is no scientific basis for
Kook's description of the two types of souls.

Evidently, Kook must have felt that the discrepancy he assumes
is too one-sided. Hence, he looked for a compensation for
women. We men must not go overboard in exaggerating our
superior status, for

while men do work effectively in impressing their deeds and influence on the world and on life, passive women also have an advantage, in the very fact of their being the recipients [of the acts of the

males]. Men, in exercising their active power, sometimes lack the requisite physical and spiritual strength and thereby step out of the path leading to the divine purpose. In the case of the passive woman, however, when her passivity has integrity, it is apt to receive and be influenced by the full measure of God's action—that action which is the manifestation of the righteousness He employed in creating the universe and man, the material and spiritual content of existence.[3]

In other words, since women do not have to strive, as men do, they are less prone to mistakes. All they must do is to receive God with open arms. Moreover, women are more apt than men to act in accord with God's will, because their willing, passive souls are the direct recipients of divine plenitude, as was determined at Creation. Kook thinks that the combination of freedom and power enjoyed by males is a danger as well as an opportunity. Men have to overcome temptations that are not put in the way of women.

Kook's convoluted commentary points to the positive and negative in the status and function of women in his halakhic version. On the positive side, he wished to confer on women an honored place in Jewish life. But his conception also has a threefold negative side. The status offered is inferior; men grant it paternalistically; and, as I said above, Kook gives short shrift to scientific evidence. However, even if Kook were to be convinced of the blatant mistakes in his reading of human biology, he would not be moved to alter a word in the blessing under discussion. In the end, for Kook, the status and role of women are in the hands of God and are unrelated to our knowledge of the human makeup. In Kook's view, the only challenge must come from the *Halakhah*. That work is now being attempted within the halakhic community. If Kook were alive today, he might be part of this development.

Those of us who prize the values of an open society must nonetheless be disturbed by the excesses to which it is prone. Freedom can be and frequently is distorted into license and moral anarchy. In any criticism of halakhic restrictions or the disproportion in relations between the sexes, this fact must be borne in mind. However, Kook's concern for feminine modesty and the sexual purity of men, which are prime objectives in the halakhic plan of sexual propriety, rests on shaky foundations. His opposition to the most innocent physical contact between males and females assumes that it would lead to feminine immodesty and masculine promiscuity. Adopting an extreme construction of the *Halakhah*, widely practiced to this day in very pious circles, Kook banned mixed dancing and handshakes between a man and a woman.

Kook refused to be alone with a woman. Alexander Dushkin, the renowned Jewish educator, tells how Kook insisted that he (Dushkin) be present during a private conversation with Henrietta Szold. This halakhic custom, apparently based on an exaggerated assessment of the magnetic sexual power of women, is a male fantasy that, if pressed to its illogical conclusion, would preclude any kind of normal relationship between the sexes. Each contact would become an occasion of unbearable tension. Kook's comment on dancing provides a good illustration of this tension:

> It is difficult even to mention the breach in the fence around our sacred Torah and the negative effect on the modesty and purity that characterize the pious among us that can be caused by inter-sexual dancing. Far be it from us to imitate the lawless and irreverent and stumble ignominiously in the slightest respect. The feeling of camaraderie and the protection of the honor of Jewish women are strengthened and made more effective in the context of a holy lifestyle. Even the daughters of other peoples, who have some cultural background, can testify as to the advantage for the honor of the woman and her high social standing that results from the purity of Jewish culture. . . .[4]

Again, this is a typical male perspective.

Nonetheless, this fear of close intersexual contacts is not completely unfounded. It is, as we have seen, based on the realization that weak-minded men or women can easily fall into a cheap sexual morality.

Having admitted the danger, we must also address the other side of the problem. By this we mean that repression of natural human drives and oversuppression of bodily, social, and psychological needs can also be costly. In Kook's outlook, woman appears as the embodiment of the evil impulse that seduces man.[5] This idea induces the very result that Kook wants to prevent. It harms the image of the modest woman and damages her honor.

It stands in the way of the natural behavior of the male, casting the suspicion that he lacks enough moral integrity to channel the sexual challenge in appropriate ways. Moreover, Kook's ban on mixed dancing (including folk dancing) presupposes that it is essentially a sexual act. He ignores completely its other facets—for example, its functions as a form of play and of esthetic and even religious expression. Kook himself participated in the wild abandon of dancing with the Torah on *Simhat Torah* and in the celebration of other happy occasions. But while he experienced the spiritual release of this form of bodily movement, he apparently could not conceive that this emotion might dominate men and women engaged together in the same activity. What constitutes feminine honor, therefore, is not to be determined by men who fear the seductive power of women. We must assume that the rabbis dreaded the *Yetzer HaRa* and lacked confidence in the ability of many men to withstand the sexual attraction of women.

Nevertheless, Kook exhibited decency in other facets of his attitude toward women. He tried as best he could, within the limits of the *Halakhah*, to protect feminine rights. A number of instances of his kindness and fairness appear in his responsa. He was always on the alert to prevent the mistreatment of wives by their husbands. He fought any attempt to make the wife a captive of her husband, and he supported wives who had come to despise their husbands because of their cruelty or lack of consideration. If a man refused to divorce his wife at her request, Kook decreed that he must at least support her according to the terms of the marriage certificate (*ketubah*). This was as far as the *Halakhah* permitted him to go in backing the cause of fairness in the marital situation. Only if the claims of the wife were proved to be deceitful was Kook prepared to release the husband from his conjugal responsibility of support for his spouse.[6]

Kook's dilemma is common to all halakhists. In a world of changing moral values and perceptions, those who are tied to the *Halakhah* cannot keep pace with the radical alterations in traditional Jewish law that would be prerequisites for its moral updating. Many halakhists are pained by the problem but seem, like Kook, to be trapped between their personal convictions and what they consider to be God's commandments. However deeply

Kook might have felt personally about right and wrong, he could not revise the halakhic status of women on a moral basis alone. Therefore, he could not deal with the questions posed above. The fact that so many women find satisfaction under the traditional system is a tribute to its virtues and an indication of the extent to which many women are still ignorant of their human potential and elementary rights. However, the countervailing fact that the overwhelming majority of Jews now view the *Halakhah* as discriminatory toward women has created one of the most serious crises that Jewish law has had to face in two thousand years.

Finally, we have to note that Kook worried about the potential breakup of the Jewish family. Women's growing participation in activities outside the home, a process that was well on its way during Kook's career, was in his eyes fraught with danger. He believed that work in such fields as science and politics—indeed, in any vocation that would remove a woman from the home— would preempt the function of the male and adopt "the ways of the gentiles." He held that "[a]mong other peoples, the family is not as profoundly the root of national life as it is among us."[7] Thus, he was adamantly opposed to any act that might affect family serenity and peace. He did not comprehend the dynamics of change in family life during the last century. The unity of many households has been disrupted, but such is the inevitable outcome of the awakening of women to what has been denied them throughout the ages. Like every revolution, the feminine uprising leaves confusion and destruction in its wake. The conservative Kook utters a necessary word of caution. The wisdom of the *Halakhah*, in this as in other matters, deserves a hearing. Kook puts it this way: "I think that our national policy has not yet departed from religion to the extent that our statesmen should arrogate to themselves the right to establish any policy in the name of all Jews in Eretz Yisrael, without due consideration to the opinions of religious authorities. . . ."[8] Some might not agree with Kook's opinion about the wisdom of the men he considered to be religious authorities, but we can appreciate his apprehension that many social changes might be made without careful consideration of their consequences.

KAPLAN'S MODERN PERSPECTIVE

Kaplan was one of the first Jewish thinkers in the twentieth century to reckon with the seriousness of halakhic discrimination
against women. He reasoned that this condition indicates the
anachronistic character of much of the halakhic tradition, and it
represents a potential danger to the social fabric of Jewish life.
Further, the status of women under the *Halakhah* hinders release
of the enormous intellectual, moral, and spiritual power that
women can harness for the welfare of the Jewish people. Kaplan
touched a raw nerve, and every time he urged equality for
women, colleagues and opponents in many walks of Jewish life
attacked his ideas.

Kaplan cherished the precious quality of the Jewish family, and
his efforts were directed to its preservation as a force for moral
purity.[9] *"Judaism exalted the institution of the family and made it the
end to be served by chastity."*[10] (Italics, MMK) Judaism treats sexual
propriety as a necessary virtue in fostering the spiritual and moral
quality of the family, but it does not regard chastity as an end in
itself. However, the emancipation of women renders impossible,
and to a significant extent undesirable, attempts to restore the
Jewish family to its traditional structure and mores. Unlike Kook,
Kaplan detected deficiencies in the halakhically directed family,
in its form and hierarchy, in its conception of the roles to be
assigned to husband and wife, and in certain aspects of its views
on sexual relations. Because he deemed the strengthening of the
family to be so crucial to the Jewish future, Kaplan called for a
reexamination of its structure and inner dynamics.

In one of his references to the status of women, Kaplan writes:

> Few aspects of Jewish thought and life illustrate so strikingly the
> need of reconstructing Jewish law as the traditional status of the
> Jewish woman. In Jewish tradition, her status is unquestionably that
> of inferiority to the man. If the Jewish woman is to contribute her
> share to the regeneration of Jewish life, and if in turn Jewish life is
> to bring out the powers for good that are in her, this status must be
> changed.[11]

Interestingly, Kaplan urged women to work for their own emancipation rather than to rely on the men who hold the power to

effect the needed changes. He knew that the latter could not be convinced to take the necessary steps until Jewish women had first emancipated their own minds and begun to articulate their pain and their aspirations. He urged his audience—his essay was first presented as a lecture before a group of women from several streams of the Jewish community—to study the *Halakhah* relating to their status and to draw their own conclusions. He was confident that they would rise in protest. It took about twenty years after this 1936 lecture before the Jewish feminist movement began to take action.

Kaplan postulated that the reticence of both men and women to revise the status of the latter stemmed from a perverted opinion of the woman's essential nature and capabilities. For thousands of years, men have regarded women in general as creatures who are essential to their welfare but whose capacities, on the whole, are limited and inferior. On the basis of this evaluation, the Jewish woman was restricted to relatively few, well-defined functions in society, most of which dealt with the home and the family. If she entered the economic arena, it was not because she was entitled to do so by virtue of her talents or because she had a unique contribution to make. Instead, she became the breadwinner in devout families because it was her responsibility to enable her husband to engage undisturbed in the study of Torah. This whole conception of the essential woman has no basis in fact.

Kaplan never retreated from his conviction that drastic change would have to occur in women's involvement in religion, law, politics, science, education—indeed, in the whole gamut of the human enterprise. Kook tried, here and there, to soften the consequences of the powerlessness of women under Jewish law, but he did not challenge the idea that the *Halakhah* was basically correct in its approach to women. Kaplan, however, declared that if we are to hold on to our talented women for the furtherance of Judaism, we must make room for them in every activity for which they are qualified. This means the recognition of the total equality of the sexes. All persons are entitled to equality of opportunity to express themselves in accordance with their individual endowments and predilections.

In 1939, after a two-year sojourn at the Hebrew University as a visiting professor in philosophy of education, Kaplan addressed a gathering of his supporters.[12] In this talk, he leveled a number of criticisms against the Jewish community in Eretz Yisrael, one of which was the charge that it had not progressed toward creating a code of civil law. He felt that the leaders of the Yishuv were evading the issue, leaving treatment of the tradition in the hands of those who were uncritically committed to it as a cultural system. The authorities did not relate to the knotty problem of how and to what degree the *Halakhah* should be adapted or applied to the conduct of a Jewish society in the homeland. Kaplan foresaw that as Jewish self-rule expanded, laws concerning women would become a central issue; even if a state might be long in the offing.[13] (In 1939, not too many Zionists were forcefully calling for Jewish statehood.) He realized that the problem could not be solved by halakhic means, and certainly not by them alone. Furthermore, he anticipated that once women awakened from their long-standing torpor, they would not be satisfied with verbal assurances of their spiritual equality. Today, we witness in Israel and the Diaspora the fact that non-Orthodox women will, as far as possible, have nothing to do with halakhic guidelines or law in matters affecting their status or their relations with men. More revealing are the growing numbers of Orthodox women who express criticism or dissatisfaction with their position under the *Halakhah*. Thus far, the halakhic experts have been unable to overcome their inability to provide the critics with satisfying solutions within the normal halakhic procedures. Nor have they arrived at a state of mind that would induce them to take the route of decrees and *horaot shaah* (special dispensations or emergency measures).

Even before the establishment of the State of Israel, Kaplan pleaded for a national solution to the problem of the status of the Jewish woman that would take into account halakhic standards but would not necessarily be bound by them. He argued, "[M]arriage from the standpoint of Jewish law is fundamentally not a religious sacrament, as with the Church, but a civil covenant sanctioned by civil law."[14] Furthermore, he warned, "[I]f voluntarism is to prevent the development of sufficient homogeneity to give rise to a commonly accepted code of civil law, there can be no national life. So long as this condition will continue to exist in Palestine, there is no possibility of getting Jews in the Diaspora to foster internal adjustment of conflicting interests by means of arbitration, or with the aid of any commonly accepted Jewish code, whether of ethics or of law."[15]

Kaplan's warning fell on deaf ears. The situation in Israel today is such that statutes dealing with women's rights are generally unacceptable to secular, Orthodox, or liberal religious Jewish women. To add to the absurdity of the matter, the legal status of women has been and is determined by a majority of Knesset members who do not live according to halakhic standards. Everyone in Israel knows that current laws of personal status are not supported by a national consensus and arouse bitterness in all sectors of the population. As for diaspora Jewry, inasmuch as it is independent of political decisions made in Israel, it can and does find its own solutions to the role of women. Unfortunately, lacking a common communal framework, each denomination develops its own procedures, which are often rejected by one stream or another. This contributes to the widening gap between Jews in Israel and those living in other parts of the world and to the difficulty in defining Jewish identity.

The major and potentially explosive debate within Jewish ranks might well be about matters of personal status. As time goes on, understanding of the nature of women and their needs and rights is bound to broaden. As we have noted, Kook tries to defend the Halakhah, both in its theoretical perception of the humanity of women and in its practical application to their legal status. In contrast, Kaplan sees this issue as an important test of the Jewish people's ability to respond intelligently and creatively to the revolutionary changes that continue to take place in human self-understanding. He writes:

> The basic issue in Jewish life today is: What shall be done with the law? Shall it be defended, or amended? Those who are Orthodox insist on upholding the law in all its details, despite the radical changes that have rendered many of those details contrary to our notions of social and spiritual welfare. The early Reformists, who abjured Jewish peoplehood, consistently declared the prerogative of administering law in human relationships as outside the scope of modern Judaism. In the face of these two untenable positions, as illustrated by the pressing problem of the civic and juridical status of the Jewish woman in modern Jewish life, it is impossible to build Jewish society on any other lines than those implied in Judaism as

a living social process, in which the right to amend traditional law and to legislate anew is accepted as indispensable to the very life of the Jewish people and as the only guarantee of its future.[16]

Kaplan did not rest with analysis. He turned with great earnestness to Jewish women, stating,

> It is high time for the Jewish women throughout the world to inaugurate a movement that will aim to remove the religious, civic and juridical disabilities which traditional Jewish law imposes on them and that will win for them the status of equality. This change in the status of Jewish women is an immediate and urgent need for Eretz Yisrael Jewry. Without such change, Jewry in the Diaspora is bound to grow culturally sterile and spiritually anemic.[17]

This message was uttered six decades ago and reflected Kaplan's thinking from an even earlier period. However, it came at a time when few people in the Jewish community were prepared to listen. Henrietta Szold, with whom Kaplan had a long, mutually respectful relationship, was one of the few women in her day who dared to publish criticism of the rabbis for their listlessness in facing the problem of equality of the sexes. But Kaplan's barbs were not directed primarily at the contemporary generation of rabbis. He realized that the limited flexibility of the *Halakhah* and the mood of caution that had fallen over its practitioners in the age of enlightenment would restrain even those halakhists who were aware of the needs of the hour. Instead, Kaplan addressed the large, open-minded Jewish public and urged it to overcome its lethargy in regard to modernizing Jewish society. The call was ignored for at least two decades.

Kaplan, too, was not omniscient. No one can completely escape from the bonds of time. Kaplan did not anticipate the emergence of feminist theologies and the accompanying efforts to introduce feminist themes into the liturgy. Although he was always disturbed by the disparity between the language of prayer and the beliefs of most present-day Jews, his concern was how to devise a poetic and emotionally appealing liturgy appropriate to a naturalist theology. Had he lived to see the current efforts to introduce feminine terminology into the prayers, he would in all likelihood regard this development in two ways. He would have seen the feminist critique of masculine-oriented theology and prayer as a helpful critique of traditional ideology. However, he would have felt that the feminist trend missed the point. God is no more She than He or It. The problem is far more profound. (It is important, therefore, to note that both male and female liturgists are now attempting to devise a gender-free liturgy. Kaplan would have approved of this trend, while Kook, a religious poet, would have regarded it as a sign of spiritual hunger. However, inasmuch as Kook saw no need to change the content of the *Siddur*, he would have opposed the introduction of the new rhetoric into the synagogue service. I cannot expand on these speculations, but it has to be said that Kaplan was after bigger game than gender neutrality. He was troubled by the whole purpose and function of prayer and the theological problems that cannot be solved by elimination of gender bias.)

The changes in Jewish life have undoubtedly occurred at a faster rate than Kaplan foresaw. For all his support for the cause of women, he did not, until the late 1960s, argue for the training of women rabbis and cantors, although he embraced this step when it was taken by the Reform and Reconstructionist movements and later by the Conservatives. Even he was constrained to some extent by the social conventions of his day. To the best of my knowledge, Kaplan only slowly came to grasp the full scope of the revolution to which he had contributed a small share, but he was pleased when the newly formed Reconstructionist Rabbinical College (1968) ordained women rabbis and when he observed the increasing involvement of women in the Jewish civil service and their rise to top positions in lay activity.

The empowerment of the Jewish woman is not an isolated phenomenon. It was and is part of the evolving consciousness and conscience of the entire Jewish community. The feminist revolution is now accelerating, with little or no recognition accorded to Kaplan for his part in its early stages. This is particularly regrettable, because leaders of the revolution should be more familiar with Kaplan's vision of Jewish life than they are. That vision will be supportive of women's aspirations and will equip them to contribute maximally to Jewish life as a whole. Kaplan's broad and balanced program deserves careful study by those who wish for the full equality of men and women in all facets of Judaism.

NOTES

1. FAJ, p. 511. Kaplan is aware of this phenomenon. He comments that despite the many discriminatory and even oppressive *halakhot*, the lot of the Jewish woman in traditional society was happier than might have been expected from their legal restrictions. Mutual love generally prevailed between husbands and wives, and, as Kaplan says, "A happy lot often goes together with a status of subjection" (FAJ, p. 405).

2. OR, Vol. 2, p. 71. Similarly, in an open letter to the Mizrachi organization (5680), in connection with whether or not women should be permitted to vote for the delegates to the National Assembly of Jews in Eretz Yisrael, Kook writes, "[T]he duty of public service on a regular basis falls upon the male. For it is his nature to exert dominion and not that of the woman (Yevamot 65b). Functions of office, law and bearing witness are not in her domain. Her glory is internal" (p. 189).

3. Ibid., pp. 71–72.

4. EK, R. 30, p. 128.

5. This is the reasoning behind Kook's ban on a woman's singing in the presence of men, particularly in the synagogue. He writes, "It is forbidden to recite the *Sh'ma* ("Hear, O Israel, the Lord is our God, the Lord is One") when one hears the sound of a woman's singing, just as it is forbidden to recite it in the presence of any sexual immorality. . . . It is especially necessary in a holy place to distance oneself from anything that is apt to cause one to commit a sin or even to think about it. For the more sacred a place is, the more powerful is the Evil Impulse. . . ." (*Orah Mishpat, The Way of Law* [Jerusalem: Mosad HaRav Kook, 5699, R. 35, p. 48]). How much more "illegitimate is the introduction of a communal practice that would necessarily bring about a massive mixing of the sexes, in groups and in person-to-person contacts, in the course of ongoing public life" (MR, p. 189).

6. EK, R. 56, pp. 208–209.

7. MR, p. 192.

8. Ibid., p. 191.

9. JC, p. 420.

10. Ibid., p. 421.

11. FAJ, p. 402.

12. The increasing participation of women in public worship, their determination to introduce feminist themes and semantics into theological discourse and into prayer, and their entrance into the rabbinate and *hazzanut* are all unstoppable consequences of the revolution occurring before our eyes.

13. "Palestine Jewry: Its Achievements and Shortcomings," in *The Reconstructionist*, Vol. 5, No. 11, September 29, 1939.

14. Ibid., p. 14.

15. Ibid., p. 15.

16. FAJ, p. 411.

17. Ibid., p. 412.

15

Judaism and Esthetics

ONE OF THE MOST STRIKING RESULTS of the resettlement of the Jewish people in Eretz Yisrael has been the flowering of the arts—painting, sculpture, architecture, crafts, music, theater, dance, poetry, and literature. Israel's Jewish artists have succeeded in producing an original genre that reflects both the sights and the sounds of the landscape of Israel and the values of the historical Jewish tradition. Out of the particularity of Jewish peoplehood is emerging an esthetic culture of universal proportions. In addition to absorbing the beauty of Japheth into the tents of Shem, Israel's Jews are creating beauty out of the sources of Judaism. The soul of a vital and creative people is seeking esthetic expression. It is unnecessary to list the large number of Israeli Jewish novelists, poets, artists, composers, and musicians, whose works are enjoyed wherever men and women appreciate esthetic sincerity and talent. The works of Israeli writers are translated into many languages; Israeli musical compositions are part of the repertoires of major orchestras; the paintings of Israeli artists hang in many museums, galleries, and private salons; and buildings planned by Israeli architects dot the landscapes of many countries. This esthetic explosion is the natural accompaniment of the reconstruction, under freedom, of Jewish life in the national homeland. A living people creates unique forms of beauty.

The relative paucity of Jewish artistic creativity for many centuries has been attributed to two factors—fear of idolatry and the effect of sensual creations on the moral norms of Judaism, and national mourning over the destruction of the ancient Temple. This reticence about expressing the feeling for beauty persists to this day in extremely pious circles. However, to be fair to halakhic Judaism, we should note that the Rabbis and Sages never turned their backs on beauty. They simply limited it to the adornment of the *mitzvot*. This restriction undoubtedly diverted the attention of many talented persons from thinking about the possibilities of creativity in the plastic arts. Nevertheless, we must not underestimate the real sense of beauty that underlay the Rabbis' sublimating it to the service of spirituality. Throughout the centuries, Jews would adorn their homes with artistically designed candlesticks for use on Sabbaths and holidays, uniquely designed candelabras for *Hanukkah* and illuminated *Haggadot* for Pesah. The poorest Jew would always purchase the most perfect *ethrog* (citron) that he could find for the *Sukkot* celebration. Synagogues were built with great attention to their appearance and to the beauty of the ritual objects used during worship. A rich musical tradition was developed for worship and folk occasions of all kinds. Whatever artistic creations delighted the senses and did not offend or threaten the good taste of pious Jews were accepted as enhancing the quality of Jewish life.

KOOK'S ESTHETICISM

Kook took note of the widening interest that Jews in Eretz Yisrael were displaying in various art forms. He hoped to channel this interest to the advantage of religion and to ensure that the new creativity would not digress from halakhic boundaries. As Zvi Yaron stated, "Art in itself has no particular value or standing in the teaching of the Rav. He rejects outright the idea of 'art for art's sake.' According to him, art is the expression of the inner soul of man. When a person articulates an impure thought, he pollutes beyond measure his literary creation."[1] What Yaron says about Kook's attitude toward literature applies in equal measure to the other arts as well.

Yaron maintains that only one other Orthodox thinker besides Kook, Nathan Birnbaum, regarded the cultivation of beauty as a religious duty, and Birnbaum held this view only up to his turn to Orthodoxy. We need not wonder at the fact that halakhists closed an eye to estheticism. Art was a subject related to the materialism and idolatry of Hellenism, as they understood Greek culture to be. Indeed, in every society, the danger always exists that biological drives can take hold of many artists and overrun their sense of intellectual, moral, and spiritual responsibility. The result is permissiveness, pornography, licentiousness, and ugliness. Kook was right when he wrote:

> The highest virtue is that intellect should be so complete and the forces of morality so strong that they will produce a feeling for multi-colored beauty, to a point where it [the sense of beauty] will add splendor to the true perfection of goodness, the holiness of Providence and the knowledge of God as expressed in the fear and love of Him.[2]

However, what are complete or perfect intellect and spiritual power? Is intellect perfect if it forbids the painting or photographing of the human bust? If we argue that it is the *Halakhah* and not the mind that issues the ban, free artists will not give credence to a rule accusing them of an idolatry that never enters their soul. Everyone has daily contact with countless human beings, and, for the artist, they become the inspiration for the revelation of esthetic insights that escape most other human beings. Thus, far from opening the door to idolatry, the search for beauty reveals in the physical world depths of meaning that await their release in the works of talented artists.

Of course, if we take the Second Commandment literally as the word of God, all of this philosophizing becomes pointless. For if God has forbidden the painting or sculpting of the human image, then the role of the mature or pure intellect is irrelevant. With one utterance, Kook encourages the founders of Bezalel and their fellow artists; with another word, he wants them to restrain their artistic imagination to what is halakhically permissible. Kook's concerns about the ability of artists to withstand the temptations of the senses are understandable, but they are part of a mind-set that fears freedom of expression.

Our description of Kook's esthetic theory has thus far not disclosed anything particularly startling or new. To understand Kook's depth of thinking, we must look beyond his traditionalism. First of all, the mere fact that he includes beauty as an independent category of Judaism—more than the embellishment of the *mitzvot*—indicates that he is onto something new in halakhic tradition He holds beauty to be a natural facet of reality. Kook states:

> [T]he observation of God's works reveals the laws of beauty that guide all material and spiritual reality. . . . The laws also determine

the flow of time. Thus, by observation, we come to understand the order of all events, including those about which we feel no sense of beauty. Nevertheless, these phenomena enhance beauty and move toward a perfected order.[3]

Beauty is immanent in all cosmic phenomena that follow the divine order. The beautiful is not defined as that which pulls at the heartstrings; rather, it is the form of a phenomenon that is true to the laws that apply to its inherent nature. It is in obedience to these laws that chaos becomes order; the same organicity evokes beauty out of formlessness or distortion.[4] Beauty cannot exist by itself. It participates in the same organic order that marks the reality of truth and goodness. Individuals and peoples have their own beauty. Kook's estheticism leads him to find divine providence in the fact that no phenomenon is left without the formative influence of God's Wisdom.[5]

Just as Kook sees prayer, repentance, goodness and truth, and the Torah in its entirety, as cosmic processes, so it is with beauty. The force of beauty, alongside that of the other processes in human maturation, impels us to try and repair the universe. Of course, we can easily lose our sense of direction, leave the straight path, and wander off senselessly. Apprehending or creating beauty is thus only partially attainable in the short run; but since the world is God's creation, everything will exhibit its beauty at some point. Kook provides a strange and unexpected substantiation for his theory:

> For example, wars are not beautiful, at all, but they nonetheless contain some good for the future. For the conflicts between small nations eventuated in the formation of large ones. This is a contribution to the larger union of mankind, that, in turn, will bring about its ultimate unification and universal peace. And although wars are not beautiful in themselves, the Holy One, blessed be He, from time immemorial, has given them a certain charm in men's eyes. The latter view the sword as an ornament of bravery. In war it is a glory to him who holds it—but it will be beautiful only until the knowledge of God's wisdom will show him that he has no need for it.[6]

This passage is made difficult by the relativism it displays. If beauty is characterized by its determination according to cosmic laws, we must conclude that it is necessary. If it is necessary, it must be so by divine command. Therefore, if God gives a "certain charm" in human eyes, Kook should have identified it as a beautiful step in the direction of cosmic perfection. For if wars are designed to push us toward peace, they must in some way be beautiful. Kook's hesitations show that he recognizes the complexity of his problem. Wars are not beautiful, but, he tells us, they have an element of beauty, if only during the transitionary period, until they are no longer required. Is war ugly only in the eyes of men and women but not because it is the antithesis of God's essence? What did Isaiah mean when he declared that God "makes peace and creates evil" (Is. 45, 7)? Is there no distinction in the Being of God between the two? Is it all a matter of the relative way in which human beings see things? Or must we say that God hates violence? But then, how can we say that we have to resort to war to attain peace? Does this not suggest that there is a contradiction between God's power and His goodness?

The above questions are not merely semantic exercises, and Kook cannot answer them within his own theological system. The cosmic laws of beauty, about which he speaks, cannot be autonomous. Their regularity is only apparent but can be set aside at God's will, as is true of all existence. Therefore, Kook cannot overcome the contradiction between seeing beauty as an autonomous cosmic drive and perceiving it as a subjective human reaction to the esthetic quality of every entity.

The category of the ugly is a problem for every philosophy of esthetics. A talented artist can give esthetic expression to phenomena of evil and ugliness, as is evident in great novels that deal with human cruelty, avarice, and thirst for power or in paintings or sculptures that freeze into forms of rare beauty a single moment in an act of violence or savagery. Kook looked ugliness in the face but did not accord it independent esthetic status. Although ugliness will eventually vanish, in the meantime it is present and thus it, too, must belong to God's scheme. The question arises: For what reason does God spoil the beauty of His universe? Kook leans on a weak reed, as is usually the case when supernaturalists try to solve the conundrum of a good, omnipotent God who causes or permits the torture of innocent men and women. Kook regards the ugly as one of God's tools in the long process of hewing out the good. He looks upon the decorative sword as one way in which human beings attempt to cover over the ugliness of war, but this seeming beauty will give way to the beautiful goodness of peace. An esthetic category finds its justification as a step toward the fulfillment of the good. It follows that the beautiful has no permanency unless it is in tune with the good. Kook would not dignify the esthetic as a category on the same level as the true and the good. The good, like the ugly, can be a means to an end, but it can never be an end in itself.

Kook deserves much credit for assigning such a significant role to beauty in the striving for human salvation. As we noted, past generations of Jews feared the idolatrous and pagan consequences of estheticism. In view of the thick wall that the *Halakhah* erected to prevent the entrance into Judaism of serious attention to the dimension of beauty, the openness to the subject of a halakhist like Kook is daring. Naturally, Kook set limits. In no way did he license artistic development not authorized by Jewish law in spirit and in practice. Nonetheless, to the extent that the *Halakhah* permits, he opened the door partway so that even Orthodox Jews could explore the spiritual possibilities in the search for beauty.

Traditional Judaism, as compared with many other religions, is unusually earthy. It does not repress the natural bodily or spiritual urges of normal men and women. It rejects asceticism in favor of pointing these drives toward constructive purposes. In this spirit, Kook calls upon Jews to take proper advantage of their will to live abundantly. He affirms the desirability of seeking an attractive wife—we must never forget Kook's masculine perspective— living in a beautiful and comfortable home, and using esthetically pleasing dishes and cutlery. All these, he believes, help to broaden a person's horizons. As long as one is not excessive in these matters, one's behavior should be esthetically admirable. But Kook balances the scales by cautioning everyone to remember that the dimension of beauty is subordinate to the knowledge and demands of Torah. To complete one of Kook's thoughts that we have mentioned before,

[a]lthough the entire universe and all thoughts and feelings are infused with divine light and the holiness of supernal life . . . nevertheless, the fount of basic illumination is hidden in Torah. Thus,

when one is studying while walking along the road and permits the sight of a beautiful tree or field to interfere with his reflections that have raised him to the level of meditation about God, he forfeits his soul. At least, the intent [of the rabbinic statement] is to stress the gravity of one's loss of concentration. After all, while the light of life shines from the entire universe, it is in Torah that life abounds. One should not abandon original, profound holiness for a lesser, secondary sanctity.[7]

Up until now, we have not paid attention to the branch of art that Kook considered most likely to endanger the purity of Judaism—literature in general and belles-lettres in particular. When Kook writes about literature, he usually refers to toraitic writings—research, ethics, philosophy, mysticism, and the like. He is careful not to overlook poetry and those branches of literature that bear a heavy esthetic load, but he fears the secularization of creative writing. In a letter on yeshivah education, sent in 1908 to Rabbi Yitzhak Isaac Halevi, Kook declares:

> [T]he *Yeshivah* must supply the nation whatever it lacks. Since literature and poetry are today so attractive and so influential in our lives, we must try to insure that this branch, too, is of us and for us. Let us not submit to the assumption ab initio, that every one who has a literary talent and every prominent poet has to be a heretic and sinner. We have to dispense with this deceitful stance and to show all humanity the poetic majesty and the literary charm that will flourish when drawn from the natural, trustworthy source of our national life—the living waters of God.[8]

Every word written by a scholar, poet, or novelist must breathe the spirit of Torah.

Kook believes that authors in all branches of creative writing will fulfill his hopes, provided they drink heavily from the spring of Torah. However, Kook sets forth clear restrictions. He opens the door to censorship by the religious establishment, which he foresees. Literature, in the eyes of its open-minded savants, is glorified as an instrument of social criticism. Writers are expected to be free to disclose and criticize distortions of truth or justice in the tradition, to add to its content, and to create new substance for Jewish thought and practice. This does not mean that literature itself is to be considered immune from critical attack from within or without. Kook does not hesitate to express his disagreement with authors whom he wants to bring into the traditional fold. He does not perceive that criticism based solely on traditional criteria is subjective and apt to drive away men and women of initiative and talent. Art in the service of the true, the good, and the beautiful has to be free.

KAPLAN ON ART

The similarity between the views of Kook and Kaplan in certain areas of esthetic theory is striking. Both try to understand the dynamic interplay of goodness, truth, and beauty. Kaplan observes, "Every emotion experienced by the Jew in the past, from the mirth of Purim to the elegiac mood of *Tish'ah B'Av*, found aesthetic expression in musical modes, art forms, poetry and ritual."[9] He asks: "Can Judaism in our day make the tragic experience of Jews in the present meaningful and edifying to future generations through expression in the arts?"[10]

The response of Jews to their incomparable experiences in the twentieth century—particularly the Holocaust and the establishment of the State of Israel—has, indeed, been a flowering of Jewish art. Even before these events occurred, Kaplan wrote:

> Not only religious but other human values, not only those derived from the past of the Jewish people but those drawn from contemporary Jewish life, must find expression in art forms. Furthermore, the gamut of artistic expression must be widened to include poetry and song, music, drama, dance, painting, sculpture and architecture. *When Judaism has acquired the potency of multiple appeal, not even extreme diversity of belief will threaten its integrity.*[11] (Italics, MMK)

Thus, in spite of the possibility that freedom of artistic expression might introduce forms and themes that threaten traditional norms, Kaplan, unlike Kook, felt that the risk had to be taken. Without novelty, the tradition itself would atrophy. A living people has no choice but to venture toward new horizons. Art must be no less honest than any other form of human expression. Artists, it is true, can mislead, but placing artificial restraints on their

integrity will certainly deprive humanity of the measure of goodness, truth, and beauty their talents can produce.

   According to Kook, the goodness, truth, and beauty embedded
in the Torah cannot be matched by employing any other instrument. Kaplan is at one with Kook in ascribing to the toraitic
tradition the power of raising the Jew to the highest level of the
human potential. But it has to be approached in the right way.
*"Though the modern Jew cannot believe that God revealed the Torah to
Israel, he cannot deny the historic fact that the Torah revealed God to
Israel."*[12] (Italics, MMK) Nonetheless, Kaplan continues:

> The recognition of the truth that the Torah is a human document
> gives it a different, not necessarily a less important, significance to
> the Jew. The content of that document is Israel's quest for God and
> the discoveries made in that quest. The record of a people's attempt
> to find meaning and worth in life, to see in it the evidence of a
> spirit that makes for truth, goodness and beauty, is always signifi-
> cant. Perfect it is not, since the quest for God is endless. But the
> very imperfections can be valuable, since we learn truth by dis-
> covering our errors.[13]

   Whoever accepts Kaplan's premise will have to accompany him
in his objection to confining the artist within halakhic restraints.
Kaplan hopes that the Jewish artist will explore the national heritage for its hidden treasures. However, a free spirit will seek many
sources of inspiration and will also respond to those that he or she
comes upon by chance. No people has a monopoly on truth,
beauty, or goodness; individually and collectively, humans must
learn and borrow from one another. It is legitimate to caution
against drinking carelessly from strange waters, for they might
contain harmful substances. However, an experienced people is
capable of adapting foreign-born ideas, values, and practices to its
own culture. This ability has been one of Jewry's strengths in its
struggle for survival.

   Kaplan and Kook resemble one another in seeing beauty as an
intrinsic quality of the cosmos and its process of regularity and
mysterious novelty. Kook, of course, regards the order in the universe as the fruit of God's continuing, active Wisdom and Providence. Nothing happens without God's making it possible.
Although we might not know the reason for this or that phenom-

enon, the whole is planned and executed with consummate orderliness. Events do not always occur in accordance with the
tenets of human logic, but this is merely indicative of creaturely
limitations and an inability to fathom God's purposes.

In contrast to this vision, Kaplan argues:

> The progress of mankind is a movement from the notion that the
> world is governed by arbitrary whim to the realization that this is a
> law-governed world. Law-mindedness is that attitude of mind
> which seeks out the inherent nature of the realities it copes with in
> order to discover their potentialities for the achievement of truth,
> beauty or goodness. The attitude of law-mindedness toward physi-
> cal realities has given us science. . . . Law-mindedness in matters of
> human creativity has given us the arts. It was due to the discovery
> of the great uniformities in the physical form of man, and the un-
> sparing self-discipline which the Greeks cultivated in the arts, that
> they became the world's exemplars in human creativity. The long
> years of training and apprenticeship to which the musician, painter
> and sculptor must submit in order to achieve success proves that
> those laws which its devotees conform to have not been arbitrarily
> devised by a few master artists, but are inherent in the very nature
> of the beauty which man seeks to create.[14]

Kaplan's analysis leads to the conclusion that each human discipline has its own laws. These laws, in turn, are organically related
in and to the overall cosmic order. The scientist, the artist, and
the theologian are engaged, each in his or her own field, in
searching for and uncovering different aspects of existence. Each
one has to undergo special training for his or her field. These
enterprises are all part of the human search for fulfillment. They
supplement one another and have to be fitted together in an organic way, if they are to play constructive roles in the composition
of a decent humanity. This is a formidable task. Consider, for a
minute, the fact that even within a single discipline such as physics
or chemistry, research has become so specialized that communication between colleagues who are involved in different aspects of
their common field has become a major problem. Sometimes,
they do not understand each other's language, to say nothing of
comprehending another branch of science. Attempting to inte-
grate all of human knowledge into a single field theory or Gestalt
is an exercise in futility. That is one of the main reasons why one

should be hesitant about attacking the integrity of others in matters relating to their areas of interest and expertise. In Kaplan's view, artists are entitled to a reasonable amount of independence in giving tangible form to their esthetic visions. They have to be free to discover the laws of their disciplines and to apply them to their creative activity. Simultaneously, Kaplan warns against the arrogance of the artist, as was exemplified in the Tower of Babel myth, and of the critic who often lacks the sharp insight of the creator.

It is understandable that a religion that regards the arts as its handmaidens would not grant them autonomy. Every artist, as seen from this point of departure, is potentially given to serving impure purposes, even idolatry. Therefore, halakhic Jews discouraged the furtherance of the plastic arts, except insofar as they could beautify the synagogue or ritual articles. The ban on the use of musical instruments in the synagogue prevented pious Jewish composers from giving free rein to their musical imagination. As long as men feared a sexual threat in female voices, not only were these voices muted, but songs that might have been composed for the feminine range were never realized. "Nevertheless," Kaplan writes, "with all these limitations, there was . . . a Jewish art in the ghetto, not a sumptuous or luxurious art, but one that was sincere and moving in its simplicity."[15]

Modern Jewish art is impressive but still in its infancy. Its future promise is great, but like all infants, its movements have not yet been defined. Kaplan differentiates between Jewish art and art by Jews. The religious art that Jews created in the Diaspora during the long Exile was Jewish, inasmuch as it sprouted in the soil of Jewish national and religious life. Although limited in scope, it was, nevertheless, an authentic response of the people to its hardships. Nor must we forget that moments of joy were also symbolized in this religious art and, to some extent, in folk music as well.

In his evaluation of Jewish religious art, Kaplan seems to pay insufficient attention to environmental influences on its form and content. For instance, even a cursory glance at the architecture of synagogues in different countries demonstrates that Jewish architects absorbed the criteria of structural beauty and utility from their non-Jewish fellows. Or, even more dramatically, the melodies of synagogue prayers abound in the sounds of Russia, Italy,

Germany, France, England, the United States, and all lands of the Dispersion. This same borrowing from foreign folk and religious sources holds for the illumination of the Pesah *Haggadah* and for the shaping of *Kiddush* cups, spice boxes, candelabras, and Torah decorations. This does not imply that Jewish artists were unoriginal or that imitation or borrowing is illegitimate. Wherever peoples live together, they learn from one another. Jewish influences on non-Jewish art can also be easily traced, as evidenced by the Gregorian chant and its derivation from the tradition of Torah-cantillation. Thus, Kaplan justifiably identifies Jewish religious art as Jewish because it arose out of the inner need of Jews to find an esthetic outlet for their spiritual emotions and thoughts. But we must always be aware that in art, too, no one is alone and that it is an activity of human interdependence.

Compared to the heavy weight of traditional Jewish religious art, Kaplan claims,

> *Today we have many Jewish artists, but almost no Jewish art.* Jews, ever since the Emancipation have thrown themselves enthusiastically into a mastery of artistic techniques, but their work is, for the most part, irrelevant to Jewish life. It does not originate in, or contribute to, the enrichment of that life. It does not express an aesthetic reaction to those experiences which Jews go through by reason of their being Jews.[16] (Italics, MMK)

For Kaplan, esthetic expression is an intrinsic part of human fulfillment and, for the Jew, no less essential than the study of Torah, praying, or observing the other *mitzvot*. The arts assist the Jew in the search for the beauty in what appears to lack form or to be distorted; they provide release from feelings of pain, depression, and suffering, and they celebrate courage; they express rapture in the renewed contact of the Jewish people with the soil and landscape of Eretz Yisrael; and they articulate anguish at the unspeakable slaughter of innocent Jews during the Shoah and at today's cruel terrors. The list of experiences is long and continuously supplemented. Kook and Kaplan disagree as to the amount of release that can be expected from recourse to traditional sources alone. As stated, Kaplan wants to give the artist free rein to seek the proper forms for the esthetic embodiment of these varied experiences that range from the debasement of man to his exaltation.

Without such freedom, the ability of the Jewish people to un-
cover the depths of the beautiful and the ugly will be truncated.
Halakhic restraints will inevitably suppress talents that are essential
to the revitalization of all aspects of Jewish life in the cradle of
Jewish civilization and in those countries of the Diaspora where
Jews are eager to contribute their share to creative Jewish survival.

Kook's realization of the importance of the esthetic dimension
was not broad enough to permit him to see that in the interplay
of the true, the good, and the beautiful, the last might have a
critical function to play regarding the other two concerns. From
an esthetic perspective, for example, the opinion that a woman's
voice is a stimulus to licentiousness is not only a sin against beauty
but is also damaging to truth and goodness. Depriving women of
vocal self-expression is a crime against their humanity and a false
reading of their psychological and physiological needs and capacities. In parallel fashion, the social injustice that leads to the development of city slums is easily inferred from their ugliness.
Wherever we find houses unfit for human habitation, we know
there is no truth and no justice.

Artists fulfill two functions in the drive toward salvation. They
enable both themselves and the community at large to expand the
amount of beauty in the world and to disclose, by means of esthetic criticism, pockets of untruth and injustice. Paintings and
photographs of poverty, especially when skillfully executed,
arouse the conscience of the observer. At the same time, a prosaic
representation of such scenes is less likely to attract the attention
and to prick the conscience of the viewer.[17] Consumers of art, of
course, must be as free as the artists themselves, and their appreciation or criticism of the artists' works is no less a phase of the
esthetic process than the creative activity of the artists. Neither
can legitimately be ordered to do their jobs by obeying rules that
are not inherent in the esthetic mode.

Kaplan agrees with Kook that truth and goodness should guide
the creator and the consumer of art. Kaplan muses:

> The classification of values into the good, the true and the beauti-
> ful, formulated by the Greeks, has become traditional. Its inade-
> quacy becomes apparent the moment we realize the term "good"
> is not coordinated with the other two. Plato identifies the Idea of

the Good as the supreme idea, thereby making truth and beauty phases of it. I would therefore have "good" coextensive with value or meaning in all its aspects conceived affirmatively, that is as conducive to the fullness of human life.[18]

Clearly, Kaplan, like Kook, regards goodness as the central, determining value of the Greek-inspired trinity.

However, whereas Kook thinks that the definition of the good is embedded in the classic rabbinic texts, Kaplan looks upon art as another means of defining what is good. He would have us be aware that "[a]rt possesses the magic whereby it is able to express the seemingly ineffable and to communicate what is ordinarily regarded as incommunicable."[19] To be able to transpose feeling into an artistic form is a rare skill. Genius cannot be ordered to exist, but we can at least prepare the soil in which it can grow. Therefore, Kaplan exerted great effort in urging Jewish educators on all rungs of the educational ladder to introduce an esthetic dimension into the curriculum, in order to cultivate a sophisticated sense of beauty, to uncover hidden talents, and to encourage the appreciation of artistic creations and the release of untapped esthetic resources in each pupil and student. Prayer and ritual observance are not the only forms of spiritual expression.

Art is a two-edged sword. The Jewish people today, in Israel and the Diaspora, has to choose between an unfettered Jewish art and one appropriate to halakhic standards. Under the latter, the Jewish people will probably be saved from much of the danger of the permissiveness, shallowness, and perversity of modern mass culture. Artistic freedom, on the other hand, while exposing us to these potential dangers, is likely to lend new color to Judaism and to awaken talented men and women to enrich Jewish life with a beauty it has never known before. The esthetic front turns out to be a crucial arena in determining the parameters and limits of human freedom.

Notes

1. *Mishnato shel HaRav Kook* (*The Philosophy of HaRav Kook*) (Jerusalem: World Zionist Organization, 1974, p. 18).
2. Quoted by Sh. Z. Shragai in a selected list of Kook's letters, in

ZR, p. 62. Kook's opinion enables us to understand his objection to any change in the customs of earlocks and wigs. (See "Israel's Mission and Its Nationalism," *HaPeles*, 5661, pp. 155–156.)

3. ZR, pp. 62–63.
4. Ibid., p. 63.
5. Ibid.
6. Ibid.
7. OH, p. 45.
8. KL, L. 149, p. 195.
9. FAJ, p. 343.
10. Ibid.
11. JC, p. 486.
12. FAJ, p. 346.
13. Ibid.
14. MG, p. 316.
15. FAJ, p. 352.
16. Ibid.
17. Kaplan writes: "The aesthetic and ethical ideals are not unrelated, although neither can be wholly derived from the other. The refinement of the emotions, the capacity for recognizing qualitative differences that do not lie on the surface, is of deep ethical significance" (FAJ, p. 355).
18. *Diaries*, August 14, 1935.
19. FAJ, p. 357.

16

An Excursion to the Future

ALTHOUGH I AM ABOUT TO CONCLUDE this book, the study and analysis of Kook's and Kaplan's works will continue—both by me and, hopefully, by many others. Commentators will differ as to the messages of the two men and their relevance to the Jewish present and future. Researchers will delve into the sources of their ideas and examine aspects of their thinking that I have omitted in this work. I am tempted to add a few more chapters of my own, but I believe that I have written enough to introduce Israeli readers (through my original volume in Hebrew) and readers of English (through this translation and revision) to what I consider to be the two reasonable ends of the spectrum of philosophies of Judaism and programs for Jewish life. Whatever the differences between Kook and Kaplan may be—and we have noted that they are many and profound—their disciples can and must engage in reasoned, honest, and respectful dialogue, if the centrifugal forces threatening Jewish solidarity are not to have their way. I realize that I have only begun the dialogue, but I hope that I have opened it in the proper spirit.

All of us have to stake out our positions in life. We have to be as objective as possible in reaching our conclusions, but we dare not be neutral and leave it to extremists and "true believers" to fill the vacuum left by our reluctance to take a stand. Unless we use the reasoning power that is the hallmark of our human makeup and act upon its imperatives, we cannot be free and independent. Fear of making mistakes is not a justifiable excuse for inaction; passivity, too, is frequently erroneous in its way. Neither Kook nor Kaplan followed the path of least resistance. They were both forthright, and that is part of their magnetism. But disciples must learn from their masters that convictions, however strongly held, must not become absolutes and must be open to reexamination, especially in response to the opinions of fair-minded critics. Approving of Kaplan does not mean that one should not learn from Kook, and vice versa. Let us, then, examine the structure of Jewish life, as it might appear if we were to choose one system or the other.

Throughout this study, I have repeatedly emphasized the organic character of the two ideologies. Both Kook and Kaplan saw the interrelatedness of all facets of Jewish civilization. Israel's God, its Land, and its Torah are one. This oneness, however, is a dynamic one. Both men felt the need to try and explain how Jewish continuity and unity can be maintained while all Jews are in constant movement, and the entire people is in perpetual metamorphosis. What principles account for the dynamism of the group and can, at the same time, hold the parts together?

Kook and Kaplan agreed that Judaism without God at its center is a distortion. A Jewish theology that does not relate to the strengthening of Jewish peoplehood and the rebuilding of Eretz Yisrael is like a disembodied soul. A Jewish people without its Land is like a body lacking vital organs and limbs. And an Eretz Yisrael that fails to give birth to a wise religion is apt to seduce the Jewish people into idolatrous chauvinism. While they were ardent nationalists, Kook and Kaplan opposed sociolatry; for them, God is the measure. Psychologically and existentially, however, it is the fate of the Jewish people that stands at the center of concern of loyal Jews. Jewish identity, the national will to live, the quality of Jewish culture—these are only a few of the motivating forces that animate the Jew as he or she confronts life. In the search for answers to these questions, Jews must constantly reexamine their relationship to God, to their Jewish heritage and to their path in life. Up to this point, Kook and Kaplan walk together. From then on, they head in different directions.

THE FUTURE ACCORDING TO KOOK

What would Jewish life look like if we were to follow Kook's vision? Any response to such a question must, of course, be rendered with great reservation. However, we have a right, on the basis of the massive evidence of Kook's writings, to guess at his direction. He would join and perhaps lead the religious parties in Israel in pressing for the extension of religious control over areas of life not yet in the hands of the religious establishment, or not sufficiently under its hegemony. He would most likely press for full halakhic determination of Jewish identity under the Law of Return, for stricter control of traffic on Sabbaths and holidays, for a wider presence of Orthodox values in the general educational system, and for the evolution of a more traditional public domain. However, one must keep in mind that Kook also opposed legislation that would be unacceptable to the majority. Thus, while he would most likely seek, by means of persuasion rather than political maneuvering, to influence legislation in the Knesset, his main thrust would be to increase public respect for the *Halakhah*. Kook would attempt to persuade his colleagues to act with dispatch to liberalize Jewish law wherever possible. He would hope to demonstrate that by being flexible and showing a genuine desire to improve the quality of life for all, halakhic scholars would convince even secular-minded legislators to give greater credence to halakhic standards.

Kook would untiringly endeavor to induce non-Orthodox Jews to enter the halakhic fold. I believe he would encourage Orthodox teachers to seek posts in the general educational stream and, through legitimate exercise of their educational role, bring about a revolution in the spirit of the traditional Jewish school. This revolution would also include the religious trend, where Kook would call for greater attention to science, foreign languages, and the study of other cultures. On the other hand, Kook would oppose any effort to introduce non-Orthodox religious interpretations of Judaism into any branch of the educational system. If Kook were with us today, I think he might sense the need for Israel's Jews to learn Arabic and to gain greater insight into Arab culture.

In brief, Kook would embrace all Jews with his love but would deny the legitimacy of "non-kasher" Judaism. He would call upon all deviants to repent, and he would keep them at arm's length until they did. In other words, Kook's style would be far more congenial to non-Orthodox Jews than that of most of Israel's current rabbinical leadership, but his commitment to the demands of the *Halakhah* would not differ substantially from theirs.

Kook was not a religious liberal. There is no basis for the assumption of well-meaning Jews that, if Kook were to be resurrected or if someone like him were to become the Chief Rabbi of the State of Israel, its religious problems would be readily solved. On the contrary, Kook's love of his people would blind the Jewish public to the fact that neither he nor any of his followers are likely to refrain from trying to use the institutions of democracy for purposes such as those mentioned above. Never mind that parliamentary legislation is not conducted in a halakhic spirit or method. If it can restore some of the authority and content of traditional Judaism, why not use it, even if it means traducing the spirituality of the religionists and turning them into professional politicians?

We cannot afford to hide the disparity between the *Halakhah* and democracy. The *Halakhah* purports to come from heaven; democracy is from the people. Any attempt to blur this distinction distorts both systems. Although many democratic seeds are scattered in its soil, the *Halakhah* is an authentic plant of its own, the characteristics of which I have tried to sketch briefly in the chapter devoted to the subject. These qualities often anticipate the spirit of democratic values, but in many instances they oppose democratic concepts and commitments. Kook was not a democrat. As a halakhist, if he were alive today, he would be forced to resist the acceptance of important democratic principles. Consistent with halakhic standards of Jewish polity, he would have to regard non-Jewish residents of Israel as *gerei toshav*, resident aliens, but not as equal citizens. They would be the beneficiaries of an enlightened paternalism, but they would not be seen as full partners in the making of a pluralistic state. Christians, Moslems and Druse, Palestinians, and other non-Jewish citizens and permanent residents would all be respected and protected. However, some radical changes would have to be made in Jewish law before these non-Jews could be permitted to acquire additional property for the building of new homes and the extension of their economy. One need only refer to the limitations placed upon the growth of Arab communities in Jerusalem and Karmiel to perceive how the halakhic tradition affects Israel's secular government. How much more so would the straitjacket be tightened in the hands of halakhic authorities!

If Kook were to apply his philosophy, diaspora Jewry would be considered to be living in an impure world, as is stipulated in the talmudic view. He would undoubtedly do everything in his power to help them deepen their Jewish loyalty, in the hope that they would come to live in Israel. Although not denying their Jewish identity, Kook would regard the best of them as flawed and as suffering from the damaging influences of exile. He would see them as unnatural; their continued residence in the Diaspora would be viewed as preventing the redemption of the Jewish people. All that might be expected of Jews outside Eretz Yisrael is that they should resist assimilation as long as possible. Kook would press them quickly to come on *aliyah*.

The core of Kook's Jewish nationalism is his belief in election. I have emphasized that the Jewish doctrine of chosenness is a many-faceted concept, encompassing questions of theology, ethics, history, psychology, politics, and demography. Kook believed that Israel's chosenness is both a promise of national redemption and God's way of guaranteeing the salvation of all humankind. There is no contradiction, he thought, between the particular assignment God gave to Israel and the universal goal of bringing all men and women under the wings of the Almighty. But we cannot glide so smoothly over the sense of superiority that is implicit in this ethically motivated apologetic for chosenness. Straight thinking should convince us that we cannot have it both ways. A people can choose as a vocation to become a light to the nations. In this case, it must take full responsibility for the path it chooses. However, a chosen people can only agree to the terms set for its election by God. It cannot negotiate those terms. Israel is subject to the Torah and, according to the acceptance of its dictates, cannot uproot any of its principles or initiate new terms that might not be congruent with the original contract.

In the traditional account, Israel could have rejected the covenant, but since it did not, it is eternally bound by it. And if, as some thinkers maintain, the people is expected to develop the Torah in response to changing conditions of life, the boundaries of its freedom of decision are set not by its generations but by God. It is this very bond with God, however, that confers on Israel a sense of superiority. The more difficult the mission entrusted to one by an authority one respects, the greater the feeling of one's worth at having been so selected. It appears to me that election is a weak intellectual reed on which to hang Jewish morale or on which to pin our national vocation. It can serve only those whose fulfillment as Jews depends on whether or not the Jewish people are not only unique, which is true of every individual and every group, but also in some way superior.

The Future According to Kaplan

Kaplan also dealt with the above matters. His devotion to the Jewish people was so strong, emotionally and intellectually, that he has been accused of opening the door to the very sociolatry and chauvinism that he repeatedly castigated. Recently, for instance, the noted theologian David Hartman wrote of Kaplan:

> Although I agree with Kaplan's elevation of the concept of peoplehood to a position of prime importance in his analysis of Judaism, I refuse to allow for the possibility of the Jewish people's becoming the object of a modern form of idolatry. What serves the Jewish state or contemporary Jewish civilization ought not to become the sole criterion of authentic Judaism. There must be a tension underlying Jewish commitment; one should not sacrifice the Jewish people to God or to Torah, nor should one abandon God and Torah in favor of glorification of the Jewish people.[1]

Hartman's remarks are, to put it mildly, a total misreading of what Kaplan wrote and what he intended. In 1934, Kaplan had already published the following: "The task of modern Judaism must not end with the readjustment of its folk religion. As the emphasis placed on its folk religion increases, it is essential to guard against the chief misuse that folk religion is open to its apotheosis into a consecrated chauvinism."[2] Kaplan repeated this warning throughout his career. The moral behavior of groups, he reiterated, is always in need of the vigilance of social critics who are capable of rising above collective self-interest. He stated, "Personal religion, with its element of universalism, will therefore have to act as a check and corrective"[3] for excessive nationalism. "Furthermore," he continued, "we must remember that folk religion necessarily moves on the plane of popular intelligence and crowd emotions. It cannot breathe in those reaches of mysticism where the more highly developed mind dwells. Since modern mysticism presupposes a highly-trained metaphysical grasp of reality, folk religion will lack the metaphysical and mystical elements with which the more advanced mind cannot dispense."[4]

Kaplan delved deeply into the problem of theology and its implications for the moral conduct of any people. Precisely because of his awareness of the danger of chauvinism and sociolatry, he insisted that every nation must subject itself to universal moral norms that are recognized by enlightened men and women as divine. Kaplan knew, though, that even this appeal to enlightenment cannot be devoid of some subjectivism and error. However, a theology that recognizes that man is the measurer—not the measure—at least starts from a self-critical acknowledgment. If man is the initiator and sponsor of national claims, the latter automatically raise suspicions of hubris. Only those who are conscious of the potential subjectivity in all human thought are likely to take honest criticism seriously.

We have referred several times to Kaplan's critique of the chosen people doctrine and to the self-pride it engenders or of which it is the result. One of the main components of the doctrine is its advocates' belief in the unadulterated truth and justice of Israel's Torah and the destiny of Israel to lead all humankind to redemption. Under chosenness, this leadership is not only national purpose but also national destiny or divine vocation imposed from above on Israel alone. The sacred pages of Jewish tradition have already recorded the way to peace and international fellowship. All that remains to be done is for Israel to faithfully follow the prescribed tenets and for the other nations to approximate them. Then the Kingdom of God will be established on earth.[5] Israel's role is thus of cosmic dimensions.

Contrary to this concept of human destiny, Kaplan held that while Israel has a crucial role to play in the redemptive process, it is merely *its* unique part. All other nations are similarly obligated to play their roles as called for by their unique circumstances. No one can tell in advance how the parts will fit together.

Israel's chosenness is directed not only outward, determining its place in the international society, but also inward, thereby informing the national character, including its relationship to God, the ingathering of all Jews in Eretz Yisrael, and the spirit of the national culture. All these are not merely a Zionist dream. They are vital steps in God's plan for human destiny.

Kaplan, on the other hand, conceives the national vocation to be a function of social craftsmanship and a decisive element in Israel's strategy of survival. Although he regards Eretz Yisrael as indispensable to the creative continuity of the Jewish people, his idealism is wide open to the many changes that have taken place in the civilized world and that make the hope of concentrating the entire nation in the homeland totally unrealistic. New locales for Jewish continuity have been found and new strategies for creative Jewish existence are constantly being devised. With the rise of democracy, the spread of freedom, and the growing interdependence of states and nationalities, men and women everywhere are beginning to share cultural experiences and to respect one another's individuality. In this kind of world, the ingathering of the exiles loses some of its peremptoriness. Taking this international setting into account and considering the psychological need for a centripetal point of national concentration, Kaplan calls upon Jews to define themselves as a transterritorial people, centered in Eretz Yisrael as the site of its primary culture. In the Diaspora, each segment of Jewry will engage in its own form of Jewish civilization, in keeping with the potential opportunities available in each country. It will be up to world Jewry to devise the instruments needed to hold this vast voluntary enterprise together.

Kaplan was one of the few Zionist theoreticians to view the total picture of Jewish life as a prelude to a realistic appraisal of Eretz Yisrael's position in fabricating the Jewish future. He refused to fall into the trap of negating the *golah*, but neither did he dodge the enormous difficulties that Jewish minorities have to overcome to survive under freedom.

If Kaplan were among us today, he would be continuing his fight for the democratization of Jewish life. His philosophy demands equality for all citizens in the state of a Jewish majority, regardless of nationality, religion, race, or sex. As a Zionist, he would teach the need for maintaining a Jewish majority in the State of Israel, but not through antidemocratic means such as preventing minority groups from settling in certain areas or from purchasing new land. These strategies intended to discourage the natural growth of Israel's minorities should have no place in a democratic state. Kaplan's method would be educational, so that with the spread of enlightenment, both Jews and non-Jews would tend to keep their birth rates within reasonable proportions.

Kaplan would support the Law of Return as a temporary but probably long-term measure. As long as anti-Semitism is prevalent in many countries throughout the world, the State of Israel must serve as a haven for Jews, as well as the main setting for the revitalization of Jewish civilization. Also, as long as deep-seated animosity for Israel persists in the Arab world, Jewish sovereignty in Israel must also be protected. However, the Jewishness of the State of Israel must be asserted on its own merits and not at the expense of full human and civil rights for its Arab citizens and other minorities. Non-Jews should be able to attain high public office and freely cultivate their cultures and religions in accordance with the laws of the state.

As for Kaplan's program for Judaism in all of its facets—theological, cultic, moral, literary, and artistic—we need not elaborate. He matched Kook's breadth of scope in envisaging Judaism as a religious civilization. However, Kook could not conceive of a Jewish future outside the framework of the halakhic system. On this subject, there were no grounds for discussion with non-halakhic Jews. Kook's intellectual argument was with those fellow traditionalists who were blind to what was happening in the world around them and were devoid of the pathos that he felt in the face of the changing reality. Kook never deviated from the halakhic path, but his critics were justified in their judgment that he must have been disturbed by the ever-increasing cogency of certain currents of modern thought.

Kaplan was certain of the way of reason and enlightenment, but he knew that many Jews were not ready to follow its twists and turns. They were incapable of employing the methods of democracy, voluntarism, pluralism, compromise, and the like. Their reluctance made it clear that progress would be slow. But Kaplan's courage and his profound belief in the efficacy of rationality convinced him that the route to a better future could not be found by retreating to the past. The application of the Kaplanian system today would make for an adventurous Judaism, fit only for the strong of heart and for those who are prepared to live with uncertainty.

We cannot be sure what the face of Jewish life would be like if we were to faithfully follow either of our two teachers. Men and women choose their spiritual masters according to their own temperaments. Persons who gravitate toward mysticism and emotionalism will find Kook to be inspiring, while they will regard Kaplan as a "cold Litvak," that is, unfeeling. Men and women who are realistic and open-minded will flock to Kaplan and regard Kook as having a beclouded sense of reality and a narrow perspective on Jewish existence. Both of these perceptions are superficial. Kook and Kaplan cannot be placed neatly in pigeonholes. A better way of describing the two men would be as follows: Kook is like a flowing stream, whose direction is permanently determined by its two banks. Its flow is fast but one-directional. In the end, it will reach its predestined outlet in a lake or an ocean. Kaplan is like a hiker who sets out to reach a certain site but becomes interested in the scenery and sights along the winding route. He might be tempted to turn aside if he comes across a path that seems to be more attractive than the one he originally chose, even to the point of pursuing a goal that may be more enchanting than his original one.

Whoever wants a life filled with ancient treasures that can be lovingly caressed will find it in the Judaism of Kook. Those in search of adventure will accompany Kaplan. Those who look to a Creator, a supreme Judge, and a Dispenser of loving-kindness will pray with Kook. Those who want to discover the order in immanent and transcendent existence that makes their quest for fulfillment plausible will pray with Kaplan.

These men represent the two ends of the reasonable spectrum of Judaism. Jews will have to choose either one or the other or perhaps some combination of the two. There may be other visions worthy of consideration, but I believe no one can afford to ignore either Avraham Yitzhak Hakohen Kook or Mordecai Menachem Kaplan.

NOTES

1. *Conflicting Visions* (New York: Schocken, 1990, p. 202).
2. JC, p. 348.
3. Ibid., pp. 348–349.
4. Ibid.
5. See Kook's interpretation of Hanukkah (OR, Vol. 1, pp. 132–135).

GLOSSARY

"Adon Olam" (**"Eternal Lord"**). Popular, philosophically inspired hymn.

Aggadah. Literally, tale. Homiletical section of Rabbinic literature.

Avat Yisrael. Love of fellow Jews.

Aliyah. Literally, ascent. Migration to Eretz Yisrael out of a sense of Jewish national obligation and a desire to live Judaism as one's primary civilization.

Amidah. Literally, standing. The prayer is generally known as the Shemoneh Esrei (Eighteen Benedictions) or Hatefillah, the prayer par excellence. Actually, the number of benedictions differs, depending on whether the prayer is recited on a weekday, Sabbath, or holiday.

Diaspora. Dispersion, referring to all Jewish communities outside of Israel.

Eretz Yisrael. The Land of Israel, Palestine.

Halakhah. Traditional Jewish law as it has developed from the Bible until today.

Halutzim. Pioneers, particularly referring to early Zionist settlers on the soil.

Haredim. Literally, pious ones. Extreme traditionalists. In Israel, they represent about 6 percent of the population who want to replace the democratic state with an halakhic polity.

Havdalah. Literally, separation or differentiation. The benediction recited at the moment of passing from the Sabbath to week days.

Hillul Shabbat. Desecration of the Sabbath. Violation of halakhic rules of Sabbath observance.

Kabbalah. Literally, tradition passed from generation to generation. Designation for various schools of Jewish mysticism.

Kavvanah. Devotion, intention, attention. The complete and sincere concentration demanded of a person at prayer or engaged in performing a religious act.

Kiv'yakhol. As it were, so to speak.

Mahzor. Prayer book for a Jewish holiday. Each holiday has its own Mahzor, which contains mandatory liturgy for all the sacred days plus prayers on the theme or themes of the particular holiday.

Mezuzah. A small parchment containing verses from Deuteronomy 5:4–9 and 11:13–17. The parchment is placed in a decorative box and affixed to the doorposts of Jewish homes as a sign of devotion to Judaism.

Milhemet Mitzvah. Mandatory war, either to fill out the borders of Eretz Yisrael or to defend the country against enemy attack.

Minhago Shel Olam. Cosmic order. The usual behavior of the physical universe.

Minyan. Quorum. The ten adults whose presence is required to establish a public prayer service. Among Orthodox Jews, the minyan must be completed by at least ten males.

Mithnagdim. Opponents of the Hasidim. More strict in their construction of Rabbinic tradition.

Mitzvah. Literally, precept. Divine command (pl. mitzvot). Observance of halakhic social and ritual law. Performance of a good deed.

Mitzvot Maasiyot. Ritual and behavioral practices.

Shemittah. Sabbatical (seventh) year, during which the land is to remain fallow.

Shiv'ah. Seven days of mourning for close relatives.

Shulhnn Aeukh. Literally, table set for a meal. Authoritative code of Jewish law, prepared by R. Joseph Karo in the sixteenth century.

Siddur. Shortened form of Siddur (or Seder) Hatefillot, the prayer book.

Talmud. The major text of the Halakhah. There are two versions of the Talmud. One originated in Eretz Yisrael and is called the Yerushalmi. The other was edited in Babylonia and is known as the Bavli. Each Talmud is a compendium of legal debates among the Sages, homiletical interpretations, historical references, folk customs, and so forth—a virtual encyclopedia of Jewish life in the five or six centuries before and after the destruction of the Second Temple (70 CE).

Talmud Torah. Study of the Jewish classics.

Teshuvah. Repentance, return.

Tikkum. Repair. Restoring the universe to its perfect state. Refers to the kabbalistic conception of overcoming the imperfections that remained imbedded in the physical world when God created it through His act of self-contraction.

Torah. Literally, instruction, teaching, law, theory. Variably referring to the Pentateuch or the whole range of Jewish law and wisdom.

Torah Lishman. Studying Torah for its own sake.

Yeshivah. A school for the study of Talmud and other Rabbinic texts.

z'l. Zikhrono or Zikhronah Liv'rakhah. "May his (her) memory be a blessing." Added to the name of beloved and respected deceased persons.

INDEX